THE PROPHECIES OF NOSTRADAMUS

THE PROPHECIES

Translated, Edited and Introduced by

OF NOSTRADAMUS

ERIKA CHEETHAM

A WIDEVIEW/PERIGEE BOOK

Perigee Books
are published by
G.P. Putnam's Sons
200 Madison Avenue
New York, New York, 10016

First published in Great Britain by Neville Spearman Ltd.
Copyright © 1973 by Erika Cheetham

Twenty-third Impression

ISBN 0- 399-50345-5
Library of Congress Catalog
Card Number: 73-78597

PRINTED IN THE UNITED STATES OF AMERICA

To Alexander and Jamie

INTRODUCTION

In the autumn of 1939, soon after Germany had declared war on Europe, Frau Dr. Goebbels was lying in bed reading an obscure book on occult literature. It contained some predictions made by a certain Nostradamus, printed in 1568. Her husband was asleep, but Frau Dr. Goebbels was so excited by what she had read that she woke him and made him read the relevant passages. He was sufficiently impressed to arrange that his Propaganda Ministry hired the services of an astologer named Krafft who was soon to be found reproducing material based on Nostradamus' Prophecies, using them to some effect psychologically in occupied Europe. How could an obscure medieval French doctor cause such consternation in both Goebbels and Himmler's Departments? How could he also cause the British Secret Service to spend a reputed sum of £80,000 on retaliatory propaganda?

He was Michel de Nostredame, more commonly known by the Latinized form of his name, Nostradamus, born at noon on 14th December 1503 by the old calendar, in St. Rémy de Provence. His family were not the illustrious line of Jewish-Italian doctors working at the Courts of King René of Anjou and of his son, as has commonly been claimed, but people of simple lineage from around Avignon. His grandfather was Peyrot or Pierre de Nostredame, an established grain-dealer, who married a Gentile girl named Blanche. Their son Jaume or Jacques, Nostradamus' father, moved to St. Rémy in 1495 and gave up the family trade. Here he married Reyniere de St. Rémy who was the granddaughter of an ex-doctor, turned tax-collector. The family were converted from Judaism to the Catholic faith by the time Nostradamus was nine years old, as his parents are listed in 1512 as being part of the new Christian community. It is important to remember the Jewish element of Nostradamus' childhood when trying to decipher the Prophecies, as he was greatly influenced by occult Jewish literature. Nostradamus was the oldest son, and had four brothers; of the first three we know little; the youngest, Jean,

5

wrote a great many ribald Provençal songs and commentaries, and eventually became Procureur of the Parliament of Provence.

Nostradamus' great intellect became apparent while he was still very young, and his education was put into the hands of his grandfather, Jean, who taught him the rudiments of Latin, Greek, Hebrew, Mathematics and what Nostradamus calls celestial science, Astrology. When this grandparent died the boy returned to his parents' house in the rue de Barri and his other grandfather endeavoured to continue his education. Soon, however, Nostradamus was sent to Avignon to study, and probably stayed with some of the many cousins he had in the town.

He already showed a great interest in astrology and it became common talk among his fellow students. He upheld the Copernican theory that the world was round and circled around the sun more than 100 years before Galileo was prosecuted for the same belief. His parents were quite rightly worried by this attitude because theirs was the age of the Inquisition, and as ex-Jews they were more vulnerable than most. So they sent him off to study medicine at Montpellier in 1522. Nostradamus was now nineteen years old and had the advantage of some of the most progressive medical minds in Europe to stimulate him. He obtained his bachelor's degree (baccalauréat) after three years, with apparent ease, and once he had his licence to practise medicine he decided to leave the University and go out into the countryside and help the many victims of the plague.

Plague was endemic in Southern France during the 16th Century, in particular a very virulent form known locally as '*le charbon*' because of the great black pustules that appeared on the body of the victim. Nostradamus had many detractors throughout his lifetime but not one has ever denied his courage in facing disease, his humanity, his kindness towards the sick, and his generosity towards the poor. It was at this early stage, 1525, that his reputation as a healer became known. Nostradamus went from town to stricken town dispensing his own cures, the prescriptions for some of which are found later in a book he published in 1552. He was very unsettled and went from Narbonne to Carcassonne where incidentally he prescribed an elixir of life for the local bishop, which if it did all the author claimed for it would be the salvation of every jaded man! Next we hear of him at Toulouse in the rue de la Triperie, again at Bordeaux where the plague was severe and then back to Avignon where he remained studying for some months. His interest in magic and the occult may spring from this period of his life, for the library at Avignon held many occult books. At the same time he managed to concoct a delicious recipe for quince jelly for the Papal Legate and the Grand Master of the Knights of Malta who were then in the town. It is a good recipe but with rather too much sugar for modern tastes.

After nearly four years of sporadic travelling he returned to Montpellier to complete his doctorate and re-enrolled on 23rd October 1529. Nostradamus had some trouble in explaining his unorthodox remedies and treatments, for his success and renown had made him enemies among the faculty. Nevertheless his learning and ability could not be denied and he obtained his doctorate. He remained teaching at Montpellier for a year but by this time his new theories, for instance his refusal to bleed patients, were causing trouble and he set off upon another spate of wandering, moving from place to place as his work and fancy took him. Throughout his life he was to suffer from this wanderlust. Dressed in his dark scholar's cap and gown he must have looked the epitome of the Wandering Jew.

While practising in Toulouse he received a letter from Julius-César Scaliger, the philosopher considered second only to Erasmus throughout Europe. Apparently Nostradamus' reply so pleased Scaliger that he invited him to stay at his home in Agen. This life suited Nostradamus admirably, and *circa* 1534 he married a young girl 'of high estate, very beautiful and admirable', whose name unfortunately has not come down to us. He had a son and a daughter by her and his life seemed complete. His practice was famous and profitable and he had the brilliant mind of Scaliger to help sharpen his wits. Then a series of tragedies struck. The plague came to Agen and, despite all his efforts, killed Nostradamus' wife and two children. The fact that he was unable to save his own family had a disastrous effect on his practice. Then he quarrelled with Scaliger and lost his friendship—a not unlikely happening, as Scaliger quarrelled with all his friends sooner or later. His late wife's family tried to sue him for the return of her dowry and as the final straw, in 1538, he was accused of heresy because of a chance remark made some years before, which had been reported to the authorities. To a workman casting a bronze statue of the Virgin, Nostradamus had commented that he was making devils. His plea that he was only describing the lack of aesthetic appeal inherent in the statue was ignored and the Inquisitors sent for him to go to Toulouse. Nostradamus, naturally having no wish to stand trial nor to suffer the rack or the stake, immediately set out on his wanderings again, keeping well clear of the Church authorities for the next six years.

We know very little about this period of his life. From references in his later books we know that he travelled in the Lorraine and went to Venice and Sicily, making a point of meeting the apothecaries of each place and noting down those who were efficient or bad for his book, the Traité des Fardmens.

It was probably around this period that he started to translate the Horapollo of Philippus from the Greek into French. It is nothing but a collection of treatises on ethics and philosophy and is of no great literary merit. Legends about Nostradamus' prophetic powers also start to appear at this time. Apparently when in Italy he saw a young monk who had been a swineherd pass by him in the street, and immediately knelt down and called him 'Your Holiness'. Felice Peretti became Sextus V in 1585, long after Nostradamus' death.

There is another amusing tale concerning a certain Seigneur de Florinville, who was discoursing with Nostradamus about prophecy and asked him to put his gift to the test by telling him the fates of the two suckling pigs in his yard. Nostradmus replied that the Seigneur would eat the black pig and a wolf the white one. Immediately de Florinville went to his cook and ordered the white pig to be killed for that night's dinner, which it duly was. Unfortunately a tame wolf-cub, belonging to the lord's men, stole the meat. The terrified cook killed the black pig and served it for dinner. Seigneur de Florinville then told Nostradamus that they were now eating the white pig. When Nostradamus insisted that it was the black one, the cook was sent for and confessed to the whole incident.

By 1554 Nostradamus had settled in Marseilles. In November of that year, Provence experienced one of the worst floods of its history. The plague redoubled in virulence, spread by the waters and the polluted corpses. Nostradamus worked ceaselessly. Most doctors had fled with those people who were still well enough to move, thus carrying the infection farther. According to contemporary memoirs, the plague was particularly bad at Aix, the capital of Provence, and the city sent for his help on 1st May. Nostradamus was alone throughout the epidemic, working among the sick, curing many, and insisting on fresh air and unpolluted water. The sense of hopelessness was so great when he first arrived in the city that he saw one sick woman sewing herself into her own shroud because she knew there would be no one to do it for her when she was dead.

Once the city had recovered, Nostradamus moved on to Salon, which he found so pleasant a town that he determined to settle there for the rest of his life. But almost immediately the city of Lyons sent for him to cure a pestilence which may, in fact, have been an epidemic of whooping cough. Whatever it was, once over, Nostradamus returned home laden with yet more gifts from the grateful citizens. Characteristically, he gave many away to the poor of the town before leaving. It is difficult to separate truth from legend in these reports of his great generosity but they almost certainly have some foundation in fact.

Back home in Salon in November, he married Anne Ponsart Gemelle, a rich widow. The house in which he spent the remainder of his days can still be seen off the Place de la Poissonnerie. Now Nostradamus seems to have led a quieter existence. His interest in the occult was strong and presumably he was still experiencing odd flashes of prophetic insight. He does not seem to have practised much medicine at this period, and appears to have concentrated more upon his writings. After 1550 he produced a yearly Almanac —and after 1554 The Prognostications—which seem to have been successful, and encouraged him to undertake the much more onerous task of the Prophecies.

Nostradamus converted the top room of his house at Salon into a study and as he tells us in the Prophecies, worked there at night with his occult books. He also mentions later that he burnt a lot of them once he had finished with them, but it is difficult to believe that a true scholar could possibly do this. It was more probably an attempt to mislead the Church authorities. The main source of his magical inspirations was a book called *De Mysteriis Egyptorum*, a copy of which was published at Lyons in 1547, and which Nostradamus almost certainly possessed, as he quotes from it line for line in his prophecies.

It was also about this time, 1554, that Jean Aymes de Chavigny, a former mayor of Beaune, gave up his position in that city and came to Nostradamus as a pupil to study judicial astrology and astronomy. He wrote several books about Nostradamus after the prophet's death and certainly helped to edit the first complete edition of the Prophecies, but, like Nostradamus' son César, he seems to have exaggerated his own importance with regard to the prophet. The evidence for this lies in Nostradamus' will, a long and detailed document referring not only to to his money but detailing all his possessions. There is no reference to Chavigny concerning Nostradamus' papers which he states specifically are to be left to whichever of his sons on reaching maturity 'has drunk the smoke of the lamp' i.e. is a true scholar. Chavigny did, however, edit a great many of Nostradamus' papers, probably with the consent of his widow.

By 1555 Nostradamus had completed the first part of his book of prophecies that were to contain predictions from his time to the end of the world. The word Century has nothing to do with one hundred years; it was so called because there were a hundred verses, or quatrains, in each book, of which Nostradamus intended to write ten, making one thousand quatrains in all. For some unknown reason, the Seventh Century was never completed, and there are indications among his papers that Nostradamus was considering adding an Eleventh and Twelfth Century, which were prevented by his death.

The verses are written in a crabbed, obscure style, with a polyglot of vocabulary of French, Provençal, Italian, Greek and Latin. In order to avoid being prosecuted as a magician, Nostradamus writes that he deliberately confused the time sequence of the Prophecies so that their secrets would not be revealed to the non-initiate.

It is extraordinary how quickly the fame of Nostradamus spread across France and Europe on the strength of the Prophecies, published in their incomplete form of 1555. The book contained only the first three Centuries and part of the fourth. At this time books were an expensive luxury and were usually owned and read only by the rich, for most of the population were illiterate. The Prophecies became all the rage at Court, and one or two seemed to invoke a certain uneasiness among the courtiers, particularly the one which appeared to predict the king's death (I. 35). Be that as it may, the Queen, Catherine de' Medici, sent for Nostradamus to come to Court, and he set out for Paris on 14th July 1556. The journey took only one month because the Queen had horses posted for him, instead of the more usual eight weeks. On 15th August, Nostradamus booked a room at the Inn of St. Michel, near Notre Dame. The Queen must have been very anxious to see him because she sent for him the next day and the Chief Constable took him to the Court of St. Germain en Laye.

One could only wish that there had been a witness to record their meeting. Nostradamus and the Queen spoke together for two hours. She is reputed to have asked him about the quatrain concerning the king's death and to have been satisfied with Nostradamus' answer. Certainly she continued to believe in Nostradamus' predictions until her death. The king, Henri II, granted Nostradamus only a brief audience and was obviously not greatly interested, although he sent Nostradamus one hundred golden crowns, and Catherine sent another thirty. This seemed poor recompense to Nostradamus, who had expended one hundred crowns on his journey alone. However, his lodgings were exchanged for the grandeur of the palace of the Archbishop of Sens, where he remained for some two weeks seeing people who came for advice, drawing up horoscopes, and offering prophetic guidance. The Queen then sent for him a second time and now Nostradamus was faced with the delicate and difficult task of drawing up the horoscopes of the seven Valois children, whose tragic fates he had already revealed in the Centuries. All he would tell Catherine was that all of her sons would be kings, which is slightly inaccurate since one of them, François, died before he could inherit. If on the other hand what he actually said was that he saw four kings to come, then the prediction was accurate because Henri III was king of Poland before returning to be king of France.

Soon afterwards Nostradamus was warned that the Justices of Paris were enquiring about his magic practices, and he returned quickly to Salon. He was welcomed home as a person of importance. From this time on, suffering from gout and arthritis, he seems to have done little except draw up horoscopes for his many distinguished visitors and complete the writing of the Prophecies. Apparently he allowed a few manuscript copies to circulate before publication, because many of the predictions were understood and quoted before the completed book came off the printing press in 1568, two years after his death.

The reason for this reticence was probably the king's death in 1559. Nostradamus had predicted it in I. 35 and may have felt that it was too explicit for comfort and that it would be advisable to wait a few more years until things had quietened down. But the following year, 1560, King Francis II, married to Mary Queen of Scots, died, and this time the courtiers openly quoted quatrain 39 of Century X.

'The eldest son; a widow of an unfortunate marriage with no children; two islands in discord; before eighteen still a minor; for the other one the betrothal will take place when even younger.' Francis II was Henri II's eldest son. He died six weeks before reaching the age of eighteen leaving a widow, Mary Queen of Socts, whose return to her country was to put two realms at discord. Francis' younger brother, Charles, had been betrothed at the early age of eleven to Elizabeth of Austria.

In 1564 Catherine, now Queen Regent, decided to make a Royal Progress through France with her second son Charles IX and the rest of her family. The progress was to take two years and the court entourage was reduced to a minimum of eight hundred people. While travelling through Provence Catherine naturally came to Salon to see Nostradamus. He dined with the King and Queen and she also visited him at his house and admired his children. This time Catherine gave Nostradamus three hundred gold crowns and the title Physician in Ordinary, which carried with it a salary and other fringe benefits, which doubtless pleased him.

Another interesting incident occurred during this visit to Salon when Nostradamus asked to see the moles on the body of a young boy in the entourage. This was a common form of prediction, but the child was shy and ran away. Nostradamus went to see him the next day while asleep and declared that he would one day be king of France, although Catherine still had two sons living. The boy was Henri of Navarre, who later became Henri IV.

By now the gout from which he suffered was turning to dropsy and Nostradamus, the doctor, realized that his end was near. He made his will on 17th June 1566 and left the large sum, for those days, of 3,444 crowns over and above his other possessions. On 1st July he sent for the local priest to give him the last rites, and when Chavigny took leave of him that night, told him that he would not see him alive again. His body was found the next morning, as he himself had predicted, 'trouvé tout mort pres du lit & du banc'. He was buried upright in one of the walls of the Church of the Cordeliers at Salon, and his wife Anne erected a splendid marble plaque to his memory. Nostradamus' grave was opened by superstitious soldiers during the Revolution but his remains were reburied in the other church at Salon, the Church of St. Laurent, where his grave and portrait can still be seen.

HISTORY OF THE CENTURIES SINCE PUBLICATION

In evaluating the works of anyone who claims to have prophetic powers it is essential to know which of those writings attributed to him are really his own, and which publication dates are genuine. Nostradamus in particular has been the victim of many forgeries over the centuries which may help to account for his undeservedly bad reputation.

There is great confusion about all the early editions of Nostradamus' works, including the Prophecies, because they were first printed in two parts, in 1555 and 1568. Several of the oldest editions are undated and there are several counterfeit 'first' editions which have altered texts and were printed more than one hundred years later than the date on their frontispiece.

There are so many editions of the Prophecies that it is impossible to list them here, but Nostradamus is probably the only author who could claim that his work has never been out of print for over four hundred years, apart from the Bible. The interest he generates is extraordinary. On an average about thirty books, either editions of the Prophecies, or critical appreciations of them, have been published each century since his death. Of course, times of crisis, such as the French Revolution, and the First and Second World Wars, produce a spate of such books. Some are frankly bad, and make no attempt at impartiality of judgment and often change the text to suit themselves. Others are sceptical and critical, but none manage wholly to dismiss out of hand the small hard core of Nostradamus' accurate predictions.

Nostradamus was used as a propaganda machine as early as 1649 and as late as 1943. In 1649 the opponents of Cardinal Mazarin, who felt he had too great an influence in the French Court, published an edition of the Prophecies, dating it 1568, in which they planted two obvious quatrains against the Cardinal. When the Bastille was stormed on 14th July 1789, the Revolutionaries recognized themselves in the Preface to the Prophecies, for apparently a copy was laid open on a table in the prison, and for ten days the people filed past, to read confirmation of their achievements. Napoleon's attention was drawn to the Prophecies by the Empress Josephine, but he was also the victim of an unscrupulous forgery which was declared to have been written by Nostradamus, called the Prophecies of Olivarius. It was a fake and its true date is *circa* 1820. A later similar forgery appeared in 1839 called the Prophecy of Orval. Neither of these works have anything to do with Nostradamus.

His fame was not confined to France. Editions of the Prophecies appeared all over Europe within twenty-five years of their first publication. Again it is impossible to list them all here, but if one mentions that twenty-six known editions and four forged ones were published in Europe between 1555 and 1643, at a time when books were valuable, one is given some idea of the strength of Nostradamus' popularity, which has continued to the present day.

From 1860 onwards a provincial French curé, called the Abbé Torné to which he added the surname Chavigny after Nostradamus' pupil, produced a series of interpretations of Nostradamus' quatrains which shook France and affected many political decisions of the time. He was convinced that the Bourbon line would be restored to the French throne. Equally he was certain that in the next war France would be invaded by means of Switzerland, and it was because of this information that the then French Chief of Staff ordered the drawing up of the disastrous Maginot line on the strength of Quatrain 80 in Century IV. Incredible but true.

Hitler's interest in Nostradamus was first aroused by the notorious Hister quatrains discovered by Frau Dr. Goebbels who, as I have mentioned, drew her husband's attention to them in 1939. By May 1940 onwards, the Germans were dropping from aircraft crude forgeries of various quatrains from the Prophecies which predicted that Hitler would be victorious and that the war would not affect South-eastern France. By this means the Germans hoped to clear the roads to Paris and the Channel ports. In retaliation, British Intelligence, 'inspired' by Louis de Wohl, who was probably as great a charlatan as any, spent an enormous sum on anti-German propaganda, carefully composing and imitating selected German Nostradamus quatrains which Allied pilots dropped over France and Belgium. This occurred as late as 1943. Books have continued to be written about Nostradamus ever since.

The final problem remaining with regard to Nostradamus is as to whether the man was a prophet or fraud. He believed himself to possess certain powers, although there is reason to believe he could not draw on these to order. They certainly sometimes let him down in the Prophecies. The reader must decide whether it is possible to believe in prediction, whether a man who wrote over four hundred years ago could possibly glimpse incidents in the future, or whether it is just inspired guesswork. It is essential for thinking man to believe in free will, to believe that his future can be changed by thought and action. Prophecy denies this and declares that all futures are immutable and fixed, that nothing man strives towards is relevant, as is already preordained by whatever governs his future, be it God or Destiny. I believe that mankind must have free will; but also I must admit the disturbing fact that although I can dismiss ninety-five per cent of Nostradamus' predictions as historical coincidence, there remain a few quatrains which are hard to reconcile with this. What about the one describing Louis XVI's flight to Varennes, the ones mentioning Napoleon and Hitler? What about the verses giving the actual month and year of an occurrence, such as that which describes the obscure treaty between the Persians and the Turks in October

1727, or another which gives the day and month of the assassination of a Prince? (III. 96) I find this type of quatrain difficult to explain away completely. They appear to me to be more than coincidence.

The modern disciples of Einstein recognize nothing but an eternal present which was also what the ancient mystics believed. If the future exists already then precognition is a fact. The whole trend of advanced knowledge is to place the laws of physics in a four dimensional continuum, that is, the eternal present. If this is so then past, present and future exist simultaneously. Perhaps it is only our consciousness that moves? One day we may know and then precognition would become an accepted fact.

But, on the other hand, the answer may lie in Dunne's concept of alternative variable futures which run parallel to each other. Each man receives the future dependent upon his earlier actions. Nostradamus could have glimpsed these parallels of time which may or may not have occurred, depending upon the earlier freely determined actions of other men. No man can be in any sense an island; all our actions affect someone else. Thus if Louis XVI had done the sensible thing and stayed in Paris instead of fleeing in a panic to Varennes, there would have been another incomprehensible quatrain in this book. Equally, however appalling it may appear, if Hitler's attention had not been drawn to the Prophecies and the connection between Poland and Britain, would he have gone to war at that time?

The reader can try to reconcile the concept of free will with the mathematical probability of chance. By means of E.S.P. or some similar faculty, possibly the future may be vaguely seen and grasped at—a future conditioned by the education of the man who receives it. Humanity does seem to repeat its mistakes, or as Dr. Inge says, resemble itself to a remarkable degree. This is proven by the fact that some of the quatrains—the ones I call split quatrains—will quite accurately predict events separated by over a century in time. But it seems that if we wish to avoid the gloomy future that Nostradamus foresees for mankind, we must break away from our present behaviour pattern, conditioned over the last few hundred years, and grow outwards towards a new concept of worldwide peace and brotherhood, and away from Nostradamus' medieval concepts of famine, war and tragedy.

THE TEXT, TRANSLATION AND COMMENTARY

Throughout this edition I have used the text of the first edition, published by Benoit Rigaud in 1568. The concessions I have made to the reader are mainly in the realm of spelling. I have changed *u* to *v* when required, *y* to *i*, *f* to *s*, and added *n* or *m* when only indicated by an accent, e.g. *côplaire = complaire*. I have copied the same punctuation, accents and capital letters as the original.

Opposite each quatrain I have given a very literal translation, which may seem nonsensical at first sight because I have kept as closely as possible to the Latin style of the original. I explain proper names and obscure words in footnotes. Below the translation is a prose commentary with a heading summarizing the subject matter when possible, for those who wish to skip quickly through the book. In the list of subjects at the beginning of each quatrain I have marked the interesting ones with an asterisk and those that possibly apply to our future, or which are especially intriguing, with an F? or an *. Those quatrains which I cannot decipher I leave to the ingenuity and patience of the reader.

I have omitted the Preface to the first edition and the Epistle to Caesar, which is placed before the Seventh Century because of length and obscurity. I will deal with them in detail in the companion book to this one on Nostradamus' life and beliefs.

January 1972

CENTURY I

1	Nostradamus' method of divination
2	Divination
3*	French Revolution, 1789
4*	Napoleon and Pius VII
5	Huguenot struggles in Provence, 1562–98
6	French occupation of Italian towns, 1601
7*	Dreyfus case, 1894
8	Henri IV. Siege of Paris, 1590
9	Henri IV. Siege of Malta, 1565
10	Fates of Children of Catherine de' Medici and Henri II
11	
12	
13	Conspiracy of Amboise, 1560
14	French Revolution, 1789
15	Difficulties facing the Church
16F?	War towards end of Century
17	Floods and drought
18	Second World War
19	Catherine de' Medici
20	Occupation of Loire towns
21	
22	Medical
23*	Battle of Waterloo, 1815
24*	Napoleon at Villa Nova, 1795
25*	Louis Pasteur
26	Kennedy assassinations
27	
28	Tobruk. Second World War, 1941
29*	Polaris or SUBROC
30	
31*	Downfall of Spanish monarchy, Second World War
32*	Napoleon at St. Helena
33	

34*   Hitler and France, 1938/40
35*   Death of Henri II, 1559
36*   Death of Henri III, 1588
37   Pius VI and France
38*   Waterloo, 1815
39   Death of Louis Bourbon Condé, 1830
40
41
42*   Institution of Gregorian Calendar, 1582
43
44   Cult of Reason, 1793, during French Revolution
45
46
47*   League of Nations
48   Dating of prophecies
49   Events around 1700
50*F?   Third Antichrist?
51F?   Events 1702–1802. Possible war 1995?
52   Death of Sultan Selim III, 1807/8
53*   Disestablishment of clergy during French Revolution, 1790
54*   Two revolutions followed by a war
55*
56
57*   Execution of Louis XVI, 1793
58   Napoleon and the Bourbons
59
60   Napoleon
61
62
63*F?   Air travel followed by war. 20th Century
64*   Air battle. 20th Century
65
66
67*F?   World Famine
68
69
70
71
72*   French casualties. Second World War
73   France and Common Market?
74
75

76*   Napoleon I
77*   Battle of Trafalgar. 1805
78
79
80
81
82*   Austria, 1914–18
83   Italian Occupation of Greece, 1940
84   Murder of Duke de Berry, 1820
85*   Fate of the de Guise family, 1588
86*   Flight of Mary Queen of Scots, 1568
87*F? New York?
88*   Charles I and Parliament
89   Peninsular Wars, 1808
90
91*F? Future war devastating America?
92   Franco-Prussian war
93*   Napoleon's Italian Campaign, 1795
94   Lepanto, 1571
95
96   Religious revival
97*   Assassination of Henri III, 1589
98   Napoleon's Expedition to Egypt, 1798
99
100   Comte de Chambord

KEY: * Of interest. F? Possibly referring to the future.

Estant assis de nuict secret estude
Seul reposé sur la selle d'aerain;
Flambe exiguë sortant de soli-
tude
Fait prosperer qui n'est à croire
vain.

Sitting alone at night in secret study; it is placed on the brass tripod. A slight flame comes out of the emptiness and makes successful that which should not be believed in vain.

DIVINATION

Both this and the following quatrain describe Nostradamus' method of divination, they are not predictions. Nostradamus used the methods of the 4th Century neo-Platonist Iamblichus, a reprint of whose book *De Mysteriis Egyptorum* was published at Lyons in 1547 and almost certainly read by Nostradamus. It may well have been the source of his experiments with prophecy, for soon afterwards his almanacs started to appear.

All the ingredients for magical practices are in this quatrain. It is night. Nostradamus is alone in his study reading the secret forbidden books which inspire his prophecies; the brass tripod is a method used by Iamblichus—on it was placed a bowl of water into which the seer gazed until the water became cloudy and pictures of the future were revealed. *Flambe exiguë* is the light of inspiration which seizes Nostradamus as he begins to prophesy.

2

La verge en main mise au milieu
des BRANCHES[1]
De l'onde il moulle[2] *& le limbe*[3]
& le pied:
Un peur & voix fremissant par les
manches:
Splendeur divine. Le divin pres
s'assied.

The wand in the hand is placed in the middle of the tripod's legs. With water he sprinkles both the hem of his garment and his foot. A voice, fear; he trembles in his robes. Divine splendour; the god sits nearby.

DIVINATION

Nostradamus continues to explain his method. He touches the middle of the tripod with his wand, and then moistens his robe and his feet with the water placed on it. This is the same method as was used to obtain inspiration by the Apollonian prophetess at the

[1] *Branches*—Capitals in original = (*a*) The three limbs or branches of the tripod. (*b*) Indirect reference to the prophetess of Branchus.
[2] *moulle*—Modern french *mouille* = to moisten.
[3] *limbe*—Latin, *limbus* hem of a garment.

oracles of Branchus in Classical times. Nostradamus is afraid of the power he evokes when it comes to him; he hears it, as well as sees it; it appears to speak to him and he writes down the prophecies. He is unafraid once the gift has possessed him. This dual aspect of his vision is most important when interpreting the centuries.

3

Quand la licture du tourbillon versee,
Et seront faces de leurs manteaux convers:
La republique par gens nouveaux vexée,
Lors blancs & rouges jugeront à l'envers.

When the litters are overturned by the whirlwind and faces are covered by cloaks, the new republic will be troubled by its people. At this time the reds and the whites will rule wrongly.

FRENCH REVOLUTION

The French Revolution of 1789, which Nostradamus calls the Common Advent, the coming of the ordinary men in the Preface, is here described. The aristocracy were always carried in litters, and this, their symbol, is overturned by the violent whirlwind of revolution. Could the line mentioning the heads covered by cloaks refer to the many exiles who fled from France, or possibly to the heads which fell from the guillotine and were hidden from sight? It is interesting that Nostradamus should here refer to France as a republic, and to one that was greatly troubled by its new rulers. The era of Danton, Murat and Robespierre during the terror springs vividly to mind. White was the colour of the Bourbon kings and red, of course, that of the revolutionaries. The last line 'à l'envers' may also imply that the law givers, i.e. the church and aristocracy, were judged by the populace who were unsuited for this work.

4

Par l'univers sera faict un monarque,
Qu'en paix & vie ne sera longuement,
Lors se perdra la piscature[1] barque,
Sera regie en plus grand detriment.

In the world there will be made a king who will have little peace and a short life. At this time the ship of the Papacy will be lost, governed to its greatest detriment.

[1] piscature—Latin, piscature = fishing, but a common synonym for the Papacy.

Napoleon crowned himself king and Emperor of France on 18th May 1804 and abdicated in April 1814, ruling for the short time of ten years. Peace was certainly not a characteristic of his era. Pius VII (1800–23) first came to France to crown Napoleon an Emperor, but on his second visit he came as a prisoner. The French army, under General Miollis, captured Rome in 1809 and the Papal States were joined to the French Empire in 1810; the Pope was held prisoner by Napoleon and only released by the abdication at Fontainbleau on 23rd January 1814. The last line refers to the general religious anarchy that existed in France from the time of the dissolution of the Clergy in 1792.

5

Chassés seront pour faire long combat,	They will be driven away for a long drawn out fight. The
Par le pays seront plus fort grevés:	countryside will be most griev-
Bourg & Cité auront plus grand debat,	ously troubled. Town and country will have the greater
Carcas[1] *Narbonne auront coeur esprouvéz.*	struggle. Carcassonne and Narbonne will have their hearts tried.

HUGUENOT STRUGGLES IN PROVENCE, 1562–98

The whole of southern France was greatly afflicted by the religious wars which broke out between Huguenots and Catholics before the accession of Henri IV. Carcassonne declared itself for the Catholic League but the Huguenots seized part of the town, and Narbonne also suffered a great deal of fighting. A general quatrain covering a wide period of over thirty years. Nostradamus was always greatly interested in the fate of France and those towns he knew and had lived in during his wanderings.

6

L'oeil de Ravenne sera destitué,	The eye of Ravenna will be forsaken, when his wings will
Quand à ses pieds les ailles failliront:	fail at his feet. The two of
Les deux de Bresse auront con- stitué,	Bresse will have made a con- stitution for Turin and Ver-
Turin, Derseil[2] *que Gaulois foule- ront.*	celli, which the French will trample underfoot.

[1] Apocope of Carcassonne.
[2] Read *Versail* = Vercelli, Piedmont, Italy.

FRENCH OCCUPATION OF BRESSE, 1601,
TURIN, 1640 etc. VERCELLI 1904 etc. CAPTURED
FROM THE PAPAL STATES

Ravenna has been part of the Papal States since 1509, and the most likely interpretation of this quatrain concerns the fates of the states mentioned above, Bresse, Turin and Vercelli, which were all occupied by the French at some period. Bresse was ceded to France in 1601, Turin was taken by the French in 1640 and 1798–1814. Vercelli was also captured in 1704 and 1798–1814. All that is certain is that each of these places, except for Ravenna, suffered French occupation after the Centuries were written.

7

Tard arrivé l'execution faicte,[1]	Arrived too late, the act has been done. The wind was against them, letters intercepted on their way. The conspirators were fourteen of a party. By Rousseau shall these enterprises be undertaken.
Le vent contraire lettres aux chemin prinses:	
Les conjurez xiiii d'une secte:	
Par le Rousseau semez[2] *les entreprinses.*	

DREYFUS CASE, 1894–1906.
M. WALDECK ROUSSEAU, 1899

Alfred Dreyfus, a Jewish French soldier was condemned for treason, selling military secrets to the Germans in 1894, and publicly degraded and transported to a penal colony, l'Ile du Diable in 1895. In 1899 he was brought back to France for a public retrial but due to strong anti-semitic influences was again found guilty, but with extenuating circumstances. President Loubet pardoned him ten days later and the courts ordered further investigation of the case. The letters which convicted him were declared forgeries and Dreyfus innocent. The case troubled French society for some years to come. Nostradamus describes the proof of Dreyfus' innocence as arriving too late, for his sentence has already been passed and he is in the penal colony. *Vent contraire* is interpreted as political, i.e. anti-semitic, feeling running high against Dreyfus. The minister who was called upon to revise the Dreyfus case in 1899 was M. Waldeck Rousseau, whose name is given in the last line. He was violently anti-Dreyfus, finding him guilty a second time until the

---

[1] *faicte*—Normal spelling of the period for fait.
[2] Two alternatives. Either *semez*, to spread, which I accept, or *senez* = wise.

public pardon. The number of conspirators may well have been fourteen, but it is impossible to prove at this date.

8

Combien de fois prinse cité solaire	How often will you be cap-
Seras changeant les loix barbares &	tured, O city of the sun? Chang-
vaines:	ing laws that are barbaric and
Ton mal s'approche. Plus sera	vain. Bad times approach you.
tributaire,	No longer will you be enslaved.
La grand Hadrie[1] recourira des	Great Hadrie will revive your
veines.	veins.

Combien de fois prinse cité solaire
Seras changeant les loix barbares &
  vaines:
Ton mal s'approche. Plus sera
  tributaire,
La grand Hadrie[1] *recourira des*
  veines.

How often will you be captured, O city of the sun? Changing laws that are barbaric and vain. Bad times approach you. No longer will you be enslaved. Great Hadrie will revive your veins.

HENRI IV. SIEGE OF PARIS, 1590

After his accession to the French throne Henri IV de Navarre had to besiege Paris for six months before he could enter the city in September 1590. It is called Solaire, city of the sun, a suitable epithet if one thinks of Louis XVI, the Sun King. The barbarous laws refer to the innovations of the Seize which was the first truly revolutionary faction to govern Paris. '*Ton mal s'approche*'; the siege occurred less than thirty years after Nostradamus' death and he seems to feel the accession of a Huguenot king deeply. The last line is interesting in that throughout the siege from April to September Henri IV allowed food to be passed through the lines to the starving people of Paris. Perhaps this line is to be taken in its most literal form, or more metaphorically in that the new line of the Navarre family will revive the greatness of France and the French kings?

9

De l'Orient viendra la coeur
  Punique
Facher Hadrie & les hoirs[2]
  Romulides
Accompagné de la classe[3] *Libyque*
Temples Mellites[4] *& proches isles*
  vuides.

From the Orient will come the African heart to trouble Hadrie and the heirs of Romulus. Accompanied by the Libyan fleet the temples of Malta and nearby islands shall be deserted.

[1] *Hadrie*—Henry by anagram, one letter being altered according to Nostradamus' rules.

[2] *hoirs* = heirs. The heirs of Romulus are of course the Italians.

[3] *classe*—Latin, *classis* = fleet.

[4] *Mellites* = adjective, Maltese.

1. HENRI IV AND THE DUC DE PARME.
2. THE SIEGE OF MALTA

This quatrain should be divided into two parts. Lines 1–2 continue from the last verse and refer again to Henri IV. The man who troubles him from the East is the Duke of Parma who compelled Henri to raise his siege of Paris in 1590 in order to meet the Spanish army advancing from Flanders. This annoyed the Pope (the heir of Romulus) who favoured the Navarre claim and was hostile to Spanish policy at this point.

Lines 3–4 most probably refer to the siege of Malta in 1565 and the Libyan fleet is then the Turkish navy which roamed the Mediterranean. These are not quite contemporary events.

10

Serpens[1] transmis dans la caige de fer,
Ou les enfans septaines[2] du Roy sont pris:
Les vieux & peres sortiront bas de l'enfer,
Ains mourir voir de fruict mort & cris.

A coffin is put into the vault of iron, where the seven children of the king are held. The ancestors and forebears will come forth from the depths of hell, lamenting to see thus dead the fruit of their line.

FATES OF VALOIS CHILDREN AND HENRI III's DEATH, 1610

This complicated quatrain refers to the fall of the House of Valois and in particular to the removal of the remains of the last Valois king, Henri III, in 1610 to the family sepulchre at Saint Denis. The theme of the seven Valois children of Catherine de' Medici, Queen of France, wife of Henri II, recurs several times in the quatrains. Nostradamus seems clearly aware that the line will die out although it is only fair to admit that Henri III was not the last to die, as Marguerite de Navarre lived until 1615. Line three is a poetic reference to the family ghosts who return to mourn the end of the Valois line.

[1] Serpens—From serpos, Gk. = Shroud.
[2] enfans septaines = (a) François II, 1549–60. (b) Elisabeth 1545–68. (c) Claude 1547–75. (d) Charles IX 1550–74. (e) Henri III 1551–89. (f) Marguerite 1552–1615. (g) François duc d'Alençon 1554–84.

Le mouvement de sens, coeur, pieds & mains,	The motion of senses, heart, feet and hands will be in agreement between Naples, Lyon and Sicily. Swords, fire, floods, then the noble Romans drowned, killed or dead because of a weak brain.
Seront d'accord Naples, Lyon,[1] *Sicille:*	
Glaves, feux, eaux puis aux nobles Romains,	
Plongez tuez mors par cerveau debile.	

All the places mentioned, if one accepts the reading Leon for Lyon, were part of the Spanish Hapsburg Empire. The weak mind may imply that some Pope would cause trouble between the Vatican and the Empire?

12

Dans peu dira faulce brute fragile,	There will soon be talk of a treacherous man, who rules a short time, quickly raised from low to high estate. He will suddenly turn disloyal and volatile. This man will govern Verona.
De bas en haut eslue promptement:	
Puis un instant desloyale & labile,	
Qui de Veronne aura gouvernement.	

From 1405–1562 Verona was governed by podestas, the office of a captain which was meant to change yearly. After that date it was ruled by a council of proveditors. The last podesta was Jacapo Sansebastiani 1539/62, but he was not a traitor.

13

Les exilez par ire, haine intestine,	Through anger and internal hatreds, the exiles will hatch a great plot against the king. Secretly they will place enemies as a threat, and his own old (adherents) will find sedition against them.
Feront au Roy grand conjuration:	
Secret mettront ennemis par la mine,	
Et ses vieux siens contre aux sedition.	

CONSPIRACY OF AMBOISE, 1560 (?)

This is a generally worded quatrain concerning the Conspiracy of Amboise 1560. The coming to power of the Guise family in France, caused other parties, in particular the Montmorencys and the Bourbons, to conspire to kill the Duc de Guise and kidnap the

[1] *Lyon*—Alternative reading = Leon.

King, Francis II. However the plot leaked out in advance and was suppressed.

14

De gent esclave[1] chansons, chants & requestes,	From the enslaved populace, songs, chants and demands,
Captifs par Princes & Seigneur[2] aux prisons:	while Princes and Lords are held captive in prisons. These
A l'avenir par idiots sans testes,[3]	will in the future be received
Seront reçus par divines oraisons.	by headless idiots as divine prayers.

FRENCH REVOLUTION, 1789

Most commentators accept this quatrain as referring to the songs and demands of the populace while Louis XVI was imprisoned with his family in the Temple. The idiots who lose their heads are the early ringleaders of the terror who in their turn will follow the aristocracy to the guillotine, but who are regarded at first as inspired leaders of the Revolution.

15

Mars nous menace par la force bellique,[4]	Mars threatens us with the force of war and will cause
Septante fois fera le sang espandre:	blood to be spilt seventy times.
Auge[5] & ruine de l'Ecclesiastique,	The clergy will be both exalted
Et plus ceux qui d'eux rien voudront entendre.	and reviled moreover, by those who wish to learn nothing of them.

DIFFICULTIES FACING THE CHURCH

Commentators of the early 19th Century, such as Nicollaud, take lines 1–2 as referring to Napoleon (Mars) and the many wars of the Empire. The church was both humbled and exalted during this period. In 1792 the clergy were disbanded and religion almost vanished from France during the early days of the Directoire. However by 1804 Napoleon had recognized the Pope and the position of the clergy in order to legitimize his coronation. The troubles facing the Catholic Church in the future is a common theme through the Prophecies. Religious practice is certainly declining in most western countries at the present time.

[1] *esclave* = (*a*) enslaved, (*b*) Slav or Russian?
[2] Singular use of *Seigneur* may indicate King Louis XVI.
[3] *testes*—O.F. for *têtes* = heads.
[4] *bellique*—Latin, *bellicus* = warlike.
[5] *Auge*—Latin, *augere* = to increase.

Faulx[1] *à l'estang*[2] *joint vers le Sagitaire,*[3]
En son hault AUGE[4] *de l'exaltation,*
Peste, famine, mort de main militaire,
La siecle approche de renouvation.

A scythe joined with a pond in Sagittarius at its highest ascendant. Plague, famine, death from military hands; the century approaches its renewal.

POSSIBLE WAR TOWARDS THE END OF THE CENTURY?

When Saturn and Aquarius are in conjunction with Sagittarius in the ascendant, towards the end of a century, we should expect a great war, together with disease and famine. This description is so general that it could fit our century as well as any other. Nostradamus does refer later in Centuries to the possibility of a third war towards the end of this Century. See I. 91, II. 41, 46, 62, VI. 97, VIII. 59, 77, X. 49, 72, 74, 75.

Par quarante ans l'Iris n'apparoistra,
Par quarante ans tous les jours sera veu:
La terre aride en siccité croistra,
Et grans deluges quand sera aperceu.

For forty years the rainbow will not be seen. For forty years it will be seen every day. The dry earth will grow more parched, and there will be great floods when it is seen.

FLOODS AND DROUGHT

This must be left to the reader. There is no record of a forty-year drought followed by forty years of flooding. One of the general quatrains of gloom and doom.

Par la discorde negligence Gauloise,
Sera passaige à Mahommet ouvert:
De sang trempé la terre & mer Senoise,
Le port phocen[5] *de voiles & nefs convert.*

Because of French discord and negligence an opening shall be given to the Mohammedans. The land and sea of Siena will be soaked in blood, and the port of Marseilles covered with ships and sails.

[1] *Faulx* = a scythe, the sign of Saturn.
[2] *l'estang* = a pond, or water sign, i.e. Saturn in Aquarius.
[3] *Sagitaire* = (Nov.–Dec.) sign of the Zodiac.
[4] *Auge*—Latin, *augere* = increase.
[5] *phocen* = Marseilles, founded by the people of Phocaea, the mother city in W. Asia Minor.

FRANCE AND NORTH AFRICA.
SECOND WORLD WAR

This refers to the chaos in France during 1940 which allowed the Italian armies to march into North Africa without hindrance. The Italian blood spilt would refer to the battles in the desert; the harbour at Marseilles was constantly operative, although in German hands.

19

Lors que serpens viendront cir-cuir[1] l'are,[2]	When the snakes surround the altar, and the Trojan blood is troubled by the Spanish. Because of them, a great number will be lessened. The leader flees, hidden in the swampy marshes.
Le sang Troyen vexé par les Espaignes:	
Par eux grand nombre en sera faicte tare.	
Chef fruict,[3] caché aux mares[4] dans les saignes.[5]	

CATHERINE DE' MEDICI

Catherine de' Medici, Queen mother of France, changed her emblem after her husband's death to a serpent biting its tail curled round a star, not an altar. Trojan blood is the usual Nostradamus description of Royal blood derived from the medieval legend that the French Royal family were descended from Francus, a mythical son of Priam. The French trouble with Spain did not really occur until the interregnum 1589–94, and the later war of the Spanish succession. Another suggestion is that the snakes refer to the Huguenots pressing hard around the Catholic altar, but the reference to Trojan blood links it to Catherine de' Medici and the French royal line. The last line is unclear.

20

Tours, Orleans, Blois, Angiers, Reims, & Nantes,	The cities of Tours, Orleans, Blois, Angers, Reims and Nantes are troubled by sudden change. Tents will be pitched by (people) of foreign tongues; rivers, darts at Rennes, shaking of land and sea.
Cités vexées par subit changement:	
Par langues estranges seront ten-dues tentes,[6]	
Fleuves, dards Rones, terre & mer tremblement.	

[1] *circuir*—Latin, circuire = to encircle.
[2] *are*—Latin, ara = altar. [3] *fruict*—fuit = flee.
[4] *mares*—O.F. = swamp marsh. [5] *seigne*—O.F. = swamp, marsh.
[6] *tentes* = (a) Tents pitched by invaders. (b) Latin, *tentare*, to attack. These cities will be attacked by invaders. The meaning is substantially the same.

All the cities, except for Reims, are situated on the Loire and have suffered several foreign invasions, mainly the Prussian and Russian armies in 1815, the Prussians again in 1871 and 1940, and also the Americans in 1917–19 and 1944–5. There is no record of an earthquake at Rennes since publication.

21

Profonde argille blanche nourrit rochier,	The rock holds in its depths white clay which will come
Qui d'un abisme istra[1] lactineuse:[2]	out milk-white from a cleft.
En vain troublez ne l'oseront toucher,	Needlessly troubled people will not dare touch it, unaware that
Ignorans estre au fond terre argilleuse.	the foundation of the earth is of clay.

No connection with local historical events can be found to explain this odd verse. I wonder whether the language has alchemistic undertones?

22

Ce que vivra & n'ayant ancien sens,	A thing existing without any
Viendra leser à mort son artifice:	senses will cause its own end
Austun, Chalan, Langres & les deux Sens,	to happen through artifice. At Autun, Chalan, Langres
La gresle & glace fera grand malefice.	and the two Sens there will be great damage from hail and ice.

MEDICAL? *c.* 1613

A very interesting solution to this quatrain occurs in Garancières. He states that in 1613 a petrified embryo was removed by operation (artifice) from the womb of a woman called Colomba Chantry who lived at Sens. This quite a rare event; examples can be found in medical textbooks, and a woman living in Italy two years ago was found to have been carrying a petrified embryo well into her sixties; an interesting medical sideline from Nostradamus the doctor. All the towns mentioned belong to the Duchy of Burgundy. The reference to the weather seems very general, the quatrain implying that it occurred around the same period, 1613. The second town of Sens is near Louhans.

[1] *istra*—O.F. = *aller* to go (ira).
[2] *lactineuse*—Latin, *lac* = milk. *lacticineum* = milk food.

Au mois troisiesme se levant le soleil
Sanglier, Liepard au champ Mars pour combattre:
Liepard laissé, au ciel extend son oeil,
Un aigle autour du Soleil voit s'esbattre.

In the third month, at sunrise, the Boar and the Leopard meet on the battlefield. The fatigued Leopard looks up to heaven and sees an eagle playing around the sun.

BATTLE OF WATERLOO. 18th JUNE 1815.
NAPOLEON'S 100 DAYS

This is one of Nostradamus' most fascinating quatrains. The background to the battle of Waterloo was that Blücher, the Prussian Boar, had been beaten back at Ligny and the joining up of the British and Prussian forces had therefore not been able to take place when Wellington decided to make his stand at Waterloo. This was in June, just over three months after Napoleon's return from Elba in February 1815 (*au mois troisiesme*). It may also contain a reference to Napoleon's reign of 100 days which this battle brought to an end. Equally, dating from the March solstice, which Nostradamus would have done, we are given the month of June for the date of the battle. This is a typical example of Nostradamus' convoluted style where meaning after meaning appears to be contained in one phrase. The French troops battered the English Leopard all day from sunrise to evening while Wellington waited for his ally Blücher to turn the French flank. Wellington's position was facing south so he would have seen Napoleon's Imperial eagles flying against the sun. As the day drew to a close, the British were exhausted. A cloud of dust was seen. Napoleon thought it was Grouchy, but it was Blücher. The end had come. This is a vivid and poetic quatrain of a much higher standard than most. The Imperial Eagle is often used in the Centuries as a synonym for Napoleon himself. On this occasion it refers both to the standards and to the man. Napoleon used to call the English heraldic lion the Leopard of England.

A cité neufue pensif pour condemner,	At the New City he is thought-
L'oisel de proye au ciel se vient	ful to condemn; the bird of
offrir:	prey offers himself to the gods.
Apres victoire à captifs pardonner,	After victory he pardons his
Cremone & Mantoue grands maux	captives. At Cremona and
aura souffert.	Mantua great hardships will
	be suffered.

NAPOLEON AT VILLA NOVA, AND THE
SIEGE OF MANTUA, 1796–97

During Napoleon's Italian campaigns 1795–7, he arrived at Villa Nova uncertain how to proceed, having received no orders from the Directoire in France. In June 1796 Napoleon besieged Mantua which, despite terrific bombardments, held out until February 1797. Napoleon is reputed to have treated the prisoners generously on their defeat. Cremona is situated near Mantua and must have suffered from the French invasion. Mantua's peace, however, lasted a very short time. In 1799 it was again taken by the Austrians and, although restored to the French in 1801 (Lunéville) it became Austrian again from 1814 to 1866. Cremona and Mantua both suffered severe political persecution as did the whole of Lombardy between 1849–59 after the peace of Villafranca. Note again the use of the metaphor of the bird of prey, the eagle, for Napoleon.

Perdu trouvé, caché de si long siecle,	The lost thing is discovered,
Sera Pasteur demi Dieu honoré:	hidden for many centuries.
Ains que la lune acheve son grand	Pasteur will be celebrated
siecle,	almost as a god-like figure.
Par autres vents sera deshonoré.	This is when the moon com-
	pletes her great cycle, but by
	other rumours he shall be
	dishonoured.

LOUIS PASTEUR, 1822–95.
FOUNDING OF INSTITUTE, 1889

Another fascinating quatrain which contains not only the name of Pasteur but also a very specific dating although not apparent at first. Pasteur's discovery that germs polluted the atmosphere was one of the most important in medical history, and led to Lister's theory of sterilization. The Encyclopaedia Britannica says that

Pasteur, the 'demi-Dieu', 'was now the acknowledged head of the greatest chemical movement of the time'. He founded his Institute Pasteur on 14th November 1889; the cycle of the moon ran from 1535 to 1889. The rumours that dishonoured him may mean the violent opposition to his methods which were roused among powerful members of the Academy, against the new practices of the Institute such as vaccines against hydrophobia etc.

26

Le grand du fouldre tumbe[1] d'heure diurne,	The great man will be struck down in the day by a thunder-
Mal & predict par porteur postu- laire:	bolt. An evil deed, foretold by the bearer of a petition. Accord-
Suivant presage tumbe[1] d'heure nocturne,	ing to the prediction another falls at night time. Conflict at
Conflict Reims, Londres, Etrusque pestifere.	Reims, London, and pestilence in Tuscany.

ASSASSINATION OF J.F.K., 1963 AND R.F.K., 1968

The first three lines here may apply to the assassinations of the two Kennedy brothers. John F. Kennedy was shot down (thunderbolt) in broad daylight at Dallas, Texas on 22nd November 1963 by the psychopath, Lee Harvey Oswald. The other man linked with him who is killed at night, was his brother Robert F. Kennedy who was shot down on 5th June 1968 in the early morning while celebrating his victory in the presidential primary elections at an hotel. Line 2, the fact that the assassination had been told by the bearer of a petition may refer to the many death threats John F. Kennedy and his brother received during their terms of office. The troubles in France, England and Italy would refer to the world repercussions to these assassinations. See VIII. 46, 77.

27

Dessouz de chaine[2] Guien du ciel frappé,	Beneath the oak tree of Gienne, struck by lightning,
Non loing de là est caché le tresor:	the treasure is hidden not far from there. That which for
Qui par longs siecles avoit esté grappé,	many centuries had been gathered, when found, a man
Trouve mourra, l'oeil crevé de ressort:	will die, his eye pierced by a spring.

[1] *tumbe—tombe* = fall.

[2] *chaine*—O.F., *chene*, but could possibly mean *chaine* = a chain of mountains.

There are several puzzling quatrains linking the finding of a tomb, a man dead for many centuries, and a treasure, see quatrain IX. 7, but none of them make much sense. Guienne was an ancient province of South-west France, therefore this quatrain cannot refer to the opening of Nostradamus' tomb, which was done during the Revolution when his remains were transferred to the chapel of Notre Dame in the church of St. Laurent, as Salon is not in that province. *Guien* could stand for *gui*, meaning mistletoe, which alters the first line to 'beneath the mistletoe covered oak tree etc.'. However, this gets us no further in solving the quatrain, or the riddle of the spring guarding the tomb. I wonder whether the treasures could be the many antiquarian treasures of southern France, most of which were not seriously excavated until the end of the 19th Century.

28

La tour de Boucq craindra fuste[1] barbare
Un temps, long temps apres barque hesperique:[2]
Bestail, gens, meubles tous deux feront grand tare[3]
Taurus & Libra quelle mortelle picque?[4]

Tobruk will fear the barbarian fleet for a time, then much later the Western fleet. Cattle, people, possessions, all will be quite lost. What a deadly combat in Taurus and Libra.

TOBRUK. SECOND WORLD WAR, 1941

It is possible that Tour de Boucq was the nearest Nostradamus could get to the place name Tobruk. The first line refers to Tobruk's chequered history as a trading port between Greeks and Libyans until the Italians became interested in it for strategic reasons. Tobruk then suffered the British invasion of 1941. Hesperique is a difficult word to interpret in the Centuries. It can mean either Western or Spanish, but I feel it cannot here mean Spain, and therefore is more applicable to America. Although it was the British Army which was fighting the Italians at Tobruk in January 1941, the attack upon Pearl Harbour occurred in November of that year in the same month as Tobruk was retrieved, and so Hesperique can refer to the American fleet. Rommel reached

[1] *fuste* = a low draught galley with sails and oars.
[2] *hesperique*—Spanish, Western or American.
[3] *tare* = loss.
[4] *?* —printers' error for *!*, if necessary at all.

Tobruk on 8th April (Taurus) and besieged it until November 1941, when it was relieved by British reinforcements. Libra is October, so Nostradamus was a month out in his calculations.

29

Quand la poisson terrestre & aquatique,	When the fish that travels over both land and sea is cast up on
Par forte vague au gravier sera mis:	to the shore by a great wave, its shape foreign, smooth and
Sa forme estrange sauve & horri-fique,	frightful. From the sea the enemies soon reach the walls.
Par mer aux mure bien tost les ennemis.	

POLARIS OR SUBROC

This is a perfect description of a Polaris ballistic missile fired from a submerged submarine, causing an enormous upheaval of water. Alternatively it describes the American equivalent, SUBROC, which although fired under water flies through the air to its target.

30

La nef estrange par le tourment marin,	Because of the storm at sea, the foreign ship will approach an
Abourdera pres de port incogneu:	unknown port. Notwithstand-ing the signs of the palm
Nonobstant signes de rameau pal-merin,[1]	branches, afterwards there is death and pillage. Good advice
Apres mort pille bon avis tard venu.	comes too late.

A very general quatrain. The *rameau palmerin* means palm branches indicating peaceful intent which is later reversed. It appears that the ship suffers the damage rather than the port, which lures it in feigning peaceful intentions.

31

Tant d'ans les guerres en Gaule dureront	The wars in France will last for so many years beyond the reign
Outre la course du Castalon[2] monarque:	of the Castulon kings. An un-certain victory will crown three
Victoire incerte trois grands couron-neront,	great ones, the Eagle, the Cock, the Moon, the Lion, the Sun in
Aigle, coq, lune, lion, soleil en marque.	its house.

[1] *palmerin*—Latin, *palmarius* = of a palm tree.
[2] *Castulon* = ancient Iberian city, standing for Spain.

DOWNFALL OF THE SPANISH MONARCHY

There are many ingenious interpretations offered for this quatrain concerning the French Revolutionary struggles and the Spanish Empire after the death of Charles V. It seems to indicate a great war in France after the downfall of the Spanish monarchy. Although some Spanish monarchs resigned and others were deposed, the real downfall of the monarchy must be dated from the founding of the Spanish Republic in 1923. This brings us to the 1930–40s, the period of the Second World War in which France was totally involved in *guerres en Gaule*. The three great powers who won an uncertain victory are America (Eagle), France (Cock), and Britain (Lion). The final capitulation of the Japanese which ended the war was proffered on 12th August (in Leo the Sun sign).

32

Le grand empire sera tost translaté,[1]	The great Empire will soon be
En lieu petit, qui bien tost viendra croistre:	exchanged for a small place, which soon will begin to grow.
Lieu bien infime d'exigue comté,	A small place of tiny area in the
Ou au milieu viendra poser son sceptre.	middle of which he will come to lay down his sceptre.

NAPOLEON I. ELBA AND ST. HELENA

The great Empire of the Imperial Napoleon (note the use of the word empire, not kingdom) is soon changed into the tiny island of Elba. However, on Napoleon's escape and the victorious 100 Days his empire begins, but only begins, to grow again. From here he is sent to an even smaller realm of no account, St. Helena, where he finally relinquishes all claims to power. This is one of the better quatrains, succinct and moving in its simplicity.

33

Pres d'un grand pont de plaine spatieuse,	Near a great bridge near a spacious plain the great lion
Le grand lion par forces Cesarees:[2]	with the Imperial forces will
Fera abbattre hors cité rigoureuse,	cause a falling outside the aus-
Par effrai portes lui seront reserées.[3]	tere city. Through fear the gates will be unlocked for him.

[1] *translaté*—Latin, *translatus* = transferred, exchanged.
[2] *Caesareus*—Latin = imperial.
[3] *reserées*—Latin, *reseratus* = unlocked.

The austere city of line 3 is probably Geneva, home of Calvinism. The plain may be Lombardy, and the Lion the commander of the Imperial forces. But if Nostradamus hoped for the fall of Geneva through the pressures of the Holy Roman Empire he was grievously wrong. The bridge is probably to be interpreted as a mountain pass. One must remember Nostradamus' strong pro-Catholic, anti-Huguenot feelings which seem to come out periodically in the prophecies.

34

L'oiseau de proie volant à la semestre,[1]	The bird of prey flying to the left, before battle is joined with the French, he makes preparations. Some will regard him as good, others bad or uncertain. The weaker party will regard him as a good omen.
Avant conflict faict aux François pareure:[2]	
L'un bon prendra l'un ambigue sinistre,	
La partie foible tiendra par bon augure.	

HITLER AND FRANCE. c. 1938/40

Nostradamus is describing one of the great warmongers of all time, Hitler, as a bird of prey, which name he also gives to Napoleon. The former seems more appropriate here however. The left would mean nothing to Nostradamus other than in a geographical sense, that is the Low Countries. Hitler invaded France through Holland and Belgium having made his preparations (*pareure*) well in advance. The third line refers to the corruption and uncertainty rife among French politicians in the early days of the war, culminating in the Pétainists who accept Hitler's authority and the Vichy cabinet (*partie faible*).

[1] *semestre*—Latin, *sinistre* = left.
[2] *pareure*—O.F. = preparation.

Le lion jeune le vieux surmontera,
En champ bellique par singulier
  duelle:
Dans caige d'or les yeux lui
  crevera,
Deux classes une, puis mourir,
  mort cruelle.

The young lion will overcome the older one, in a field of combat in single fight: He will pierce his eyes in their golden cage; two wounds in one, then he dies a cruel death.

DEATH OF HENRI II, 10th JULY 1559

This quatrain was understood in France during Nostradamus' lifetime, and was one of the verses that caused Catherine de' Medici to send for Nostradamus to interpret it. The Italian prophet Luc Gauric had warned Henri II that both the beginning and the end of his reign would be marked by a duel. The first took place soon after his accession, so it seems strange that the king did not take more care in the tournaments held in honour of the double marriage of his sister Elizabeth to Philip II of Spain, and Marguerite his daughter to the Duke of Savoy in the summer of 1559. During the festivities, which lasted for three days, the king joined in the competitions in the lists at the rue St. Antoine. He was victorious for the first two days, but on the third rode against Montgomery, the captain of the Scottish guard. Henri failed to unseat his opponent and insisted on refighting the bout. On the third try they splintered lances successfully, but Montgomery failed to pull up his lance in time, and the splintered shaft pierced the king's gilt helmet and entered his head just above the eye. Some reports say that he suffered a second wound in the throat. Henri's end was cruel indeed, he lay in agony for ten days before death released him. Montgomery was seven years younger than Henri who was forty when he died. Henri sometimes used the lion as his emblem. The word *classes* is understood here to come from the Greek *klasis* meaning a break, or fracture, rather than the Latin *classis*, a fleet.

*Tard la monarque se viendra
repentir
De n'avoir mis à mort son adversaire:
Mais viendra bien à plus hault
consentir,
Que tout son song par mort fera
deffaire.*

Too late the king will repent
that he did not put his adversary to death. But he will soon
come to agree to far greater
things which will cause all his
line to die.

HENRI III. DEATH OF GUISE BROTHERS
AT BLOIS 1588. LOUIS XVI?

This is a quatrain which seems to fit two historical events equally
well. The first and most probable interpretation is that it refers to
Henri III and his determination to quash the influence of the
Guise family in French politics. The king caused both the Duke
and his brother Louis to be murdered at Blois on 25th December
1588. However he did not kill the third brother, the Duc of
Mayenne, the real ringleader, and was forced to further action to
eliminate their power (*à plus hault consentir*). Other commentators
prefer to interpret it as describing Louis XVI and his brother and
adversary, the Duke of Orléans. Certainly Orléans intrigued
against the king and was a sworn enemy of the Queen, Marie
Antoinette. At one point he debated joining up with the revolutionaries. Here line 3 then refers to the constitutional monarchy that
Louis was forced to accept and the later imprisonment of himself
and his family, leading to their deaths on the guillotine. But Louis'
brother did not die, *tout son sang*: he returned to France in 1814 as
Louis XVIII so this is rather a less satisfactory interpretation.

*Un peu devant que le soleil
s'excuse,
Conflict donné grand peuple dubiteux:
Profliges, port marin ne faict
response,
Pont & sepulchre en deux estranges
lieux.*

Shortly before sun set, battle is
engaged. A great nation is
uncertain. Overcome, the sea
port makes no answer, the
bridge and the grave both in
foreign places.

I cannot explain this quatrain but offer these possible clues to the
ingenuity of the reader. *Pont* in line 4 often stands for Pontifex,
Pope, in Nostradamus. If it is so in this case, one might connect the

Pope who died away from Rome in a foreign grave, with Pius VI, who died at Valence in 1799, captured by the French. His death occurred in August so could the first line mean the summer? The French nation were still *dubiteux* in 1799; the Directoire had suffered defeats both in Italy and Germany and Napoleon's Egyptian campaign was by no means completed. I can only suggest a reference to French naval action in Egypt for line 3; it cannot refer to the British fleet which were scouring the seas for Napoleon's ships.

38

Le sol & l'aigle an victeur paroistront	The Sun and the Eagle will appear to the victor. An empty
Response vaine au vaincu l'on asseure:	answer is assured to the defeated. Neither bugle nor
Par cor ne cris harnois n'arresteront,	shouts will stop the soldiers. Liberty and peace, if achieved
Vindicte paix par mors si acheve à l'heure.	in time through death.

WATERLOO, 1815

This quatrain probably followed on I. 23 in the original. It continues the vivid description of Waterloo with Napoleon, the Imperial Eagle, coming out of the mist into the sun to attack the victor, Wellington. Both sides knew this was a fight to the finish, but for Napoleon it was the final stand after the frantic 100 Days. No reasonable terms awaited him if he lost (*response vaine*), nothing but life exile on St. Helena. Once the men joined in battle they could not be stopped. Napoleon's Grenadiers fought until the last man dropped, and refused to retreat. Freedom and peace can once again come to Europe but only by means of the bloody slaughter of battle, and possibly also Napoleon's end, his political, if not actual, death.

De nuict dans lict le suspresme[1]
estrangle,
Par trop avoir sejourné, blond
esleu:
Par trois l'empire subrogé[2] exanche,[3]
A mort mettra carte, et pacquet ne
leu.[4]

At night the last one will be
strangled in his bed because
he became too involved with
the blond heir elect. The
Empire is enslaved and three
men substituted. He is put
to death with neither letter nor
packet read.

DEATH OF LOUIS BOURBON CONDÉ, 1830

The last of the Condés, Louis, was found strangled one night in
1830, not however in his bed, but hanging in his bedroom. He was
probably murdered for the support he gave to the cause of the
Duke of Bordeaux, the Comte de Chambord, whom Nostradamus
rightly describes as *esleu* as he was the grandson of Charles X and
heir to the French throne. The three who usurped power can be
interpreted either as the three regimes which followed Charles X,
Louis Philippe, the Republic and then the Bonapartes, or it could
refer more specifically to the three men who intrigued against the
Condé family, Charles X, the Duke of Angoulême and the Duke of
Bourgogne. Le Pelletier says that Condé was fair-haired and had
written a will (*carte et pacquet*) in favour of the Duke of Bordeaux.
This is said to have been replaced by an earlier will written in
favour of the Duke of Aumale, son of Louis Philippe who became
king in 1830.

La trombe[5] fausse dissimulant
folie,
Fera Bisance[6] un changement de
loix:
Istra d'Egypte qui veut que l'on
deslie,
Edict changeant monnaies & alois[7].

The false trumpet concealing
madness will cause Byzantium
to change its laws. From
Egypt there will go forth a man
who wants the edict withdrawn,
changing money and standards.

[1] *supresme* = either great or last, both meanings possible here.
[2] *subrogé*—Latin, *subrogatus* = substitute.
[3] *exanche*—Latin, *exancilatus* = enslaved.
[4] *leu.*—O.F., lu = read.
[5] *trombe*—Misprint, *trompe* = trumpet.
[6] *Bisance* = Byzantium.
[7] *alois* = alloy, standard (of metal).

I cannot interpret the first line. The quatrain seems to refer to a political situation between the Ottoman Empire (Bisance) and Egypt. Some commentators think that the last two lines refer to Napoleon's return from Egypt and the establishment of totally new values in France under the Directoire of money, laws, the Church, etc.

41

Seige en cité est de nuict assaillie,
Peu eschapés non loin de mer conflict:
Femme de joie,[1] retours fils defaillie,
Poison & lettres cachees dans le plic.

The city is besieged and assaulted by night; few have escaped; a battle not far from the sea. A woman faints with joy at the return of her son, poison in the folds of the hidden letters.

This quatrain has been given many explanations by commentators who either refer it to the French invasion of Italy in 1556–47 or even to Dunkirk, 1940, where the Third Republic becomes the woman, the prostitute, and the poison the constitution (lettres) of the Nazi doctrines. None of these appears at all convincing.

42

Le dix Kalende[2] d'Avril de faict Gothique,
Resuscité encor par gens malins:
Le feu estainct assemblé diabolique,
Cherchant les os du d'Amant & Pselin.

The tenth day of the April Calends, calculated in Gothic fashion is revived again by wicked people. The fire is put out and the diabolic gathering seek the bones of the demon of Psellus.

INSTITUTION OF THE GREGORIAN CALENDAR SYSTEM, 1582. DIVINATION

It is believed that the last line should read 'cherchant les os du Demon et Psellus', but that Nostradamus suppressed it for fear that the authorities might accuse him of magic practices. There is a description of a similar evocation of spirits in Michael Psellus' book De Demonibus. Nostradamus seems to have understood the change of the Calendar from the old style to the Gregorian system, which took place (after his death) in 1582. The tenth day of the Kalends

---

[1] Femme de joie = either a woman (fainting) with joy, or a prostitute.
[2] Kalende—Calend = 1st day of Roman month.

of April would be 10th April, as the Calends was the first day of the Roman month. When the Gregorian system was introduced ten days were removed, so possibly Nostradamus means 1st April, new style. Good Friday was regarded as the best day for magical evocations, and it is possible that Nostradamus is implying that this was the day on which he started using these methods to inspire the prophecies. Psellus mentions the use of a bowl of water 'which seems to boil over and a faint voice murmurs words which contain the revelation of future events'. Nostradamus may therefore have begun writing the Prophecies on a Good Friday which fell on 10th April, old style.

43

Avant qu'advienne le changement d'Empire	Before the Empire changes a very wonderful event will take place. The field moved, the pillar of porphyry put in place, changed on the gnarled rock.
Il adviendra un cas bien merveilleux:	
Un champ mué, le pillier de paphire[1]	
Mis translaté sur le rocher noilleux.	

Line 1 probably places this quatrain before 1789. There is another reference to a pillars of porphyry in IX. 32.

44

En bref seront de retour sacrifices,	In a short time sacrifices will be resumed, those opposed will be put (to death) like martyrs. There will no longer be monks, abbots or novices. Honey shall be far more expensive than wax.
Contrevenans seront mis à martyre:	
Plus ne seront moines, abbez, ne novices,	
Le miel sera beaucoup plus cher que cire.	

THE CULT OF REASON, 10th NOVEMBER 1793.
ABOLITION OF CLERGY

The French Revolutionary government abolished the worship of God in 1793. The sacrifices in line 1 mean a restoration of paganism. On 10th November the Cult of Reason was established and in 1794 this was followed by a Festival of the Supreme Being, 8th June. The Constitution of 1790 declared the dissolution of the Clergy (no more monks) and of ecclesiastical orders. Many who refused to embrace the new ideology were persecuted, and all

[1] paphire = porphyry—a type of red or white crystallized feldspar.

priests who refused to accept the Civil Constitution of the Clergy were expelled. The last line is a generalization implying that lack of demand for beeswax for church candles makes its price less than that of the honey it holds, a new state of affairs in France.

45

Secteur de sectes grand peine au delateur,
Beste en theatre, dresse le jeu scenique,
Du faict antique ennobly l'inventeur,
Par sectes monde confus & schismatique.

A founder of sects, much trouble for the accuser: A beast in the theatre prepares the scene and plot. The author ennobled by acts of older times; the world is confused by schismatic sects.

This is probably a tirade against Calvinism, like I. 33.

46

Tout aupres d'Aux, de Lestoure & Mirande,
Grand feu du ciel en trois nuicts tumbera:
Cause adviendra bien stupende & mirande,
Bien peu aupres la terre tremblera.

Very near Auch, Lectoure and Mirande a great fire will fall from the sky for three nights. The cause will appear both stupefying and marvellous; shortly afterwards there will be an earthquake.

All three towns mentioned are in the Departement of Gers in south-western France. Perhaps Nostradamus is referring to a hail of meteorites, which make the earth tremble, or which are followed by a minor earthquake?

47

Du lac Leman[1] les sermons fascheront,
Les Jours seront reduicts par les sepmaines:[2]
Puis mois, puis an, puis tous deffailliront,
Les magistrats damneront leurs loix vaines.

The speeches of Lake Leman will become angered, the days will drag out into weeks, then months, then years, then all will fail. The authorities will condemn their useless powers.

[1] Leman = Lake Geneva.
[2] sepmaines—semaines = weeks.

LEAGUE OF NATIONS, 1919–47

Geneva was important as the setting of the League of Nations whose first assembly was held there on 15th November 1920. The quatrain describes vividly the years of fruitless argument and failure until the final formal disbandment after the war in August 1947, although in fact it ceased to be effective after early 1940. See also V. 85.

48

Vingt ans du regne de la lune passez,	When twenty years of the Moon's reign have passed
Sept mil and autre tiendra sa monarchie:	another will take up his reign for seven thousand years. When
Quand le soleil prendra ses jours lassez,	the exhausted Sun takes up his cycle then my prophecy and
Lors accomplit & mine ma prophetie.	threats will be accomplished.

DATE OF PUBLICATION AND COMPLETION OF PROPHECIES

According to Roussat the cycle of the Moon lasted from 1535–1889, which places the date of the first line as 1555, the publication date of the first part of the Centuries. Nostradamus seems to envisage another 7,000 years from that date to the cycle of the sun when all will be accomplished. According to astrologers we have now entered the reign of Aquarius. This quatrain is interesting in that it gives the date of publication and associates this with the completion of the prophecies. It is as though Nostradamus believes the Centuries are written at the start of a new era lasting 7,000 years. It was a commonly held theory in the Middle Ages that the world would come to an end at the beginning of the seventh millennium. This information originated from the book of Enoch which was general reading during the first and second centuries but removed by the Church from the Canon in AD 300. Nostradamus also refers to 7,000 years in quatrain X. 74, but no commentator is able to agree on the date from which to start calculating, and this theory does not agree with the statements of some of the other prophecies.

Beaucoup avant telles menees,	Long before these happenings
Ceux d'orient par la vertu lunaire:	the people of the East, in-
L'an mil sept cens feront grands	fluenced by the Moon, in the
emmenees,	year 1700 will cause many to
Subjugant presque le coing Aquilo-	be carried away, and will
naire.[1]	almost subdue the Northern
	area.

EVENTS AROUND 1700

The astrologer Roussat also believed the year 1700–2 would show the start of great upheavals, but this seems a prophecy where both he and Nostradamus are wrong. It could apply to various invasions in the North (*Aquilonaire*). In February 1700, August II invaded Livania. Peter the Great took Azov and Kouban from the Turks; Charles XII occupied Iceland and Peter the Great then declared war on Sweden, but none of these actions reduced the North sufficiently in the sense Nostradamus means it.

De l'aquatique triplicité[2] *naistra.*	From the three water signs will
D'un qui fera le jeudi pour sa feste:	be born a man who will
Son bruit, loz,[3] *regne, sa puissance*	celebrate Thursday as his
croistra,	holiday. His renown, praise,
Par terre & mer aux Oriens	rule and power will grow on
tempeste.	land and sea, bringing trouble
	to the East.

THIRD ANTICHRIST?

This describes a person with the three water signs of Aries, Cancer and Aquarius dominant in his birth chart, presumably not a Christian, *jeudi pour sa feste*, whose power becomes so great that he brings trouble to countries in the East.

It may refer to the Third Antichrist. See II. 5, 62, 89, IV. 50, VI. 33, VIII. 77, X. 66, 72, 74, 75.

[1] *Aquilonaire*—Latin, *aquilonaris* = northern.
[2] *aquatique triplicité* = the three water signs of the Zodiac.
[3] *loz*—Latin, *laus* = praise.

Chef d'Aries, Jupiter & Saturne,	The head of Aries, Jupiter
Dieu eternel quelles mutations?[1]	and Saturn. Eternal God, what
Puis par long siecle son maling[2]	changes! Then the bad times
temps retourne	will return again after a long
Gaule, & Italie quelles emotions?[1]	century; what turmoil in
	France and Italy.

13th DECEMBER 1702. WAR OF SPANISH SUCCESSION, AND FRANCE, 1802

The conjunction of Jupiter and Saturn in Aries took place on 13th December 1702 during the War of the Spanish Succession under Louis XIV. The great changes of line 2 are the French Revolution which will occur before the century mentioned in line 3 is completed. By 1802 France is embroiled in the Italian campaign and it was in January of that year that Napoleon was declared President of the Italian Republic. The next time this conjunction occurs will be 2nd September 1995.

Les deux malins de Scorpion con-	Two evil influences in con-
joinct,	junction in Scorpio. The great
Le grand seigneur meutri dedans sa	lord is murdered in his room.
salle:	A newly appointed king per-
Peste à l'Eglise par le nouveau roy	secutes the Church, the lower
joinct	(parts of) Europe and in the
L'Europe basse & Septentrionale.	North.

DEATH OF SULTAN SELIM III, 1807/8, AND NAPOLEON'S CONQUESTS

The two evil influences in Scorpio are Mars and Saturn, but this conjunction has occurred fourteen times since 1555. It happened in 1807 when Selim III of Turkey, one of whose titles incidentally was Seignior, was deposed in 1807, although he was not murdered until the following year. The troubles suffered by the Church are those caused by Napoleon who, having restored the Catholic hierarchy in France, at the same time held Pius VII prisoner. By this period, Napoleon had defeated Austria and Prussia (lower Europe) and Russia (Septentrionale) and France was at the height of her powers.

[1] *?* printers' error for *!*
[2] *maling—malin,* old spelling.

Las qu'on verra grand peuple tourmenté,	Alas, how we will see a great nation sorely troubled and the
Et la loi saincte en totale ruine:	holy law in utter ruin. Christ-
Par autres loix toute la Christienté,	ianity (governed) throughout
Quand d'or, d'argent trouve nouvelle mine.	by other laws, when a new source of gold and silver is discovered.

DISESTABLISHMENT OF CLERGY, 1790.
CREATION OF ASSIGNATS, 1789

This quatrain again tells of the disestablishment of the French Clergy, 14th July 1790, and of its subsequent persecution during the Revolution. The laws other than Christian that governed France were those of the Cult of Reason, see quatrain I. 44. The last line is interesting. In 1789 the National Assembly passed a decree on 19th December creating an issue of 400 million assignats. This currency was in fact based on the confiscated goods of the clergy which were used as security for the notes, and was certainly a new source of wealth on which the country could draw.

54

Deux revolts faicte du maling[1] falcigere,[2]	Two revolutions will be caused by the evil scythe bearer mak-
De regne & siecles faict permutation:	ing a change of reign and centuries. The mobile sign thus
Le mobil signe[3] à son endroit si ingere,[4]	moves into its house: Equal in favour to both sides.
Aux deux egaux & d'inclination.	

TWO REVOLUTIONS AND WAR
STARTING IN AUSTRIA

The evil scythe bearer is Saturn, and the two great Revolutions occurring in different centuries due to his malign influence are of course the French Revolution at the end of the 18th Century and the Russian Revolution in the early 20th Century. The mobile sign is Libra, the Balance, which governs Austria according to the

[1] *maling*—O.F. spelling = malin.

[2] *falcigere*—Latin, *falcam gerens* = bearing a scythe; the scythe was a sign of Saturn.

[3] Libra = the balance.

[4] *ingere*—Latin, *ingerere (se)* = to enter, penetrate. The *si* may be a misprint for *se*.

astrologers. Apparently the influence of Libra was not strong enough to tip the balance in favour of Austria (*aux deux egaux*) and so the malign influence of Saturn is able to cause war in that country following on the second revolution. Nostradamus is referring to the assassination of the Arch Duke Ferdinand at Sarajevo, 1914 and its consequence, the First World War.

55

Soubs l'opposite climat Baby-lonique,	In the land with a climate opposite to Babylon there will
Grand sera de sang effusion:	be great shedding of blood.
Que terre & mer, air, ciel sera inique,	Heaven will seem unjust both on land and sea and in the air.
Sectes, faim, regnes, pestes, con-fusion.	Sects, famine, kingdoms, plagues, confusion.

This is a very obscure quatrain, the only point of interest being the use of the word *air* in line 3. Nostradamus obviously comprehends that man will move in this dimension in the future, see quatrains I. 63, 64, II. 29, III. 69 etc.

56

Vous verrez tost & tard taire grand change,	Sooner and later you will see great changes made, dreadful
Horreurs extremes, & vindications:	horrors and vengeances. For
Que si la lune conduicte par son ange,	as the moon is thus led by its angel the heavens draw near to
Le ciel s'approche des inclinations.	the Balance.

Another astrological quatrain promising disaster in Libra, either the country, Austria, or using the sign as a date. It may follow on from the last verse, I. 55.

57

Par grand discord la trombe[1] *tremblera*	The trumpet shakes with great discord. An agreement broken:
Accord rompu dressant la teste au ciel:	lifting the face to heaven: the bloody mouth will swim with
Bouche sanglante dans le sang nagera,	blood; the face anointed with milk and honey lies on the
Au sol la face ointe[2] *de laict & miel.*	ground.

[1] *trombe = trompe,* trumpet.
[2] *ointe*—Latin, *unctus =* anointed.

49

In 1793 amidst the horrors and discords of the Revolution Louis XVI accepted the constitution decreed by the National Assembly, (*accord rompu*). As Louis went to his execution he is recorded as having recited the Third Psalm—*exaltus caput meum (dressant la tête)*. When a victim is guillotined the blood rushes out through the mouth of the corpse. Nostradamus is nothing if not meticulous about detail. Louis is described as anointed with milk and honey because he was actually so anointed as part of the coronation service. See also VI. 89.

58

Tranche le ventre, naistra avec deux testes,	Through a slit in the belly a creature will be born with two
Et quatre bras: quelques ans entiers vivra:	heads and four arms: it will survive for some few years.
Jour qui Alquiloie[1] celebrera ses festes,	The day that Alquiloie celebrates his festivals Fossana,
Fossen, Turin, chef Ferrare suivra.	Turin and the ruler of Ferrara will follow.

NAPOLEON AND THE BOURBONS

This is an involved quatrain dealing with both Napoleon and the Bourbon family. It is possible to interpret the first line literally as a Caesarian section, but it is more likely to refer to Louis XVI as the belly. *Tranche* is the same adjective that Nostradamus uses for the king's death elsewhere, from whom come the two comparatively short ruling heirs, Louis XVIII and Charles X (*deux testes*). The four arms are understood to be the Dukes of Angoulême, Normandy, Berry and Bordeaux. Alquiloie, the rule of the Eagle, connects them with Napoleon by whom the family was deposed, and the ruler of Ferrare was the Pope who 'followed' Napoleon back to France as a prisoner; the rest of Italy Fossana and Turin followed metaphorically, in that they were captured by the French. This is one of the quatrains in which Nostradamus has reversed the time sequence.

[1] *Alquiloie* = (*a*) *Aquila lex*, the rule of the eagle. (*b*) *Aquilene*, one of the great cities of the Roman Empire.

Les exilez deportez dans les isles,	The exiles deported to the
Au changement d'un plus cruel monarque	islands at the advent of an even more cruel king will be mur-
Seront meurtris:[1] *& mis deux les scintiles,*[2]	dered. Two will be burnt who were not sparing in their
Qui de parler ne seront estez parques.[3]	speech.

Nicollaud ascribes this to the events of the Coup d'Etat in 1857, when many members of French secret societies were deported to the Cayenne Islands. The new king was Napoleon III, who caused people who spoke against the regime (*ne seront estez parques de parler*) to be imprisoned and deported. All the lines fit, but I am not convinced by the interpretation. Some commentators, such as Roberts, ascribe it to the cremation of the Jews, but this is impossible if one reads the line (*mis deux les scintiles*); not even Nostradamus would reduce six million tragedies to two.

60

Un Empereur naistra pres d'Italie	An Emperor will be born near
Qui a l'Empire sera vendu bien cher:	Italy, who will cost the Empire very dearly. They will say,
Diront avec quels gens il se ralie,	when they see his allies, that he
Qu'on trouvera moins prince que boucher.	is less a prince than a butcher.

NAPOLEON I, 1769–1821

This is one of the famous quatrains predicting Napoleon, the Emperor born near Italy in Corsica. He cost France dearly in both manpower and strength. The third line may be a reference to the Creole origins of his first wife, Josephine, or to his own brothers whom he raised to positions of great honour, kings of Naples and Spain, Holland and Westphalia. The reference to butchery also covers the enormous number of men who died in the Napoleonic campaigns.

[1] *meutrir*—O.F. = to kill.
[2] *scintiles*—Latin, *scintilla* = sparks, flames.
[3] *parques*—Latin, *parcus* = sparing, economic.

La republique miserable infelice[1]
Sera vastee[2] *de nouveau magistrat:*
*Leur grand amus de l'exile male-
fice,*
Fera Sueve[3] *ravir leur grand
contracts.*

The wretched, unfortunate republic will again be ruined by a new authority. The great amount of ill will accumulated in exile will make the Swiss break their important agreement.

The fourth line makes this quatrain difficult to interpret. Sueve is derived from the Latin Suevi, the German Swiss, which is hard to connect with a French republic devastated by a new government, characterized by the sending of many people into exile. The nearest to this is the rule of the Prince-President Louis Bonaparte III, 1852–70. If Sueve, the Swiss, can be understood as German/Prussian, then the reference may be to the Franco-Prussian war which started in the year of Napoleon III's deposition, 1870.

*Le grande parte las que feront les
lettres,*
Avant le cycle de Latona[4] *parfaict:*
*Feu grand deluge plus par ignares
sceptres,*
*Que de long siecle ne se verra
refaict.*

Alas! what a great loss there will be to learning before the cycle of the Moon is completed. Fire, great floods, by more ignorant rulers; how long the centuries until it is seen to be restored.

Nostradamus visualizes scholarship as suffering a great loss before the end of the Moon's cycle (1889). This may be open to two interpretations. First, that a work of scholarship becomes lost before that date, and reappears after many calamities after a century or so (*de long siecle*); second, a more general meaning that Nostradamus regarded scholarship as becoming vulgarized by the changing of scholastic standards and its availability to what he would have called the common people. Like all scholars of his time, Nostradamus regarded himself as one of an élite.

[1] *infelice*—Latin, *infelix* = unhappy.
[2] *vastee*—Latin, *vastatus* = ruined devastated.
[3] *Sueve*—Suevi = German Swiss tribe.
[4] *Latona* = mythological mother of Apollo and Diana; the Moon.

Les fleurs[1] passés diminue le monde,
Long temps la paix terres inhabi-tées:
Seur marchera par ciel, serre, mer & onde:
Puis de nouveau les guerres sus-citées.

Pestilences extinguished, the world becomes smaller, for a long time the lands will be inhabited peacefully. People will travel safely through the sky (over) land and seas: then wars will start up again.

AIR TRAVEL. 20th CENTURY

It is not clear whether the age of pestilence refers to disease or war, but it is remarkable that Nostradamus envisages the world as a smaller place, presumably because of the ease of air travel mentioned in line 3 as well as more orthodox means by land and sea. Air travel specifically puts this quatrain into the 20th Century, and we are told that war will break about again after a long interlude of peace. This may be the third Great War of this century, which Nostradamus prophecies to follow the Hitler wars. The prophecies are mostly concerned with Europe and the last twenty-seven years are the longest era of peace it has known this century. If for nothing else, this and the following quatrain are noteworthy for their reference to air travel.

64

De nuict soleil penseront avoir veu,
Quand le pourceau demi-homme on verra:
Bruict, chant, bataille, au ciel battre aperceu:
Et bestes brutes à parler lon orra.

At night they will think they have seen the sun, when they see the half pig man: Noise, screams, battles seen fought in the skies. The brute beasts will be heard to speak.

AIR BATTLE. 20th CENTURY

This seemingly nonsensical quatrain is one of the most interesting. Nostradamus describes a vivid picture of a battle in the air. The sun, appearing at night, is the searchlight piercing the sky, or possibly bombs exploding. The pig-like man, which no commentator to date has ever deciphered, seems a clear picture in silhouette of the pilot in oxygen mask, helmet and goggles. The oxygen breathing apparatus would look just like a pig's snout to Nostradamus. The air battle is a remarkable enough description for the 16th Century, and the screams may be the sound of the

---

[1] *fleurs*—read *fléaux* = plague, pestilence.

dropping bombs as they whine to earth. The battle is watched by people on the ground (*aperceu*) and it is important to understand the wording of the last line. The pilots (*brutes bestes*) are heard talking to others; could this be a forecast of radio? This quatrain convinces me that Nostradamus' inspiration was certainly partly visual and he describes as best he can in his limited vocabulary the puzzling glimpses of a future he didn't always understand.

65

Enfant sans mains jamais veu si grand faudre,
L'enfant royal au feu d'oesteuf blessé:
Au pui[1] brises[2] fulgures[3] allant mouldre,
Trois souz les chaines[4] par le milieu troussés.[5]

A child without hands, never so great a thunderbolt seen, the royal child wounded at a game of tennis. At the well lightning strikes, joining together three trussed up in the middle under the oaks.

A definite quatrain about a specific event and a deformed royal child which has not been realized to date.

66

Celui qui lors portera les nouvelles,
Apres un peu il viendra respirer
Viviers, Tournon, Montferrand & Pradelles,
Gresle & tempestes les fera soupirer.

He who then carries the news, after a short while will (stop) to breath: Viviers, Tournon, Montferrand and Pradelles; hail and storms will make them grieve.

67

La grande famine que je sens approcher,
Souvent tourner, puis estre universelle:
Si grand & long qu'un viendra arracher,
Du bois racine & l'enfant de mamelle.

The great famine which I sense approaching will often turn (in various areas) then become world wide. It will be so vast and long lasting that (they) will grab roots from the trees and children from the breast.

[1] *pui*—well, or possible O.F. *puy* = hill? It does not help to interpret the quatrain.
[2] *brises*—O.F., *briser* = to fracture, break.
[3] *fulgures*—Latin, *fulgur* = flash of lightning.
[4] *chaines*—Either oak tree or *chaine* = chain of hills.
[5] *troussés*—Some interpreters translate this as carry off.

The shortage of food throughout the world and particularly in the underdeveloped countries seems clear to Nostradamus. He describes local famines, however dreadful, whether those of France, 1709, Ireland, 1846, Biafra, 1969, India, 1971, as appearing small in comparison with the problem of world hunger which will develop and become universal.

68

O quel horrible & malheureux
tourment,
Trois innocens qu'on viendra à
livrer:
Poison suspecte, mal garde tradiment,[1]
Mis en horreur par bourreaux
enivrez.

O to what a dreadful and wretched torment are three innocent people going to be delivered. Poison suggested, badly guarded, betrayal. Delivered up to horror by drunken executioners.

69

La grand montaigne ronde de sept
stades,[2]
Apres paix, guerre, faim, innondation:
Roulera loin abismant grands contrades,[3]
Mesmes antiques, & grand fondation.

The great mountain, seven stadia round, after peace, war, famine, flooding. It will spread far, drowning great countries, even antiquities and their mighty foundations.

This probably describes a flood in southern France which may reveal many Graeco-Roman archaeological treasures sited somewhere near a mountain. Sites such as Glanum near the mountains of Les Beaux, very near Salon, may be indicated.

70

Plui, faim, guerre en Perse non
cessée,
La foi trop grand trahira le
monarque:
Par la finie en Gaule commencee,
Secret augure pour à un estre
parque.

Rain, famine and war will not cease in Persia; too great a faith will betray the monarch. Those (actions) started in France will end there, a secret sign for one to be sparing.

[1] tradiment—O.F. = treason, betrayal.
[2] stade—Latin, stadium = measure roughly a furlong in length, seven stades would be just under a mile in circumference.
[3] contrades—Provençal, contrad = country.

France and Persia have been at war, with France an ally of Turkey, on several occasions, but it is difficult to relate this to a specific incident.

71

La tour marine trois fois prise & reprise,	The marine tower will be captured and retaken three times by Spaniards, barbarians and Ligurians. Marseilles and Aix, Arles by men of Pisa, devastation, fire, sword, pillage at Avignon by the Turinese.
Par Hespagnols, Barbares, Ligurins:[1]	
Marseilles & Aix, Arles par ceux de Pise,	
Vast,[2] feu, fer, pillé Avignon des Thurins.	

This is an irritating quatrain because it appears to be indecipherable despite all the proper names given. The main problem is the identity of the marine tower, which could then be related to conflict between the French and the Italians. Could it refer to the Tour de Bouq I. 78. ?

72

De tout Marseille des habitants changee,	The inhabitants of Marseilles completely changed, fleeing and pursued as far as Lyons. Narbonne, Toulouse angered by Bordeaux; the killed and captive are almost one million.
Course & poursuitte jusqu'au pres de Lyon,	
Nalbon[3] Tholoze par Bordeaux outragee,	
Tuez captifs presque d'un million.	

FRANCE AND CASUALTIES. SECOND WORLD WAR

The enormous number of dead places this quatrain in modern times, possibly in the last war, for which the official casualty lists give a figure of 675,000 Frenchmen dead or wounded. This sum does not include the Allies who fought alongside the French, so Nostradamus' total may be nearer the mark. When the German army entered Paris, June 1940, the French Government fled to Bordeaux. Narbonne, Toulouse and Lyons were all cities under the puppet Vichy régime. Marseilles, under German occupation, certainly had its *habitants changees*.

[1] *Ligurins* = people of Liguria in Italy.
[2] *vast*—Latin, *vastus* = laid waste.
[3] Apocope for Narbonne.

France à cinq pars[1] par neglect assaillie,[2]	France shall be accused of neglect by her five partners.
Tunis, Argel[3] esmuez par Persiens:	Tunis, Algiers stirred up by the Persians. Leon, Seville and
Leon, Seville, Barcelonne faillie	Barcelona having failed, they
N'aura la classe[4] par les Venetiens.	will not have the fleet because of the Venetians.

FRANCE AND COMMON MARKET.
LIBYAN REVOLUTION, 1969

Line 1 may refer to France during the end of de Gaulle's presidency, when she was under pressure from her five Common Market partners. This agrees in time with the trouble in North Africa, the 1969 Revolution in Libya which deposed King Idris. The reference to Persia is interesting. In Nostradamus' day Persia was part of the Ottoman Empire, an area which is now part of the U.S.S.R., and so, by implication, the Soviets are involved in the Middle Eastern troubles. The last two lines are unclear.

Apres sejourné vogueront en Epire	After a rest they will travel to
Le grand secours viendra vers Antoche:	Epirus, great help coming from around Antioch. The
Le noir[5] poil crespe tendra fort à l'Empire,	curly haired king will strive greatly for the Empire, the
Barbe d'aerain se roustira en broche.	brazen beard will be roasted on a spit.

Both Epirus and Antioch were part of the Turkish Empire until the 19th Century. As the footnote states, 'noir' is continually used as an anagram of 'roi', king, in the Centuries. This dark-haired king recurs in other quatrains as does the red-bearded man. There was a family of Algerian corsairs named Barbarossa, whose plunderings were contemporary to Nostradamus. Other commentators refer this to Philip II of Spain who had a blondish beard, but his enigmatic fate is incomprehensible.

[1] *pars*—Used throughout Nostradamus to mean partner, rather than part. *See* IX. 20.

[2] *assaillir*—Literally assault. France has only been attacked on five sides once in 1813/4 and then by the European allies.

[3] *Argel*—Anagram or misprint for Alger = Algiers.

[4] *classe*—Latin, *classis* = fleet.

[5] *noir*—Anagram for *roi*. IX. 20 etc.

Le tyran Sienne occupera Savone,
Le fort gaigné tiendra classe
marine:
Les deux armees par la marque
d'Ancomme,
Par effrayeur le chef s'en examine.

The tyrant of Siena will occupy Savona, having won the fort he will restrain the marine fleet. Two armies under the standard of Ancona: the leader will examine them in fear.

Siena was a free town and held out with French help against the Florentine states until April 1555. Savena was a protectorate of the Genoese Republic, and Ancona was part of the Papal States.

D'un nom farouche tel proferé sera,
Que les trois soeurs[1] auront fato[2]
le nom:
Puis grand peuple par langue &
faict dira
Plus que nul autre bruit & renom.

This man will be called by a barbaric name that three sisters will receive from destiny. He will speak then to a great people in words and deeds, more than any other man will have fame and renown.

NAPOLEON BONAPARTE

This verse is always interpreted as fitting Bonaparte, because of the derivation of his name from the Greek NEAPOLLUON, which means destroyer or exterminator. The name was still spelt in this way during his lifetime, as the inscription of 1805 in the Place Vendôme shows, NEAPOLIO. IMP AUG. Napoleon was barbaric in a more general sense, being the younger son of a Corsican family whose language and standards were not those of Parisian society. He was also renowned for the great speeches made to his troops (*par langue dira*) before battle.

Entre deux mers dressera pro-
montaire,
Que plus mourra par le mords du
cheval:
Le sien Neptune pliera voille
noire,
Par Calpre & classe aupres de
Rocheval.

A promontory stands between two seas: A man who will die later by the bit of a horse; Neptune unfurls a black sail for his man; the fleet near Gibraltar and Rocheval.

[1] The three Fates. In classical mythology they spin the web of a man's destiny.

[2] *fato*—Latin, *fatum* = fate, destiny.

BATTLE OF TRAFALGAR, 21st OCTOBER 1805

The promontory separating the seas is Gibraltar between the Mediterranean and the Atlantic. The French and English fleets fought the battle of Trafalgar between Gibraltar and Cape Roche (Rocheval), Trafalgar itself being a point between two bays. The leader of the French fleet, Admiral Villeneuve, was reputedly strangled by one of Napoleon's Mamelukes with the bridle of a horse at an inn in Rennes in 1806, when he returned to France having been taken prisoner by the English. When Nelson was mortally wounded his ship raised a black sail on its return voyage to England. Rocheval may just be an anagram for *roche*, rock, which is the name given to mean Gibraltar.

78

D'un chef naistra sens hebeté	To an old leader will be born
Degenerant par savoir & par armes:	an idiot heir, weak both in
Le chef de France par sa soeur redouté,	knowledge and in war. The leader of France is feared by
Champs divisez, concedez aux gendarmes.	his sister, battlefields divided, conceded to the soldiers.

This has been referred to Marshal Pétain, who took over the government of France from Reynaud in 1940, but the sister is unsatisfactory and the whole quatrain too general.

79

Bazaz, Lestore, Condon, Ausch, Agine,	Bazas, Lectoure, Condom, Auch and Agen are troubled by
Esmens par loix querelle & menopole:	laws, disputes and monopolies.
Car[1] Bourd, Toulouze Bay[2] mettra en ruine.	Carcasonne, Bordeaux, Toulouse and Bayonne will be ruined when they wish to renew
Renouveller voulant leur tauropole.[3]	the massacre.

All these towns are in the south-west of France. It may contain a reference to a trading dispute and the granting of rights to monopolies in the locality. The massacre or sacrifice is unclear.

[1] *Car*—Either apocope of Carcassonne, or *car* = because.

[2] *Bay*—Bayonne, as above.

[3] *tauropole*—Latin, *Taurobolium* = sacrifice of a bull; metaphorically, massacre, slaughter.

De la sixieme claire splendeur celeste,	From the sixth bright celestial light it will come to thunder
Viendra tonner si fort en la Bourgongne:	very strongly in Burgundy. Then a monster will be born
Puis naistra monstre de treshideuse beste,	of a very hideous beast: In March, April, May and June
Mars, Avril, Mai, Juin grand charpin[1] & rongne.	great wounding and worrying.

Saturn being the sixth planet, apparently these portents will occur during the time governed by him. Some commentators date it as spring 1918.

D'humain troupeau neuf seront mis à part,	Nine will be set apart from the human flock, separated from
De jugement & conseil separez:	judgment and advice. Their
Leur sort sera divisé en depart,	fate is to be divided as they
Kappa,[2] Thita,[3] Lamda,[4] mors bannis esgarez.	depart. K. Th. L. dead, banished and scattered.

This has been applied by at least one commentator to the death of the three Soviet cosmonauts. It is very obscure.

Quand les colomnes de bois grande tremblee,	When the great wooden columns tremble in the south
D'Auster conduicte couverte de rubriche:	wind, covered with blood. Such a great assembly then pours
Tant videra dehors grand assemblee:	forth that Vienna and the land of Austria will tremble.
Trembler Vienne & le Pays d'Austriche.	

AUSTRIA, 1914-18

In the autumn of 1918, when the trees trembled in the wind, Austria was overturned and the new revolutionary (rubriche) rule replaced the autocratic order of the Habsburgs. The great

---

[1] *charpin*—O.F., rags to dress wounds. Wounds.
[2] Letter of the Greek alphabet K.
[3] Letter of the Greek alphabet Th.
[4] Letter of the Greek alphabet L.

assembly of the world Powers, which troubles Austria is the Triple Entente. Austria's troubles first started in the south (Auster) in Turkey and the Balkan States.

83

La gent estrange divisera butins,	The alien nation will divide the
Saturne en Mars son regard furieux:	spoils. Saturn in dreadful aspect in Mars. Dreadful and foreign
Horrible estrange aux Tosquans & *Latins,*	to the Tuscans and Latins, Greeks who will wish to strike.
Grecs qui seront à frapper curieux.	

ITALIAN OCCUPATION OF GREECE, 1940

The last two lines seem to refer to the Greek struggles with the Italian occupying forces of 1940. The booty taken by the Germans was proverbial; it is still reappearing in sale rooms throughout the world, *divisera butins*. Mars is the God of War, and Saturn indicates a bad aspect, which indeed it was for the Italians who allied themselves with the losing side.

84

Lune obscurcie aux profondes tene-bres	The moon obscured in deep gloom, his brother becomes
Son frere passe de couleur ferru-gine:[1]	bright red in colour. The great one hidden for a long time in
Le grand caché long temps soubs les tenebres,	the shadows will hold the blade in the bloody wound.
Tiedera[2] fer dans la plaie sanguine.	

MURDER OF THE DUKE DE BERRY.
13th FEBRUARY 1820

The Count of Artois is the man obscured, he was in exile, whose brother Louis XVI died (*passe*) in blood on the guillotine. D'Artois remained in exile for a long time before his return as Charles X, with his family. His son, the Duke de Berry, was attacked and fatally stabbed at the Opera on the night of 13th February 1820. As he died, he clutched the hilt of the knife and is reputed to have said, 'I am murdered. I am holding the hilt of the dagger.' See C. III. 96, IV. 73.

[1] *ferrugine*—Latin, ferruginus = rusty, blood-coloured.
[2] *Tiedera*—Read, *tiendra*.

Par la response de dame Roi troublé,	The king is troubled by the queen's reply. Ambassadors
Ambassadeurs mespriseront leur vie:	will fear for their lives. The
Le grand ses freres contrefera doublé,	greater of his brothers will doubly disguise his action, two
Par deux mourront ire, haine, ennui.	of them will die through anger, hatred and envy.

MURDER OF THE DUKE DE GUISE
AND HIS BROTHER, 1588

Catherine de' Medici, the Queen Mother, was furious at her son Henri III's action in killing not only the Duke de Guise, but also his brother the Cardinal because of their political power. The *Ambassadeurs* are probably the Estates whom the king assembled to meet him at Blois and who remonstrated strongly about the murders. The greater brother who survives was the Duke de Mayenne who then led the Catholic League, and became Lieutenant-General of France, *contrefera doublé*.

La grande roine quand se verra vaincue,	When the great queen sees herself conquered, she will
Fera excés de masculin courage:	show an excess of masculine
Sus cheval, fleuve passera toute nue,	courage. Naked, on horseback,
Suite par fer: à foi fera outrage.	she will pass over the river pursued by the sword: she will have outraged her faith.

FLIGHT OF MARY QUEEN OF SCOTS, 1568

This is a very close description of the flight of Mary Queen of Scots, in May 1568, when having been defeated a second time by Murray she fled to England possessing nothing but the clothes she wore, *toute nue*. Mary crossed the river by ferry, but fled on horseback, and had outraged her faith, whether the Catholics, or the Scots, by her behaviour with Bothwell.

Ennosigee¹ feu du centre de terre.	Earthshaking fire from the
Fera trembler au tour de cité neufue:	centre of the earth will cause tremors around the New City.
Deux grands rochiers long temps feront la guerre,	Two great rocks will war for a long time, then Arethusa will
Puis Arethuse² rougira nouveau fleuve.	redden a new river.

ATTACK ON NEW YORK?

An explosion in the centre of the city of New York making the land tremble, or could *tour* here mean towers or skyscrapers? The two great rocks are the immutable great powers who will eventually open war. Ingenious commentators interpret Arethusa as coming from Ares, God of War, and U.S.A. The new river is presumably blood see X. 49.

Le divin mal surprendra le grand prince,	The divine wrath overtakes the great Prince, a short while
Un peu devant aura femme espousee.	before he will marry. Both
Son appuy & credit à un coup viendra mince,	supporters and credit will suddenly diminish. Counsel, he will
Conseil mourra pour la teste rasee.	die because of the shaven heads.

CHARLES I AND PARLIAMENT

Divine wrath overtook Charles I of England when he was sentenced by his own Court, but the trouble with Parliament broke out originally around the time of his marriage in 1625 to Henrietta Maria of France. On his actual wedding day, Charles directed that persecution of the Catholics should cease. Parliament refused this and demanded subsidies for the war against Spain. This led to his death, demanded by the Roundheads (*teste rasee*) in 1649. *See* IX. 49.

¹ *Ennosigaeus*—Greek = earth-shaking, a name given to Neptune.
² *Arethusa* = a Greek nymph who in one legend changed into a stream.

Tous ceux de Ilerde[1] seront dans la Moselle,
Mettant à mort tous ceux de Loire & Seine:
Le cours[2] marin viendra pres d'haute velle,
Quand Espagnols ouvrira toute veine.

Those of Lerida will be in the Moselle, killing all those from the Loire and Seine. The seaside track will come near the high valley, when the Spanish open every route.

PENINSULAR WARS, 1808–14

This seems to be a general quatrain about the Peninsular Wars when Wellington pushed up through Spain and Portugal across the Pyrenees to Bordeaux. James Laver suggests that *haute velle* is Nostradamus groping towards the name of Wellington.

90

Bourdeaux, Poitiers au son de la campane,
A grand classe ira jusques à l'Angon:
Contre Gaulois sera leur tramontane,
Quand monstre hideux naistra pres de Orgon.

Bordeaux and Poitiers at the sound of the bell will go with a great fleet as far as Langon. A great rage will surge up against the French, when an hideous monster is born near Orgon.

This specifies an invasion by the French, great resistance, and the birth of a monstrous child near Organ, probably like the two-headed one Nostradamus saw and described in another book. In *The Times*, 20th November 1971, a report was given of the birth of a two-headed boy, so that Nostradamus is not completely in the realms of fantasy.

91

Les dieux feront aux humains apparence,
Ce qu'il seront auteurs de grand conflict:
Avant ciel veu serein espee & lance
Que vers main guache sera plus grand affict.

The gods will make it appear to mankind that they are the authors of a great war. Before the sky was seen to be free of weapons and rockets: the greatest damage will be inflicted on the left.

[1] *Ilerde* = Lerida, city in Spain.
[2] *cours* = path, progress.

FUTURE WAR AFFECTING AMERICA?

Nostradamus declares that we will not know which side starts the next world war although in later quatrains he places blame for the start of the war upon China. After a peaceful interlude (I. 63) the air will be full of weapons and fighting, rockets pointing like lances to the skies. The left hand side of the world on a map is America and the country will suffer great losses. However in IV. 95, he states that the victor will be born in America.

92

Sous un la paix par tout sera clamee	Under one man peace will be
Mais non long temps pillé &	proclaimed everywhere, but
rebellion:	not long after will be looting
Par refus ville, terre, & mer	and rebellion. Because of a
entamee,	refusal, town, land and sea will
Mors & captifs le tiers d un	be broached. About a third of
million.	a million dead or captured.

FRANCE AND THE FRANCO-PRUSSIAN WAR, 1870–1

The universal peace described here is the French Empire, bearing in mind Napoleon's statement, '*L'Empire, c'est la paix*'. The Franco-Prussian war is depicted in the rest of the quatrain, starting with the King of Prussia's refusal to agree to the humiliating French demands. The Encyclopaedia Britannica gives the figures of dead and wounded in this war as 299,000 which is very close to Nostradamus' estimate of 333,000.

93

Terre Italique pres des monts	The Italian lands near the
tremblera,	mountains will tremble. The
Lyon & coq non trop confederez:	Cock and the Lion not strongly
En lieu de peur l'un l'autre	united. In place of fear they
s'aidera.	will help each other. Freedom
Seul Catulon[1] & Celtes moderez.	alone moderates the French.

NAPOLEON'S ITALIAN CAMPAIGN, 1795

The mountains are the Alps and this is Napoleon's Italian Campaign which started in 1795. After capturing Toulon he set out on the Italian wars and France (*Coq*), saw the start of enmity which grew up between her and England (*Lion*). This is followed by a period of mutual alliance, after the accession of Louis XVIII, the French (*Celtes*) regaining their freedom from tyranny.

[1] *Castulon* = Liberty.

65

Au port Selin le tyran mis à mort,
La Liberté non pourtant recouvree:
Le nouveau Marc par vindicte &
*   remort*
Dame par force de frayeur honnoree.

The tyrant Selim will be put to death at the harbour but Liberty will not be regained, however. A new war arises from vengeance and remorse. A lady is honoured through force of terror.

BATTLE OF LEPANTO, 1571

At the battle of Lepanto fought on 7th October 1571 Ali Pasha, the Admiral of the Turkish fleet, was killed while on board his ship. Selim II was not killed himself but his aggression in the Mediterranean was finally crushed by the defeat at Lepanto. However, Liberty was not regained as had been hoped by the crusade of Christian countries to put down Turkish influence—this continued for some centuries. See IX. 42. The Pope formally ascribed the victory of Lepanto to the intercession of our Lady, line 4.

Devant moustier[1] trouvé enfant
*   besson,[2]*
De heroic sang de moine &
*   vestutisque:[3]*
Son bruit par secte langue &
*   puissance son,*
Qu'on dira fort esleue ie vopisque.

In front of a monastery will be found a twin infant from the illustrious and ancient line of a monk. His fame, renown and power through sects and speech is such that they will say the living twin is deservedly chosen.

Apparently the twin son of a monk will grow to be an important leader. Many commentators refer this to the Man in the Iron Mask who was possibly the son of Queen Anne and Cardinal Mazarin.

Celui qu'aura la charge de des-
*   truire*
Templus, & sectes, changez par
*   fantasie:*
Plus aux rochiers qu'aux vivans
*   viendra nuire,*
Par langue ornee d'oreilles res-
*   sasie.*

A man will be charged with the destruction of temples and sectes, altered by fantasy. He will harm the rocks rather than the living, ears filled with ornate speeches.

[1] *moustier*—Provençal = monastery.
[2] *besson*—Provençal = twin.
[3] *vestutisque*—Latin, *vestutus* = old.

RELIGIOUS REVIVAL

A man will come whose religious destiny is concerned with people rather than the buildings, temples, bricks and mortar of accepted religions. It is possible that the rock in line 3 is the Rock of Peter, the Vatican, in which case this revival would harm the Catholic church.

97

Ce que fer, flamme n'a sceu paracheuer,	That which neither weapon nor flame could accomplish will
La douce langue an conseil viendra faire:	be achieved by a sweet speaking tongue in council. Sleeping,
Par repos, songe, le Roy fera resver,	in a dream, the king will see the enemy not in war or of
Plus l'ennemy en feu, sang militaire.	military blood.

ASSASSINATION OF HENRI III, 1589

Henri III was killed not while at war but in council. The monk, Jacques Clément came to the king at St. Cloud saying he had a secret letter, and leaning towards Henri, as though to speak confidentially, he stabbed him in the stomach. Henri died the next day. The fact that he had dreamed of his death is well authenticated; he told his courtiers three days before his death that he saw the royal regalia, his blue cloak, two crowns, sceptre, sword and spurs all trodden underfoot by monks and the populace. An example of double precognition; by Nostradamus and the victim himself. Is the *douce langue* in line 2 a play on words on the name Clément? It would be a typical Nostradamus double meaning, as the two words mean the same in French.

98

Le chef qu'aura conduit peuple infiny	The leader who will conduct great numbers of people far
Loing de son ciel, de meurs & langue estrange:	from their skies, to foreign customs and language. Five
Cinq mil en Crete & Thessalie fini	thousand will die in Crete and Thessaly, the leader fleeing in
Le chef fuyant, sauvé en marine grange.[1]	a sea going supply ship.

NAPOLEON'S EXPEDITION TO EGYPT, 1798/9

When Napoleon left Egypt, he successfully eluded the British Navy to land in France, leaving behind for the Turks an army

---

[1] *grange*—Fr. = literally, barn.

reduced to around 5,000 men. The Turks ruled Thessaly and Crete at this time, and Napoleon did flee in a wooden ship. This fact prevents the prophecy applying to the British Expeditionary forces in Crete and Thessaly in 1940, when ships were made of metal and the figures were also much greater.

99

Le grand monarque que fera compagnie, *Avec deux rois unis par amité:* *O quel soupir fera la grand mesgnie,[1]* *Enfans Narbon à l'entour quel pitié.*	The great king will join with two kings, united in friendship. How the great household will sigh: around Narbon what pity for the children.

100

Longtemps au ciel sera veu gris oiseau, *Aupres de Dole & de Touscane terre:* *Tenant au bec un verdoyant rameau,* *Mourra tost grand & finera la guerre.*	For a long time a grey bird will be seen in the sky near Dôle and the lands of Tuscany. He holds a flowering branch in his beak, but he dies too soon and the war ends.

COMTE DE CHAMBORD, 1820

The grey bird is both the dove of peace and the Comte de Chambord, son of the Duchess de Berry and last legitimate heir to the French throne. At his birth he was called the dove of peace, but unfortunately he was usurped by the Orléans family and exiled to Venice, near Dôle, and Modena, near Tuscany. He also married the daughter of the Duke of Tuscany in 1846. He died without regaining the French throne, but he and the Comte de Paris, Duke d'Orléans, the pretender, were reconciled when the latter was also sent into exile by the new republic. The death of the Comte de Chambord saved the possibility of another war between republicans and monarchists.

[1] *mesgnie*—O.F. = household, court.

CENTURY II

1*   Dardanelles, 1915
2
3*F?   Atomic explosion in Aegean sea?
4F   *continued*, conditions in France
5*F?   The Third war? 1996? and its originator
6*   1945 Nagasaki and Hiroshima
7
8   Religious Revival
9
10   French Revolution
11   Napoleon?
12*   Suppression of Religion, *c.* 1790
13   Nostradamus' religious beliefs
14*   Regency of Catherine de' Medici
15
16   Italy in Second World War
17
18   Henri III, 1587–9
19
20   Henri II, 1557
21
22*F? NATO fleet off Britain
23
24*   Hitler
25*   Capitulation of Metz, 1870
26
27
28*   A man whose name begins with HO, HAN or DA
29*   Man from East. Air travel to France
30
31
32
33

34
35
36
37
38   Russia and Allies, *c.* 1940
39*   Europe in 1939 and Germany
40*   Second World War
41*F?   Third World War, 1986?
42*   Death of Robespierre, 1794
43*   Triple Alliance, 1881
44   France, 1813/14
45
46*F?   Third World War, 1986
47
48
49
50*   1568. Revolt Netherlands
51*   1666. Great Fire of London
52*   War with United Provinces, 1665–7?
53*   Great Plague of London, 1665
54
55   France, 1594
56
57   John F. Kennedy?
58
59
60
61
62*F?   Third World Leader
63*   Battle of Ivry, 1550
64   Cevennes, *c.* 1685
65*   7th December 2044
66*   Napoleon's 100 days
67*   James II, William III, 1688–90
68*   *continued*
69*   *continued*
70*   Napoleon, 1815
71
72
73
74
75   General famine
76*   Talleyrand, 1754–1838

```
77
78
79*     Battle of Lepanto, 1571?
80
81F?
82
83*     Lyons, 1795
84
85      Napoleon?
86*     Napoleon in Egypt
87*     Accession of George I, 1714
88**    Seven children of Catherine de Valois and accession of
             Henri IV, c. 1590
89**F?  America, Russia and Third Antichrist?
90*     Hungarian Revolution, 1956
91*F?   Attack on U.S.A. or Russia?
92*     Napoleon III, 1870
93F?
94*     Napoleon
95F?    Kennedys?
96
97*     1799. Death of Pius VI
98
99*     Napoleon's Campaign in Russia, 1812
100
```

KEY: * = of interest. F? = possibly future.

Vers Acquitaine par insuls Britan-niques	Towards Aquitaine, by British assaults, and by them also
De pars eux mesmes grands incur-sions	great incursions. Rains and frost make the terrain unsafe,
Pluies gelées feront terroirs uniques,	against Port Selin they will
Port Selin fortes fera invasions.	make mighty invasions.

THE DARDANELLES. FIRST WORLD WAR, 1915

An important quatrain. When France (Aquitaine) and Britain were deadlocked on the Western Front during 1915, Winston Churchill persuaded the Allies to open a new front against Turkey (Port Selin is Constantinople, and Turkey, by extension). It was planned to attack the Dardanelles in order to reach Constantinople. The dreadful weather suffered by troops during the First World War is referred to in line 3.

2

La teste bleu fera la tete blanche	The blue leader will inflict
Autant de mal que France a faict leur bien,	upon the white leader as much damage as France has done
Mort à l'anthene grand pendu sus la branche,	them good. Death from the great antenna hanging from
Quand prins des siens le Roy dira combien.	the branch, when the king will ask how many of his men have been captured.

Obscure but interesting in that the antenna may be understood as an aerial from which the King obtains information; an attempt to describe radio communications or something similar?

3

Pour la chaleur solaire sus la mer	Because of heat like that of the
De Negrepont les poissons demi cuits:	sun upon the sea the fish around Negrepont will become half
Les habitans les viendront entamer,[1]	cooked. The local people will
Quand Rhod, & Gannes leur faudra le biscuit.	eat them when in Rhodes and Genoa there is a lack of food.

ATOMIC EXPLOSION?

To produce such heat on the sea surface implies a very strong explosion, possibly of atomic force, somewhere in the Aegean sea,

---

[1] *entamer*—Literally to cut up, therefore = to eat.

as Negrepont is the Italian name for the Island of Ruboea. The second implication that in Italy and other parts of Greece people are starving, indicates either conditions of famine or war. Nostradamus mentions this explosion again in V. 98, when he says its source comes from the sky.

4

Depuis Monach[1] jusque aupres de Sicile
Toute la plage demourra desolée:
Il n'y aura fauxbourg, cité ne ville,
Que par Barbares pillé soit &
volée.

From Monaco as far as Sicily all the coast will remain deserted. There will be no suburbs, cities nor towns which have not been pillaged and robbed by barbarians.

This may be a continuation of the last quatrain, II. 3. extending the area of the disaster through Italy to France. Nostradamus would describe as barbarian either Arab, Negro, Russian or Chinese, but from later quatrains the latter is the most likely interpretation.

5

Qu'en dans poisson, fer & lettres enfermée,
Hors sortira qui puis fera la guerre:
Aura par mer sa classe[2] bien ramée,
Apparoissant pres de Latine terre.

When weapons and documents are enclosed in a fish, out of it will come a man who will then make war. His fleet will have travelled far across the sea to appear near the Italian shore.

THE THIRD WAR, 1996? AND ITS ORIGINATOR

The fish is interpreted as a submarine rather than a ship as a fish travels under water; this one carries weapons and important papers as well as the man who is responsible for starting a new war. He is described as actually coming out (*hors sortira*) of the fish as are the hostile soldiers in I. 29, where the submarine is also called a fish by Nostradamus. The fleet brought by this unnamed man has travelled a great distance to appear in either the Mediterranean or Adriatic sea. It is tempting to link him with the man Nostradamus calls the Third AntiChrist whom he believes will start a third war in this century. The date may actually be given to us, because the first line contains a second, astrological meaning, 'When Mars and Mercury are in conjunction in Pisces'. According to Norab the

[1] *Monach*—Latin, *Monoceus* = Monaco.
[2] *classe*—Latin, *classis* = fleet.

next time this occurs is 23rd March 1996. and Nostradamus dates the war as starting around 1995 in I. 51, in 1993 in II. 41, and mentions it indirectly in I. 16, all of which are uncomfortably close and consistent.

6

Aupres des portes & dedans deux cités	Near the harbour and in two cities will be two scourges,
Seront deux fléaux & oncques n'apperceu un tel:	the like of which have never been seen. Hunger, plague
Faim, dedans peste, de fer hors gens boutés,	within, people thrown out by the sword will cry for help from
Crier secours au grand Dieu immortel.	the great immortal God.

THE BOMBINGS OF NAGASAKI AND HIROSHIMA, 1945
Both Nagasaki and Hiroshima are on the sea and experienced the plague of radiation which had never been seen before on earth. Two bombs were dropped (*deux fléaux*) and the survivors would have looked very similar to victims of the plague in Nostradamus' day, which turned them black, and for this was known as '*le charbon*'. Radiation burns turn black too, and there was hunger among the miserable survivors who were thrown out of the cities by the sword of war. The last line speaks for itself.

7

Entre plusieurs aux isles deportés,	Among many people deported to the islands will be a man
L'un estre nay à deux dents en la gorge:	born with two teeth in his mouth. They will die of hunger
Mourrant de faim les arbres esbrotés,	having stripped the trees. A new king will pass new laws for
Pour eux neuf Roy, nouvel edict leur forge.	them.

The islands are either the French penal colonies such as Ile du Diable in South America or those along the south coast of France which are used for the detention of dangerous criminals. It is quite common for children to be born with some teeth already formed. The last line may predict the closing of the penal settlements; most of the tropical ones are no longer in use.

Temples sacrez prime facon Romaine
Rejecteront les goffres[1] fondements
Prenant leurs loix premieres & humaines,
Chassant, non tout des saincts les cultements.

Temples consecrated in the early Roman fashion, they will reject the broken foundations; taking their early human laws, expelling almost all the cults of the saints.

A RELIGIOUS REVIVAL

A general quatrain predicting a return to the simpler religious precepts and practices, and a rejection of the elaborate cult of saints in the Roman Catholic Church. It may have been intended for the Huguenots of Nostradamus' own time.

9

Neuf ans le regne le maigre en paix tiendra,
Puis il cherra[2] en soif si sanguinaire:
Pour lui grand peuple sans foi & loi mourra,
Tué par un beaucoup plus debonnaire.

For nine years the thin man will keep a peaceful rule, then he will fall into so bloody a thirst that a great nation will die for him without faith or law; killed by a much better natured man.

Three specific elements combine in this quatrain, which do not seem to have occurred as yet. A very thin ruler will, after a nine year peace, plunge his nation into a disastrous war. His death, in turn, will be caused by someone with right or good on his side. It has been suggested that this could be the Nazi party coming to power in the elections of 1930, and that Roosevelt is the good-natured opponent, but this gives a wrong time factor.

10

Avant long temps le tout sera rangé,
Nous esperons un siecle bien senestre
L'estat des masques & des seuls bien changé,
Peu trouverant qu'à son rang vueille estre.

Before long everything will be organized; we await a very evil century. The state of the masked and the solitary ones greatly changed, few will find that they wish to retain their rank.

[1] *Goffre*—Romance = deep, broken.
[2] *cherra*—O.F., *choir* = to fall.

A general description of the French Revolution in which the state of two particular social orders was dangerous to maintain and became greatly changed. The first were the Court (*masques*), and the second the Clergy, who were abolished in 1790. Both classes suffered financial loss and many faced death because of their social rank or function throughout the early years of the Revolution.

11

Le prochain fils de l'aisnier parviendra, Tant esleue jusque au regne des fors:[1] Son apre gloire un chacun la craindra, Mais ses enfans du regne gettez[2] dehors.	The following son the elder will succeed, very greatly raised to a kingdom of privilege. His bitter renown will be feared by all, but his children will be thrown out of the kingdom.

NAPOLEON?

The first line is extremely difficult because of the multitude of possible meanings of *prochain* and *aisnier*. *Prochain* may mean next, nearest, younger or favourite, and *aisnier* either elder or a falcon (*l'ainier*) giving a metaphor of a bird of prey similar to Napoleon, the eagle. If it does refer to Napoleon, he was the second son and he was elected to a kingdom and privilege, from being the son of a Corsican middle-classs family he became Emperor. He was feared in Europe and his children were deprived of kingship by Louis XVIII. However, Napoleon's nephew, Louis Napoleon, re-established himself in 1852 and ruled until the Third Republic of 1871.

12

Yeux clos, ouverts d'antique fantasie, L'habit des seuls seront mis à neant: Le grand monarque chastiera leur frenaisie, Ravir des temples le tresor par devant.	Their eyes closed, open to the old fantasy, the habit of priests will be abolished. The great monarch will punish their frenzy, stealing the treasure in front of the temples.

[1] *fors*—O.F., Privileges.
[2] *gettez*—Alternative spelling of jettez = to throw.

SUPPRESSION OF THE CLERGY, *c.* 1790

Nostradamus seemed greatly worried by the fate of the Catholic Church and its priests during the French Revolution and there are many references to it. The eyes of the people were closed to Christianity and the Cult of Reason was established in 1793. In 1789 the wearing of ecclesiastical costume was suppressed. The monarch can be interpreted either as Louis XVI, who had already helped despoil the monasteries, or as Napoleon, who continued to do so with great vigour until the time of his Coronation when he needed the Pope and found it necessary to restore the Roman Catholic religion to France.

13

Le corps sans ame plus n'estre en sacrifice.	The body without a soul no longer at the sacrifice. At the
Jour de la mort mis en nativité:	day of death it is brought to
L'esprit divin fera l'ame felice,	rebirth. The divine spirit will
Voyant le verbe en son eternité.	make the soul rejoice seeing the eternity of the word.

RELIGIOUS BELIEFS

This is an ambiguous statement of Nostradamus' religious beliefs. Once dead, he can no longer communicate with the spirits, whether he means the Mass or some magical rite by the word sacrifice is impossible to say. His soul will be reborn at his death into happiness. The word ('*verbe*') is either Christ as is used in the Christmas Gospel, *the word was made flesh*, or may be a promise made to Nostradamus in his magic studies which he expects to be fulfilled eternally at his death. If there is any occult meaning in this quatrain it is very deliberately hidden. Nostradamus foretold his own death to his confessor, Frère Vidal, and to his pupil, Chavigny, but he may have been able to do this by a medical diagnosis. He died on 1st July 1566.

14

A Tours, Gien, gardé seront yeux penetrans,	At Tours and Gien watchful eyes will be guarded, they will
Descouvriront de loing la grand seraine:	spy far off the serene Highness. She and her suite will enter the
Elle & sa suitte au port seront entrans.	harbour, combat joined, sovereign power.
Combat, poussez, puissance souveraine.	

Tours and Gien are both on the Loire. This probably refers in general terms to the regency of Catherine de' Medici and the wars of religion which troubled France from 1562–98. The Queen died in 1599 having seen her three sons predecease her, as predicted.

15

Un peu devant monarque trucidé[1]	A short while before a king is
Castor, Pollux en nef, estre crinite[2]	murdered, Castor and Pollux
L'erain[3] *public par terre & mer*	in the ship, a bearded star.
vuidé,	Public treasure emptied on land
Pise, Ast, Ferrare, Turin, terre	and sea, Pisa, Asti, Terrara and
interdicte.	Turin are forbidden lands.

The second line of this quatrain gives a form of dating. Castor and Pollux, the twins, stand for Gemini, the ship is for Argo, and the bearded star is a comet. Linked with these is an assassinated king, a great war effort, money being raised on land and sea, and the Italian states being placed under interdict. This last thing has never happened since publication, and seems unlikely now to be fulfilled.

16

Naples, Polerme, Sicille, Syracuses,	In Naples, Palermo, Sicily and
Nouveau tyrans, fulgures[4] *feux*	Syracuse new tyrants, thunder
celestes:	and lightning in the skies. A
Force de Londres, Gand, Bruxelles,	force from London, Ghent,
& Suses,	Brussels and Susa: a great
Grand hecatombe, triomphe faire	massacre, then triumph and
festes.	festivities.

ITALY'S PART IN SECOND WORLD WAR

The new tyrants in the Italian towns are the Mussolini régime of the Fascisti. The thunder and lightning become the sound of war in Italy. London goes out in force against them, allied to Brussels, and wins the war after great slaughter.

[1] *trucidé*—Latin, *trucidare* = to slaughter.
[2] *crinite*—Latin, *crinitus* = bearded.
[3] *erain*—Latin, *eranus* = public fund.
[4] *Fulgures*—Latin, *fulgur* = lightning.

Le camp du temple de la vierge
vestale,
Non esloingé d'Ethne & monte
Pyrenées:
Le grand conduict est caché dans la
male[1]
North[2] getez fleuves & vignes
mastinées.[3]

The field of the vestal virgin's
temple is not far from Ethne
and the Pyrenees. The great
one led is hidden in a trunk.
In the North, the rivers over-
flow and the vines destroyed.

Ethne is probably a greek anagram for Elne, *th* in Greek being one letter. Elne lies near the Pyrenees between the Tech and the Réart which flow into the Mediterranean. I cannot decipher this quatrain further.

18

Nouvelle & pluie subite impeteuse,
Empechera subit deux excercites:
Pierre ciel, feux faire la mere
pierreuse,
La mort de sept terre & marin
subites.

News; unexpected and heavy
rain will suddenly prevent two
armies. Stones and fire from
the skies will make a sea of
stones. The death of the seven
suddenly by land and sea.

HENRI III 1587–9

The clue to this quatrain lies in the last line, the death of the seven, the Valois children of Catherine de' Medici. When Henri III left Paris in 1587 the city was invaded by 35,000 German and Swiss troops. The Duc de Guise rushed with his troops of the League to Montargis, but the decisive battle was prevented by a violent rainstorm. In the following year, 1589, Henri III, the last of the Valois kings was assassinated; his death was the direct result of his clash with the Leaguers and the assassinations of the two Guise brothers.

[1] male—(a) malle = trunk, or possibly, (b) mal = evil.
[2] North = very rare use of English by Nostradamus.
[3] mastiner—O.F. = to bruise, destroy.

Nouveau venus lieu basti sans defence.
Occuper la place par lors inhabit-able:
Pres, maisons, champs, villes prendre à plaisance,
Faim, Peste, guerre arpen[1] long labourable.

Newcomers will build a place without defences, occupying a place inhabitable until then. Meadows, houses, fields, towns will be taken with pleasure. Famine, plague, war, extensive arable land.

Freres & soeurs en divers lieux captifs,
Se trouveront passer pres du monaique;
Les contempler ses rameaux[2] enten-tifs,
Desplaisant voir menton, front, nez, les marques.

Brothers and sisters captives in differing places will find themselves passing before the monarch. His attentive offspring will look at them, displeased to see the signs on their chins, foreheads and noses.

HENRI II 1557

The commentator Jaubert applies this to an event which occurred soon after publication. In September 1557 some Huguenots were captured in Paris during a raid and Henri II went to see them, taking his children. The King is reputed to have been angry that the captives had been wounded and bruised. But it is so general that it may apply to other similar events.

L'ambassadeur envoyé par biremes,
A mi-chemin d'incogneus repoulsez:
De sel renfort viendront quatre triremes,
Cordes & chaines en Negre pont troussez.

The ambassador sent by the biremes is repulsed half way by an unknown man. Four triremes come reinforced with salt; he is bound with cords and chains to Negrepont.

Biremes are oared galleys with two bridges, and triremes larger ones with three. Salt in the Centuries often stands for taxation, because of the famous French salt tax, the gabelle, or for wisdom in the Biblical sense. Negrepont is the Italian name for Euboea which belonged to the Turks until 1831, when it became part of Greece.

[1] *arpen*—O.F. = measure of land, just under 1 acre.
[2] *rameaux*—Literally branches, therefore offspring.

Le camp Ascap[1] d'Europe partira,	The aimless army will depart
S'adjoignant proche de l'isle sub-	from Europe and join up close
mergée:	to the submerged island. The
D'Arton[2] classe[3] phalange pliera,	NATO fleet folds up its stan-
Nombril du monde plus grand voix	dard, the navel of the world in
subrogée.[4]	place of a greater voice.

NATO FLEET OFF BRITAIN

Nostradamus writes of the submerged island again in IX. 31 where it is identified with Britain. The army is described as aimless; could this mean that it, just like the NATO fleet, had no warlike intent as they were both only on exercises? This view is reinforced by the fact that the fleet folds up its standards showing no signs of war. The navel of the world, and its centre, may be understood as Italy, presumably the centre of the direction of operations. But again, Nostradamus implies that NATO will be taken over (*subrogée*) by a more powerful agency. European countries do combine at the present time to hold naval and military exercises both in Europe and in the English Channel under the auspices of NATO.

23

Palais, oiseaux, par oiseau des-	Birds at the palace, chased out
chassé,	by a bird very soon after the
Bien tost apres le prince parvenu:	upstart prince. How many of
Combien que hors fleuve ennemi	the enemy are repulsed beyond
repoulsé,	the river, the upheld bird
Dehors sousi trait d'oiseau soustenu.	seized from without by a trick.

This is very vague. Probably the birds are courtiers or supporters of one prince where power is taken by an upstart who is finally captured by a trick. Some interpret line 4 as 'captured outside, a shaft held by a bird', i.e. by an arrow.

[1] *Ascop*—Greek, *askopos* = incredible, aimless.
[2] *Arton*—Either anagram for NATO or Greek, *artos* = bread.
[3] *classe*—Latin, *classis* = fleet.
[4] *subrogée*—Latin, *subrogatus* = substituted.

Bestes farouches de faim fleuves tranner,[1]	Beasts wild with hunger will cross the rivers, the greater
Plus part du champ encontre Hister sera.	part of the battlefield will be against Hitler. He will drag the
En caige de fer le grand fera treisner,	leader in a cage of iron, when the child of Germany observes
Quand rien enfant de Germain observera.	no law.

HITLER

One of Nostradamus' most remarkable series of quatrains, with the name Hitler given in anagram as Hister. There can be little doubt that Hitler is implied; who else could be so well described by the last line, the German who observed no law? In 16th-Century handwriting the resemblance is even closer with the use of the long *s*, Hifter. Commentators before 1930 understood the Hister to be the river Danube, from its latin name Ister. But Hitler recognized himself in these quatrains by the mid 1930s and Goebbells made great propaganda out of them in the pre-war party years. Evidence for this is found in many sources, chiefly Ellic Howe's book 'Nostradamus and the Nazis'. During the first year of the Second World War the development of the war was to a great extent dependent upon the rivers crossed by the Germans who came into Europe in a never-ending stream looting and pillaging (*farouches de faim*).

La garde estrange trahira forteresse	The foreign guard will betray
Espoir & umbre de plus hault mariage:	the fortress the shadowy hope of an important marriage. The
Garde deçeue,[2] fort prince dans la presse,	guard deceived, the fort taken in the crush. Loire, Saône,
Loire, Son, Rosne. Gar à mort oultrage.	Rhône, Garonne outraged to death.

CAPITULATION OF METZ, 1870

The defender of a fortress who betrays his trust chasing the illusion of a higher post (*plus hault mariage*) may be Bazaine who in 1870 handed over the fortress of Metz and his troops to the Germans,

---

[1] *tranner*—Latin, *tranare* = to swim across.
[2] *deçeue* = deceived, or Latin, *decisus* = to cut down.

and thus allowed them into the French interior during the Franco-Prussian War.

Pour la faveur que la cité fera,
Au grand qui tost prendra camp de
* bataille,*
Puis le rang Pau Thesin versera
De sang, feux mors noyés de coup de
* taille.*

Because of the fervour that a city will show towards a great man who later loses on the battlefield, the ranks will flee, rushing into the Po and the Tessin, blood, firing, dead men drowned and slashed.

Le devin verbe sera du ciel frappé,
Qui ne pourra proceder plus avant:
Du reserant[1], le secret estoupé[2]
Qu'on marchera par dessus &
* devant.*

The divine voice will be struck by heaven and he will not be able to proceed further. The secret is hidden with the revelation so that people will walk over and ahead.

One of the several quatrains which indicate some secret locked up with the grave. Someone over whom one can walk (*par dessus & devant*) in French means to be buried at the foot of a wall, or chained in an underground cell. Some person will be struck down and not be able to reveal his information. He may be a theologian or religious man (*le divin verbe*).

Le penultiesme du surnom du
* prophete,*
Prendra Diane pour son jour &
* repos:*
Loing vaguera par frenetique teste,
Et delivrant un grand peuple
* d'impos.[3]*

The last but one of the prophets' name, will take Monday for his day of rest. He will wander far in his frenzy delivering a great nation from subjection.

NAME BEGINNING HO, HAN OR DA

Is Nostradamus referring to Mahomet or Mohamed, or even to himself, Nostradamus? A man whose name begins with one of these sets of initials will apparently declare Monday, the day of Diana the moon, his Sabbath or day of rest. Could this be related

---

[1] *reserant*—Latin *resarare* = to unlock.
[2] *estoupé*—O.F. = to shut up.
[3] *impos*—O.F., *impost* = taxation.

to the next quatrain 29? One is not given any indication as to which nation this new leader will free from subjection.

29

L'Oriental sortira de son siege,	The man from the East will
Passer les monts Apennins voir la Gaule:	come out of his seat and will cross the Apennines to see
Transpercera le ciel les eaux & neige,	France. He will cross through the sky, the seas and the snows
Et un chacun frappera de sa gaule.	and he will strike everyone with his rod.

MAN FROM THE EAST?

This is a curious verse. The word *sortira* for *ira* indicates that the Easterner does not usually leave his country; could this refer to the North Vietnamese talks in Paris? France (*la Gaule*) to which he comes, was one of the few countries to maintain diplomatic relations with China until its acceptance into United Nations in October 1971. The third line seems to indicate air travel—he goes through the air to his destination. The last line is very ambiguous. The word *gaule* means a stick or rod, it could mean a weapon, it also means France and might be an indirect reference to the name of de Gaulle, which would certainly date the quatrain. There is a curiously threatening quality in the last line, as though no one is expecting any harm to come from the visitor. See also V. 54.

30

Un qui des dieux d'Annibal infernaux,	A man who revives the infernal Gods of Hannibal, the terror
Fera renaistre, effrayeur des humains:	of mankind. Never more horror nor the papers tell of worse in
Oncq' plus d'horreur ne plus dire journaulx,	the past, then will come to the Romans through Babel.
Qu'avint viendra Babel aux Romains.	

The infernal Gods of Hannibal imply North Africa and the near Middle East, from which a man will bring trouble to the world. The word for newspapers is interesting as there were none in Nostradamus' time; this line is a definite reading from the first edition of Benoist Rigaud, 1568. Pamphlets existed, of course, and the word may be used in this sense. Babel implies a confusion of languages and is also the Hebrew word for Babylon which some commentators feel that Nostradamus uses when he means Paris.

The quatrain may describe a relapse into paganism which brings terror to Rome and the Catholic Church.

31

En Campanie le Cassilin[1] fera tant,	In Campanie the Cassilin
Qu'on ne verra que d'aux des	(river) will do so much that
champs couvers:	one will see only fields covered
Devant apres le pluie de long temps,	in water. Before and after the
Hors mis les arbres rien l'on verra	long lasting rain nothing green
de vert.	will be seen except for the trees.

This general quatrain predicts a flood of the Volturno river, perhaps of the town of Capua itself, in that it was built on the ruins of the Roman town of Casilinum.

32

Laict, sant grenouilles escoudre[2] en	Milk, blood, frogs will be pre-
Dalmatie,	pared in Dalmatia: battle
Conflict donné, peste pres de	engaged, plague near Balennes.
Balennes	A great cry will go up through-
Cri sera grand par toute Esclavonie,	out Slavonia, then will a
Lors naistra monstre pres & dedans	monster be born near Ravenna.
Ravenne.	

This prophecy covers both sides of the Adriatic, but it is unclear what is to happen in the first line. Dalmatia is on the Eastern Adriatic, Balennes was Trebula Balliensis near Capua, Ravenna is in Central Italy. The former province of Slavonia is now part of Northern Yugoslavia and part of the Hungarian Empire.

33

Par le torrent qui descent de	Through the torrent which
Veronne,	pours down from Verona there
Par lors qu'au Pau guidera son	where the entry is guided to the
entrée:	Po, a great wreck, and not less
Un grand naufrage, & non moins	so in Garonne when the people
en Garonne	of Genoa will march against
Quand ceux de Gennes marcheront	their country.
leur contree.	

This is similar to the last quatrain describing three 16th-Century states, France, Venice and Genoa. Verona is on the river Adige,

[1] *Cassalin* = a town on the Volturno river.
[2] *Escoudre*—Latin, *excudere* = to prepare.

which enters the Adriatic parallel to the Po about ten miles distant. The flood may be connected with II. 31.

34

L'ire insensee du combat furieux	The senseless rage of a furious
Fera à table par freres le fer luire:	struggle will cause the brothers
Les despartir, blessée, curieux,	to draw their weapons at table.
Le fier duelle viendra en France	A wounded man parts them,
nuire.	curious: the proud duel will
	bring harm to France.

The duel that affects France must occur between her princes or statesmen. Several French kings, including Henri III and Louis XIV have hated their brothers but none have actually duelled together.

35

Dans deux logis de nuict le feu	Fire will take hold in two houses
prendra,	at night, several people inside
Plusieurs dedans estouffes & rostis:	suffocated or burnt. It will
Pres de deux fleuves pour seul il	happen near two rivers for sure
adviendra:	when the sun, Sagittarius and
Sol, l'Arq & Caper tous seront	Capricorn are all diminished.
amortis.	

This event could occur on 22nd December of any year, for this is the day that the sun moves out of Sagittarius into Capricorn. It is difficult to distinguish a town on two rivers, there are so many. Commentators who lived *c.* 1600 all related it to a fire at Lyons in 1582, and this town is situated at the mouth of two rivers.

36

Du grand Prophete les lettres	The letters of the great prophet
seront prinses,	will be intercepted and fall into
Entre les mains du tyran deviendront:	the hands of the tyrant. His
Frauder son Roy seront ses entre-	efforts will be to deceive his
prinses,	King, but soon his thefts will
Mais ses rapines bien tost le	trouble him.
troubleront.	

The Abbé Torné, a great interpreter of Nostradamus, believed this verse referred to him. It may just as well be Nostradamus talking of some personal vendetta of his own.

De ce grand nombre que l'on envoyera, *Pour secourir dans le fort assiegez,* *Peste & famine tous les devorera,* *Hors mis septante qui seront profligez.*[1]	Of the great number that are sent to relieve the besieged fort, disease and hunger will destroy them all except seventy who will be killed.

Des condamnez sera fait un grand nombre, *Quand les monarques seront conciliez:* *Mais l'un deux viendra si malencombre*[2] *Que guere ensemble ne seront reliez.*	There will be a great number of condemned people when the monarchs are reconciled. But one of them will be so unfortunate that they will hardly remain allies.

RUSSIA AND ALLIES?

This may be interpreted as a general quatrain about the alliance of Hitler and Stalin between the years 1939–41? Others apply it to the breakdown of the Yalta conference of 1945, and interpret line one as referring to the Nuremberg Trials and the misfortune as the commencement of the Cold War by Russia.

Un an devant le conflict Italique, *Germains, Gaulois, Hespaignols pour le fort:* *Cherra l'escolle maison de republique,* *Ou, hors mis peu, seront suffoque mors.*	A year before the war in Italy, Germans, French and Spanish will be for the strong one; the school house of the republic will fall, where, except for a few, they will suffocate to death.

EUROPEAN ATTITUDES TOWARDS GERMANY, *c.* 1939

This quatrain summarizes very succinctly the general situation in Europe during 1939, the year before Italy was involved in the Second World War, which she declared on 10th June 1940. The Spanish were certainly on the German side, and there was a definite pro-German element in France as was proved by the Vichy régime. The strong man was Hitler who had enormous support in Germany at this time. The school-house republic which falls and crushes so many of its people could be either

---

[1] *profligez*—Latin, *profligare* = to destroy, kill, ruin.
[2] *malencombre*—O.F., 13th Century, *malencontre* = misfortune.

France or Italy. It is difficult to understand the meaning of the adjective here. This quatrain seems to continue on to the following one with the claim that after these alliances between Germany, Spain and France there will be world battles on land and sea, which were part of the Second World War.

40

Un pres apres non point longue intervalle	Shortly afterwards, not a very long interval, a great tumult
Par mer & terre sera faict grand tumulte:	will be raised by land and sea. The naval battles will be
Beaucoup plus grande sera pugne[1] navalle,	greater than ever. Fires, creatures which will make more
Feux, animaux, qui feront plus d'insulte.[2]	tumult.

SECOND WORLD WAR

Should this quatrain be linked with II. 39 it becomes a continuation of the description of the Second World War. The importance of power at sea was obvious, submarines played a great part in the war game, and are probably described as the creatures of line 4, as in I. 29, II. 5 etc. *Feux* could be translated as firing, making them creatures with weapons.

41

La grand estoille par sept jours brulera,	The great star will burn for seven days and the cloud will
Nuée fera deux soleils apparoir:	make the sun appear double.
Le gros mastin fera toute nuict hurlera,	The large mastiff will howl all night when the great pontiff
Quand grand pontife changera de terroir.	changes his abode.

THIRD WORLD WAR, c. 1986–93?

There are several Popes who have changed their abode in the past, notably Pius VI who died in Valence, and Pius VII, who was forcibly detained by Napoleon before returning to Rome. However the reference to the two suns, plus the great star, which is probably a comet, may bring the quatrain to 1986 when Halley's comet will reappear and when the next Pope but one, predicted by Malachy, may well be in the Vatican whose motto is given as

[1] *pugne*—Latin, *pugna* = battle.
[2] *insulte*—O. Provençal = insult. Tumult, upheaval.

de laboris solis, the toil of the sun. Could this describe an atomic bomb which was referred to as a 'second sun' as early as 1947? This all fits in with Nostradamus' description of a Third World War towards the end of this century. The then Pope might well have to leave the Vatican, or even Europe, if this should arise. Perhaps the seven days stand for seven years, which brings Nostradamus to 1993, nearer the date given in other prophecies, *see* II. 46, 62, VIII. 59, 77, X. 49, 72, 74, 75.

42

Coq, chiens & chats de sang seront repeus	The cock, cats and dogs will be replete with blood when the
Et de la playe du tyran trouvé mort.	tyrant is found dead of a
Au lict d'un autre jambes & bras rompus,	wound in the bed of another, both arms and legs broken, he
Qui n'avait peur de mourir de cruelle mort.	who was not afraid dies a cruel death.

DEATH OF ROBESPIERRE, 1794

The cock is the emblem of France, and the dogs and cats the rabble who have had enough of the reign of Terror under the committee led by Robespierre. Between 12th–28th July 1,285 victims died on the guillotine. Robespierre was a tyrant but so were many others of his committee. On 26th July 1794, he said the Terror should be ended and the Committee of Public Safety renewed. Robespierre was arrested but freed by troops of the Commune who took him to the Hôtel de Ville (strange bed). Then the National Guard captured Robespierre; he was shot in the jaw (not arms and legs) and after a long night of agony he was executed without further trial on 29th July at the Place de la Revolution.

43

Durant l'estoille chevelue[1] apparente,	During the appearance of the bearded star, the three great
Les trois grans princes seront faits enemis:	princes will be made enemies. The shaky peace on earth will be
Frappés du ciel paix terre tremulante,	struck from the skies, the Po, the winding Tiber, a serpent placed
Pau, Timbre undans, serpent sus le bort mis.	upon the shore.

[1] *estoille chevelue* = comet.

Pope Leo XIII is given the motto 'Lumen in Caelo' by the prophet Malachy, and on his coat of arms was a comet (*estoille chevelue*). He is also referred to as this in VI. 6 by Nostradamus. During Leo XIII's reign the Triple Alliance (three great princes) was formed in 1881 by Germany, Austria and Italy against France. The fact that peace was disturbed is probably a reference to the Triple Entente, which ultimately led to the First World War. The snake which constricted the French leaders was that of the Triple Alliance.

44

L'aigle pousée entour de pavillions,	The eagle driven back around
Par autres oiseaux d'entour sera chassée:	the tents will be chased by other birds around him. When
Quand bruit des cymbees, tubes & sonaillons,	the sound of cymbals, trumpets and bells will restore sense to
Rendront le sens de la dame insensée.	the senseless woman.

FRANCE, c. 1813–14

The Eagle is, as always, Napoleon, here driven back from Moscow and surrounded by the other birds of prey, Russia, Austria and Prussia. The last two lines may hold two separate interpretations. First, they may refer to the martial music of the armies which bring France back to her senses, that is, restore to her King Louis XVIII, or they refer to Napoleon's second marriage to Marie Louise of Austria and the grief and madness of the discarded Josephine (*dame insensée*). It was a common popular belief that Napoleon's luck deserted him when he discarded Josephine Beauharnais.

45

Trop le ciel pleure l'Androgyn[1] procrée,	The heavens weep too much for the birth of Androgeus, near
Pres de ciel sang humain respondu:	the heavens human blood is
Par mort trop tard grand peuple recrée,	spilt. It is too late for the great nation to be revived because of
Tard & tost vient le secours attendu.	the death, soon, yet too late, comes the awaited help.

[1] *Androgyn* = (*a*) hermaphrodite. (*b*) Androgeus, son of Minos of Crete, killed by the young people of Athens because he won all the prizes at the Pantheon.

Androgin implies an hermaphrodite who causes some form of aerial warfare in the second line? The rest is very generalized.

46

Apres grand troche[1] *humaine plus grand s'appreste,*	After great misery for mankind an even greater approaches
Le grand moteur des Siecles renouvelle:	when the great cycle of the centuries is renewed. It will
Pluie, sang, laict, famine, fer & peste,	rain blood, milk, famine, war and disease: In the sky will be
Au ciel veu feu, courant long estincelle.	seen a fire, dragging a trail of sparks.

THIRD WORLD WAR, *c.* 1986?

The great catastrophe of war that Nostradamus predicts here is linked with a comet appearing at the end of a century. The most likely is Halley's comet, last seen in 1910 and due to reappear in 1986, which is consistent with the other dates given by Nostradamus. He is obviously not exactly clear when this war will break out and dates between the late 70s and 1999 are given. Comets were important to 16th-Century philosophers and had significance according to their place in the zodiac. It does not seem to apply to the 1910 dating, because Nostradamus specifies that a great war has already taken place before the comet appears. See I. 91, II. 41, 62, 91, IV. 97, VIII. 59, 77, X. 49, 72, 74, 75.

47

L'ennemi grand vieil dueil meurt de poison,	The enemy watches with grief the old man dead from poison;
Les souverains par infiniz subjugez	the kings are overcome by an immeasurable (number). It
Pierres plouvoir, cachez soubz la foison,	rains stones, hidden under the fleece; vainly articles are
Par mort articles en vain sont alleguez.	asserted by the dead man.

[1] *troche*—from the Greek, *trukos* = misery.

La grand copie[1] *qui passera les monts,*	The great army which will pass over the mountains when
Saturne en l'Arq tournant du poisson Mars:	Saturn is in Sagittarius and Mars moving into Pisces.
Venins caches soubs testes de saulmons,	Poison hidden under the heads of salmon, their chief in war
Leur chef pendu à fil de polemars.[2]	hung with a cord.

The conjunction mentioned in line 2 is rare and has apparently only occurred once since publication, 17th July 1751. Its next occurrence will be 13th July 2193. The mountains may be the Alps but the third line seems incomprehensible. A *saumon* in Provençal means a donkey head, but gets one no further.

Les conseilleurs du premier monopole,[3]	The advisers of the first conspiracy, the victors won over
Les conquerants seduits par la Melite:	on behalf of the Maltese; Rhodes and Byzantium opening
Rodes, Bisance pour leurs exposant pole,[4]	their towns for them, the pursuers in flight will need land.
Terre faudra les poursuivans de suite.	

The connection between Istanbul (Bizantium) Rhodes, Malta and a conspiracy is obscure. It almost certainly refers to an incident during the Ottoman Empire.

Quand ceux d'Hainault, de Gand[5] *& de Bruxelles,*[6]	When the people of Hainault, Ghent and Brussels see siege
Verront à Langres le siege devant mis:	laid before Langres: Behind their flanks will be dreadful
Derrier leurs flancs seront guerres cruelles	wars, the former wound being worse than their enemies.
La plaie antique fera pis qu'ennemis.	

[1] *copie*—Latin, *copia* = forces.

[2] *polemars* = (*a*) Greek *polemarches*, he who leads in war. (*b*) Provençal *polomar*, twine or thick string.

[3] *monopole*—Greek, *monopolum* = conspiracy.

[4] *pole*—Greek, *polis* = town.

[5] *Gand* = Ghent, chief city of Flanders.

[6] *Bruxelles* = Brussels, chief city of Brabent.

REVOLT IN NETHERLANDS, 1568

Hainault, Flanders (Ghent) and Brabant (Brussels) were the richest provinces of the 16th-Century Netherlands. Nostradamus sees them as involved with a siege upon Langres, which was an important city on the frontier during the Hapsburg wars. The third line then indicates the uprising of the Netherlands in 1568, but it is unclear what is meant by the 'former wound'; possibly some form of internal dissension?

51

Le sang de juste à Londres fera faulte,
Bruslés par fouldres de vingt trois les six:
La dame antique cherra de place haute,
Des mesme secte plusieurs seront occis.

The blood of the just will be demanded of London burnt by fire in three times twenty plus six. The ancient lady will fall from her high position, and many of the same denomination will be killed.

GREAT FIRE OF LONDON, 1666

The only fire in London occurring in a year '66 is the great one of 1666. This is one of Nostradamus' more interesting quatrains where he gets very close to giving an accurate dating that can be checked historically. The 'dame antique' who falls is interpreted as the Cathedral of St. Paul's, which was destroyed, and the others of the same denomination, either the churches or their occupants. Many people did flee from their wooden homes hoping to escape the flames in the stone-built churches, but the heat was so intense that even these buildings did not escape. The blood of the just is understood to mean that the victims of the fire were undeserving of their fate. This quatrain is linked with II. 53, by the words 'sang de juste' and 'dame antique'.

52

Dans plusieurs nuicts la terre tremblera:
Sur le printemps deux effors suite:
Corinthe, Ephere aux deux mers nagera,
Guerre s'esmeut par deux vaillans de luit.[1]

For several nights the earth will shake; in the spring two great efforts in succession. Corinth and Ephesus will swim in the two seas; war will be stirred up by two valiant in combat.

[1] luit—Romance = fight, combat.

93

England was engaged in a naval war with the United Provinces from 1665-7, and if one can accept that they are represented by Corinth and Ephesus, even though the link is quite obscure, then this, the preceeding and following quatrains become a trio covering the same period.

53

La grande peste de cité maritime,	The great plague in the maritime city will not stop until death is avenged by the blood of a just man taken and condemned for no crime; the great lady is outraged by the pretence.
Ne cessera que mort ne soit vengée	
Du juste sang par pris damné sans crime,	
De la grand dame par feincte n'outragée.	

PLAGUE OF LONDON, 1665

Nostradamus clearly shows in the second line that he believes the Great Plague and Fire of London to be the result of the killing of Charles I; *see also* quatrain IX. 49, where it is predicted in detail. The maritime city is a description often used for London, and the plague broke out the year before the great Fire. It is suggested that the lady who is outraged, and was interpreted as St. Paul's Cathedral in II. 51, stands for the Church because soon afterwards Protestantism became re-established in England under William III, and Nostradamus was a fervent Catholic. His views towards all Protestant forms of religion are very hostile throughout his writings, probably a reflection of the development of Calvinism during his own lifetime. Again in this verse is the theme that the people suffering from the plague are those of '*juste sang*', the people of II. 51, who are described as being in London.

54

Par gent estrange, & Romains lointaine,	By a foreign people, far from the Romans, their great city will be greatly damaged by water. A girl without a greatly different estate taken by the leader, the lock not having been removed.
Leur grand cité apres eaue fort troublée:	
Fille sans trop different domaine,	
Prins chef, ferreure[1] n'avoir este riblée.[2]	

[1] *ferreure*—This may be read in variants as *serreure*.
[2] *riblée*—O.F., *ribler* = to rob, pillage.

This quatrain indicates that Rome will be attacked by a distant invader after or during a time of flooding. Whether the girl is to be understood literally or metaphorically is not clear.

55

Dans le conflict le grand qui peu valloit,
A son dernier fera cas merveilleux:
Pendant qu'Hadrie verra ce qu'il falloit,
Dans le banquet pongnale l'orgueilleux.

In the conflict the great man who is of little worth will perform an astonishing deed at his end. While Hadrie sees what is needed, during a banquet he stabs the proud.

FRANCE, 1594

By 1594 the revolutionary ideas of the Paris Seize (Peoples' Parliament) were becoming too strong for the League to cope with, and the Duke de Mayenne, claimant to the throne through the House of Guise, carried out a *coup d'état*. He invited all the leaders of the Seize to a banquet in order to lull their suspicions and had them all killed on the following night. Mayenne hoped that he would be able to hold Paris for the Catholic league but Henri IV (Hadrie) realizing the situation, saw that he had to become Catholic and thus unite France.

56

Que peste & glaive n'a sceu definer,[1]
Mort dans le puis sommet du ciel frappé:
L'abbé mourra quand verra ruiner,
Ceux du naufrage l'escueil voulant grapper.

One whom neither plague nor sword could kill will die on the top of a hill, struck from the sky. The abbot will die when he sees the ruin of the people in the shipwreck trying to hold on to the reef.

57

Avant conflict le grand tombera,
Le grand à mort, mort, trop subite & plainte,
Nay imparfaict: la plus part nagera,
Auprès du fleuve de sang la terre tainte.

Before the battle the great man will fall, the great one to death, death too sudden and lamented. Born imperfect, he will go the greater part of the way; near the river of blood the ground is stained.

---

[1] *definer*—O.F. = die, finish, decide.

Mort, trop subite probably implies an assassination, and *nay imparfaict* a leader born with a deformity. If it were not for the deformity I would apply this to J. F. Kennedy's stand against Khrushchev over Cuba. The Russian fleet did come 'the greater part of the way', and it was after this confrontation that Kennedy was killed at Dallas *trop subite & plainte*.

58

Sans pied ne main dend aiguë & forte,	Without either foot or hand, with strong and sharp teeth through the crowd to the fortified harbour and the elder born. Near the gates, treacherous, he crosses over; the moon shines but little, great pillage.
Par Globe[1] *au fort de port & lainé nay:*	
Pres du portail desloyal transporte,	
Silene[2] *luit, petit grand emmené.*	

Some interpret the last line as 'the moon shines, the great little man is carried off' meaning Napoleon. They apply the same interpretation to '*petit grand*' in II. 85.

59

Classe Gauloise par appuy de grande garde,	The French fleet with the support of the main guard of great Neptune and his trident warriors; Provence scrounged to sustain this great band, moreover, fighting at Narbonne with javelins and arrows.
Du grand Neptune, & ses tridens souldars:	
Rongée Provence pour soustenir grand bande,	
Plus Mars Narbon, par javelots & dards.	

Neptune apparently refers to Turkey, the dominant power in the Mediterranean during Nostradamus' lifetime. The trident warriors are probably French allied troops. Toulon was used as a base against the Habsburgs during the 1540s but not later, and there does not seem to have been any trouble in Narbonne at this period.

[1] *Globe*—Latin, *globus* = a crowd, throng.
[2] *Silene*—Greek, *selene* = moon, but the spelling *selin* is more normal for Nostradamus, so this may be an anagram.

La foy Punicque en Orient rompue	Faith with Africa broken in the
Grand Jud.[1] & Rosne, Loire &	East, Great Jordan, Rosne,
Tag[2] changeront.	Loire & Tagus will change.
Quand du mulet la faim sera repue,	When the hunger of the mule is
Classe espargie,[3] sang & corps	sated, the fleet is scattered and
nageront.	bodies swim in blood.

At the time of some discord between Africa and an Eastern country the rivers Jordan in Palestine, Rosne and Loire in France, Tagus, Spain and Portugal will change. This may mean the borders of the parent countries change, and is in some way allied with a great naval disaster. Line three is completely obscure.

Euge,[4] Tamins,[5] Gironde & la	Bravo, men of the Thames,
Rochele,	Gironde and la Rochelle; O
O sang Troyen Mort ay port de la	Trojan blood killed by an
flesche:	arrow at the harbour. Beyond
Derrier le fleuve au fort mise	the river the ladder put against
l'eschele,	the port, flashes of fire, great
Pointes feu grand meutre sur la	slaughter in the breach.
bresche.	

The French Royal Family is referred to by Nostradamus as being of Trojan blood, see I. 19, but it did not exist by the time that Englishmen fought side by side with Frenchmen. There is no record of a prince of the blood being killed or wounded at a harbour.

Mabus puis tost alors mourra,	Mabus will then soon die and
viendra,	there will come a dreadful
De gens & bestes une horrible	destruction of people and
defaite:	animals. Suddenly vengeance
Puis tout à coup la vengeance on	will be revealed, a hundred
verra,	hands, thirst and hunger, when
Cent, main, soif, faim, quand	the comet will pass.
courra la comete.	

[1] *Jud*—Short for Jordan.
[2] *Tag*—Short for Tagus.
[3] *espargie*—O.F., *espargier* = to sprinkle.
[4] *Euge*—Latin = bravo!
[5] *Tamins*—Syncope of Tamisiens = people of the Thames?

THIRD WORLD LEADER?

Again we have the reference to a comet. If this is the same comet as in II. 41 and 46, this could be a reference to a future war. It is possible that Mabus is an anagram of the leader's proper name Nostradamus as a doctor would know that most diseases do not kill people as well as animals, yet in this verse he specifically says it will happen. It has been suggested that he is referring to atomic fallout which kills all living creatures equally dreadfully (*horrible defaite*).

63

Gaulois, Ausone[1] *bien peu sub-jugera,*	The French will subdue Ausonia in a little, while Pau
Par, Marne & Seine fera Perme l'vrie:	Marne and Seine Perme will make drunk. He who raises the
Qui le grand mur contre eux dressera,	great wall against them, the great one will lose his life from
Du moindre au mur le grand perdra la vie.	the least at the wall.

BATTLE OF IVRY, 1590

There does not seem to be much connection between Parme in Russia and this quatrain. However, if line 2 reads *Parme l'vrie* there is a most interesting possibility. In 1590 the Duke of Parma was ordered to France from the Netherlands to help the Catholic Leaguers against Henri of Navarre. Parma was defeated by Henri at the Battle of Ivry, 1590. However he did not die until 1592 from wounds received at another battle.

64

Seicher de faim, de soif, gent Genevoise,	The people of Geneva will dry up with thirst and hunger,
Espoir prochain viendra au defaillir:	hope at hand will come to failure; the law of the Cevennes
Sur point tremblant sera loi Gebenoise.[2]	will be at breaking point, the fleet cannot be received at the
Classe au grand port ne se peut acuillir.	great port.

CEVENNES, c. 1685

After the revocation of the Edict of Nantes 1685 by Louis XIV, the people of the Cevennes revolted, so deeply rooted was their

---

[1] *Ausone*—Ausonia, Southern Italy.
[2] *Gebenoise*—Cevennes mountain chain in Switzerland.

Calvinist faith. Presumably the fleet would be bringing supplies across Lake Geneva.

65

Le parc enclin grande calamité.	In the feeble lists, great cala-
Par l'Hesperie & Insubre fera:	mity through America and
Le feu en nef peste et captivité,	Lombardy. The fire in the
Mercure en l'Arc Saturne fenera.	ship, plague and captivity;
	Mercury in Sagittarius, Saturn
	warning.

7th DECEMBER 2044?

According to Wöllner the next date for this configuration is 7th December 2044, the last being 1839. Insubria is definitely either Milan or Lombardy but the dangers to it and America (Hesperie I. 28) are not clear.

66

Par grans dangiers le captif eschapé,	The captive escaped great dangers, his fortune greatly
Peu de temps grand a fortune changée:	changed in a short time. The people are trapped in the
Dans le palais le peuple est attrapé,	palace, by good omen, the besieged city.
Par bon augure la cité assiegée.	

NAPOLEON'S 100 DAYS, 1st MARCH–28th JUNE 1815

The captive who escapes great dangers and whose fortune changes so dramatically in a short time, is Napoleon after his escape from Elba on 1st March 1815. The line can also be read inversely with the meaning that the good fortune will very soon change back again, meaning the defeat at Waterloo on 18th June. The third line is interesting. On Napoleon's victorious return to Paris after his escape, the Parisian mob invaded the palace and court of King Louis XVIII and carried their hero, Napoleon, on their shoulders into the private chambers once occupied by the king, and reinstated him themselves physically. Apparently the crowd was so enormous that no one could get in or out for some hours. The final line is interpreted as meaning that Paris, the city besieged by the Allies, will find its monarch restored (*par bon augure*) as he was on 8th July 1815.

Le blond an nez forchu viendra commettre,
Par le duelle & chassera dehors:
Les exilés, dedans fera remettre,
Aux lieux marins commettant les plus fors.

The blond one will come into conflict with the hooknosed one, in a duel and will drive him out. He will have restored the exiles committing the strongest to the marine places.

JAMES II AND WILLIAM III, 1688–9

The blond man was understood even by contemporary pamphlets to stand for William of Orange, who was in fact also fair-haired. William's party drives out James II in 1688, but the Stuart party (*les exilez*) decided to reinstate him and put all their efforts into a sea battle. James based himself in Ireland and was aided by the French fleet. In 1690 the Allies were badly beaten at sea off Beachy Head but on the same day William III won the Battle of the Boyne and James was forced to flee to France, from which he never returned. The British fleet did not finally subdue the French and assure her maritime supremacy for another two years at Cap la Hague in 1692.

De l'aquilon[1] les efforts seront grands.
Sus l'Ocean sera la porte ouverte:
Le regne en l'isle sera reintegrand,
Tremblera Londres par voille descouverte.

In the North great efforts will be made, across the seas the way will be open. The rule on the island will be re-established, London fearful of the fleet when sighted.

JAMES II, *continued*

This seems to continue the last quatrain, and is one of the pairs that Nostradamus overlooked when he separated them to make interpretation more difficult. The great efforts made in the North are those of the invader, William III of Orange. The British fleet was so sluggishly commanded at this time by the Earl of Torrington that he lost several sea battles to the French and Stuart fleets, particularly Beachy Head and Bantry Bay, and it was only William's strength on land that kept him the throne. There could be a second interpretation of line 2; that the seas were open and undefended allowing William to cross to England. The island, in the singular, indicates Ireland where James II took refuge; Nostradamus usually refers to the British Isles in the plural.

[1] *aquilon*—Latin = North Wind, North.

James naturally re-established Stuart rule there until displaced by the Battle of the Boyne, 1690. The last line again refers to the bad government of the British fleet under Lord Torrington. After the defeat at Beachy Head he withdrew his remaining ships to London where he was courtmartialled for lack of agressiveness, but acquitted. However, the British paid heavily for his reluctance to act during the next two years. It may also refer to the occasion in 1667 before William III came to England when his Dutch fleet sailed up the Thames on a raiding party.

69

Le Roy Gaulois par la Celtique dextre,	A Gallic king from the Celtic right hand (side) seeing the
Voyant discorde de la grande Monarchie	discord of the great monarch will flourish his sceptre over
Sus les trois pars fera florir son sceptre	the three leopards against the king of the great Hierarchy.
Contre la Cappe¹ de la grand Hierarchie.	

The clue for this quatrain is in line 3, the use of the word *pars*. In another book of his called 'the Horapollo' Nostradamus translates this word as leopards, and these are the three leopards of England, as Napoleon called the English heraldic lions. Thus we seem to continue yet again the theme of James II and William III. William is the Celtic king from Northern Gaul (i.e. Holland) (dextre is the northern side on a map) who seeing England in trouble under James II takes over the kingdom. Note that Nostradamus makes no mention of war. It was not a bloody invasion but one of invitation, William having many supporters in Britain. Cappe, as in other quatrains, is Nostradamus' version of Capet, the line of the French kings. As has been explained in the last two quatrains the French bitterly opposed William's establishment in England and allied themselves with the deposed James II and supplied him with troops and naval aid.

¹ *Cappe*—Nostradamus' version of Capet. One of the names of the French royal line until the last of the Bourbons. *See also* IX. 20 etc.

Le dard du ciel fera son estendre,	The dart from heaven will
Mors en parlant: grande execution:	make its journey; Death while
La pierre en l'arbre la fiere gent	speaking; a great execution.
rendue,	The stone in the tree, the
Bruit humain monstre purge expia-	proud nation brought down;
tion.	rumour of a human monster,
	purge and expiation.

NAPOLEON, 1815

This is often interpreted as referring to Napoleon but it seems too general in its meaning for this to be satisfactory. The theory is that the scene is Waterloo 1815, and the dart from the sky is the vengeance of heaven. The next line refers to the carnage and slaughter, and the stone to an axe cutting down the Bonaparte dynasty. Then France surrenders, is expiated, and the monster, Napoleon, is removed to St. Helena. Very ingenious if one can accept it.

Les exilés en Sicile viendront,	The exiles will come to Sicily
Pour delivrer de faim la gent	in order to deliver the foreign
estrange:	nation from hunger. At day-
Au point du jour les Celtes lui	break the Celts will fail them,
faudront	life remains by reason; the
La vie demeure à raison: Roi se	king joins in alliance.
range.	

Armée Celtique en Italie vexée,	The French army will be
De toutes pars conflict & grande	troubled in Italy, on all sides
peste:	conflict and great loss. Flee
Romains fuis, ô Gaule repoulsé,	the Italians, O France repelled;
Pres du Thesin,[1] *Rubicon pugne*[2]	near the Tessin the battle at
incerte.	the Rubicon is uncertain.

A difficult quatrain, because it sounds so specific and yet has not occurred since 1555. It is best used as an example of retroactive prophecy, that is, describing an event occurring during the prophet's lifetime or earlier and which has sunk into his subsconcious. If this is so, the first 3 lines are a good description of the Battle of

---

[1] *Thesin*—River Ticino flows into the Po below Pavia.

[2] *pugne*—Latin, *pugna* = battle.

Pavia 1525, the third line describing the strategy of the Imperial forces. But even then the outcome of Pavia was a definite victory for the Italians, not an uncertain one.

73

Au lac Fucin[1] de Benac[2] le rivage,	The shore of Lake Garda to
Prins du Leman[3] au port de l'Orguion:[4]	Lake Fucino, taken from Lake Geneva to the harbour of
Nay de trois bras predict bellique image	Orguion. Born with three arms it foretells a warlike image with
Par trois couronnes au grand Endymion.[5]	three kingdoms for the great Endymion.

A large number of wild interpretations have been made for this quatrain including (Allen 1943) that Endymion is a metaphor for the U.S.A.! The three arms and crowns may well be the triple tiara of the Pope, linking it with the Vatican States, or a state containing three kingdoms probably set in Italy.

74

De Sens, D'Autun viendront jusques au Rosne,	From Sens, from Autun they will come as far as the Rhône
Pour passer outre vers les monts Pyrenées:	to cross over the Pyrenees. The people going out from the
La gent sortir de la Marque d'Anconne,	Marches of Ancona will follow in great trails over land and
Par terre & mer suivra à grans trainées.	sea.

This quatrain is very muddled. Leoni (1961) has a clever interpretation in which he suggests that the Pyrenees are a mistake for the Alps. This would certainly help the geography, as Sens and Autun are in North Eastern France, but the Rhône is not on the way to the Pyrenees. If we interpret the mountains as the Alps the quatrain describes an invasion of Italy. The Marches of Ancona stretch from Rimini to north of Guilianova.

[1] *Fucin*—Lake Fucino, drained in 1876, in Italy.
[2] *Benac*—Lake Garda, Italy.
[3] *Leman*—Lake Geneva, Switzerland.
[4] *Orguion*—? possibly Orgon in Southern France, or Orgiano in Lombardy, not deciphered.
[5] *Endymion*—Youth in Greek mythology loved by Selene the moon, and having the gift of eternal sleep.

La voix ouie de l'insolite oiseau,	The call of the unwanted bird
Sur le carron de respiral estage:[1]	being heard on the chimney
Si hault viendra du froment le	stack; bushels of wheat will
boisseau,	rise so high that man will
Que l'homme de l'homme fera	devour his fellow man.
Antropophage.[2]	

GENERAL FAMINE

The unwanted bird on the chimney stack is an owl or similar bird of ill omen bringing warning of famine and the high price of corn, but one is given no indication as to what famine will be so dreadful that men will become cannibals. Possibly refers to the World Famine of I. 67.

Foudre en Bourgongne fera cas	Lightning in Burgundy will
portenteux,	reveal portentous events. A
Que par engin[3] *oncques ne pourrait*	thing that could never have
faire,	been done by trickery. The
De leur senat sacriste fait boiteux	lame priest will reveal matters
Fera scavoir aux ennemis l'affaire.	of the senate to the enemy.

TALLYRAND, 1754–1838

Charles Maurice de Talleyrand-Périgord fits this quatrain remarkably well. The starting point lies in the third line, the lame priest. Talleyrand became lame at the age of nearly four years when a chest of drawers fell on his foot injuring it permanently. He was destined by his family for the Church and took orders in 1778 and was Bishop of Antin by 1789. By 1790 he was totally identified with the Revolutionaries, and was banned by the Pope in the following year. By 1807 however, he resigned his position as Grand Chamberlain in Napoleon's service because he disapproved of the Emperor's policies, and secretly advised the Emperor Alexander I of Russia not to pressure Austria as Napoleon wished. By 1814 he was contemplating absolute treachery. When Alexander I came to the Hôtel Talleyrand he was advised by Talleyrand that the restoration of the Bourbons was the only solution for the future of France, and on 1st April in the same year he convened the senate (line 3) who pronounced Napoleon to have forfeited his crown.

[1] The line literally means—on the pipe of the breathing floor.
[2] *Antropophage*—Greek, *anthro-phagos* = man-eating.
[3] *engin*—Latin, *ingenium* = genius, ruse, trickery.

| Par arcs feux poix & par feux repoussés, | Repulsed by bows, burning pitch and fires, cries and shouts |

Par arcs feux poix & par feux
repoussés,
Cris hurlements sur la minuit
ouis:
Dedans sont mis par les remparts
cassez
Par cunicules¹ les traditeurs² fuis.

Repulsed by bows, burning pitch and fires, cries and shouts will be heard in the middle of the night. They will get in through the broken defences; the traitors escape through the underground passages.

A general verse concerning a city captured in the middle of the night, with its ramparts broken down, and the people who betrayed it escaping through underground passages.

Le grand Neptune du profond de la
mer,
De gent Punique³ & sang Gaulois
meslé:
Les isles à sang pour le tardif
ramer,⁴
Plus lui nuira que l'occult mal celé.

Great Neptune from the depths of the sea, of mixed African race and French blood, the islands remain bloody because of the slow one; it will harm him more than the badly concealed secret.

Neptune was used by Nostradamus in II. 59 to refer to the Turkish Moslem fleet, which brings line 2 into the Franco-Turkish agreements of Nostradamus' day. The famous Barbary pirates, whose leader Barbarossa is also referred to in I. 74 are probably the Punic people, as their base was in Northern Africa. The last two lines may apply to an event of 1558 when, according to Jaubert, the Turkish fleet attacked Minorca (*les isles*), and took Chidadela, killing and enslaving the entire population of the town. He also states that the Turks were bribed to delay co-operating with the French fleet (*tardif ramer*) and thus demoralize them instead of coming to their aid in an Italian raid.

¹ *cunicules*—Latin, *cuniculus* = rabbit, interpreted as burrow, passage, mine.

² *traditeurs*—Latin, *traditor* = traitor.

³ *Punique*—adjective for Carthage in North Africa.

⁴ *ramer*—Romance = to remain, stay.

La barbe crespe & noir par engin
Subjugera la gent cruelle & fiere:
Le grand CHIREN ostera du
longin,[1]
Tous les captifs par Seline[2] bar-
riere.

The man with the curly, black
beard will subdue the cruel and
proud nation through skill. The
great Chiren will take from afar
all those captured by the Turkish banner.

LEPANTO, 1571?

This quatrain poses a problem. All commentators have interpreted CHIREN as an anagram for HENRIC, an alternative
spelling for Henri. This verse is then ascribed to the Battle of
Lepanto 1571 which freed over 1,500 Christian slaves from the
Turkish fleet (line 4). But at the time of Lepanto, Charles X was
on the French throne, and Henri III was not to follow until 1574.
Perhaps Nostradamus is a few years out in his dates, or uses Henri
as a symbol for France? At Lepanto the Christian powers formed
the last crusade against the Turks (Seline, because of their
crescent-shaped banners). Command was given to Don John of
Austria who was dark and bearded. The third line may mean that
France benefited from the final removal of Turkish naval power
from the Mediterranean. The clue lies in a definitive interpretation of CHIREN.

80

Apres le conflict du lesé l'eloquence,
Par peu de temps se trame faint
repas:
Point l'on n'admet les grands à
delivrance,
Des ennemis sont remis à propos.

After the battle, the eloquence
of the one left behind for a
short time brings a short
respite. None of the great will
be allowed to go free, they are
left to their enemies at the
proper time.

---

[1] *longin*—Provençal, *longinc* = far off, distant.
[2] *Seline*—Greek, Selene = moon, crescent.

Par feu du ciel la cité presque aduste,	The city is almost burned down by fire from the sky, water
L'urne[1] menace encor Ceucalion,[2]	again threatens Deucalion. Sar-
Vexée Sardaigne par la Punique fuste,[3]	dinia is vexed by the African fleet after Libra has left Leo.
Apres que Libra lairra son Phaeton.	

This quatrain appears to be modern for the first line implies the destruction of a city from the air with fire, by bombing or something similar. This devastation is followed by flooding, as Deucalion was the Noah of Greek Mythology. Then follows an African raid on Sardinia or Italy, and line four gives us an astrological dating. Phaeton was the youth who drove the chariot of the sun, Leo, when struck down by Zeus. Libra usually stands for Austria in astrological geography.

Par faim la proye fera loup prisonnier,	Through hunger the prey will make the wolf prisoner, the
L'assaillant lors en extreme detresse,	attacker then in great distress;
Le nay[4] ayant au devant le dernier,	the elder having the younger in front; the great man cannot
Le grand n'eschappe au milieu de la presse.	escape in the middle of the crowd.

It is possible to invert the translation of the first line but unfortunately this does not make the quatrain any more specific.

Le gros traffic d'un grand Lyon changé	The great trade of great Lyons changed, the greater part turns
La plus part tourne en pristine[5] ruine.	into early ruin. A prey to the soldiers through a harvest of
Proie aux soldats par pille vendengé[6]	pillage. Fogs through the mountains of Jura and Switzer-
Par Jura mont & Sueve[7] bruine.	land.

[1] *urne*—Metaphor for waters, flooding.
[2] *Ceucalion*—Misprint for Deucalion in other editions, see commentary above.
[3] *fuste* = a kind of low oared galley.
[4] Probably corruption of *l'aîné* = elder.
[5] *pristine*—Latin, *pristinus* = former, early, first.
[6] *vendengé*—O.F. = vendage, harvest.
[7] *Sueve* = Switzerland, from the Latin Suevi, the German Swiss.

Nicollaud gives as the basis for interpreting this quatrain the Memoirs of the Marquis de Beauregard who says that during October 1795, when troops of the Revolution were putting down an uprising at Lyons, 'we saw large crowds of peasants ... who with great empty sacks rushed to Lyons to pillage the town'. This was after a two month long siege and many of the town's inhabitants had been massacred. The fog mentioned in the last line was not recorded.

84

Entre Campaigne, Sienne, Flora, Tustie,	Between Campania, Sienna, Florence and Tuscany, it will
Six mois neuf jours ne ploura une goutte:	not rain a drop for six months and nine days. A foreign
L'estrange langue en terre Dalmatie,	language will be spoken in
Courira sus: vastant la terre toute.	Dalmatia, it will overrun the country, devastating all the land.

When Nostradamus wrote, Dalmatia belonged to the Venetians, but was surrounded by the Ottoman Empire. Perhaps he thought it would be taken by the Turks (*estrange langue*)? It was not captured, nor has so specific a drought been recorded along the west coast of Italy.

85

Le vieux plain barbe soubs le statut severe,	Under the severe authority of the old man with the flowing
A Lyon faict dessus l'Aigle Celtique:	beard, at Lyon it is put above the Celtic Eagle. The small
Le petit grand trop autre persevere,	great one perseveres too far;
Bruit d'arme au ciel: mer rouge Ligustique.[1]	noise of weapons in the sky, the Ligurian sea is red.

NAPOLEON?

The small great man of line 3 is applied possibly to Napoleon in II. 58 and the theme may be continued here. During the 100 Days Napoleon arrived at Lyons on 10th March; the Eagle is certainly the French eagle since it is described as Celtic, which further develops the possibility. It cannot be identified with the Habsburg Imperial Eagle in this quatrain. But the stumbling block is line

[1] *Ligustique*—Ligurian, North Eastern Mediterranean.

one; who is the severe bearded man who accepts Napoleon at Lyons? Marshall Ney was not bearded, and he went over to Napoleon at Auserre. I leave this to the ingenuity of the reader.

86

Naufrage à classe[1] *pres d'onde Hadriatique,*	The fleet is wrecked near the Adriatic sea, the earth trembles,
La terre tremble esmeüe sus l'air en terre mis:	pushed into the air and falls again. Egypt trembles; Maho-
Egypte tremble augment Mahometique.	metan increase; the herald is sent to call out for surrender.
L'Herault soi rendre à crier est commis.	

1799. NAPOLEON IN EGYPT

In 1799 during Napoleon's Expedition to Egypt the British and French fleets met on the Nile and the latter were roundly defeated by the British led by Sir Richard Abercromby. It is suggested that the second line may refer to the French army who had disembarked but were frightened when they heard that the French Admiral's vessel had been blown up and the pieces strewn along the beaches. From this defeat Napoleon led his troops against the Turks at Acre, but during the siege his men were struck with the plague and so finally Napoleon decided to withdraw to Egypt, if he could not break down the Turkish resistance. A herald was sent to demand the surrender of Acre but this was refused and Napoleon was compelled to raise the siege.

87

Apres viendra des extremes contreés	Afterwards there will come from a distant country a
Prince Germain, dessus le throsne doré:	German prince upon the golden throne. Servitude met from
La servitude & eaux rencontrées,	over the seas. The lady sub-
La dame serve, son temps plus n'adore.	ordinated, in the time no longer adored.

GEORGE I, 1714

This prediction probably applies to the accession of the Hanoverian George I to the throne of England in 1714. George came from Germany, a distant country, and was a German Prince. Should the word germain be used with the second meaning of

---

[1] *classe*—Latin, *classis* = fleet.

cousin or relative, he was also a cousin of the Queen Anne, but the use of the capital letter makes the first interpretation the most likely. However, it may be one of Nostradamus' famous double meanings. The English throne was a great prize and so is described as golden. Servitude refers to the fact that George was invited to accept the throne; it was not won in battle, while the final line is probably a reference to the Mother Church (Catholicism) which was no longer to be the main religion once the Hanoverians came to the throne.

88

Le circuit du grand faict ruineux,	The completion of the great
Le nom septiesme du cinquiesme	disastrous action, the name of
sera:	the seventh will be that of the
D'un tiers plus grand l'estrange	fifth. Of the third (name) a
belliqueux,	greater, foreign warmonger,
Mouton, Lutece,[1] Aix ne garantira.	Paris and Aix will not be kept
	in Aries.

THE CHILDREN OF CATHERINE DE VALOIS AND ACCESSION OF HENRI IV

An interesting and detailed quatrain which becomes very clear on study. The clue again is the seven children of Catherine de' Medici of whom the fifth will be the seventh and last king, Henri III (*tiers*), as his younger brother the Duke d'Alençon had died earlier, and his sister Marguerite had married the foreigner of the same name, Henri IV, who would become even greater through acts of war. Henri IV was considered a foreigner because he was Prince of Navarre, separate from France at this time. He had to besiege Paris before France capitulated and accepted his rule, and he started the siege in the sign of Aries (March, April) after the Battle of Ivry in February 1590. The first line probably refers to the massacre of St. Bartholomew which really sowed the seeds of final destruction for the Valois line (*circuit*) as it was partly because of this dreadful deed (*faict ruineux*) that Henri III was assassinated by the Jesuit Clément and left the throne free for Henri of Navarre.

[1] *Lutece*—Latin, *Lutetia* = Paris.

Un jour seront demis les deux grands maistres,
Leur grand pouvoir se verra augmenté:
La terre neufue sera en ses hauts estres,
Au sanguinaire le nombre racompté.

One day the two great leaders will be friends; their great power will be seen to grow. The new land will be at the height of its power, to the man of blood the number is reported.

AMERICA, RUSSIA (?) AND THE MAN OF BLOOD.

To solve this quatrain one must first decide on the translation of the word *demis* in the first line. Nearly all versions have the word *d'amis* (friends) which is how I have translated it here, because to understand *demis* as meaning halved would make nonsense of line two. The power of the leaders cannot be seen to increase if they are halved. The two great leaders sound as though they may be the great powers, and line 3 (the New Land) links this with America as Nouvelle Lande was one of the contemporary names for America. If not, it may refer to the modern usage of the New World. When America is at the height of its power and is allied with another great power (Russia?), then the man of blood, the third AntiChrist of Nostradamus will start assessing his position, See VIII. 77 where the war is described, II. 50, III. 60 and IV. 50 where he seems to be placed in Asia. There are many other references to him.

Par vie & mort changé regne d'Ongrie,[1]
La loi sera plus aspre que service:
Leur grand cité d'hurlements plaincts & crie,
Castor & Pollux[2] ennemis dans la lice.

Through life and death the rule in Hungary will be changed, the law will become more bitter than servitude. Their great city calls out with howls and laments, Castor and Pollux are enemies in the field.

REVOLUTION IN HUNGARY, 1956

The life and death change in Hungary certainly occurred during the Revolution of 1956 after Premier Nagy renounced the Warsaw Pact on 1st November of that year, and found Russian troops

[1] *Ongrie* = Hungary.
[2] *Castor & Pollux*—Identified with Gemini or the twins.

advancing into his country on 4th November. The strictness of
the régime that followed, from which many thousands fled to the
West, is well known. There was a general policy of severe repression
and there were many executions. The great city of Budapest
was occupied and badly damaged by the fighting during the
Revolution. The last line means that the pro-Russian Hungarians
were fighting against their brother Hungarians, as indeed
happened. I do not think this is intended as an indirect form of
dating.

91

Soleil levant un grand feu l'on verra,	At sunrise a great fire will be seen, noise and light extending
Bruit & clarté vers Aquilon tendants:	towards the North. Within the globe death and cries are heard,
Dedans le rond mort & cris l'on orra,	death awaiting them through weapons, fire and famine.
Par glaive, feu, faim, mort las attendants.	

ATTACK ON U.S.A. OR RUSSIA?

This is a frightening quatrain if one applies it to the future. It
seems to imply that a Northern Country, Russia or the U.S.A.
will be bombed suddenly at sunrise, and this will be followed by
a period of great devastation. In I. 92 Nostradamus states that
America will suffer the greatest destruction. If we link this quatrain
with I. 91, II. 5, 41 and 46, we are facing a very gloomy prospect.

92

Feu couleur d'or du ciel en terre veu,	Fire the colour of gold from
Frappé du haut nay, faict cas merveilleux:	the sky seen on earth, struck by the high born one, a marvellous
Grand meutre humain; prinse du grand nepveu.	happening. Great slaughter of humanity; a nephew taken
Morte d'expectacles eschappe l'orgueilleux.	from the great one; the death of the spectator, the proud one escapes.

NAPOLEON III, 1870

The clue to this quatrain is the word nephew in line three. There
are several references to Napoleon III as the nephew of Napoleon
and this quatrain describes the German artillery; the second line
an incident on 2nd August 1870 when a bullet hit the ground by
the Prince Imperial's feet, an event much publicized by the news-

papers. Napoleon III was captured during the general French capitulation of September 1870.

93

Bien pres du Timbre presse la Lybitine:[1]	Very near the Tiber hurries death a short while before a great flood. The captain of the ship taken and put into the bilges, the castle and palace burnt down.
Un peu devant grand inondation:	
Le chef du nef prins, mis à la sentine,[2]	
Chasteau, palais en conflagration.	

The word Tiber, in Rome, linked with the captain of a ship (the Bark of St. Peter) implies that the latter is a Pope who comes to a dreadful end before a flood. The castle and palace would be St. Angelo and the Vatican.

94

GRAND Pau grand mal pour Gaulois recevra,	Great Po will receive great harm from a Frenchman, vain terror to the maritime Lion. An infinite number of people will cross the sea and a quarter of a million will not escape.
Vaine terreur du maritin Lyon:	
Peuple infini par la mer passera.	
Sans eschapper un quart d'un million.	

NAPOLEON IN ITALY AND EGYPT

As the first line says, Italy (the Po) suffered great harm from Napoleon who also terrified the maritime British lion, but vainly, because he did not manage to invade her. A great army did cross the seas to Egypt with Napoleon and certainly at least a quarter of a million men died during his campaigns.

95

Les lieux peuplez seront inhabitables:	The populated lands will become uninhabitable, great disagreement in order to obtain lands. Kingdoms given to men incapable of prudence. Then for the great brothers, death and dissension.
Pour champs avoir grand division:	
Regnes livrez à prudents incapables,	
Lors les grands freres mort & dissention.	

[1] *Lybitine*—Latin, *Libitina* = Goddess of Death.
[2] *sentine*—Latin, *sentina* = (*a*) bilges, (*b*) dregs.

This quatrain is extremely vague. Some commentators apply it to the present and near future, in which case Nostradamus' opinion of our politicians is not high. The last line might then refer to the Kennedy brothers. There is no other world-known group of brothers to link with this period. The first line would be yet another description of the third war he believes will devastate this century. See VIII 46 and 77.

96

Flambeau ardent au ciel soir sera veu,	A burning torch will be seen in the sky at night near the end and source of the Rhône. Famine and weapon; help provided too late, Persia will turn and invade Macedonia.
Pres de la fin & principe du Rosne:	
Famine, glaive: tard le secours pourveu,	
La Perse tourne envahir Macedoine.	

The last line of this quatrain, by far the most specific, seems to indicate that Nostradamus foresaw the Persians (never part of the Ottoman empire) inflicting a great defeat on the Turks (Macedonia) so as to open up the Balkans. The light in the sky if the verse is to be accepted will be seen from the source of the Rhône at the Furka Pass as far as the mouth of the river west of Marseilles.

97

Romain Pontife garde de t'appro-cher,	Roman pontiff beware of approaching a city watered by two rivers. You will spit blood in that place, both you and yours, when the roses bloom.
De la cité que deux fleuves arrouse,	
Ton sang viendras aupres de là cracher,	
Toi & les tiens quand fleurira la rose.	

DEATH OF POPE PIUS VI AT VALENCE, 1799

The Pontiff in question is Pius VI who was imprisoned at Valence by the French after they had taken Rome in 1799. The two rivers are the Rhône and the Saône near by at Lyons. The Pope did die spitting blood, he suffered from an attack of severe vomiting in the summer (when the roses bloom) and died on 29th August 1799. His people referred to in the last line were the thirty-two priests who were imprisoned with the Pope. The word rose may have a typical Nostradamus double meaning of red, and therefore revolutionary, as well as of summertime. Both interpretations fit beautifully.

98

Celui de sang reperse[1] le visage,	He whose face is spattered with
De la victime proche sacrifiée,	the blood of a newly sacrificed
Tonant[2] en Leo augure par presage,	victim. Jupiter in Leo forewarns through prediction. He
Mis estra à mort lors pour la fiancée.[3]	will be put to death for the promise.

99

Terroir[4] Romain qu'interpretoit augure,	Roman land that the augur interprets, will be greatly
Par gent Gauloise par trop sera vexée:	molested by the French nation. But the French will come to
Mais nation Celtique craindra l'heure,	dread the time of the North wind having driven their fleet
Boreas,[5] classe[6] trop loing l'avoir poussée.	too far.

FAILURE OF NAPOLEON'S RUSSIAN CAMPAIGN, 1812

The Vatican States were taken into the French Empire in 1810, the French certainly molested Italy at this point. But soon afterwards, in 1812, Napoleon is suffering the defeat of his Russian campaign due to the cold weather (Boreas) and the folly of his general overcommitment. The fleet may refer to the earlier defeat at Trafalgar.

100

Dedans les isles si horrible tumulte,	Within the islands will be so
Bien on n'orra qu'une bellique brigue	dreadful a tumult although one only hears the warlike
Tant grand sera des predateurs l'insulte,	party. So great will be the threat of the plunderers that
Qu'on se viendra ranger à la grand ligne.	they will come to join in the great alliance.

[1] *reperse*—Latin, *respergere* = to sprinkle, splash.
[2] *Tonant*—standing for Jupiter Tonans, the Thunderer.
[3] *fiancée* = (*a*) marriage, bride. (*b*) Romance—promise or assurance.
[4] *terroir*—Latin, *terra* = land.
[5] *Boreas*—Latin = North wind.
[6] *classe*—Latin, *classis* = fleet.

Malta 1565, when all the great powers of Christendom sent reinforcements and aid, the 'Grand Succorso', to La Vallette in order to save Europe. The great alliance is probably the supranational order of Malta plus the Christian powers.

CENTURY III

1	
2	Alchemy
3	
4	1556/7
5	*continued*
6	Châteauneuf, 1819
7*	Occupied France, 1940
8*	Spanish Civil War, 1936
9	
10	House of Grimaldi, Monaco
11*	Assassination of Henri IV, 1610
12	Flood
13*	Submarine fleet
14*	Louis XV
15*	Louis XV
16F?	
17	
18	
19	
20*	Spain, 1610
21	
22	
23	
24	
25*	Henri IV
26	
27	
28*	England and France, *c.* 1558
29	
30*	Count of Montgomery, 1574
31*	Lepanto, 1571
32*	Second World War
33	

34
35**   Hitler/Napoleon
36
37*   Napoleon, 1796
38
39
40
41*   Death of Louis de Condé, 1569
42   Famine
43
44*?   Wireless or electricity?
45*   Battle of Toulouse, 1814
46
47
48
49*F?   France
50*   Paris, 1588
51*   Murders of the de Guise brothers, 1588
52
53?
54*   Franco and Spanish Civil War
55*   Henri II and III of France
56
57**   England, 1603–1939
58**   Hitler
59*   French Revolution
60
61
62
63**   Italy and Germany, 1937
64
65*F?   Tomb of St. Peter and a new Pope.
66*   Jerôme Greslot, 1562–9
67   Protestant sects
68**   Franco and Mussolini
69
70**   Great Britain, 1604
71**   Blockade of Britain, 1939–45. Concentration camps
72
73**   Duke of Bordeaux, 1820–71
74
75*F?   Chemical warfare in Europe?
76   Protestant sects, 16th Century

77***   October 1727
78
79
80*   Charles I
81*   Cromwell and Pontefract
82*F?   Invasion of France?
83*   Louis XVIII
84*   Sack of Rome under Pius VI
85
86
87*   Sinking of French fleet, 1655
88*   Marseilles, 1596
89*   Cyprus and Enosis
90
91*   Duke of Bordeaux
92*?
93
94
95**F? Rise of Communism.
96**   13th February 1820
97**F? The founding of Israel and eventual defeat of U.A.R.
98
99
100*   General de Gaulle

KEY * of interest. F? Possibly referring to the future.

Apres combat & bataille navale,	After the combat and naval
Le grand Neptune à son plus haut	battle, great Neptune in his
befroi:	highest belfry; the red adver-
Rouge adversaire de peur deviendra	sary will become pale with fear,
pasle	putting the great ocean into a
Mettant le grand Ocean en effroi.	state of terror.

In II. 59 Nostradamus used Neptune as a synonym for the Turkish Algerian fleets who were then ravaging the coasts. The red adversary would be the Spanish whose colour was red, but here the quatrain fails. At the Battle of Lepanto 1571 the Spanish defeated the Turks although the Barbary Corsairs continued to dominate the Mediterranean for some time to come.

2

Le divin verbe donrra[1] *à la sub-*	The divine word will give to
stance,	the substance (that which)
Comprins ciel, terre, or occult au	contains heaven and earth,
laict[2] *mystique:*	occult gold in the mystic deed.
Corps, ame esprit ayant toute	Body, soul and spirit are all
puissance	powerful. Everything is beneath
Tant soubs ses pieds comme au	his feet, as at the seat of heaven.
siege Celique.[3]	

ALCHEMISTIC QUATRAIN

Although many commentators dismiss this verse I think it is a rare and important description of Nostradamus' beliefs and experiences. The divine word which takes on substance is either Nostradmus literally calling forth the spirit who inspires him to prophecy, or an incantation which gives him divine powers, 'the occult gold and the mystic deed'. He feels his body to be possessed of great powers and possibly the last line indicates that during his prophetic sessions he felt disembodied, that his soul was outside his body looking down on himself, at the foot of the heavenly seat. This is a common trance-like experience. Alternatively Nostradamus could mean that the spirit of inspiration came down to him and is as much present beneath his feet, and therefore under his control, as it is at its heavenly source.

[1] *donrra*—Form of *donnera* = will give.
[2] *laict*—Misprint for *faict*, deed, found in other editions.
[3] *Celique*—O.F. = celestial, heavenly.

Mars & Mercure & l'argent[1] *joint ensemble,* *Vers le midi extreme siccité:* *Au fond d'Asie on dira terre tremble,* *Corinthe, Ephese lors en perplexité.*	Mars, Mercury and the Moon in conjunction towards the south there will be a great drought. An earthquake will be reported from the depths of Asia, both Corinth and Ephesus then in a troubled state.

In quatrain II. 52 Corinth and Ephesus are understood to mean England and Holland; there is no other reference to these two countries linked together throughout the quatrains. At a time of drought in Southern France (Midi) and of earthquakes in Asia, there will be trouble in these two countries. However, it is all very general in outline; perhaps Corinth and Ephesus do mean Greece and Asia Minor in this quatrain? The first line is obviously a dating but I am unable to place it.

4

Quand seront proches de defaut des lunaires, *De l'un à l'autre ne distant grandement,* *Froid, siccité, danger vers les frontieres,* *Mesme ou l'oracle a prins commencement.*	When the downfall of the lunar ones is close they will not be very distant from each other. Cold, drought, danger around the frontiers even where the oracle had its source.

1556/7

Joubert understands the first line as meaning a year when the solar and lunar eclipse come close together and arrives at the year 1556. He states that there was no rain from April to August followed by a very severe winter in 1556–7. The danger at the frontier was the Spanish invasion of Picardy. The last line must refer either to Salon where Nostradamus lived, or to St. Rémy where he was born. At both towns there were local uprisings against the Huguenots by the peasantry, the Cabans, which continued well on into the 1560s. It is just possible that *lunaires* may mean 'people of the crescent', i.e. Mohammedans, and then the quatrain should be interpreted with regard to the contemporary struggles against the Ottoman Empire.

[1] *argent*—synecdoche for the moon. An alchemistic term used because of its colour.

Pres loing defaut de deux grands
   luminaires,
Qui surviendra entre l'Avril &
   Mars:
O quel cherté nais deux grans
   debonnaires,
Par terre & mer secourrant toutes
   pars.

Then, after the eclipse of the two great stars which will occur between April & March. Oh, what a loss! but two great good influences will help on all sides by land and sea.

1556–7 continued

The quatrain almost certainly continues on from III. 4, but it is unclear as to what might have happened between March and April. Perhaps it is prevented by the influences of two good planets or stars? Nostradamus may mean that the drought and winter of 1556–7 would have been more severe but for their influence.

6

Dans le temple clos le foudre y
   entrera,
Les citadins dedans leur fort
   grevez
Chevaux, boeufs hommes, l'onde
   mur touchera,
Par faim, soif, soubs les plus
   faibles armez.

Lightning will strike inside the closed temple and will harm the citizens inside their stronghold. Horses, cattle, men, the flood will reach the walls; through hunger and thirst beneath the weakest armed.

CHATEAUNEUF 1819?

Lightning must have struck more than one church since 1555 when Nostradamus published this verse. There is however a famous occasion in 1819 at Châteauneuf when nine people were killed and eighty-two injured among those present. But this does not have any connection with a flood around this period, nor with people and cattle retiring to a fortified place on high ground to escape the waters. It is possible that the last two lines belong to another verse, and that this is one of the 'split' verses I mention in the Introduction.

Les fugitifs, feu du ciel sus les piques.
Conflict prochain des corbeaux s'esbatans,
De terre on crie aide secours celiques,
Quand pres des murs seront les combatants.

The fugitives, fire from heaven on to their weapons, the next conflict will be that of the crows. They call on earth for help and heavenly aid when the aggressors draw near the walls.

OCCUPIED FRANCE, 1940

The quatrain is usually understood as describing the Fall of France in 1940, when the French army and multitudes of refugees were driven back in confusion along the roads to Paris. The fire from the sky may mean the aerial attacks to which they were subjected, even the refugees were heavily bombed and strafed on the roads. The aggressors are the Germans about to enter Paris.

8

Les Cimbres joints avecques leurs voisins,
Depopular viendront presque l'Espaigne:
Gens amassez, Guienne & Limosins,
Seront en ligue, & leur feront compaigne.

The Cimbrians, allied with their neighbours will come to ravage almost all of Spain. People gathered in Guienne & Limousin will be allied, and join their company.

SPANISH CIVIL WAR, 1936

The Cimbrians were a North German tribe who vanished as early as 100 BC becoming intermixed with the Teutones. This verse may refer to Germany and her neighbour Italy who supported the Fascist cause in Spain and Franco's armies, during the bloody civil war of 1936–9. The last two lines may be a reference to the wide support for Hitler's policies that existed inside France at this period, or alternatively to the many Frenchmen who came to fight for the Insurgent armies in Spain, and to the fact that the Republican Spanish army after its defeat at Teruel in 1938 was actually driven into France for a time, followed by a mass exodus of Spanish refugees into France early in 1939. See IX. 16.

Bordeaux, Rouan, & la Rochelle joints,
Tiendront autour la grand mer Occeane,
Anglois, Bretons, & les Flamans conjoints,
Les chafferont jusque au pres de Rouane.

Bordeaux, Rouen & la Rochelle allied, will hold all around the open seas; The English, Bretons and Flemish allied will drive them as far as Roanne.

Although this quatrain gives detailed names and places it remains quite obscure. Bordeaux and la Rochelle are near each other, but Rouen is to the North. Roanne is on the upper Loire.

10

De sang & faim plus grand calamité,
Sept fois s'appreste à la marine plage:
Monech[1] de faim, lieu pris, captivité,
Le grand mené croc[2] en ferree caige.

With blood and famine even greater calamity; seven times it approaches the sea shore. Monaco, from hunger, captured, in captivity. The great golden one caught, in an iron cage.

HOUSE OF GRIMALDI, MONACO

Monaco was already a semi-independent state under the House of Grimaldi in Nostradamus' time. This general quatrain could refer to any disaster occurring to Monaco since then. The last line is particularly difficult to translate.

11

Les armes battre an ciel longue saison
L'arbre au milieu de la cité tombé:
Verbine,[3] rongne, glaive en face, Tison
Lors le monarque d'Hadrie succombé.

The weapons fight in the sky for a long period; the tree fell in the middle of the city. The sacred branch cut, a sword opposite Tison, then the King Hadrie falls.

[1] *Monech*—Latin, *Moneceus* = Monaco.
[2] *croc*—(*a*) Latin, *croceus* = yellow. (*b*) O.F., *croquer* = to crunch. (*c*) Prov., *croc* = a hook.
[3] *verbine*—Latin, *verbene* = sacred branch.

ASSASSINATION OF HENRI IV, 1610

Hadrie is one of Nostradamus' anagrams for Henri IV, which seems at first sight to clash with line one, which suggests a modern battle in the air. But apparently when Henri was assassinated by Ravaillac on 14th May 1610 according to Guynaud there appeared in the *Mercure Français* of 1619 the story of a ghostly army marching in the skies at the time of the killing. It may have been a similar phenomenon to the Angels of Mons. Henri is the tree chopped down in the centre of the city of Paris, and he is also the last of the direct Valois family tree, as Louis XIII was the son of his second wife Marie de' Medici. He is described as sacred because he was anointed at his coronation; he was actually stabbed with a knife in the rue Ferronnierre, not far from the corner of which runs the Rue Tison. Nostradamus gives us another obscure but graphic proper name which helps sort out the whole quatrain.

12

Par la tumeur de Heb, Po, Tag, Timbre & Rome[1]	Because of the overflow of the Ebro, Po, Tagus, Tiber and
Et par l'estang leman[2] & Arentin[3]	Rhone and by the lakes of
Les deux grands chefs & citez de Garonne,	Geneva and Arezzo the two great and chief cities of the
Prins mors noyez. Partir humain butin.	Garonne taken, dead, drowned. Human booty divided.

FLOOD

The flooding described in this quatrain is so vast that it covers Spain and Portugal (Ebro and Tagus), Italy (Po and Tiber) and France (Rhône). Lake Geneva is in Switzerland and Lake Trasimine is near Arezzo. The two chief cities of the Garonne are Bordeaux and Toulouse. There are other quatrains of this type predicting a vast general flood.

[1] *Rome*—Misprint for Rhône, although it may be the city that is intended.
[2] *leman*—Latin, *Lemannus* = Lake Geneva.
[3] *Arentin*—Latin, *Arentius* = now Arezzo.

Par fouldre en l'arche[1] or & *argent fondu,* *De deux captifs l'un l'autre* *mangera:* *De la cité le plus grand estendu,* *Quend submergee la classe[2] nagera.*	Through lightning in the box gold and silver are melted, the two captives will devour each other. The greatest one of the city stretched when the fleet travels under water.

SUBMARINE FLEET

The first two lines are probably alchemistic and Nostradamus is referring to a chemical process that would fuse the two metals together. Line three is very obscure; the fourth line certainly indicates a fleet of submarines although it is difficult to know whether the metal of the first two lines is linked with the ships as a weapon, or a separate process.

Par le rameau[3] du vaillant per- *sonnage,* *De France infime, par le pere* *infelice:* *Honneurs, richesses, travail en son* *vieil aage[4]* *Pour avoir creu le conseil d'homme* *nice.[5]*	Through the offspring of a valiant personage, of weakened France because of the unhappy father; honours, riches, labour in his old age, because he believed the counsel of an inexperienced man.

LOUIS XV AND FLEURY

Louis XV, son of the glorious Sun King, that valiant personage Louis XIV, caused the weakening of France. He came to the throne aged five, and the Duke of Orléans exerted total power during his Regency. France was in such a poor financial state that it led to her bankruptcy under John Law in 1721. The inexperienced man who brings trouble to the king, must be Fleury, tutor and priest who did not come to power until he was seventy-two in 1726. His policies helped the general unrest leading to the attempted assassination of Louis XV by Damiens in 1757.

[1] *arche*—Latin *arx* = box ark.
[2] *classe*—Latin, *classis* = fleet.
[3] *rameau*—literally branch.
[4] *aage*—O.F. spelling = age.
[5] *nice*—Romance = simple inexperienced.

Coeur, rigeur, gloire le regne changera,	The kingdom will change in heart, vigour and glory. On
De tous points contre ayant son adversaire,	all sides having its adversary opposed. Then through death
Lors France enfance par mort subjuguera,	a child will rule over France, the great Regent will then be
Un grand regent sera lors plus contraire.	very contrary.

LOUIS XV

This quatrain continues with the subject of Louis XV. Again we get a reference to the glory of the reign of Louis XIV (the great kingdom will change in glory etc.) and a reference to the Regent, Philippe, Duke of Orléans, who was the complete opposite both in public and private life, to his predecessor (*adversaire*). There has been no other male Regent of France since the publication of the Centuries. It is possible that in the words 'then through death a child will rule over France' there is a confirmation of popular opinion of the time which stated that both the Duke of Burgundy and the Duke of Bretagne, Louis XV's grandfather and father, had been poisoned by the Regent in order to obtain control over the throne.

Un prince Anglais Mars a son coeur de ciel,	An English prince, Mars has his heart in the heavens, will
Voudra poursuivre sa fortune prospere:	wish to follow his prospering fortune. In two duels, one will
Des deux duelles l'un percera le fiel,	pierce him in the gall bladder,
Hai de lui, bien aimé de sa mere.	hated by him, but well loved by his mother.

A quatrain which seems unfulfilled to date. There have been very few English princes, and even the Scottish ones do not satisfy this prediction. It seems unlikely that duels will take place in the future so this is probably a failure.

Mont Aventine brusler nuict sera veu,	Mount Aventine will be seen burning at night, the sky in Flanders will be suddenly obscured. When the King drives out his nephew their churchmen will commit scandals.
Le ciel obscur tout à un coup en Flandres:	
Quand le monarque chassera son nepveu,	
Leurs gens à Eglise commettront les esclandres.	

Mount Aventine is one of the seven hills of Rome and therefore probably stands for the city itself. The sudden obscurity of the sky in Flanders may mean an eclipse of the sun, but I am unable to link it with a king driving out his nephew plus atrocities being committed in the Church. It sounds vaguely Napoleonic but Napoleon did not actually drive out his nephew, Napoleon III, however, he was driven out from Holland as a child when his father, King Louis, abdicated. The church scandals would relate to the Cult of Reason during the Revolutionary excesses. Presumably the first line may refer to Napoleon I's troops and their successful sack of Rome?

Apres la pluie laict assez longuette	After the rather long milky rain, several places in Reims will be touched by lightning. Oh what a bloody battle is approaching them, fathers and sons' kings will not dare approach.
En plusieurs lieux de Reims le ciel touché:	
O quel conflict de sang pres d'eux s'appreste,	
Peres & fils Rois n'oseront approcher.	

The reference to a rain of milk is puzzling. It also occurs in the following quatrain, III. 19.

En Luques sant & laict viendra plouvoir,	In Lucca it will come to rain blood and milk, shortly before a change of governor. Great plague and war, famine and drought will be seen, far from where the prince and ruler dies.
Un peu devant changement de preteur:[1]	
Grand peste & guerre, faim & soif fera voir.	
Loing où mourra leur Prince recteur.[2]	

[1] *preteur*—Latin, *praetor* = governor.
[2] *recteur*—Latin = leader, governor, instructor, ruler.

Lucca was a duchy between Tuscany and Modena. It is impossible to try and identify the governor and the prince. Apart from the rain of milk we now also have a rain of blood, a favourite of Roman historians, but which can occur when red dust clouds meet rain clouds and the resultant drops fall red coloured. After the atomic bombs were dropped in 1945 the rain fell black, full of atomic dust.

20

Par les contrees du grand fleuve Bethique[1]	Through the lands of the great river Guadalquivir far from
Loing d'Ibere[2] *au royaume de Grenade:*[3]	Spain to the kingdom of Grenada; the cross spurned by
Croix repoussees par gens Mahometiques,	the Mohammedans, a man from Cordova will betray his
Un de Cordube trahira la contrade.[4]	country.

SPAIN

Grenada, the last Moorish outpost of Iberia, North Eastern Spain, was conquered in 1492. It is south of the Guadalquivir river. The Jews in this area were allowed to remain after the conquest provided they accepted Christianity. In 1610, the remainder of the Jewish colony were accused of lack of sincerity in their religious practices and turned out of Spain by Philip II, despite the fact that a contract had been drawn up by Ferdinand and Isabella of Spain with Gonsalvo Fernandez de *Cordova* who helped negotiate the treaty. Here is another proper name produced by Nostradamus.

21

Au Crustamin[5] *par mer Hadriatique,*	Near the (river) Conca by the Adriatic sea will appear an
Apparoistra un horrible poisson	horrible fish with human features and an aquatic purpose,
De face humaine & la fin[6] *aquatique,*	it will be caught without the hook.
Qui se prendra dehors de l'amacon.	

[1] *Bethique*—Latin, *Baetis* = Guadalquivir river.
[2] *Ibere*—Greek for Spaniards around river Ebro.
[3] *Grenada*—Southern Spain.
[4] *contrade*—Provençal = country.
[5] *Crustamin*—Latin, *Crustumius* flows into the Adriatic, now called river Conca.
[6] *fin*—Either means end or purpose.

Garencières (1672) says in his commentary that a mermaid-like creature, perhaps a manatee or dugong was seen near Rome in 1523 and by Rondeletius in 1531. But Edgar Leoni states in his commentary that the records of Cattolica, where the Conca flows into the Adriatic, shows no such event. Even Garencières seems to have been carried away by hearsay events in this case.

22

Six jours l'assaut devant cité donné:
Livree sera forte & aspre bataille:
Trois la rendront & à eux pardonné,
Le reste à feu & sang tranche traille.

Six days the assault is made in front of the city. It will be freed in a strong and bitter fight. Three will hand it over, and to them pardon, to the rest fire and bloody slaughter and slashing.

Too general to be specifically identified.

23

Si France passes entre mer ligustique,[1]
Tu te verras en isles & mers enclos:
Mahommet contraire, plus mer Hadriatique,
Cheveux & d'Asnes tu rongeras les os.

If, France, you cross the Ligurian sea, you will find yourself besieged among islands and seas. Mahomet against you, more so the Adriatic, you will gnaw the bones of horses and asses.

Another general prediction of disaster for contemporary France, particularly where the Ottoman Empire was concerned.

24

De l'entreprinse grande confusion,
Parte de gens, tresor innumerable:
Tu n'y dois faire encore tension[2]
France à mon dire fais que sois recordable.[3]

From the expedition great confusion, immense loss of men and treasure. You must never attempt to expand there again, France, try to remember my prediction.

This is almost certainly a continuation of the warnings contained in the preceding verse.

[1] *ligustique*—Latin, *ligusticus* = Ligurian.
[2] *tension*—Latin, *tensio* = extension.
[3] *recordable*—O.F. = memorable.

Qui au Royaume Navarrois par- viendra, *Quand de Sicile & Naples seront joints:* *Bigore & Landres par Foix loron tiendra,* *D'un qui d'Espaigne sera par trop conjoint.*	He who attains the kingdom of Navarre when Sicily and Naples are allies; he will hold Bigorre and Landes through Foix and Oloron from one who will be too strongly allied with Spain.

HENRI IV

The man who inherits Navarre is Henri IV; Sicily and Naples
were joined together sporadically for centuries but the title was
only formalized three times, first by Philip of Spain when he
was due to marry Mary Tudor in 1554, later by Joseph Buona-
parte and Joachim Murat in the 19th Century. Henri became
king of Navarre in 1562 and king of France in 1594. All the places
mentioned in line 3 are in Navarre, and Bigorre has a double
meaning as Bigorro was the rallying cry of the Huguenot armies.
The person too strongly allied with Spain from whom Henri IV
keeps Navarre, is presumably his cousin Elizabeth, daughter of
Henri II who married Philip of Spain in 1558. A rather generalized quatrain in many ways.

26

Des Rois & Princes dresseront simulacres, *Augures, cruez eslueuz aruspices:*[1] *Corne, victime dorée, & d'azur, d'acre,* *Interpretez seront les extipices.*[2]	They will raise up idols of kings and princes, augurers and hollow priests elevated. A vic- tim, its horns gilded with gold, azure, dazzling, the entrails will be interpreted.

27

Prince libinique puissant en Occi- dent, *François d'Arabe viendra tant enflammer,* *Scavans aux lettres sera conde- scendant,* *La langue Arabe en François translater.*	The Libyan prince will be powerful in the West, the French will become so ena- moured of Arabia; learned in letters he will condescend to translate the Arab Language into French.

[1] *aruspices* = auspices.
[2] *extispicus* = soothsayer, inspector of animal's entrails.

Nostradamus seems to use the term Libyan very loosely for North Africa in general, and of course the French made great use of the Barbary corsairs of Tunis and Algeria in their fight against the Turks. The literature line is puzzling—the first French Arabic dictionary came out in 1505 and one cannot think of any other great work of literary merit that was translated under these conditions.

28

De ferre faible & pauvre paren-
tele,[1]
Par bout & paix parviendra dans
l'Empire:
Long temps regner une jeune
femelle,
Qu'oncques en regne n'en survint
un pire.

One possessing few lands and of poor parentage through efforts and peace will attain to the empire. For a long time a young woman shall reign, never has a worse influence remained on the kingdom.

ELIZABETH OF ENGLAND, 1558, AND HENRI OF NAVARRE, 1594

This is regarded by most commentators as a 'split' quatrain referring to two different people. The first two lines refer to Henri of Navarre whose court was renowned for its poverty and simplicity. Elizabeth and Henri only reigned contemporaneously between the years of 1594 and 1601, but Elizabeth's confirmation of Protestantism would rate the epithet 'worse influence' from the pro-Catholic Nostradamus. Elizabeth ruled for nearly half a century which was an extremely protracted reign for that period. However, the first two lines could perhaps refer to the lowly origin of Anne Boleyn, Elizabeth's mother, and the poverty to which she was subjected to as a child.

29

Les deux nepveux en divers lieux
nourris:
Navale pugne,[2] *terre peres tombez:*
Viendront si haut esluuez enguer-
ris,[3]
Venger l'injure ennemis succombez.

Two nephews will be brought up in different places, a naval battle, fathers fallen to the ground. They will be greatly elevated by making war, to avenge their injury, the enemies overcome.

---

[1] *parentele*—O.F. = parentage.
[2] *pugne*—Latin, *pugna* = battle.
[3] *enguerroier*—O.F. = to make war.

The nephews mentioned here may be two of one of the many Popes, or alternatively the nephews of the then Constable of France, Anne de Montmorency, Coligny, Chatillon and d'Andelot; however there is nothing to show which of them were intended here.

30

Celui qu'en luitte & fer au faict bellique,	He who in the struggle with a weapon in deed of war will
Aura porté plus grand que lui le prix:	have carried off the prize from one greater than he; At night
De nuict au lict six lui feront la pique,	six will bring harm to his bed, naked without his armour he
Nud sans harnois subit sera surprins.	will suddenly be surprised.

COUNT OF MONTGOMERY, 1574

The Count of Montgomery, Captain of Henri II's Scottish Guard, who unwittingly killed his king in a friendly joust, is the hero of this quatrain. Although Henri had pardoned him, Catherine demanded Montgomery's life, determined to avenge her husband. He fled to England as a Huguenot and came back to Normandy to lead the rebelling Protestants. After various successes, he was surrounded by the Marshal de Matignon at Domfront and compelled to yield. Under the terms of surrender his life was to be spared but Catherine secretly sent six men of the royal guard to arrest him. He was taken in his bedroom on 27th May 1574 and sent to the Conciergerie at Catherine's command. Note that Nostradamus does not mention his death, only the circumstances of his capture.

31

Aux champs de Mede, d'Arabe & d'Armenie,	On the (battle)fields of Media, Arabia and Armenia, two great
Deux grans copies[1] trois fois s'assembleront:	armies will assemble three times; near the border of
Pres du rivage d'Araxes la mesgnie,[2]	Araxum the establishment of great Suliman will fall to the
Du grand Soliman en ierre tomberant.	ground.

LEPANTO, 1571

A great deal has been written about this quatrain referring it to battles which had already occurred during Nostradamus' life-

---

[1] *copies*—Latin, *copiae* = forces.

mesgnie—O.F. = household, establishment.

time, in particular to the Battle of Araxes of 1514 or to the fighting with the Turks in Armenia and Media—but not Arabia—which continued until the general peace of 1555. It appears more probable that James Laver's interpretation is the correct one. The Battle of Lepanto, fought in 1571 in which Don John of Austria crushed Selim II, the son of Soliman (part of his establishment). Lepanto was fought off Cape Papa, then known as Cape Araxum, in the Mediterranean.

32

Le grand sepulchre du peuple Aquitanique,	The huge grave for the French people will approach from the
S'approchera aupres de la Toscane:	direction of Italy. When war is
Quand Mars sera pres du coing Germanique,	near the German corner and in the lands of the Italian
Et au terroir de la gent Mantuane.	people.

SECOND WORLD WAR

A general quatrain, but one which can best be applied to the Second World War because of Nostradamus' insistence on the involvement of Italy and Germany in a war that would kill many Frenchmen. Aquitaine stands for France, as do Tuscany and Mantua for Italy.

33

En la cité où le loup entrera,	Into the city which the wolf will enter, the enemies will be
Bien pres de là les ennemis seront:	very close by; A foreign army
Copie estrange grand pays gastera,	will devastate the great
Aux murs & Alpes les amis passeront.	country, the friends will pass the walls and Alps.

A quatrain involving wars between Italy and France with a third friendly party, possibly crossing the Alps?

34

Quand le deffaut du Soleil lors sera.	Then when the eclipse of the sun will be in broad daylight
Sur le plain jour le monstre sera veu:	the monster will be seen. It will
Tout autrement on l'interpretera,	be interpreted quite differently;
Cherté n'a garde mil n'y aura pourveu.	they will not care about expense, none will have provided for it.

This quatrain is almost impossible to interpret because we are given no date for the eclipse of the sun, other than the coming of a monster which may be interpreted literally or metaphorically. The last line indicates an unexpected famine or drought for which no provision will have been made.

35

Du plus profond de l'Occident d'Europe	In the deepest part of Western Europe a child will be born of poor family, who by his speech will entice many peoples. His reputation will grow even greater in the Kingdom of the East.
De pauvres gens un jeune enfant naistra:	
Qui par sa langue seduira grande troupe,	
Son bruit au regne d'Orient plus croistra.	

HITLER OR NAPOLEON

This is an excellent example of the ambiguous quatrain, one that seems to apply equally satisfactorily to two distinct historical events, here separated in time by over a century. Perhaps this is an example of history repeating itself? It seems that throughout history certain situations have recurred which appear very similar when described only in general terms. Therefore we may take this quatrain as describing either Hitler or Napoleon. I prefer the former interpretation as Austria is better described as in deepest Europe, i.e. almost at the limits of the continent; Corsica is less apt in this context although it is near the borders of Africa; one must translate *profond* as lowest, if Corsica is preferred. Hitler came of lowly stock, as did Napoleon. Both were renowned for their personal magnetism and their famous speeches to their armies. Where Hitler is concerned we can see examples of this in the Nuremberg rallies on contemporary films. The crowd were completely in his hand. It is the last line which convinces me that the German leader is described here. The kingdom of the East, Japan, joined Hitler as an ally and his reputation there was obviously held in great esteem. As far as Napoleon was concerned the East means the Middle East, Egypt, and refers to the fact that Napoleon came to power on the Coup d'État on the 18th Brumaire 1798, on his return to France.

Enseveli non mort apopletique,	Burned, apoplectic but not
Sera trouvé avoir les mains man-	dead, he will be found to have
gees:	his hands gnawed; when the
Quand la cité damnera l'heretique,	city will condemn the heretic
Qu'avoit leurs loix se leur sembloit	who, it seemed to them, had
changees.	changed their laws.

The word apoplectic obviously indicates a person in a state of coma or stroke during which he is buried, believed dead. There are several medical cases on record of this having occurred. Presumably the hands of the wretched person are chewed by rats before he returns to consciousness, or bleed as he struggled to get out of the coffin. This event is meant to occur when a city revolts against its leader, but this is unfortunately not specific enough to identify it.

Avant l'assaut l'oraison[1] *pro-*	Before the assault a speech is
noncee,	proclaimed; Milan, deceived
Milan prins d'aigle par embusches	by the ambush is captured by
decevez:	the Eagle. The ancient walls
Muraille antique par canons enfon-	are breached by cannon; in fire
cee,	and blood few receive quarter.
Par feu & sang à mercy peu	
receus.	

NAPOLEON DURING THE ITALIAN CAMPAIGN, 1796

Here again, Napoleon I is described as the Eagle, the rapacious bird of prey. He took Milan twice, first on 15th May 1796, and then on 2nd June 1800. However, the first attack is referred to here, when Napoleon made that famous speech to his troops before the battle which echoed around Europe. 'Soldiers, you are ill-fed and half-naked. The government owes you much but can do nothing for you . . . Soldiers of Italy, are you wanting in courage?' This speech so rallied his men that the defending Austrians retired without trying to hold the city. The last two lines may refer to the following battle of Pavia whose inhabitants rose up against the French. The city walls were bombarded and breached and the city totally sacked.

[1] *oraison* = (*a*) Speech. (*b*) Prayer.

La gent Gauloise & nation estrange,	The French people and a foreign nation beyond the
Outre les monts, morts prins & profligez:	mountains will be captured, killed and overcome. In a
Au mois contraire & proche de vendage,[1]	different month, near harvest time, by the Lords they will be
Par les Seigneurs en accord redigez.[2]	put back into order.

This is accepted by Jaubert as describing the peace declared between the Pope and the Spanish in September 1557, which could be either harvest time itself, or a month later, the grape harvest. In this peace the interests of the troops of the Duke de Guise belonging to the Pope, who were mainly French and Swiss, were completely ignored.

39

Les sept en trois mois en concorde,	The seven are in agreement for
Pour subjuguer des Alpes Appenines:	three months to subjugate the Apennines. But the storm and
Mais la tempeste & Ligure couarde,	the cowardly Ligurian destroy them in sudden ruin.
Les profligent en subites ruines.	

This quatrain seems to refer to one of the leagues of 16th-Century Italy, probably the Holy League of 1576, and it implies that their agreement is upset by Genoa (Liguria).

40

Le grand theatre se viendra se redresser,	The great theatre will be raised up again, the dice
Les des jettez & les rets ja tendus:	thrown and the nets already cast. The great one who tolls
Trop le premier en glaz viendra lasser,	the death knell will become too tired, destroyed by bows split
Par ares prostrais[3] *de long temps ja fendus.*	a long time ago.

The second line referring to the dice and the nets is reminiscent of Ancient Rome but the quatrain remains completely obscure.

---

[1] *vendage* = either harvest time, or the time of the vintage.
[2] Alternative translation. Drafted in agreement?
[3] *prostrais*—Latin, *prostratus* = destroyed, ruined.

Bossu sera esleu par le conseil,	The hunchback will be elected
Plus hideux monstre en terre	by the counsel, a more hideous
n'apperceu,	monster on earth was never
Le coup[1] voulant[2] crevera l'oeil,	seen. The deliberate shot will
Le traitre au Roi pour fidelle reçu.	pierce his eye, the traitor whom
	the king received as loyal.

DEATH OF LOUIS DE CONDÉ. 13th MARCH, 1569

This quatrain is one of Nostradamus' more notable successes and had been recognized by many commentators. Prince Louis de Condé was a hunchback and was proclaimed chief of the Huguenot Assembly in 1560. He was reconciled with the king several times (and made a public confession of his loyalty to Charles IX in 1560 and 1562) but continued to plot against him. He was eventually taken at the battle of Jarnac, 13th March 1569, and was deliberately shot by Montesquiou in the head, although a prisoner.

L'enfant naistra à deux dents en la gorge,	The child will be born with two teeth in his mouth; stones
Pierres en Tuscie par pluie tomberont:	will fall like rain in Tuscany. A few years later there will be
Peu d'ans apres ne sera bled ni orge,	neither wheat nor barley, to satisfy those who will weaken
Pour saouler ceux qui de faim failliront.	from hunger.

FAMINE

There is also a reference to famine and a person born with two teeth already formed in II. 7. Possibly it could refer to Louis XIV who reputedly was born with some of his teeth fully grown, as there were local famines during his reign?

Gens d'alentour de Tarn Loth, & Garonne,	People from around the Tarn, Lot and Garonne, beware of
Gardez les monts Apennines passer:	crossing the Apennine mountains. Your tomb is near Rome
Vostre tombeau pres de Rome & d'Anconne,	and Ancona; the man with the dark, curly hair will set
Le noir poil crespe fera trophee dresser.	up a trophy.

[1] coup = (a) Blow. (b) Shot.
[2] voulant = deliberate. Variant, volant = flying.

There are two other references to the elusive *noir poil crespu* in I. 74, and II. 79, if one disregards the Aenobarbe quatrains. The Lot and Tarn are both tributaries of the Garonne, and Ancona is situated on the eastern coast of central Italy. In the two earlier quatrains the blackbeard applied very aptly to the Turks but they had no hold on central Italy which proved disastrous to the French.

44

Quand l'animal à l'homme domes-tique,	When the animal tamed by man begins to speak after
Apres grands peines & sauts viendra parler,	great efforts and difficulty, the lightning so harmful to the rod
De fouldre à vierge¹ sera si malefique,	will be taken from the earth and suspended in the air.
De terre prinse & suspendue en l'air.	

WIRELESS COMMUNICATION AND ELECTRICITY

It is possible that Nostradamus is trying to describe wireless communication in this quatrain. He often used the word 'animal' to describe machines which have some of the qualities of life, i.e. that move or make a noise. Perhaps the tamed animal here is the discovery of the sound waves and the wireless as a form of communication. The lightning that is hostile to the rod, implies that the rod is either a radio mast sending out electric charges, or that it is being threatened by some electrical force, and the mast contains this force in the air. Some forms of electrical charges during storms go from the earth to the sky, although it is normally the other way round. One could alternatively interpret the last two lines as implying that the rod is a lightning conductor. Franklin discovered electricity by means of iron conducting rods in 1752, nearly two hundred years later.

45

Les cinq estranges entrez dedans le temple	The five foreigners having entered the temple; their blood
Leur sang viendra la terre pro-phaner:	will desecrate the land. The example made of the Toulous-
Aux Tholousains sera bien dur example,	ians will be very hard, made by the man who comes to wipe
D'un qui viendra les lois exter-miner.	out their laws.

¹ *vierge*—O.F. spelling; *verge* = rod or wand.

In this quatrain the five strangers are understood to be the five great powers who allied against Napoleonic France, England, Austria, Russia, Spain and Prussia. France is the land desecrated by their invasion. The battle of Toulouse fought by Wellington was very brutal and there were great casualties. The man who wipes out the laws is again the Allied Powers because they bring with them the end of Napoleon's reign.

46

Le ciel (de Plancus la cité) nous presage,	The heavens foretell, concerning the city of Lyons by means
Par clers insignes & par estoilles fixes:	of clear skies and fixed stars, that suddenly the time of
Que de son change subit s'aproche l'aage,	change approaches, neither for its good nor evil fortune.
Ne pour son bien ne pour ses malefices.	

Plancus is Lyons, so called after its foundation by Lucius Munatius Plancus in 43 BC. The quatrain is very general and similar to II. 83 in its prediction of a gloomy future.

47

Le vieux monarque dechassé de son regne	The old king chased out of his realm will go to seek help from
Aux Orients son secours ira querre:	the people of the East: For fear
Pour peur des croix ployera son enseigne,	of the crosses he will fold his banner; he will travel to
En Mitylene ira par port & par terre.	Mitylene by land and sea.

A specific quatrain which fits no event to date. An old king chased from his kingdom will seek aid from the East. He will fold his banner for fear of the cross and take refuge in Greece or on the island of Lesbos. Could the crosses possibly refer to the swastika rather than the Christian cross? It is a possibility.

Sept cens captifs estachez rude-
*   ment,*
Pour la moitié meurtrir, donné le
*   sort:*
Le proche espoir viendra si prompte-
*   ment,*
Mais non si tost qu'une quinziesme
*   mort.*

Seven hundred captives roughly bound, the lots are drawn for half to be murdered; sudden hope will come so quickly, but not fast enough for about fifteen dead.

No definite information has come to light about this very general quatrain, despite the specific numbers of prisoners and dead involved.

Regne Gaulois tu seras bien changé,
En lieu estrange est translaté
*   l'empire:*
En autres moeurs & lois seras
*   rangé,*
Roan, & Chartres te feront bien
*   du pire.*

Kingdom of France you will be greatly changed, the Empire expands to foreign places. You will be set up with other laws and customs; Rouen and Chartres will do their worst towards you.

FRANCE AS AN EMPIRE AND ITS FUTURE

This is important because Nostradamus here calls France an Empire rather than a kingdom and clearly sees a change in the future from one form of ruler to another. Rouen is in Normandy, Chartres in the Orléanais and it is implied that possible future trouble for France will come from these places. The last part of this prophecy may not yet be completed.

La republique de la grande cité,
A grand rigeur ne voudra consentir:
Roi sortir hors par trompette cité.
L'eschelle ay mur, la cité repentir.

The people's government of the great city will not consent to severe repression. The king, summoned by trumpets to leave the city, the ladder at the wall, the city will repent.

JOURNÉE DES BARRICADES. 12th MAY 1588

The Leaguers in France took Paris into their power after the Day of the Barricades when the people drove out the King, Henri III, and his followers. Henri retaliated by joining up with Henri of

Navarre at St. Cloud and resolved to besiege Paris. Before he could do this he was assassinated by Jacques Clément.

51

Paris conjure un grand meurtre commettre,	Paris conspires to commit a great murder. Blois will ensure
Blois le fera sortir en plain effect:	that it is fully carried out. The
Ceux d'Orleans voudront leur chef remettre,	people of Orléans will want to replace their leader; Angers,
Angiers, Troye, Langres leur feront un meffait.	Troyes and Langres will do them a disservice.

THE MURDERS OF THE DUKE DE GUISE AND HIS BROTHER, 1588

Henri III murdered the two brothers de Guise on 23rd December 1588. He planned the assassination in Paris and it was carried out at Blois whence the Duke de Guise had fled. He was killed by the king's bodyguard outside the royal appartment and the Cardinal, his brother, was killed the next day. At the same period the town of Orléans rose up against the governor, Balzac d'Entragues, and Charles de Lorraine, a prominent Leaguer and supporter of the Guise cause, took over. The line is inaccurate; both Angers and Langres allied themselves with the League and Troyes remained neutral.

52

En la campaigne sera si longue pluie,	In Campania there will be rain for so long and such a great
Et en la Pouille si grand siccité:	drought in Apulia; the cock
Coq verra l'Aigle, l'aesle mal accompli	will see the Eagle, its wing badly finished put into diffi-
Par Lyon mise sera en extremité.	culties by the Lion.

The Cock stands for France; it was the emblem both of the Gauls and of the French Revolutionaries. The Eagle may refer either to the Hapsburg Empire or to Napoleon. If the latter version is acceptable then the Lion stands for Britain who causes Napoleon's downfall. The rain and drought are not recorded but may possibly be metaphorical references to Napoleon's conquest of Italy.

Quand le plus grand emportera le pris,	When the greatest man carries off the prize of Nuremburg,
De Nuremberg, d'Auspourg & ceux de Basle	of Ausburg and those of Basle, Frankfurt retaken by the leader
Par Agrippine[1] chef Frankfort repris:	of Cologne: they will go through Flanders as far as
Traverseront par Flamant jusqu'au Gale.	France.

The only factor the places mentioned have in common is that they are all part of the Holy Roman Empire. Did Nostradamus think that after a new Emperor was elected France would be invaded from the North through Belgium? It is just possible that this quatrain connects with Hitler through the Nuremburg rallies. At that time he became the leader of Germany and did invade France from the North.

L'un des plus grands fuira aux Espaignes	One of the great men will flee to Spain which will bleed with
Qu'en longue playe apres viendra saigner:	a great wound thereafter. Troops will pass over the high
Passant copies par les hautes montaignes,	mountains devastating everything, then he will reign in
Devastant tout & puis en paix regner.	peace.

GENERAL FRANCO AND THE CIVIL WAR IN SPAIN, 1936–9

In 1936 General Franco was exiled from Spain to the Canary Islands as military governor. He then flew (*fuira*) to Morocco and back to Spain to start the rebellion that led to the Spanish Civil War. The wound from which Spain suffered so much was the war, with its appalling casualties 611,000 men in all. The armies who crossed the Pyrenees, Spain's border, were the 50,000 Italians and 10,000 Germans who fought for Franco's Nationalist party, and the 20,000 Russian soldiers sent to support the Loyalist Republican army. It is ironic that after the Civil War Spain did, in a sense, remain in peace, in that she was neutral throughout the Second World War.

[1] *Agrippine*—Latin, *Colonia Agrippina* = Cologne.

En l'an qu'un oeil en France regnera,	In the year that France has a one-eyed king the court will
La court sera à un bien facheux trouble:	be in very great trouble. The great man from Blois will kill
Le grand de Blois son ami tuera,	his friend, the kingdom put
Le regne mis en mal & doubte double.	into difficulty and double doubt.

THE DEATH OF HENRI II AND THE REIGN OF HENRI III, 1559–89

This famous quatrain was understood by Nostradamus' contemporaries. The one-eyed king was Henri II killed in the duel of 1559 (see I. 35) being wounded in the eye by Montgomery and dying after ten days of agony. The last two lines describe his son Henri III, who assassinates the de Guise brothers at Blois and the general civil unrest which followed this action. *Doubte double* probably refers to the two factions, the Leaguers and the Royalists.

Montauban, Nismes, Avignon & Besier,	Montauban, Nîmes, Avignon and Béziers, plague, lightning
Peste tonnere & gresle à fin de Mars:[1]	and hail at the end of March. Of the bridge at Paris, the
De Paris pont, Lyon mur, Montpellier,	wall at Lyons and Montpellier, since six hundred and seven
Depuis six cens & sept vingts trois pars.[2]	score three pairs.

The dating of this verse from the last line, see footnote, is extremely difficult. All the towns in the first line are in Southern France, but there does not seem to be much connection between the bridge of Paris and the walls of Lyons.

[1] Or in the wake of war.

[2] There are several possible readings for this. As above, which is 746 i.e. 1746 or 2301 (1555 plus 746) or 'six hundred and seven twenty three pairs' which gives 1653, or 2208 if added to 1555.

Sept fois changer verrez gent Britannique	Seven times you will see the British nation change, dyed in
Taintz en sang en deux cents nonante an:	blood for two hundred and ninety years. Not at all free
Franche non point par appuy Germanique,	through German support, Aries fears for the protectorate of
Aries doubte son pole Bastarnien.	Poland.

BRITISH HISTORY 1603–1939

The great problem for this verse is to find the date from which to calculate the 290 years and the seven great changes which affect Britain. If the year 1603 is taken as the starting point, quite arbitrarily, the whole verse fits, including the last line which clearly links Poland (*Bastarnien*) with Britain in some manner connected with a war. Aries the first sign of the Zodiac rules the East. Nostradamus indicates that there will be a critical state of affairs in Poland at the same time as Britain faces a great crisis connected with Germany. It also implies that the royal family on the throne at that time will be the last British dynasty of any note.

1 1603. New Stuart Monarch, James I.
2 1649. Death of Charles I and declaration of a Republic.
3 1660. Restoration of the Stuarts in Charles II.
4 1689. Usurpment of Stuarts by William of Orange.
5 1702. Restoration of Stuarts under Queen Anne.
6 1714. Hanoverian accession to British throne under George I.
7 1939. Pronouncement of war after the German invasion of Poland.

Aupres du Rhin des Montaignes Noriques,	Near the Rhine from the Norican mountains will be
Naistra un grand de gens trop tard venu.	born a great man of the people, come too late. He will defend
Qui defendra Saurome & Pannoniques,	Poland and Hungary and they will never know what became
Qu'on ne sçaura qu'il sera devenu.	of him.

HITLER

Hitler was born in Noricum, that is Austria, and he was the son of simple parents. He came too late in Nostradamus' view because his type of Empire was outdated. The third line must be read as describing Hitler's motives, his so-called 'defensive' attacks on

Poland and Hungary to 'save' them from the Allies. The final line is interesting. Could Hitler possibly have escaped after all from the bunker at Berlin? Were the bodies found those of his mistress and himself? There has always been doubt about this question in many people's minds despite Hugh Trevor-Roper's very thorough research into the facts of Hitler's death at the end of the war.

59

Barbare empire par le tiers usurpé,	The barbarian empire is
Le plus grand part de son sang	usurped by a third, the greater
mettre à mort:	part of its people being put to
Par mort senile par lui le quart	death. The fourth man, senile,
frappé,	struck dead by his country, fears
Pour peur que le sang par le sang	lest the line of his blood be
ne soit mort.	dead.

THE FRENCH REVOLUTION. THE TIERS ÉTAT
The third is usually accepted as meaning the Tiers État of the French Revolution 1789, although one wonders why Nostradamus calls the Bourbons barbaric. There were also three Committees of Public Safety during the Reign of Terror, those of Danton, Robespierre and the Directoire. The fourth man is Napoleon who took over from the Directoire in 1799 and died a senile death, from old age, on Saint Helena. Napoleon always feared that his line would not be continued and made himself an hereditary monarch.

60

Par toute Asie grande proscription,	Throughout Asia there will be
Mesme en Mysie, Lysie, &	great proscription, also in
Pamphylie:	Mysia, Lycia and Pamphilia.
Sang versera par absolution,	Blood will flow because of the
D'un jeune noir[1] rempli de felonnie.	absolution of a young dark
	man, filled with evil doing.

The countries mentioned in line 2 are all to be found in Asia Minor which implies that Asia in line 1 is the East as we understand the word. The great proscription might describe China's military system very aptly—whereby everyone has to be in the army for a certain period of their lives—but the Eastern influence has not yet travelled to Asia Minor, that is Modern Turkey, Iran, Iraq, etc. It is probable that this quatrain has not yet been completed

---

[1] *noir* = (*a*) A young dark-haired man or a Negro. (*b*) The usual Nostradamus anagram for roi, king.

and the bloodshed and villainy of the last two lines have yet to
come.

61

La grand band & secte crucigere, *Se dressera en Mesopotamie:* *Du proche fleuve compagnie legiere,* *Que telle loi tiendra pour ennemie.*	The great following of the sect of the cross will arise in Meso- potamia. Light company of the nearby river who will regard such a law as inimical.

The solution to this quatrain obviously lies in the identification of
the *secte crucigere*. Did Nostradamus mean the Crusades or even the
swastika, the *croix gammée*, as it was known in France. Mesopotamia
is Iraq and the two rivers are the Tigris and the Euphrates. However some commentators insist that Mesopotamia stands for Paris
between the rivers Seine et Marne and that this quatrain thus
refers to the German occupation of France in 1940.

62

Proche del duero par mer Cyrrene
  close,
Viendra percer les grands monts
  Pyrenées:
La main plus courte & sa percee[1]
  gloze,[2]
A Carcassonne conduira ses menées.
	Near the Douro closed by the
	Cyrenian sea he will come to
	cross the great mountains of
	the Pyrenees. The shortest
	hand and his opening noted he
	will take his followers to
	Carcassonne.

The river Douro rises in the mountains around Burgos in Spain
and the Cyrenian sea is the Mediterranean. Apparently some leader
will come across Spain into France. The third line is practically
untranslatable, see footnote, and the fourth could carry the second
meaning 'He will hatch his plots at Carcassonne'. Perhaps by the
shortest hand means that this leader crossed the Carcassonne by
the shortest route?

63

Romain pouvoir sera du tout abas, *Son grand voisin imiter les vestiges:* *Occultes haines civiles & debats,* *Retarderont aux bouffons leurs* *folies.*	Roman power will be quite put down following the footsteps of its great neighbour. Secret hatreds and civil disputes will delay the crassness of these buffoons.

[1] *percee*—O.F., *perce* = stake pole, or opening.
[2] *gloze*—O. Provençal, *gloza* = commentary, notes.

This describes accurately the state of Italy under Mussolini and its relations with its great neighbour Hitlerian Germany after 1937, in whose footsteps Mussolini tried to follow. The name Mussolini literally means muslin maker—a craft regarded as the lowest of the low, and yet this man is dictator of Italy. The word 'buffoons' describes these two dictators horribly well with their histrionics and projects of Aryan purity and world domination. Hitler was certainly unbalanced and it is probable that Mussolini was also in his later years.

64

Le chef de Perse remplira grande Olchade,[1] *Classe Frireme contre gent Mahometique: De Parthe, & Mede, & piller les Cyclades, Repos long temps aux grand port Ionique.*	The Persian leader will fill up great Spain. A fleet of triremes against the Mohammedans from Parthia and Media, he will pillage the Cyclades: then a long wait in the great Ionian harbour.

The trireme fleet is one with three banks of oars, probably Italian or Venetian. Parthia and Media are both parts of Persia, presumably they are the country of the invading leader who sacks the Greek islands of the Cyclades around Delos in the Aegean. The great harbour in which he shelters in the Ionian sea could be one of many—the sea lies between Greece and Sicily. It is unclear as to whether the trireme fleet is destroyed by the Persian before he retires to port or not.

65

Quand le sepulcre du grand Romain trouvé, Le jour apres sera esleu Pontife: Du Senat gueres il ne sera prouvé, Empoisonné son sang au sacré scyphe.	When the tomb of the great Roman is found a pope will be elected the next day; he will not be approved of by the Senate, his blood poisonous in the sacred chalice.

THE TOMB OF ST. PETER AND A NEW POPE

This indicates that after the finding of a tomb, possibly that of St. Peter, a Pope will be elected who will turn out to be highly unsuitable, disliked by the Synod and possibly very wicked if his

---

[1] *Ochlades*—Latin = race living in Southern Spain near Cartagena.

lood was poison to the sacred chalice. Alternatively this line may
ndicate that this Pope will be poisoned. It also indicates that the
omb which was found recently and suggested to be that of St.
'eter may not be so after all.

66

Le grand Baillif d'Orleans mis à mort,	The great Bailiff of Orleans is condemned to death by one vindictive for blood. He will not die a deserved death, nor one by jurors; they will keep him captive inefficiently (bound) by his hands and feet.
Sera par un de sang vindicatif.	
De mort merite ne mourra, ne par sort,	
Des pieds & mains mal le faisoit captif.	

JERÔME GRESLOT, 1562–9

The Bailiff of Orleans was an hereditary post for the Greslot
family since 1530, so Nostradamus clearly intended it for someone
of the family. A certain Jerôme Greslot was put to death having
opened the gates of the town in April 1562, but he was not condemned to death for this until 1569. Presumably this is what
Nostradamus means by his being inefficiently guarded, a gap of
seven years between action and execution?

67

Une nouvelle secte de Philosophes,	A new set of philosophers despising death, gold, honours and riches will not be limited by the mountains of Germany, in their following will be crowds and support.
Mesprisant mort, or, honneurs & richesses:	
Des monts Germains ne seront limitrophes,	
A les ensuivre auront appuy & presses.	

PROTESTANT SECTS

Nostradamus is probably referring to the sects of the Anabaptists
which had been almost wiped out around 1536, and it seems as
though he is expecting a revival of these or some similar Protestant
sects from the direction of Germany.

Peuple sans chef d'Espaigne &
d'Italie,
Morts, profligez[1] dedans le Cher-
ronesse:[2]
Leur dict[3] trahi par legiere folie,
Le sang nager par tout à la
traverse.

Leaderless people from Spain
and Italy dead and overcome
in the Peninsula. Their dictator betrayed by stupid folly
blood will flow all about in the
area.

SPAIN AND ITALY IN THE 20th CENTURY

This is an interesting quatrain in that Nostradamus gives us the
two countries of Spain and Italy without their kings but with
dictators, so this verse definitely describes the 20th Century. The
dictator who is betrayed is Mussolini and a fascinating possibility
is that by *à la traverse*, he was referring to Mussolini's being
hanged. *La traverse* also means a cross roads, the usual place for a
gibbet and is a typical Nostradamus play on words.

Grand excercite conduict par jouven-
ceau,
Se viendra rendre aux mains des
ennemis:
Mais la vieillard nay au demi-
porceau,
Fera Chalon & Mascon estre amis.

The great army led by a young
man, will come to give itself
up into the enemy's hands. But
the old man born to the half
pig will make Châlon and
Mâcon into friends.

The half pig turns up also in I. 64 where Nostradamus describes
a man wearing an oxygen mask. Probably here it is derived from
the false etymology of Milan which according to legend derived
its name from the finding of an animal half sheep, half pig at its
foundation. Both Mâcon and Châlon are in Burgundy.

[1] *profliges*—Latin, *profligatus* = overcame.
[2] *Cherronesse*—From the Greek word meaning peninsula.
[3] *dict*—Alternative, *duict* = leader, but meaning remains unaltered.

La grande Bretagne comprinse
l'Angleterre,
Viendra par eaux si haut à
inonder
La ligue neufue d'Ausonne[1] fera
guerre,
Que contre eux ils se viendront
bander.

Great Britain, including
England will be covered by
very deep floods. The new
league in Ausonne will make
war so that they will ally
against them.

GREAT BRITAIN 1604-7

A very interesting quatrain. England did not become Great
Britain until the unification of the English and Scottish thrones
under James I. He assumed the title of King of Great Britain on
24th October 1604. In January 1607 there were great floods
recorded around Bristol and in Somerset, the country being
covered for an area of approximately ten leagues, or thirty miles.
The last two lines then refer to the renewal of the Holy League in
1606, Ausonia standing for Italy.

Ceux dans les isles de longtemps
assiegez,
Prendront vigeur force contre
ennemis:
Ceux par dehors mors de faim
profligez,
En plus grand faim que jamais
seront mis.

Those besieged in the islands
for a long time will take
strong measures against their
enemies. Those outside, overcome, will die of hunger, by
such starvation as has never
occurred before.

BLOCKADE OF BRITAIN 1939-45. CONCENTRATION CAMPS

The blockading of Britain by the German navy during the Second
World War is vividly portrayed in this verse, as are the strong
countermeasures taken by her, described in line 2, which opened
the Atlantic routes for supplies. Britain apparently never had more
than six weeks of food supplies in the country at one time, and all
that was strictly rationed. The two final lines indicate that while
the British islanders did not starve there was great famine abroad.
This refers to Europe and to the appalling concentration and
labour camps of the Nazi régime where starvation was a matter of

[1] *Ausonne* = Ausonia. Southern Italy, especially Naples but also used
poetically for the whole country.

policy and a convenient means of killing off those millions who did not go to the gas chambers.

72

Le bon vieillard tout vif enseveli,	The good old man is buried while still alive, near a great river through false suspicion. The newcomer is old, ennobled by wealth, having taken all the ransom gold on the way.
Pres du grand fleuve par fausse souspeçon:	
Le nouveau vieux de richesse ennobli,	
Prins a chemin tout l'or de la rançon.	

The theme of someone being buried alive is also found in III. 36. but both quatrains are very obscure.

73

Quand dans la regne parviendra la boiteux,	When the lame man comes into the kingdom, a bastard, close to him will compete with him. Both he and the kingdom will be greatly trimmed before he recovers, so that his action will be too late.
Competiteur aura proche bastard:	
Lui & le regne viendront si fort roigneux,	
Qu'ains qu'il guerisse son faict sera bien tard.	

THE DUKE OF BORDEAUX, 1820–71

This is an excellent quatrain full of interesting facts. The Duke of Bordeaux was the heir of Charles X of France. He became lame as the result of a riding accident in 1841. His close competitor was the Count Paris, who was the illegal pretender to the throne. The trimming away of the kingdom refers to the Franco-Prussian war, so that by the time the Duke came to an agreement with the French they had declared the Third Republic and would not accept his terms, and he died in exile, as did the Count of Paris.

74

Naples, Florence, Favence & Imole,	Naples, Florence, Faenza and Imola will be on terms of such disagreement that to comply with the wretches of Nola they complain that they had mocked its chief.
Seront en termes de telle fascherie:	
Que pour complaire aux malheureux de Nolle	
Plainct d'avoir faict à son chef moquerie.	

Nothing can be made of this quatrain. Faenza and Imola were in the Papal States; Florence, the capital of Tuscany, and Naples of the Two Sicilies. Nola is some eighteen miles East of Naples.

75

Pau, Verone, Vicence, Sarragousse,
De glaives loings terroirs de sang
humides.
Peste si grance viendra à la grand
gousse,[1]
Proche secours, & bien loing les
remedes.

Pau, Verona, Vicenza, Saragossa, swords dripping with blood from distant lands. A very great plague will come with the great shell, relief near, but the remedies far away.

CHEMICAL WARFARE IN EUROPE

The cities here come from France, Italy and Spain, and Nostradamus implies that they will be invaded, possibly by the man from the East of the other quatrains. The third line is uncomfortably close to chemical warfare and perhaps the near relief is death, since help is far away.

76

En Germanie naistront diverses
sectes,
S'approchant fort de l'heureux
paganisme,
Le coeur captif & petites receptes,
Feront retour à payer le vrai disme.

Various sects will arise in Germany which will come near to a happy paganism. The heart captive, the returns small, they will return to pay the true tithe.

PROTESTANT SECTS, 16th CENTURY

This is another of Nostradamus's obsessions, the many Lutheran, Anabaptist and Calvinist sects that were springing up in Northern Europe throughout the 16th Century. He seems to imply in the last line that they will return to the true faith, Catholicism, which hardly seems likely at the present.

77

Le tiers climat sous Aries comprins,
L'an mil sept cens vingt & sept en
Octobre:
Le Roy de Perse par ceux d'Egypte
prins:
Conflit, mort, perte: à la croix
grand approbre.

The third climate included under Aries, in the year 1727 in October the king of Persia, captured by those of Egypt: battle, death, loss: great shame to the cross.

[1] gousse = shell, scab, husk.

Here is a quatrain with not only the year, but the actual month and place! Nostradamus must have overlooked it when he went through the quatrains to make them more difficult to interpret. It is quite correct. In October 1727 a peace was concluded between the Turks and the Persians. Egypt belonged to the Ottoman Empire and stands for the Turks. The loss to Christianity is explained by the fact that the Shah Ashraf, in return for the recognition of his dynasty, gave the lands of Emvan, Tauris and Hamadan to the Turks and recognized the Sultan as legitimate successor to the Caliph. The Ottoman power continued in strength until this century, and no more Crusades were ever raised by the Christians.

78

Le chef d'Escosse avec six d'Alemaigne,	The leader from Scotland with six Germans will be captured by Eastern seamen. They will pass Gibraltar and Spain presented in Persia to the new dreadful king.
Par gens de mer Orienteaux captif:	
Traverseront le Calpre & Espaigne,	
Present en Perse au nouveau Roy craintif.	

79

L'ordre fatal sempiternal par chaisne,	The fatal and eternal order of the cycle will turn in due order. The chains of Marseilles will be broken, the city taken and the enemy at the same time.
Viendra tourner par ordre consequent:	
Du port Phocen[1] sera rompu la chaisne,	
La cite prinse, l'ennemi quant & quant.	

The first two lines are astrological and extremely obscure making it impossible to date the downfall of Marseilles.

80

Du regne Anglois l'indigne dechassé,	The unworthy man is chased out of the English kingdom. The counsellor through anger will be burnt. His followers will stoop to such depths that the pretender will almost be received.
Le conseiller par ire mis à feu:	
Ses adhera iront si bas tracer,	
Que le batard sera demi receux.	

[1] *Phocen* = Marseilles, after the Phocenses who founded the city.

CHARLES I, 1600–49

Charles lost his kingdom mainly due to his own behaviour and irresponsibility towards Parliament. Of his counsellors Stafford was beheaded and Archbishop Laud burnt for treachery, the former in 1641, and the latter in 1645. His followers who stooped so low were the Scots who sold the king back to Parliament in 1646. The Pretender, or bastard, who is almost received in the kingdom is Oliver Cromwell, a man who has no true right to rule and who becomes Lord Protector, not king.

81

Le grand crier sans honte audacieux,	The great speechmaker, shameless and bold will be elected governor of the army. The boldness of his contention, the broken bridge, the city faint from fear.
Sera esleu gouverneur de l'armee:	
La hardiesse de son contentieux,	
Le pont rompu cité de peur pasmee.	

PONTEFRACT AND CROMWELL

The key to this quatrain lies in the broken bridge. If one can accept this as Pontefract from the Latin pons, a bridge, fractus, broken, then we have a description of this town which held out for Charles I and suffered two severe sieges during the Civil War. The speechmaker who takes over the army is Cromwell, for whom Nostradamus has little liking, as is apparent in other quatrains.

82

Friens, Antibor, villes autour de Nice,	Frejus, Antibes, the towns around Nice will be greatly devastated by land and sea; the locusts, by land and sea, the wind being favourable, captured, dead, trussed up, plundered without law of war.
Seront vastees fort par mer & par terre:	
Les saturelles terre & mer vent propice,	
Prins, morts, troussez, pillés, sans loi de guerre.	

INVASION OF FRANCE?

An invasion of the coast of Southern France by air is probably implied by this quatrain. As we have seen, Nostradamus describes all his machines as types of animals, and locusts, if read literally, could not cause the death and destruction of the final line.

Les longs cheveux de la Gaule Celtique,	The long-haired people of Celtic Gaul, joined by foreign
Accompaignez d'estranges nations:	nations will capture the people
Mettront captif la gent Aquitanique,	of Aquitaine in order that they
Pour succomber à Internitions.[1]	should succumb to their plans.

LOUIS XVIII 1755–1824

Louis XVIII of France was known contemporarily as *le Chevelu*— the long-haired one, his long hair being a great contrast to the short cropped hair of the Revolutionaries and Bonapartists. The foreign nations who help him are the Allied Armies who defeat Napoleon. The last two lines are unclear. In IX. 6 Aquitaine means England or an English colony.

La grand cité sera bien desolee,	The great city will soon be
Des habitans un seul n'y demoura:	quite deserted, not a single one
Mur, sexe, temple & vierge violee,	of the inhabitants will remain. Wall, sex, temple and virgin
Par fer, feu, peste, canon peuple mourra.	violated, people will die from the sword, fire, plague and cannon shot.

SACK OF ROME UNDER PIUS VI, 1775–1799

If the word is *sexe* an abbreviation of Sextus, which it could well be, this verse then applies to the Sack of Rome by Napoleonic troops. Many commentators think the city is Paris.

La cité prinse par tromperie & fraude,	The city is taken by trickery and deceit, captured by means
Par le moyen d'un beau jeune attrappé:	of a handsome young man. An assault is made by Raubine
Assaut donne Raubine pres de LAUDE,	near LAUDE, he and all of them dead, for having deceived
Lui & tous morts pour avoir bien trompé.	so well.

The interpretation of this stanza is connected with the river Robine, a tributary of the Aude, and presumably the city which is taken lies upon either of these.

---

[1] *Internitions*—Read intentions in all other texts.

Un chef d'Ausonne aux Espaignes ira,	A leader from Italy will go to Spain by sea and he will make a stop at Marseilles. He will linger a long time before dying, after his death great wonders will be seen.
Par mer fera arrest dedans Marseille:	
Avant sa mort un long temps languira	
Apres sa mort on verra grand merveille.	

This implies that a ruler of any Southern Italian state, or of the two Sicilies in particular, because that was the home of the Ausones in ancient times, will die a lingering death at Marseilles. This does not seem to have occurred.

Classe Gauloise n'approches de Corsegne,	French fleet, do not approach Corsica; even less Sardinia, you will regret it. You will all die, the help from the cape in vain, captive, swimming in blood you will not believe me.
Moins de Sardaigne tu t'en repentiras:	
Trestout mourrez frustrez de l'aide grogne,	
Sang nagera, captif ne me croiras.	

SINKING OF PART OF FRENCH FLEET, 1655

In 1655 part of the French fleet, under the command of the Chevalier de la Ferrière, was sunk in the Gulf of Lyons while sailing past the islands of Sardinia and Corsica. Many were lost because they were unable to reach the nearby Cap de Porceau. This is an interesting double meaning. Grogne can mean a cape, or the snout of a pig. Nostradamus uses it to describe two things with extreme economy of words. Le Captif was the name of the pilot, Jean de Rian, who had been earlier captured and taken as a galley slave by the Algerian corsairs.

De Barcellonne par mer si grand armee,	From Barcelona' such a great army by sea, all Marseilles will tremble with terror. The islands seized, help cut off by sea, your traitor will swim on land.
Tout Marseille de frayeur tremblera:	
Isles saisies de mer aide fermee,	
Ton traditeur en terre nagera.	

On this day in 1596, Philip II of Spain sent a fleet to Marseilles under the command of Charles Doria to divide French interests between the Leaguers and the king. It occupied the islands of Château d'If and Ratonneau and thus prevented help coming into Marseilles by sea. A certain Charles de Casau tried to betray Marseilles to the Spanish but was found out and assassinated by Pierre Libertat; he was killed by the sword and literally drowned in his own blood.

89

En ce temps là sera frustree Cypres,	At that time Cyprus will be deprived of its help from those
De son secours de ceux de mer Egee:	of the Aegean sea. Old men slaughtered, but by cannons
Vieux trucidez, mais par mesles[1] & lyphres[2]	and supplications, the king is won over, the queen more
Seduict leur Roy, Royne plus out-ragee.	outraged.

ENOSIS AND CYPRUS

This quatrain may describe Cyprus during the Troubles of the 1950s, when union with Greece was the great political problem. The quatrain clearly shows that Cyprus will not attain complete union with Greece, that the King (Constantine?) will be misled, and the Queen, probably Frederika, greatly upset by their enforced exile.

90

Le grand Satyre & Tigre d'Hyr-canie,	The great Satyr and Tiger of Hyrcania; gift presented to the
Don presenté à ceux de l'Occean:	people of the Ocean: the leader
Un chef de classe istra de Carmanie,	of a fleet will come forth from
Qui prendra terre au Tyrren Phocean.	Carmania and land at the Phocea of Tyre.

The key to this quatrain is in the last line. Phocea is Marseilles but it is not situated on the Tyrrhenian sea so Nostradamus is probably intending another seaport associated with the early Phoenician colonists of Tyre. Carmania and Hyrcania were both provinces of Persia but the expedition would have to cross by land as well

---

[1] *mesles*—Probably variant O.F., *masle* = cannon ball.
[2] *lyphres*—Possibly Greek, *lypros* = a supplication.

as sea, as there was no Suez canal at this period. An uncertain quatrain.

91

L'arbre qu'estoit par long temps mort seché, *Dans une nuict viendra à reverdir:* *Cron[1] Roy malade, Prince pied estaché,[2]* *Criant d'ennemis fera voile bondir.*	The tree which had been dead and withered for a long time will flourish again in one night. The Cronian king will be sickly. The prince with a damaged foot, fear of his enemies will make him hoist sail.

BIRTH OF THE DUKE DE BORDEAUX 1820, HIS EXILE & DEATH, 1838

The tree which sprouts again miraculously overnight is the line of the Bourbons, when the Duchesse de Berry gave birth to a son, the Duke de Bordeaux on 29th September 1820 seven months after her husband was assassinated. He was a sickly child and injured his foot in a fall from his horse in Austria which resulted in a permanent limp. He went into exile in 1830 with his grandfather Charles X and despite long negotiations with Republican France, did not succeed in regaining the throne.

92

Le monde proche du dernier periode, *Saturne encor tard sera de retour:* *Translat empire devers nation Brodde,* *L'oeil arraché à Narbon par Autour.*	The world is near its final period, Saturn will again be late on his return. The empire will shift towards the Brodde nation; An eye at Narbonne plucked out by a goshawk.

This is an astrological quatrain dealing probably with the future of the African nations, as *Brodde* in old French means either black or dark brown. It also contains the meaning of decadent. Nostradamus speaks several times of an '*Empire translaté*' when referring to Napoleon. Here he implies that more power will be given to African nations as is happening at the present, before the final cycle of the world occurs. It might also mean that French power

[1] *Cron*—From the Latin, *Cronus* = Saturn, an old man, in this case his grandfather.

[2] *estaché*—O.F. = stump, club foot.

shifts towards Africa—which it did until France left Algeria. In which case we are now approaching this final period.

93

Dans Avignon tout le Chef de l'empire
Fera arrest pour Paris desolé:
Tricast[1] tiendra l'Annibalique ire,
Lyon par change sera mel consolé.

In Avignon, the leader of all the Empire will make a stop because Paris is deserted. Tricast will contain the African anger, the Lion will be poorly consoled by the change.

The quatrain hints at a great enemy of France, possibly also of Rome, in that Avignon belonged to the Vatican until 1791. The British lion will dislike this enemy in Africa—there is a temptation to link this quatrain with the British campaigns in Africa during the Second World War.

94

De cinq cent ans plus compte l'on tiendra
Celui qu'estoit l'adornement de son temps:
Puis à un coup grand clarté donra,
Que par ce siecle les rendra tres contens.

For five hundred years more they will take notice of him who was the ornament of his age. Then suddenly a great revelation will be made which will make people of that (same) century well pleased.

This has been used by almost every interpreter of Nostradamus' quatrains to date as a guarantee of the inspired nature of their works. No further comment is needed. The commentator has not yet appeared.

95

La loy Moricque on verra deffaillir,
Apres un autre beaucoup plus seductive:
Boristhenes[2] premier viendra faillir,
Par dons & langue une plus attractive.

The Moorish law will be seen to fail, followed by another that is more pleasing. The Dnieper will be the first to give way through gifts and tongues to another more appealing.

[1] *Tricast—Tricasses* = city of Troyes.
[2] *Boristhenes*—Latin = the river Dnieper in the U.S.S.R.

The prophecy states that a creed, founded near the river Dnieper
in the U.S.S.R. will have a widespread success before it declines.
In Nostradamus' own day this was one of the most backward
areas of Europe. It is probable that he is forecasting the rise
of Communism but interesting in that he also predicts its eventual
failure.

96

Chef de Fosan aura gorge coupee,	The leader from Fossano will
Par le ducteur du limier &	have his throat cut by the man
laurier:	who exercised the bloodhounds
La faict patre par ceux de mont	and greyhounds. The deed will
Tarpee,	be committed by those of the
Saturne en Leo 13 de Fevrier.	Tarpean rock, when Saturn
	is in Leo on 13th February.

13th FEBRUARY 1820

To trace the leader from Fossano is difficult. If he is the Duke de
Berry then he is called this because his maternal grandfather was
King of Fossano in Sardinia. The rest of the quatrain fits very
accurately. The assassin was Louvel, who worked in the royal
stables. He was a Republican, hence the reference to the Tarpean
rock from which Republican Rome threw her criminals. Saturn
rules Aquarius, so when it is in the opposite sign of Leo it should
be understood as maleficent. The Duke de Berry was stabbed on
13th Febrary 1820, as Nostradamus stated, when leaving the
Opéra. See I. 84.

97

Nouvelle loi terre neufve occuper,	A new law will occupy a new
Vers la Syrie, Judee & Palestine:	land around Syria, Judea and
Le grand empire barbare corruer,	Palestine. The great barbarian
Avant que Phoebus son siecle	Empire will crumble before
determine.	the century of the sun is
	finished.

THE CREATION OF ISRAEL AND FINAL DEFEAT
OF U.A.R. 20th CENTURY

The first two lines speak for themselves and describe the creation
of the state of Israel. By barbarian Nostradamus means Arabic or

non-Christian and implies here that Israel will eventually triumph over her Arab enemies before the end of the 20th Century—the century of the sun.

98

Deux royals freres si fort guer-roierent,	Two royal brothers will fight so fiercely and the feud be-
Qu'entre eux sera la guerre si mortelle:	tween them will be so deadly that both will live in fortified
Qu'un chacun places fortes occu-peront,	places. Their great quarrel will concern their lives and the
De regne & vie sera leur grand querelle.	kingdom.

This is a fairly straightforward prophecy which suits the king of France, Henri III, and the Duc d'Alençon most closely (1574–84), but also fits Louis XIII and his brother the Duke of Orléans around the period 1632. A very good example of history, and prophecy, repeating themselves!

99

Aux champs herbeux d'Alein et du Vaineigne,	In the green fields of Alleins and Vernegues of the Luberon
Du mont Lebrou proche de la Durance,	mountains near Durance, the fighting on both sides will be so
Camps de deux parts conflict sera si aigre	bitter for the armies that Mesopotamia shall cease to be
Mesopotamie defaillira en la France.	found in France.

It is from the last line of this quatrain that commentators refer to Mesopotamia throughout the Centuries as referring to Paris. Both places in line one are villages near Salon, Nostradamus' home; the Luberon mountains are near the river Durance.

100

Entre Gaulois le dernier honnoré,	The man least honoured
D'homme ennemi sera victorieux:	among the French will be
Force & terroir en mouvement exploré	victorious over his enemy. Strength and lands he explored
D'un coup de traict quand mourra l'envieux.	in action, when suddenly the envious one dies from the shot.

GENERAL DE GAULLE?

This quatrain is normally applied to de Gaulle and the man who is assassinated is then identified as Admiral Darlan, who was killed on 24th December 1942. *Le traict* is the normal word for the shot of an arrow, but here may mean gunshot.

CENTURY IV

1	
2*	War of Spanish Succession, 1701–13
3	
4	
5*	War of Spanish Succession, 1701–13
6	
7	
8*	St. Quentin, 1557
9	
10	
11	
12	
13*	Duke of Parma, 1580
14*	J. F. Kennedy
15**	Britain 1939–45. Submarines
16	
17	
18	
19	
20	
21*	France 1940–4. De Gaulle
22	
23*	Greek fire
24	Persecution of Clergy
25	Occult quatrain
26**	*Coup d'État* of 18th Brumaire, 1799
27	
28	Occult quatrain
29	Occult quatrain
30	Occult quatrain
31	Occult quatrain
32*	Decline of Communism
33	Occult quatrain

34
35
36
37*   Napoleon, 1800
38?   Machine?
39**   U.S.A. and U.A.R.
40*?   Bunker at Berlin, 1945
41
42
43?   Aerial warfare
44
45
46
47*   24th August 1572
48
49
50**F? America and Asia
51
52
53
54*   Napoleon
55
56
57
58
59?   Iran?
60
61*   Marshal Pétain, 1940–4
62*   Oliver Cromwell. Colonel Gadalfi of Libya.
63   France, 1702–4
64
65*   Napoleon III
66
67
68**   Tripartite Pact. Hitler and Mussolini
69
70*   Wellington. The Peninsular War
71
72?
73*   Assassination of the Duke de Berry, 1820
74
75**   Waterloo, 1815
76

77?	
78	
79	
80*	Maginot Line. Second World War
81	
82*	Retreat from Moscow, 1812–13
83	
84?	
85*	Louis XVI and French Revolution
86	
87	
88	
89**	William III of England
90	
91	
92?	Radio Equipment
93**	The Count de Chambord, 1820
94	
95F?	U.S.A. and War?
96**	William and Mary
97	
98	
99F?	Missiles or rockets?
100*	Franco-Prussian War, 1870–1

KEY: * Of interest F? Possibly referring to the future.

Cela du reste de sang non espandu,	The remaining blood will not
Venise quiert secours estre donné,	be spilt, Venice seeks for help
Apres avoir bien long temps	to be given; Having waited
attendu,	for a very long time the city is
Cité livrée au premier cornet	handed over at the first trumpet
sonné.	blast.

This probably describes the Turkish attack on Cyprus (1560–73).
Venice received very little help and Famagusta, the capital of
Cyprus, fell to the Turks after a prolonged siege in 1571.

Par mort la France prendra voyage	Because of a death France will
à faire,	undertake a journey, the fleet
Classe par mer, marcher monts	at sea, marching over the
Pyrenées,	Pyrenean mountains. Spain
Espaigne en trouble, marcher gent	will be troubled, an army will
militaire:	march, some of the greatest
Des plus grand Dames en France	ladies brought into France.
emmenées.	

WAR OF SPANISH SUCCESSION 1701–1713

This is a comparatively successful quatrain. Philip V, grandson of
Louis XIV, inherited the Spanish throne from Charles II in 1700.
This was not popular with Austria, England, Holland, Prussia and
Savoy, who formed a coalition to support the pretensions of the
Archduke Charles. The French fleet took to the sea, and her army
crossed the Pyrenees. The war in Spain lasted for twelve years and
it was all due to two Spanish princesses who married into the
French line, the wives of Louis XII and Louis XIV respectively.

D'Arras & Bourges[1], de Brodes	From Arras and Bourges great
grans enseignes,	banners from the Dark Ones,
Un plus grand nombre de Gascons	a greater number of Gascons
batre à pied,	fight on foot. Those along the
Ceux long du Rosne saigneront les	Rhône will make the Spanish
Espaignes:	bleed. Near the mountain seat
Proche du mont ou Sagonte s'assied.	of Sagunto.

Brodes probably means dark-haired people, possibly the Spanish
Moors in this context. If Bourges is understood as Bruges then line

[1] *Bourges* = possibly Bruges.

one describes another Hapsburg invasion from the North, probably that which resulted in the Battle of St. Quentin, in 1557. The last two lines suggest that the French invaded Spain, which they did not do for another fifty years or so. The importance of Sagunto is unclear.

4

L'impotent Prince faché, plaincts & querelles,	The powerless Prince is angered, complaints & quar-
De rapts & pille, par coqz & par Libiques:	rels, rape and pillage, by the cock and by the Libyans. It is
Grand est par terre par mer infinies voilles	great on land, at sea innumer- able sails; Italy alone will be
Seule Italie sera chassont Celtiques.	driving out the Celts.

The cock is the French symbol and the Libyans are the Algerian corsairs who allied with them. The Prince is therefore probably a Hapsburg, possibly Duke Cosimo, who was in charge of the defence of Elba and the surrounding lands. These territories were ravished in 1555. The last line is confusing suggesting that the French will be defeated by the Italians but successful everywhere else. Exactly the reverse occurred. The French held their own in Italy but were defeated in the North.

5

Croix paix, soubz un accompli divin verbe,	Cross, peace under one the divine word achieved. Spain
L'Espaigne & Gaule seront unis ensemble:	and Gaul will be united. A great disaster is close, the fight-
Grand clade[1] proche, & combat tresacerbe,	ing very ferocious, no heart so brave as will not tremble.
Coeur si hardi ne sera qui ne tremble.	

SPANISH SUCCESSION, 1701–1713

Spain and France were united for the short time that Louis XIV's grandson inherited the Spanish throne. Perhaps the revocation of the Edict of Nantes is hinted at in line one? Peace achieved under the divine word could be the Papal Bull Unigenitus which was issued in 1713, the year the war ended. The great disaster following upon the union of the countries is the War of the Spanish Succession of IV. 2, and the final line is self-explanatory, just used to fill up the quatrain.

[1] *clades*—Latin = disaster.

| D'habits nouveaux apres faicte la treuve,[1]
Malice tramme & machination:
Premier mourra qui en fera la preuve,
Couleur venise insidation.[2] | After the truce is made, new clothes will be put on, malice, conspiracy and plotting. He who will prove it is the first to die, the colour of Venetian treachery. |

A very obscure quatrain. Perhaps the new clothes imply a new order of monks, and there is a shade of yellow-brown called venetian red. Perhaps this is meant rather than the city.

7

| Le mineur filz du grand & hai Prince,
De lepre aura à vingt ans grande tache,
De deuil sa mere mourra bien triste & mince,
Et il mourra là où tombe cher lache. | The younger son of a great and hated prince, will be greatly marked by leprosy by the time he is twenty. His mother will die of grief, very sad and thin, and he will die when the cowardly flesh falls (from his bones). |

There is no record to date of a younger, or youngest, son of a Royal family dying of leprosy.

8

| La grand cité d'assaut prompt & repentin,
Surprins de nuict, gardes interrompus:
Les excubies & vielles sainct Quintin,
Trucidés gardes & les pourtails rompus. | The great city will be surprised at night by a sudden and quick assault. The guards interrupted; the watch and guards of St. Quintin slaughtered, the guards and the gates broken down. |

ST. QUENTIN, 1557

There was a Battle of St. Quentin in 1557 but the city was taken not in the way Nostradamus describes it, but by a seventeen-day siege. But at least the prediction of the town's capture is correct, see IV. 3.

[1] treuve—O.F., treve = truce.
[2] insidation—O.F. = snare, trap.

Le chef du camp au milieu de la presse,	The leader of the army in the middle of the crowd is wounded
D'un coup de fleche sera blessé aux cuisses,	in the thighs with an arrow. When Geneva in trouble and
Lors que Geneve eu larmes & detresse,	distress is betrayed by Lausanne and the Swiss.
Sera trahi par Lozan & Souisses.	

Presumably another anti-Calvinist tirade by Nostradamus. He seems to foresee that Lausanne and Switzerland generally return to the Roman Catholic faith with only Geneva led by the wounded leader, holding out. A completely mistaken verse.

10

Le jeune prince accusé faulsement,	The young Prince, falsely
Mettra en trouble le camp & en querelles:	accused will put the camp into quarrels and trouble. The
Meutri le chef pour le soustenement,	leader is murdered for his
Sceptre appaiser: puis guerir escrouelles.	support to appease the crown: then he cures the king's evil.

This describes the leader of an army who supports a Prince but loses his life. A new King comes to the throne, line 4, because French and English kings were reputed to cure scrofula by their touch, particularly on the day of their coronation.

11

Celui qu'aura gouvert de la grand cappe,[1]	He who will have government of the great cloak will be led to
Sera induict à quelques cas patrer[2]	execute in certain cases. The
Les douze rouges viendront fouiller la nappe.	twelve red ones will come to spoil the cover, under murder,
Soubz meutre, meutre se viendra perpetrer.	murder will be perpetrated.

A detailed quatrain, but one that has not yet materialized. A Pope will be forced into some rash action, and then be condemned by his twelve cardinals. It is implied that they connive at the Pope's murder or will commit further murders.

[1] *cappe* = (*a*) Cloak. (*b*) Cape, standing for Pope and Vatican.
[2] *patrer*—Latin, *patrare* = to perform, execute.

Le camp plus grand de route mis en fuite,	The greatest army on the march put to flight will scarcely be pursued further. The army reassembled and the legion reduced, they will then be driven out of France completely.
Guaires plus outre ne sera pourchassé:	
Ost recampé, & legion reduicte,	
Puis hors ses Gaules du tout sera chassé.	

This is a very general quatrain and the German invasions of France in the last two wars fit it most accurately. However, there is nothing sufficiently explicit to go on.

De plus grand perte nouvelles raportées,	News of the great loss is brought; the report will astonish the camp. Bands unite against those revolting, the double phalanx will forsake the great one.
Le raport fait le camp s'estonnera:	
Bandes unies encontre revoltées,	
Double phalange grand abandonnera.	

1580, DUKE OF PARMA

This verse is normally applied to the 1580s when a rumour spread through the Duke of Parma's army of so great a defeat that they were quite demoralized and allowed the Dutch to capture Antwerp for a time. A phalanx was 800 men, so 1,600 men are understood to have revolted.

La mort subite du premier personnage.	The sudden death of the leading personnage will have changed and put another to rule. Soon, but too late come to high position, of young age, by land and sea it will be necessary to fear him.
Aura changé & mis un autre au regne:	
Tost, tard venu à si haut & bas aage,	
Que terre & mer faudre que on la craigne.	

J. F. KENNEDY

A general prophecy about a young leader who comes to power too late to alter the *status quo* of the country. It has fancifully been suggested that it may refer to J. F. Kennedy, succeeding the aged General Eisenhower, whose policies still could not lessen world tension. During the Cuba incident Kennedy's power was to be feared on land and sea.

D'où pensera faire venir famine, *De là viendra le rassasiement:* *L'oeil de la mer par avare canine* *Pour de l'un l'autre dorna huile,* *froment.*	From the place where he will think to bring famine, from there will come the relief. The eye of the sea, like a covetous dog; the one will give oil and wheat to the other.

GREAT BRITAIN 1939–45. SUBMARINES

This verse describes Britain's predicament during the Second World War very accurately. The German blockade tried to starve her out, see also III. 71, but instead, she received large quantities of American aid. 'The eye of the sea, like a covetous dog' is understood as meaning the periscope of the German U-boats, which certainly hunted down the British convoys in packs.

16

La cité franche de liberté fait serve,
Des profligés & resveurs faict
    asile:
Le Roy changé à eux non si pro-
    terve[1]
De cent seront devenus plus de mille.
	The free city of liberty is enslaved, it becomes the refuge of profligates and dreamers. The king changes and is not so ferocious towards them. From one hundred they will become more than a thousand.

Europe had many free cities when Nostradamus wrote. He may here be referring to Orange, which gave its name to the Dutch royal line, and did not belong to France until 1713. During Nostradamus' time it belonged to William the Silent, and line 2 may be intended as meaning that it had become a haven for Protestants, which it was.

17

Changer à Beaune, Nuy, Chalons &
    Dijon,
Le duc voulant amander[2] *la*
    Barrée[3]
Marchant pres fleuve, poisson, bec
    de plongeon,
Vers la queue; porte sera serrée.
	Changes at Beaune, Nuits, Chalon & Dijon, the Duke wishes to improve the Carmelites. Walking near the river, a fish, a diving (bird's) beak, towards the tail; the gate will be locked.

[1] *proterve*—Latin, *protervus* = violent.
[2] *amander*—O.F. = improve, to better.
[3] *Barrée*—This was the name for the Carmelite monks and nuns, from the O.F., *barré* = motley.

The first two lines may refer to St. Theresa who reformed the order of Carmelite nuns in Spain in 1562. But nothing can be made of the following lines.

18

Des plus lettrés dessus les faits celestes	Some of the most learned men in the heavenly arts will be
Seront par princes ignorans reprouvés:	reprimanded by ignorant Princes; punished by an Edict,
Punis d'Edit, chassez comme scelestes,	driven out as scoundrels and put to death wherever they are
Et mis à mort là où seront trouvés.	found.

Shades of the Inquisition linger over this verse, for in fact astrologers were never as grossly persecuted after Nostradamus' death as they were during the century before. However if he was also thinking of the witch hunts which bedevilled Europe they did not die out until somewhat later.

19

Devant Rouen d'Insubres mis le siege,	The Insubrians lay siege in front of Rouen, the passages
Par terre & mer enfermés les passages:	closed by land and sea. By Hainaut & Flanders, by Ghent
D'Haynault, & Flandres, de Gand & ceux de Liege,	and those of Liege, through cloaked gifts they will ravage
Par dons laenées[1] raviront les rivages.	the shores.

Rouen was first captured by the Duke of Parma who was helping de Guise against Henri of Navarre in 1592 but without much of a siege. Since Milan was part of his dominions there could have been Italians (Insubres) among his troops. Since then Rouen has never been captured by Italy, the Germans captured it in 1870 and 1940 and the Americans in 1944. All the other towns mentioned are in the Netherlands and Flanders. Although reasonably clear, this prophecy has not been fulfilled.

[1] *laenées*—Latin, *laena* = cloak, mantle.

Paix uberté[1] long temps lieu louera;	Peace and plenty for a long
Par tout son regne desert la fleur de	time the place will praise: the
lis:	fleur de lis deserted throughout
Corps morts d'eau, terre là lou	the kingdom. Bodies dead by
apportera,	water, *they* will be brought to
Sperants vain heur d'estre là	land there, waiting in vain for
ensevelis.	the opportunity of being buried.

The fleur de lis was the emblem of many other families besides the French kings so this is not much help. The obvious time that it disappears throughout the kingdom is during the Revolution and the Empire. The last two lines would then be generalities about war and death.

Le changement sera fort difficile,	The change will be very diffi-
Cité, province au change gain fera:	cult. Both city and province
Coeur haut, prudent mis, chassé lui	will gain by it. A prudent man
habile,	highly placed, will be chased
Mer, terre, peuple son estat	out by the cunning one. By
changera.	land and sea people will change
	their estate.

FRANCE, 1940–4. DE GAULLE

The first two lines of this quatrain may refer to the fall of France and Marshal Petain's 'centralized decentralization'. The prudent man is de Gaulle, who is chased out to England and the last line refers to the general state of the country and the war.

La grand copie[2] qui sera deschasée,	The great army which will be
Dans un moment fera besoing au	driven out at one moment will
Roi,	be needed by the King. The
La foi promise de loing sera	faith promised from afar will
faulsée	be broken, he will see himself
Nud se verra en piteux desarroi.	with nothing, in pitiful dis-
	order.

This is a general type of quatrain that may have occurred several times. A king quarrels with an ally, and having dismissed its forces

[1] *uberté*—Latin, *ubertas* = abundance.
[2] *copie*—Latin, *copia* = army, troops.

suddenly finds he needs them again. But because one of them breaks a promise the king is left powerless.

23

La legion dans la marine classe,	The legion in the marine fleet
Calcine,[1] *Magnes*[2] *soulphre, &*	will burn, lime, magnesia,
paix bruslera:	sulphur and pitch. The long
Le long repos de l'asseuree place,	rest in a safe place; Port Selin,
Port Selyn,[3] *Hercle*[4] *feu les con-*	Monaco will be consumed by
sumera.	fire.

GREEK FIRE

This is a very strange quatrain. The second line appears to be giving a recipe for Greek fire, the famous 'secret weapon' of the Greeks and Byzantines. Nostradamus is quite correct because after much research, Lieut.-Colonel H. Hime said that it was the presence of quicklime which distinguished Greek fire from all other known incendiaries of the period. The mixture gave rise to heat on contact with water and thus took fire spontaneously when wetted, and was used with great success in sea battles. But again, Port Selin, if I am correct in identifying it with Genoa, and Monaco, have not been attacked since Nostradamus' day. But the port of Toulon was used by Barbarossa when he helped the French against the Emperor during the 1540s.

24

Oui soubs terre saincte dame voix	The faint voice of a woman is
fainte,	heard under the holy ground.
Humaine flamme pour divine voix	Human flame shines for the
luire:	divine voice. It will cause the
Fera les seuls de leur sang terre	earth to be stained with the
tainte,	blood of celibates and destroy
Et les saincts temples pour les	the holy temples for the wicked.
impurs destruire.	

PERSECUTION OF CLERGY

An impossible quatrain because of the many variants of the first line. To which word does *saincte* belong? *Dame* is also given as

[1] *Calcine*—Latin, *calcina* = lime.

[2] *Magnes*—Latin for loadstone or magnet. Also an abbreviation of Magnesie, used loosely to describe Greek fire.

[3] *Port Selyn*—Genoa was a crescent-shaped republic and Selene means crescent in Greek.

[4] *Hercle*—Latin, *Herculeis Monacei* = another name for Monaco.

d'ame, of the soul, and *fainte* as *sainte*. The general idea seems to be the persecution of the church, perhaps personified in the Holy Lady of the first line, and its most probable fulfilment was the abolition and persecution of the clergy during the French Revolution.

25

Corps sublimes sans fin à l'oeil visibles:	The heavenly bodies endlessly visible to the eye come to cloud
Obnubiler viendront par ses raisons:	(the intellect) for their own
Corps, front comprins, sens chief &	reasons. The body, together
invisibles.	with the forehead, senses and
Diminuant les sacrees oraisons.	head all invisible, as the sacred prayers diminish.

OCCULT QUATRAIN

Some commentators regard this as referring to the invention of the telescope (1610) bringing new worlds and ideas which will be hostile to religion. But I think that Nostradamus is here describing the sensation of 'bodilessness' which he experiences when in a predictive trance, when his mind and intellect are used by the heavenly beings for their own purposes. The prayers of the last line are the invocations to the spirits made by Nostradamus. As they finish, he is possessed. See also I. 1 and 2, and III, 2.

26

Lou grand eyssame se levera d'abelhos,	The great swarm of bees will arise but no one will know
Que non sauran don te siegen venguddos:	whence they have come, the ambush by night, the sentinel
De nuech l'embousque, lou gach dessous las treilhos	under the vines, a city handed over by five tongues not naked.
Cuitad trahido per cinq lengos non nudos.	

THE *COUP D'ÉTAT* OF EIGHTEENTH BRUMAIRE
(9th NOVEMBER 1779)

This is one of the few quatrains written entirely in Provençal. It describes Napoleon's *coup d'état* of 1799 very accurately. The swarm of bees is Napoleon's emblem—they can still be seen on the embroideries at Malmaison and Fontainebleau. The five men (literally babblers), who handed over Paris were the members of the Directory who were bribed (*non nudos*) to give way to Napoleon's Consulate; they were also wearing official clothes as members of the Directory, as opposed to their everyday apparel. The coup was planned the night before it took place. Most commentators take *las treilhos* to be an anagram for the Tuileries into which Napoleon moved once he saw his action was successful. The exact French equivalent is *treilles*, but it is close enough and the quatrain fits very well in all other respects.

27

Salon, Mansol, Tarascon de SEX. *l'arc,*	Salon, Mansol, Tarascon, the arch of SEX: where the pyra-
Ou est debout encor la piramide:	mid is still standing. They will
Viendront livrer le Prince Danne- *marc,*	come to deliver the Prince of Denmark, a shameful ransom
Rachat honni au temple d'Arte- *mide.*	to the temple of Artemis.

The complicated first line stands for St. Rémy where Nostradamus was born, where there are two great historical monuments, a mausoleum with the inscription *SEX. L.M. JUILEI C.F. PAREN-TIBUS SUIS* and next to it a triumphal arch. *Mansol* is a misprint for Mausole, a priory just outside St. Rémy. The problem lies in connecting them with Dannemarc. The word may well be one of Nostradamus' better concealed anagrams which I cannot decipher.

28

Lors que Venus du Sol sera couvert,	When Venus will be covered by
Soubs l'esplendeur sera forme *occulte:*	the Sun, under the splendour will be a hidden form. Mercury
Mercure au feu les aura des- *couvert,*	will have exposed them to the fire, by a rumour of war will be
Par bruit bellique sera mis à *l'insulte.*	affronted.

OCCULT

This, and the following quatrains IV. 29, 30, 31 and 33 are all occult quatrains and probably describe Nostradamus' attempts to discover the elusive philosopher's stone which transmutes all other metals into gold, here described as the sun.

Le Sol caché eclipse par Mercure,
Ne sera mis que pour le ciel
second:
De Vulcan Hermes sera faicte
pasture,
Sol sera veu pur, rutilant & blond.

The hidden Sun eclipsed by Mercury will be placed only second in the heavens. Hermes will be made the food of Vulcan, the Sun will be seen pure, shining and golden.

OCCULT

See IV. 28. Vulcan here stands for fire.

Plus onze fois Luna Sol ne voudra,
Tous augmenté & baissez de
degré:
Et si bas mis que peu or on cendra,
Qu'apres faim, peste, descouvert le
secret.

More than eleven times the Moon will not want the Sun, both raised and lessened in degree. Put so low that one will sew little gold: after famine and plague the secret will be discovered.

OCCULT

See IV. 28. The Moon here probably means silver.

La Lune au plain de nuict sur le
haut mont,
Le nouveau sophe d'un seul cerveau
l'a veu:
Par ses disciples estre immortel
semond,
Yeux au midi, en seins mains,
corps au feu.

The moon, in the middle of the night over the high mountain, the young wise man alone with his brain has seen it. Invited by his disciples to become immortal, his eyes to the south, his hands on his breast, his body in the fire.

OCCULT

In this quatrain it is suggested that the young sage who finally makes this great discovery either comes to a violent end or is racked by mental torment.

Es lieux & temps chair un poisson donra lieu,	In those times and places that meat gives way to fish the
La loi commune sera faicte au contraire:	common law will be made in opposition. The old (order)
Vieux tiendra fort plus osté du millieu,	will hold strong, then removed from the scene, then All
Le Pánta chiona philòn mis fort arriere.	Things common among Friends put far behind.

DECLINE OF COMMUNISM

Pánta chiona philòn is the Greek for all things held in common among friends, that is, Communism in its strictest sense. Nostradamus has already described this in the U.S.S.R. in quatrain III. 95, and seems definite that its appeal will fade and there will be strong attempts to revive the old order. One wonders whether this is associated with the theory that America and the U.S.S.R. will ally together against the East, probably China? See V. 78.

Jupiter joinct plus Venus qu'à la Lune,	Jupiter joined more to Venus than to the Moon appearing in
Apparoissant de plenitude blanche:	a white fullness. Venus hidden
Venus cachée souz la blancheur Neptune	under the whiteness of Neptune struck by Mars by the engraved
De Mars frappée par la gravée branche.	wand.

OCCULT

The translation of the last line is difficult. I take gravée to mean engraved, because branche is used by Nostradamus to refer to the ceremonial wand and tripod used in his predictions therefore that the wand is engraved with hieroglyphics. The rest is very obscure.

Le grand mené captif d'estrange terre,	The great man led captive from a foreign land, chained in
D'or enchainé ay Roy CHYREN offert:	gold, offered to King Chyren. He who in Ausonia, Milan,
Qui dans Ausone, Milan perdra la guerre,	will lose the war and all his army put to fire and sword.
Et tout son ost mis à feu & à fer.	

CHYREN is an almost definite anagram for the Old French spelling of Henri, *HENRYC*, but the great problem lies in deciding which Henri these verses refer to. Many commentators favour Henri IV, others of the 19th Century in particular, a new king of France yet to come. The quatrains are not completely favourable to either idea, so maybe they have yet to be fulfilled? See II. 79, VI. 27 and 70, VIII. 54, IX. 41 etc.

35

Le feu estaint, les vierges trahiront	The fire put out, the virgins will betray the greater part of the new band; lightning in sword, lances alone will guard the king, Tuscany and Corsica, by night throats slit.
La plus grand part de la bande nouvelle:	
Fouldre à fer, lance les seulz Roi garderont	
Etrusque & Corse, de nuict gorge allumelle.	

During the Empire, Tuscany and Corsica were both bothered by the French as Tuscany was an ally and Genoa owned Corsica.

36

Les jeux nouveau en Gaule redres-sés,	New games are set up in Gaul, after the victory of the Insubrian campaign. The mountains of Hesperia the great ones tied and bound. Romania and Spain will tremble with fear.
Après victoire de l'Insubre[1] cham-paigne:	
Monts d'Esperie, les grands liés, troussés:	
De peur trembler la Romaigne & l'Espaigne.	

If *Romaigne* in line 4 stands for the Roman Empire, i.e. Germany, the best interpretation of France's victories in Spain and the north would be the Napoleonic campaigns.

37

Gaulois par saults, monts viendra penetrer:	The Gauls will penetrate the mountains in leaps and occupy the great seat of Insubria. He will make his army go deep (into the land), Genoa and Monaco will repulse the red fleet.
Occupera le grand lieu de l'Insubre:	
Au plus profond son est fera entrer,	
Gennes, Monech pousseront classe rubre.	

[1] *Insubre* = Italy, around Milan, Lombardy.

In the year 1800, Genoa was besieged by Austria, and surrendered
on 4th June. The British fleet which had been helping with a
blockade attacked Monaco on 23rd May. Earlier that month
Napoleon made his incredible crossing of the St. Bernard pass with
an army of 40,000 men, and took Milan (Insubria) on 2nd June.
A very satisfactory quatrain.

38

Pendant que Duc, Roi, Royne occupera, *Chef Bizant du captif en Samothrace:* *Avant l'assault l'un l'autre mangera,* *Rebours ferré suivra du sang la trace.*	While the Duke occupies the King and Queen, the Byzantine leader is held captive in Greece. Before the attack one will devour the other. The metalled reverse will follow the trail of blood.

MACHINE?

Does the 'metalled reverse' indicate a type of machine similar to
a Geiger counter, that will be able to follow a man's tracks?

39

Les Rhodiens demanderont secours, *Par le neglect de ses hoirs delaisseé:* *L'Empire Arabe revalera son secours,* *Par Hesperies la cause redressée.*	The people of Rhodes will demand help, abandoned by the neglect of their heirs. The Arab Empire will assess its course, its cause revived again by the West.

U.S.A. AND U.A.R.

At a time of unrest in Greece, which could refer to the present
regime, the U.A.R. will assess its position and be helped in some
way by America. Possibly this last line refers to the attitude
taken by the U.S.A. over Suez or to the complicated political
pressures now being brought to bear on the Middle East?

40

Les fortresses des assiegés serrés, *Par poudre à feu profondés en abisme:* *Les proditeurs seront tous vifs serrés* *Onc aux sacristes n'advint si piteux scisme.*	The fortress of the beseiged shut up by gunpowder sunk into its depths; the traitor will be emtombed alive, never did so pitiful a schism happen to the sextons.

The clue to this verse lies in the last line. *Sacristes* translates as sextons, which is meaningless in this context. However, if Nostradamus meant Saxons, the Germans and this is associated with a schism, a breaking up of a party, this could refer to Hitler and those pitiful few of his followers who remained in the fortified bunker to be shelled by the Allies. See also III. 58.

41

Gymnique[1] sexe captive par hostage,	A female (sex) captive as a hostage will come by night to deceive the guards. The leader of the camp deceived by her language will leave her to the people, it will be pitiful to see.
Viendra de nuit custodes decevoir:	
Le chef du camp deceu par son langage:	
Lairra à la gente, sera piteux à voir,	

An unknown woman who is abandoned to a mob after tricking the guards; very general.

42

Geneve & Langres par ceux de Chartres & Dole,	Geneva and Langres through the people of Chartres and Dôle, and Grenoble, captive at Montelimar: Seysel, Lausanne, through a fraudulent trick will betray them for sixty gold marks.
Et par Grenoble captif au Montlimard:	
Seysett, Losanne par fraudulente dole	
Les trahiront par or soixante marc.	

There are too many scattered place-names in both Switzerland and France to make this quatrain clear. A mark was 8 oz. of gold.

43

Seront ouis au ciel les armes battre:	Weapons will be heard fighting in the skies: in the same year the divine are enemies: they will want unjustly to query the holy laws, through lightning and war many believers put to death.
Celui an mesme les divins ennemis:	
Voudrant loix sainctes injustement debatre,	
Par foudre & guerre bien croyans à mort mis.	

AERIAL WARFARE?

The first line seems to indicate an air battle of some type but the divine enemies are difficult to decipher.

[1] *Gymnique*—Misprint for Greek, *gynique* = female.

Deux gros de Mende, de Rondés &
    Milhau,
Cahours, Limoges, Castres malo
    sepmano
De nuech l'intrado de Bourdeaux
    un cailhau,
Par Perigort au toc de la campano.

The two large ones of Mende,
of Rodez and Milhau, Cahors
and Limoges, Castres a bad
week: by night the entry; from
Bordeaux an insult, through
Perigord at the peal of the bell.

A quatrain of mixed Provençal and French phrases. Unfortunately
they seem to disguise little more than the names of a series of towns
in South-west France.

45

Par conflit Roi, regne abandonnera,
Le plus grand chef faillira au
    besoing:
Mors profligés peu en rechapera,
Tous destranchés un en sera tes-
    moing.

Through a battle the king will
abandon his kingdom, the
greatest leader will fail in time
of need. Dead, ruined, few will
escape it all cut down, save one
who will be a witness.

This quatrain is suggested as suitable for Napoleon I at Waterloo,
Napoleon III at Sédan or Kaiser Wilhelm II. The reader can
take his choice. A typical prophecy.

46

Bien defendu le faict par excellence,
Garde toy Tours de ta proche ruine:
Londres & Nantes par Reims fera
    defense
Ne passe outre au temps de la
    bruine.

The deed, through its excellence, strongly forbidden,
Tours, beware of your approaching ruin. London and
Nantes will make a defence
through Reims. Do not go
further afield at the time of the
fog.

47

Le noir farouche quand aura
    essayé
Sa main sanguine par feu, fer,
    arcs tendus:
Trestout le peuple sera tant
    effrayé,
Voir les plus grans par col & pieds
    pendus.

When the ferocious king will
have exercised his bloody hand
through fire, the sword and the
bended bow. All the nation
will be so terrified to see the
great ones hanging by their
neck and feet.

In line 1 *noir* is the usual anagram for *roi*, King. The savage king was the mad Charles IX, who was reputed to kill for the sake of blood when out hunting, decapitating animals which came across his path. The fear of the people refers to the massacre of St. Bartholomew, of the French Huguenots on 24th August 1572, when Admiral Coligny was killed by the mob and hung from a gibbet by one foot.

48

Planure Ausonne fertile, spacieuse,	The plains of Ausonia, rich
Produira taons si tant de sauter-	and wide, will produce so many
elles:	gadflies and grasshoppers, that
Clarté solaire deviendra nubileuse,	the light of the sun will be
Rouger le tout, grand peste venir	clouded over. They will devour
d'elles.	everything and a great pesti-
	lence will come from them.

Perhaps *sauterelles* could be translated as locusts in this context. But have they ever been found as far north as Naples (Ausonia)?

49

Devant le peuple, sang sera res-	Blood will be spilt in front of
pandu,	the people, which will not go
Que de haut ciel ne viendra esloig-	far from the high heavens. But
ner:	for a long time it will not be
Mais d'un long temps ne sera	heard, the spirit of a single man
entendu,	will bear witness to it.
L'esprit d'un seul le viendra	
tesmoigner.	

Line 2 probably implies that the spilt blood was calling to the heavens for vengeance, but the bloody deed which caused it is not clarified.

50

Libra verra regner les Hesperies,	Libra will be seen to reign in
De ciel & terre tenir la monarchie:	the West, holding the rule over
D'Asie forces nul ne verra paries,	the skies and earth. No one
Que sept ne tiennent par rang le	will see the strength of Asia
hierarchie.	destroyed until seven hold the
	hierarchy in succession.

According to this prediction, when Libra the Balance rules over America, that country will be at the height of its powers. But Asian strength will be equally strong until the seventh comes. Does this mean the seventh ruler in Asia, or the seventh decade? The last line may mean that a war between East and West may occur during the 7th decade of this Century. See II. 89, III. 60, IV. 95, VI. 21, etc. Equally it may refer to the Seven, the Common Market as it existed, until the four new members joined in 1973. See V. 40 etc.

51

Un Duc cupide son enemi ensuivre, *Dans entrera empeschant la phalange:* *Hastez à pied si pres viendront poursuivre,* *Que la journee conflite pres de Gange.*	A Duke eager to follow his enemy will enter in, hindering the phalanx. Hurried on foot they follow so closely that the day of the battle is near Ganges.

Ganges may be understood as a town in France near Montpellier, or the River Ganges. The former is more likely.

52

En cité obsesse aux murs hommes & femmes, *Ennemis hors le chef prest à soi rendre* *Vent sera fort encontre les gendarmes,* *Chassez seront par chaux, poussiere, & cendre.*	In the besieged city men and women at the walls, the enemy without, the leader ready to surrender; the wind will be strong against the armed men, they will be driven off by lime, dust and cinders.

53

Les fugitifs & bannis revoquez, *Peres & fils grand garnissant les hauts puits:* *Le cruel pere & les siens suffoquez,* *Son fils plus pire submergé dans le puits.*	The fugitives and the banished are recalled, fathers and sons strengthening the deep wells. The cruel father and his followers suffocated; His most wicked son drowned in the well.

Du nom qui onques ne fut au Roy Gaulois,	Of a name which never held by a French king, never was there
Jamais ne fut un fouldre si craintif:	so fearful a thunderbolt. Italy,
Tremblant l'Italie, l'Espaigne & les Anglois,	Spain and the English tremble; he will be greatly attentive to
De femme estrangiers grandement attentif.	foreign women.

NAPOLEON I

This is a fascinating quatrain. Napoleon brought the new name of Bonaparte to the line of French kings, for most kings had shared the same names, i.e. Louis (6), Henri (2), Charles (2), Francis (1), since Nostradamus' time. Napoleon's was the great reshaping of the map of Europe and he was very enamoured of his two foreign wives, Josephine the Créole, Marie Louise the Austrian, and possibly it also refers to his Polish mistress, Marie Walewska. The reference to his name being dreadful as a thunderbolt should be compared with IV. 82, where Nostradamus calls him the Destroyer.

Quant la corneille sur tout de brique joincte,	When the crow on a tower made of brick will do nothing
Durant sept heures ne fera que crier:	but croak for seven hours; it foretells death, a statue stained
Mort presagee de sang statue taincte,	with blood, a tyrant murdered, people praying to their Gods.
Tyran meutri, aux Dieux peuple prier.	

Both the crow, and the statue weeping blood are common omens of evil, the latter has been recorded even in this country. But the results of these omens are too general to pinpoint the stanza.

Apres victoire de babieuse langue	After the victory of the raging
L'esprit tempte en tranquil & repos:	tongue, the spirit tempted in tranquil rest. Throughout the
Victeur sanguin par conflict faict harangue,	battle the bloody victor makes speeches, roasting the tongue,
Roustir la langue & la chair & les os.	the flesh and the bones.

Ignare envie au grand Roi sup- *portee,* *Tiendra propos deffendre les* *escripitz:* *Sa femme non femme par un autre* *tentee,* *Plus double deux ne fort ne criz.*	Ignorant envy supported by the great king, he will propose forbidding the writings. His wife, not his wife, tempted by another, no longer will the double dealing couple protest against it.

It has been suggested that Nostradamus is here referring to his own writings and Henri II's cool reception of the Prophecies. The mistress would be Diane de Poitiers. There is a similar reference in VII. 9. The last line is very difficult to translate.

Soleil ardent dans le gosier coller, *De sang humain arrouser terre* *Etrusque:* *Chef seille*[1] *d'eaue, mener son fils* *filer,* *Captive dame conduicte en terre* *Turque.*	To swallow the burning sun in the throat, the Tuscan land sprinkled with human blood, the leader leads his son away, the pail of water, a captive lady led into Turkish lands.

Deux assiegez en ardente ferveur, *De soif estaincts pour deux plaines* *tasses:* *Le fort lime, & un vieillart* *resveur,* *Au Genevois de Nira monstra* *trasse.*	Two besieged in a burning heat, killed by thirst for want of two full cups; the fort filed, and an old dreamer will show the tracks of Nira to the Genevans.

IRAN?

Nira is one of the few unsolved enigmatic names in the Prophecies. It may be a corruption of Jura, the Swiss mountain range, or imply someone quite different. It is an anagram of modern Iran.

Les sept enfans en hostaige laissés, *Le tiers viendra son enfant trucider:* *Deux par son filz seront d'estoc* *percés,* *Gennes, Florence, los viendra* *encunder.*[2]	The seven children left in hostage, the third will come to slaughter his child. Two will be pierced by a hook because of his son, he will come to strike against Genoa and Florence.

[1] *seille*—O.F. = pail, bucket.

[2] *encunder*—Probably from the Latin, *incutiere* = to strike against.

It is not clear whether these seven children are the Valois children of Catherine de Medici; the rest of the quatrain does not clarify the position.

61

Le vieux mocqué & privé de sa place,	The old man, mocked and deprived of his position by the foreigner who will suborn him. The hands of his sons are devoured before his face, he will betray his brother at Chartres, Orléans and Rouen.
Par l'estrangier qui le subornera:	
Mains de son filz mangées devant sa face,	
Le frere à Chartres, Orl. Rouen trahira.	

MARSHAL PÉTAIN, 1940–4

Marshal Pétain's nickname during the Vichy régime was *Le Vieux*, and nothing could describe his position more clearly than line 2. The hands which are devoured in front of him are the forces of his régime which are destroyed. The brothers are the Allies who simultaneously reached the three towns here mentioned, Chartres, Orleans and Rouen on 19th August 1944. They were betrayed by Pétain to the Germans, who was deported to Sigmariggen on the very day of their liberation.

62

Un coronel machine ambition,	A colonel intrigues through ambition, he will seize the greater part of the army. Against his Prince a false invention; he will be discovered under his flag.
Se saisira de la plus grand armée,	
Contre son prince fainte invention,	
Et descouvert sera soubz sa ramée.	

OLIVER CROMWELL

Most commentators accept this as a general quatrain about Oliver Cromwell, who took over the greater part of Charles I's armies and fought with them under the British flag. He certainly connived in the plotting and accusations laid against the king at his trial and execution. However it would apply very neatly to Colonel Qaddafi who overthrew King Idris of Libya in 1971.

L'armée Celtique contre les mon-	The Celtic army against the
taignars,	mountaineers, who will be
Qui seront sceus & prins à la lipee:	revealed and caught in a trap.
Paysans frais pousseront tost faug-	The fresh bracken will soon
nars,	be pressed by the peasants, they
Precipitez tous au fil de l'espee.	will all perish on the sword's
	blade.

FRANCE 1702–4

This probably refers to Marshal Villar's fight against the Camisard rebels of the Cevennes who practised a very competent form of guerrilla warfare (1702–4).

Le deffaillant en habit de bour-	The defaulter, dressed as a
geois,	citizen will come to try the king
Viendra le Roi tempter de son	with his offence; Fifteen sol-
offence:	diers, for the most part outlaws,
Quinze souldartz la plupart Usta-	the end of his life and the
gois,	greater part of his estate.
Vie derniere & chef de sa chevance.	

Au deserteur de la grand forteresse,	To the deserter of the great
Apres qu'aura son lieu abandonné:	fortress, after he will have
Son adversaire fera si grand	abandoned his post, his adver-
prouesse,	sary will display such prowess
L'Empereur tost mort sera con-	that the Emperor will soon be
damné.	condemned to death.

NAPOLEON III

Napoleon III, while still Louis Napoleon, was condemned to life detention in the fortress of Ham by the French, but on 25th May 1846 escaped from the castle to England. Louis Philippe abandoned his position as king of France in the 1848 Revolution and Louis Napoleon was voted Prince-President in December of the same year. He did not, however, display great skills as an Emperor, and his policies were responsible for the Franco-Prussian war and the consequent disaster to France. He died soon afterwards in 1873. The adversaries who are so powerful are, of course, the Prussians.

Soubz couleur faincte de sept testes
  raseés
Seront semés divers esplorateurs:
Puys & fontaines de poisons
  arrousées,
Au fort de Gennes humains devora-
  teurs.

Under the false colours of seven
shaven heads several spies will
be scattered. ˙The wells and
springs will be sprinkled with
poisons, at the fort of Genoa,
they devour human flesh.

Shaven heads is sometimes used by Nostradamus to describe
Cromwell's roundheads.

L'an que Saturne & Mars esgaux
  combuste,
L'air fort seiché longue trajection:
Par feux secrets, d'ardeur grand
  lieu adust
Peu pluie, vent chault, guerres,
  incursions.

In the year that Saturn and
Mars are equally fiery, the air
is very dry, a long meteor.
From hidden fires a great place
burns with heat, little rain, a
hot wind, wars and raids.

The configuration of Saturn and Mars is a common one, so further
information is needed to understand this quatrain. The dating of
the comet or meteor is probably the key.

En lieu bien proche non esloigné de
  Venus,
Les deux plus grans de l'Asie &
  d'Affrique
Du Rhin & Hister qu'on dira sont
  venus,
Cris, pleurs à Malte & costé
  ligustique.

At a nearby place not far from
Venus, the two greatest ones
of Asia and Africa will be said
to have come from the Rhine
and Hitler; cries and tears at
Malta and the Ligurian coast.

HITLER AND MUSSOLINI. TRIPARTITE PACT

The word Venus is the clue to this quatrain. It probably stands for
Venice, thus linking Italy with Hitler. The two dictators met not
far from the city at the Brenner Pass to seal the Tripartite Pact
with Asia, that is, the Japanese. The last line refers to the blockade
of Malta by the Italians, and the trouble on the Ligurian coast,
to the Allied bombing of Genoa, and to the bombardments by
British battleships operating from Gibraltar.

La cité grande les exiles tiendront,	The exiles will hold the great
Les citadins morts meurtris &	city, the citizens are dead,
chaffés:	murdered and driven out. The
Ceulx d'Aquilee à Parme pro-	people of Aqualeia will pro-
mettront,	mise Parma to show them the
Monstrer l'entree par les lieux non	entrance by untrodden paths.
trassés.	

Aqualeia was a great city in ancient times, but nothing more than
a village by the 16th Century. Parma belonged to the Papacy and
became an hereditary duchy for the Pope's bastard in 1545.

Bien contigue des grans monts	Very near the great mountains
Pyrenees,	of the Pyrenees, a man will
Un contre l'aigle grand copie	raise a great army against the
addresser:	Eagle. Veins will be opened,
Ouvertes veines, forces exterminees,	strength disappears; the leader
Comme jusque à Pau le chef	will chase them as far as the
viendra chasser.	Pau.

WELLINGTON'S CAMPAIGN IN THE PENINSULAR WAR

This describes Wellington's approach to France through Portugal
and Spain where he is to confront the Eagle, Napoleon. The opened
veins probably indicate the lost supply lines of the French when
they were driven back as far as the Pau, despite the French victory
at Toulouse, which was of uncertain value to Napoleon.

En lieu d'espouse les filles trucidées,	Instead of a bride the girls are
Meurtre à grand faulte ne sera	slaughtered, murder with such
superstile:[1]	wickedness, there will be no
Dedans le puys vestules inondées,	survivors. The vestals are
L'espouse estraincte par hauste	drowned in the wells, and the
d'Aconite.	bride killed by a draught of
	Aconite.

Aconite is a classical poison distilled from monkshood and wolfs-
bane. Otherwise the quatrain seems completely obscure.

[1] *superstile*—Misprint for *superstite* = survivor.

Les Artomiques par Agen & *l'Estore,* *A sainct Felix feront leur parlement:* *Ceux de Basas viendront à la* *mal'heure,* *Saisir Concon & Marsan prompte-* *ment.*	The Artomiques through Agen & Lectoure will hold their parliament at St. Felix. Those of Bazas will come at an unfortunate time to seize Condon & Marsan promptly.

What the Artomiques are is not certain. Artos in Greek means bread, but there is also a resemblance to the modern word atomic.

Le nepveu grand par forces prou- *vera,* *Le pache[1] faict du coeur pusillanime:* *Ferrare & Ast le Duc esprouvera,* *Par lors qu'au soir sera le panto-* *mime.*	The nephew shall prove by great strength the crime committed by a cowardly heart. The Duke will try Ferrara and Asti; then when the comedy takes place in the evening.

ASSASSINATION OF THE DUKE DE BERRY, 1820

This event is described vividly by Nostradamus in I. 84 and III. 96 in which quatrain he gives the date as well. The Duke de Berry was killed leaving the Opéra on the evening of 13th February 1820. The nephew who benefits from this is Napoleon III who later succeeds to the throne because of the assassination of the male heir.

Du lac liman & ceux de Brannon- *ices,[2]* *Tous assemblez contre ceux d'Aqui-* *taine* *Germains beaucoup, encor plus* *Souisses,* *Seront defaictz avec ceux* *d'Humaine.[3]*	The people of Lake Geneva and of Mâcon, all gathered against the people of Aquitaine; many Germans, even more Swiss will be routed together with those of Maine.

It is just possible that by *Humaine* in the last line Nostradamus is referring to the Humanists whom he would regard as responsible for the Protestants Reformation in Switzerland.

[1] *pache*—O.F. = treaty. Variant, *peche* = crime.
[2] *Brannonices*—Latin = people from around Mâcon.
[3] *Humaine*—Variant, *ceux du Maine.*

Prest à combatre fera defection.	He who was ready to fight will
Chef adversaire obtiendra la	desert, the chief adversary will
victoire.	win the victory. The rear guard
L'arriere garde fera defension,	will make a defence, those
Les deffaillans mort au blanc	faltering, dying in a white
territoire.	country.

WATERLOO, 1815

Marshal Grouchy is the deserter of the first line. He was commander of the French cavalry whose orders from Napoleon were delayed for twelve hours, but even when he received them, Grouchy did not do as asked. Wellington is the great adversary of the French who is victorious. The famous stand of Napoleon's Imperial Guard who fought to the last man is described in the following line, while the white country may be an indirect reference to Napoleon's retreat from Moscow in 1812, and is a direct one to the sign of the white cockade of the Bourbons. It was said that after Napoleon's capture there were so many white cockades that Paris looked as though there had been a fall of snow.

Les Nictobriges[1] par ceux de	The people of Agen by those
Perigort,	of Perigord will be troubled as
Seront vexez tenant jusques au	far as the Rhône. The asso-
Rosne:	ciation of Gascons & Bigorre,
L'associé de Gascons & Begorne,	betrays the Church, the priest
Trahir le temple, le prebstre	giving his sermon.
estant au prosne.	

Both Agen and Perigord are about two hundred miles west of the Rhône. Bigorre was a Gascon town, but also a rallying cry of Henri de Navarre's Huguenots, and the verse is probably hinting at the Protestant, Catholic conflict in France in the 16th Century.

[1] *Nictobriges* = the people around Agen.

SELIN monarque l'Italie pacifique,
Regnes unis Roi chrestien du
monde:
Mourrant voudra coucher en terre
blesique[1]
Apres pirates avoir chassé de
l'onde.

Selin king, Italy peaceful, kingdoms united by the Christian
king of the world. When he
dies, he will want to lie in
Blois territory, having chased
the pirates from the sea.

This is the quatrain upon which many 19th Century royalists
built their hopes of a great French king who would come and
change the face of Europe. The key to the quatrain is the word
SELIN; it comes from the Greek *Selene*, the Moon or Diana. There
is a strong possibility that Nostradamus went completely off the
rails with this series of quatrains and intended them for Henri II
and his mistress Diane de Poitiers. Henri II also adopted the moon
as his device, but nevertheless these verses were not understood by
his contemporaries. Perhaps they are a good example of retroactive
history, as I explain in the introduction, of something that seems
unlikely now ever to take place. The notion of a Christian king
governing the world seems impossible, particularly when compared with the quatrains which describe the situation envisaged
by Nostradamus between America and the Far East.

La grand armee de la pugne civile,
Pour de nuict Parme à l'estrange
trouvée,
Septante neuf meurtris dedans la
ville,
Les estrangiers passez tous à
l'espee.

The great army of the civil war,
Parma taken at night by
foreigners. Seventy-nine murdered in the town, the foreigners all put to the sword.

Parma was an Italian duchy and an ally of the French, so the
Spanish army is the most likely interpretation for line 2.

[1] *blesique*—Med. Latin, *Blesa* = Blois.

Sang Royal fuis, Monhurt, Mas, Eguillon,	Flee, royal blood, Monheurt, Mas, Aiguillon, the Landes
Remplis seront de Bourdelois les landes,	will be full of people from Bourdeaux. Navarre, Bigorre,
Navarre, Bigorre poinctes & eguillons,	points and spurs, deeply hungry they devour acorns of the cork
Profondz de faim vorer de liege glandes.	oak.

All these places are in South-west France and have probably some connection with IV. 76, the struggle of the Huguenots and Henri de Navarre against the Catholics. As mentioned before, Bigorre was the rallying cry of the Protestants.

80

Pres du grand fleuve, grand fosse, terre egeste,	Near the great river, a great trench, earth excavated, the
En quinze pars sera l'eau divisee:	water will be divided into
La cité prinse, feu, sang, cris conflict mettre	fifteen parts. The city taken, fire, blood, cries and battle
Et la plus part concerne au collisee.[1]	given, the greater part concerned with the collision.

THE MAGINOT LINE

James Laver suggests that this is the quatrain which persuaded the Abbé Torné to insist that France erected the infamous Maginot line, which fell so quickly to the Germans. The River in line 1 is the Rhine. Hitler partially ignored the Maginot line and advanced from other directions thus fulfilling lines 3 and 4. The collision becomes the series of battles fought in France during the Second World War.

81

Pont on fera promptement de nacelles,	A bridge will quickly be built from boats, to cross the army
Passer l'armee du grand prince Belgique:	of a great Belgian Prince. Poured forth inside not far
Dans profondres[2] *& non loing de Brucelles,*	from Brussels, having passed over, seven will be cut down by
Outre passés, detrenchés sept à picque.	a pike.

[1] *collisee*—Latin, *collisus* = clash.
[2] *profondres*—Latin, *profondatus* = poured forth.

When Nostradamus wrote, the word Belgian was archaic and could only have referred to Philip II, who had been given the territory in 1554 by the Emperor Charles V. An attack on Northern France, crossing the River Scheldt was made in the 1560s.

82

Amas s'approche venant d'Escla-vonie,	A mass of men will draw near, coming from Slavonia, the
L'Olestant vieux cité ruinera:	Destroyer will ruin the old
Fort desolee verra sa Romanie.	city, he will see his Romania
Puis la grand flamme estaindre ne sçaura.	quite desolated, then will not know how to extinguish the great flame.

NAPOLEON'S RETREAT FROM MOSCOW, 1812–13

The grande armée retreated from Moscow during the bitter winter of 1812/13. The word Olestant means Destroyer and Nostradamus refers to Napoleon as this in IV. 54 when he calls him the dreadful thunderbolt. The old city is Moscow which was razed to the ground by fire. The word Romanie cannot refer to Rumania which did not exist in Nostradamus' time, but may well refer to Rome, as Napoleon's young son had just been made king of Rome, and his empire would not continue for much longer. The great flame is probably a metaphor for the war which Napoleon started and which gathered in momentum to finally defeat him.

83

Combat nocturne le vaillant capitaine,	In a night battle the brave captain is overcome and flees,
Vaincu fuira peu de gens profligé:	ruined by a few men. His
Son peuple esmeu, sedition non vaine,	people are moved, they agitate successfully, his own son will
Son propre filz le tiendra assiegé.	hold him besieged.

84

Un grand d'Auxerre mourra bien miserable,	An important man from Auxerre will die very
Chassé de ceux qui soubs lui ont esté:	wretchedly, driven out by the people who were under him.
Serré de chaines, apres d'un rude cable,	Bound in chains, then with a strong rope, the year that Mars,
En l'an que Mars, Venus, & Sol, mis en esté.	Venus and the Sun are in conjunction in the summer.

This is a very rare conjunction but has not brought forth an important man from Auxerre to date, so this quatrain may apply to the future.

85

Le charbon blanc du noir sera chassé,	The white coal is driven out by the black, made a prisoner, led to the tumbril: his feet are tied together like a rogue, when the last born will let slip the falcon.
Prisonnier faicte mené au tombereau:	
More[1] Chameau sus piedz entrelassez,	
Lors le puisné sillera l'aubereau.	

LOUIS XVI AND THE FRENCH REVOLUTION

Charbon is an anagram for Bourbon, *noir* the usual anagram for king and white the colour of the Bourbon standard. Louis XVI was the last Bourbon king before the Revolution. He was imprisoned in the Temple and dragged on a tumbril, with his feet tied, to his death on 27th January 1793. The last line probably implies that his heir, Louis XVII, about whom there has been so much speculation and doubt, may have escaped from the Temple and have lived quietly in Europe. Nostradamus refers to this theme eslewhere in the Prophecies. Louis was the second son, the last born son of the family. His elder brother Charles died in 1795.

86

L'an que Saturne en eau sera conjoinct,	In the year Saturn is in conjunction with Aquarius, and with the Sun, the very powerful king will be received and anointed at Reims & Aix. After conquests he will murder innocent people.
Avecques Sol, le Roi fort & puissant:	
A Reims & Aix sera reçeu & oingt,	
Apres conquestes meurtrira innocens.	

The astrological conjunction of lines 1 and 2 is again reasonably rare. Reims is the traditional coronation site for the French Kings and Aix that of the German and Holy Roman Emperors. No king has been crowned in both places since Nostradamus' time. This is another of the quatrains used by French Royalists to predict the return of the French royal line.

[1] *more*—Latin, *mos, moris* = custom, a practice.

Un filz du Roi tant de langues aprins,	The son of a king, having learnt many languages, different from
A son aisné[1] au regne different:	his elder in the kingdom. His
Son pere beau[2] au plus grand filz comprins	father-in-law understanding well the elder son, will cause
Fera perir principal adherent.	the main adherent to perish.

The quatrain implies that the younger son of a king will take over the kingdom, the elder, legitimate heir having been removed by his father (in law?).

88

Le grand Antoine du nom de faicte sordide	Anthony, great in name, in his actions base, at the end will be
De Phthiriase[3] à son dernier rongé:	devoured by lice. One who is
Un qui de plomb voudra estre cupide,	eager for lead, passing the harbour will be drowned by the
Passant le port d'esleu sera plongé.	elected one.

A difficult prophecy for someone named Anthony. Phthiriasis, pediculosis, is an illness caused by lice.

89

Trente de Londres secret conjureront,	Thirty Londoners will secretly conspire against their king, the
Contre leur Roi sur le pont[4] entreprinse,	enterprise on the sea. He and his courtiers will not like death,
Lui, satalites la mort degousteront.	a fair king elected, native of
Un Roi esleu blonde, natif de Frize.	Friesland.

WILLIAM III OF ENGLAND

This is a good prediction of the Glorious Revolution of 1688–9. William III insisted that those lords who supported him in England should sign a document. There were certainly a number of conspirators crossing the seas to Holland and back before William sailed with his fleet. The ones who dislike death are James II and his supporters who decide to flee rather than fight the matter out

---

[1] aisné = elder or predecessor.

[2] pere beau = father-in-law or handsome father.

[3] Phthiriase—Phthisis = consumption. Phthiriasis = suffering from lice.

[4] pont—Latin, pontus = sea, not a bridge in this context.

once the Duke of Marlborough, who led the army, deserted their cause. It is not certain whether William III was fair-haired but he did come from Friesland. What makes this prophecy so interesting is that there was no possible Dutch candidate for the English throne while Nostradamus was alive.

90

Les deux copies aux murs ne pourront joindre.	The two armies cannot join up at the walls. At that time Milan and Pavia tremble. Hunger, thirst and doubt will weigh upon them so much, they will not have a scrap of meat, bread nor supplies.
Dans cest instant trembler Milan, Ticin:[1]	
Faim, soif doubtance si fort les viendra poindre,	
Chair, pain, ne vivres n'auront un seul boucin.[2]	

91

Au duc Gauloise contrainct battre au duelle,	For the French duke compelled to fight in a duel, the ship Mellele will not approach Monaco. Wrongly accused in perpetual prison his son will attempt to reign before his death.
La nef Mollele monech n'approchera,	
Tort accusé, prison perpetuelle,	
Son fils regner avant mort taschera.	

Mellele may be a corruption of Melilla, a Moroccan sea port, but it does not fit into context very well. Perhaps this quatrain has some connection with IV. 83? The last lines are very similar.

92

Teste tranchee du vaillant capitaine,	The head of the brave captain cut off it will be thrown down in front of his adversary. His body hung from the masts of the ship, confused, he will flee using oars in a contrary wind.
Sera gettee devant son adversaire:	
Son corps pendu de la chasse à l'antenne,	
Confus fuira par rames à vent contraire.	

RADIO OR RADAR EQUIPMENT?

It is interesting that Nostradamus used the word *antenne* here instead of *mât* for the ship's mast. Perhaps he was using this word to indicate complex equipment with which he was not familiar

[1] *Ticin*—Latin, *Ticinum* = Pavia.
[2] *boucin*—Provençal = mouthful, morsel.

but which he recognized to be scientific, such as a radio mast or radar equipment?

93

Un serpent veu proche du lict royal;	A serpent will be seen near the royal bed by a lady at night,
Sera par dame nuict chiens n'abayeront:	the watchdogs will not bark;
Lors naistre en France un Prince tant royal,	Then will be born in France a Prince so royal, that all the princes will see him as a gift from heaven.
Du ciel venu tous les Princes verront.	

THE COUNT DE CHAMBORD, 1820–83

The Duchesse de Berry gave birth to a son in 1820, seven months after he husband's assassination. The legitimacy of the birth was contested by the Duke of Orléans, the snake, who had right of entry as a member of the family and so the watchdogs were not alerted. This birth of a grandson to Charles X was the cause of great rejoicing to French monarchists and the child was called 'Dieudonné', a gift from heaven, as Nostradamus so aptly puts it.

94

Deux grans freres seront chassez d'Espaigne,	Two great brothers will be driven out of Spain, the elder is beaten under the Pyrenean mountains. The sea is reddened, the Rhône, blood in Lake Geneva from Germany, Narbonne and Beziers contaminated by Agde.
L'aisné vaincu sous les monts Pyrenees:	
Rougir mer, rosne, sang lemam d'Alemaigne,	
Narbon, Blyterre, d'Agath[1] contaminees.	

A detailed qutrain containing five separate predictions:
1 Exile for two Spanish leaders.
2 Defeat for one of them near the Pyrenees.
3 A bloody naval battle.
4 An attack against Geneva from Germany.
5 A possible plague spreading from Agde, see also VIII. 21 to local towns.

[1] *Agatha*—Latin = Agde.

La regne à deux laissé bien peu tiendront,	The rule left to two, they will hold it a very short time. Three
Trois and sept mois passés feront la guerre.	years and seven months having passed they will go to war. The
Les deux vestales contre eux rebelleront,	two vestals will rebel against them; the victor then born on
Victor puis nay en Armorique terre.	American soil.

U.S.A. AND WAR?

If in this quatrain the two powers are understood to be world powers, it implies that 3 years and 7 months after the Russian/ American alliance, which Nostradamus predicts elsewhere, has taken place they will go to war against Asia. *Vestales* in line 3 is probably a corruption of *vassals*—two smaller countries disagree with this decision and perhaps stay neutral. The final victory lies in the West, with America. But see also III. 60 and IV. 50 for a possible dating in the 70s etc.

La soeur aisnée de l'isle Britannique,	The elder sister of the island of Britain will be born fifteen
Quinze ans devant le frere aura naissance:	years before her brother. Because of his promise proving to
Par son promis moyennant verrifique,	be true, she will succeed to the kingdom of the Balance.
Succedera au regne de balance.	

WILLIAM AND MARY

Mary was the elder sister of James III, who never came to the English throne, but she was in fact twenty-six, not fifteen years older than her brother. Mary acceded to the throne through her own, and her husband William of Orange's, promises to the English parliament. The Balance is Libra, the zodiacal sign, which Nostradamus seems here to apply to England although many astrologers apply it to Austria and Savoy. It also governs a trading nation, which the British certainly are. Note that again Nostradamus speaks of the British Isles and not of England which immediately dates the quatrain later than 1603.

L'an que Mercure, Mars, Venus retrograde, *Du grand Monarque la ligne ne faillit:* *Esleu du peuple l'usitant[1] pres de Gagdole,[2]* *Qu'en paix & regne viendra fort envieillir.*	In the year that Mercury, Mars and Venus are retrograde, the family line of the great King will not fail. Elected by the Portuguese people near Cadiz, who in peace will grow very old in his kingdom.

This quatrain seems to describe the Portuguese succession and is limited in time by the conjunction of line 1. It seems also to imply that the Portuguese king is elected in Spain, which never happened. But Philip II of Spain seized the Portuguese throne and ruled it until 1621, followed by his son Philip III, until the Portuguese revolted against the Spanish in 1640. However, Nostradamus did appear to understand the Spanish seizure of the Portuguese throne.

Les Albanois, passeront dedans Rome, *Moyennant Langres demipler[3] affublés,* *Marquis & Duc ne pardonnes à l'homme,* *Feu, sang, morbilles[4] point d'eau, faillir les bleds.*	The people of Alba will cross into Rome, by means of Langres the multitude are weakened. The Marquis and the Duke will spare no man, fire, blood and smallpox, no water, the crops will fail.

The word *Albanois* is hard to interpret. It probably stands for the troops of the Duke of Alba, but Albania is a possibility. The many disasters are obscure. *Langres* is in Champagne, so possibly it is the same person as in VII. 4?

[1] *usitant*—Misreading for *Lusitans* = Portuguese.

[2] *Gagdole*—Probable misprint for *Gades* = Cadiz, as the present reading doesn't even rhyme and is obviously incorrect.

[3] *demipler*—A word invented by Nostradamus, probably from the Greek, *demis-pleres* = mob-full or multitude.

[4] *morbilles*—O.F. = smallpox.

L'aisné vaillant de la fille du Roy,	The brave eldest son of a king's
Repoussera si profond les Celtiques:	daughter will drive the Celts
Qu'il mettra foudres, combien en	back very far. He will use
tel arroi	thunderbolts, so many in such
Peu & loing puis profond és	an array, few and distant, then
Hesperiques.[1]	deep into the West.

MISSILES OR ROCKETS?

The Celts referred to here are the French who are driven back by
an unidentified leader. He fights with such fearful and far-reaching weapons that they can even penetrate as far as Spain or
America, implying either mortar shells, missiles or possibly rockets
with warheads.

De feu celeste au Royal edifice,	Fire will fall from the sky on to
Quant la lumiere de Mars defail-	the royal building when the
lira:	light of war is weakened. For
Sept mois grand guerre, mort gent	seven months a great war,
de malefice,	people dead through evil,
Rouen, Eureux au Roi ne faillira.	Rouen and Evreux will not fail
	the king.

FRANCO-PRUSSIAN WAR, 1870–71

During the siege of Paris the royal palace, the Tuileries, was
destroyed by cannon fire. The glory of the Bonaparte family was
weakened and almost ended by this war. Napoleon III was to die
two years later, and France remained a republic from then on.
The Franco-Prussian war did last for seven months, July 1870 to
February 1871, an accurate prediction. The last line refers to
towns in Normandy, which part of France remained loyal to the
king and wanted to restore the monarchy through the National
Assembly.

[1] *Hesperiques*—As always, either the Western lands of Spain and
Portugal, or the U.S.A.

CENTURY V

1*   Murder of Louis XVII
2
3*   Duke of Lorraine
4*   Second World War
5*   Louis XVI and Marie Antoinette
6*   Napoleon III
7*   Louis Philippe
8*?
9*   Assassination attempt. Napoleon III
10*   Assassination attempt (*continued*)
11*   Second World War. Italy and Japan
12*   Thirty Years War
13*   Thirty Years War (*continued*)
14*   Napoleon's campaigns
15*   Pius VII and Napoleon, 1808
16*   Second World War. Africa and Greece
17
18
19
20*   Napoleon III, 1859
21
22?
23?   Two Allies
24
25*   1987?
26*   Constantine of Greece
27
28*   Assassination of King Umberto of Italy
29*   Hitler and the Vatican
30*   Sack of Rome, 1797
31
32*   Franco-Prussian War
33*   Atrocities at Nantes, 1793

34?
35
36
37
38*   Louis XV
39*   Count de Chambord
40**   U.S.A., France and the Common Market
41
42*   Return of Savoy to France
43
44
45*   Battle of Sedan, 1940
46?   New Pope?
47
48
49?   Future Pope from France
50
51**   Second World War. The Allies
52
53
54*F? Man from East?
55
56*   New Pope
57**   Montgolfier balloon, 1783
58*   1627
59
60*   Cromwell
61*   Eugène de Beauharnais
62
63
64
65
66
67*   France and the Vatican
68?
69*   Louis Philippe, 1830
70
71
72   Edict of Poitiers, 1577
73
74
75
76

77
78**F Alliance between U.S.A. and U.S.S.R.?
79*   Napoleon
80
81*?   Berlin Wall?
82
83
84
85*   League of Nations
86   France and Turkey
87
88*   1815. Savona
89
90*F? Chemical Warfare in Greece and Balkans?
91
92*   Future of the Vatican
93*   The Young Pretender
94*   Hitler and Russia
95
96
97   Man in the Iron Mask
98
99   Napoleon and the last of the Stuarts
100

KEY: * Of interest. F? Possibly referring to the future.

Avant venu de ruine Celtique,	Before the ruin of France, there
Dedans le temple deux parlementer-	will be parliamentary discus-
ont	sions about the second. Stabbed
Poignard coeur, d'un monté au	to the heart by one riding on a
coursier & pique,	charger with a lance, they will
Sans faire bruit le grand enter-	bury the great one secretly.
reront.	

THE MURDER OF LOUIS XVII (1785–95?)

There has always been much speculation about the fate of Louis XVII, the second son and heir of Louis XVI and Marie Antoinette. The King and his family were housed in the Temple in 1792, when the Revolutionary mobs appeared to be getting out of hand. The fate of the whole family was debated by the newly formed French Legislative Assembly (*parlementeront*). It is not known how Louis XVII died but Nostradamus indicates clearly that he was killed in line 4. The third line describes his killer as an unidentified soldier. He was appallingly ill-treated in prison, separated from his mother and sisters and kept in the dark for months on end, like a wild beast. In May 1795 he was declared to be seriously ill and his death was announced on 8th June. Several pretenders came forward during the next forty years claiming to be the young Prince, but if Nostradamus is correct he was buried at the Church of St. Marguerite on 10th June, as was officially announced, without even a stone to mark the spot '*sans faire bruit*'.

Seps conjurés au banquet feront	Seven conspirators at a banquet
luire,	will cause their weapons to flash
Contre les trois le fer hors de navire:	against the three who come
L'un des deux classes au grand fera	from the ship. One of the two
conduire	will take the fleet to the leader
Quand par le mail. Denier au front	when the other will shoot him
lui tire.	in the forehead through his
	armour.

Le successeur de la Duché viendra,	The successor to the Duchy will
Beaucoup plus outre que la mer de	come from far beyond the sea of
Tosquane:	Tuscany. A French branch will
Gauloise branche la Florence tiendra,	hold Florence, in its wake a
Dans son giron d'accord nautique	nautical agreement (with the
Rane.[1]	frog?).

DUKE OF LORRAINE, 1737

Florence was the capital of the Duchy of Tuscany from the rule of Alessandro de' Medici in 1531 until the death of Gian Gastone in 1737 when the Duchy was assigned to Francis, Duke of Lorraine, a Frenchman, and remained in the Lorraine family until 1859, except during the French Revolution. The reference to a nautical agreement and a frog is unclear. It may refer to the myth in which the earliest inhabitants of Tuscany were turned into frogs by Bacchus.

Le gros mastin de cité deschassé,	The great mastiff is driven out
Sera fasché de l'etrange alliance,	of the city, angered by the
Apres aux champs avoir le cerf	foreign alliance. Later having
chassé	chased the stag to the field, the
Le lous & l'Ours se donront	wolf and the bear will defy each
defiance.	other.

SECOND WORLD WAR

The other name for a mastiff in French is *le dogue anglais,* and England is probably intended in line 1. Angered by a foreign treaty England chases the stag to the battlefield where the wolf (Italy) and the Bear (Russia) are defying each other. This appears to refer to the Second World War when the Russians entered the war as British Allies.

Souz ombre faincte d'oster de	Beneath the faint pretext of re-
servitude,	moving servitude, the people
Peuple & cité l'usurpera lui	and the city will themselves
mesmes:	usurp power. He will do worse
Pire fera par fraux de jeune pute,	because of the trickery of a
Livré au champ lisant le faux	young whore, delivered in the
proesme.	field, reading the false promise.

[1] *Rane*—Latin, *rana* = a frog, possible misprint for *rame*=oar, which is more suitable.

LOUIS XVI AND MARIE ANTOINETTE

This describes the French Revolution, which replaced Louis XVI's rule with one just as autocratic. The people of Paris took over government of their city, after the revolt of the Bastille, 14th July 1789. The woman who makes things worse by her double dealing is Marie Antoinette, by her general extravagance and in particular by the affair of the diamond necklace from which her popularity never recovered. When she and Louis were later caught trying to go to St. Cloud in 1792, the family were turned back by the crowds who said to Louis XVI, 'we love you alone'. The false promises were those given by the king when he promised not to try to escape from the Temple where he and his family had been placed to protect them from the people. They fled to Varennes in 1792 and were caught. See IX. 20, and IX. 34.

6

Au roi l'Augur sur le chef la main mettre,	The Augur will put his hand on the king's head and pray for
Viendra prier pour la paix Italique:	peace in Italy. The sceptre will
A la main gauche viendra changer le sceptre	be changed to his left hand, from king he will become a
De Roi viendra Empire pacifique.	peaceful Emperor.

NAPOLEON III

The Pope was godfather by proxy to the son of Louis Napoleon, later Napoleon III. He was not too successful in his dealings with Italy and the Vatican because the Roman Revolutionaries felt he was too accommodating. The changing of the sceptre probably refers to Napoleon III's underhand manipulation of the Revolution in France of 1848 and to the fact that he declared himself Emperor on 2nd December 1851. Nostradamus views him as a peaceful monarch, which ties in well with the famous statement Napoleon III made on acquiring power. '*L'empire, c'est la paix.*' The art of Empire is peace.

7

Du Triumvir seront trouvé les os,	The bones of the Triumvir will
Cherchant profond thresor aenigmatique:	be found by those searching for a deep and enigmatic treasure.
Ceux d'alentour ne seront en repos.	Those around will not be peace-
Ce concaver marbre & plomb metallique.	ful. This hollowing of marble and metallic lead.

This describes Louis Philippe's attempt to revive his waning popularity when he brought back Napoleon's ashes from St. Helena and interred them in the Invalides. Triumvir is the key word; after the *coup d'état* of 18th Brumaire Napoleon reduced the five members of the Directory to three, and made himself first Consul. The treasure Louis Philippe was searching vainly for was Napoleon's popular appeal, some of which he hoped to gain by honouring Napoleon's ashes. The restless people are the Bonapartistes who were politically encouraged by this and insisted on helping in the task of burying the ashes. The coffin itself was of lead.

8

Sera laissé le feu vif, mort caché,	There will be let loose living fire
Dedans les globes horrible espouvantable,	and hidden death, fearful inside dreadful globes. By night
De nuict à classe cité en poudre lasché,	the city will be reduced to rubble by the fleet, the city on
La cite à feu, l'ennemi favorable.	fire, helpful to the enemy.

The dreadful object Nostradamus visualizes here is certainly no cannonball but some sort of bomb containing explosive material. Ships appear to bombard a city which, once on fire, is a landmark probably helpful to enemy aircraft.

9

Jusques au fonds la grand arq demolue,	At the foot of the great fallen arch, the friend is captured
Par chef captif, l'ami anticipé:	forestalled by the leader. A
Naistra de dame front face chevelue,	woman will bear a son whose
Lors par astuce Duc à mort attrapé.	face and forehead are covered with hair; then through cunning the Duke escapes death.

ASSASSINATION ATTEMPT ON NAPOLEON III, 1858
The first two lines are thought to refer to Napoleon III who had been involved in the Italian revolutionary movement when a young man. After some years of power in France the Italians felt he had betrayed their cause and four of them attempted to assassinate him as he left the Opéra on the night of 14th January 1858. The plot

was led by Count Orsini—the building was damaged but did not collapse as Nostradamus describes it, although several bystanders were killed. The captured friend was Pieri, a friend of Orsini's, who was arrested before the explosion. Napoleon III was only slightly hurt. The third line is obscure but the last implies that Napoleon III escaped death through foreknowledge, probably due to Pieri's arrest. This quatrain appears to lead straight on to the next one, presumably Nostradamus forgot to separate them.

10

Un chef Celtique dans le conflict blessé,	A French leader wounded in the struggle sees his subjects struck dead near the theatre. Hustled by enemies with bloody wounds, he will be saved from the four by unknown people.
Aupres de cave voyant siens mort abbatre:	
De sang & plaies & d'ennemis pressé,	
Et secourus par incognus de quatre.	

ASSASSINATION ATTEMPT, NAPOLEON III
(*continued*)

As stated in V. 9. Napoleon III was slightly wounded when Italian revolutionaries attempted to kill him with a bomb outside the Opéra. (*Cavea* is the Latin word for theatre). The ordinary people standing around him saved him by shielding him from the blast. The four conspirators were Orsini, Pieri, Gomez and Rudio.

11

Mer par solaires seure ne passera,	Those of the sun will not cross the sea in safety, the people of Venus will hold the whole of Africa. Then Saturn occupies their kingdom no longer and the part of Asia will change.
Ceux de Venus tiendront toute l'Affrique:	
Leur regne plus Saturne n'occupera,	
Et changera la part Asiatique.	

SECOND WORLD WAR. ITALY AND
THE EAST, 1941-3

Japan's flag is a sun; her ships will not be safe once she has entered the war, and caused Asian politics to change, as China then joined with the Allied Powers in 1941. The people of Venice (Venus is a common corruption for this city throughout the Prophecies) which stands for Italy, are fighting with Rommel in North Africa. The malign influence of Saturn on Italian affairs causes them to withdraw from the war in 1943.

Aupres du lac Leman sera conduite,	Near Lake Geneva he will be
Par garse estrange cité voulant trahir:	led by a foreign woman who wants to betray the city. Before
Avant son meutre à Auspourg la grande suitte,	her death a great retinue will come to Augsburg. They will
Et ceux du Rhin la viendront invahir.	come to invade the people of the Rhine.

THIRTY YEARS WAR, 1636

The Battle of Augsburg, during the Thirty Years War forced the retreat of Bernhard, Duke of Saxe Weimar, across the Rhine. This left Southern and Central Germany exposed to the attacks of the Habsburg armies of the Holy Roman Emperor, Ferdinand II. Augsburg fell to Ferdinand as did other towns along the Rhine near the Swiss border. The use of the word Auspourg by Nostradamus is probably a typical pun, containing the two key words of the Habsburg and Augsbourg. The only puzzle is the young woman.

Par grand fureur le Roi Romain Belgique	In a great rage the Roman king will wish to trouble Belgium
Vexer vouldra par phalange barbare:	with barbarian warriors. In a gnashing fury he will chase the
Fureur grinsseant chassera gent Libyque	Libyan peoples from Hungary as far as Gibraltar.
Despuis Pannons[1] jusques Hercules la hare.[2]	

THIRTY YEARS WAR

The Holy Roman Emperor Ferdinand II and Philip of Spain were allied together against Denmark, Norway and Sweden. In 1648 the Treaty of Westphalia recognized the republic of the United Netherlands, part of which is now modern Belgium. The barbarian warriors are the German Protestant powers. The Thirty Years War started as a revolt in Bohemia and spread as far as Gibraltar when Spain and France refused to recognize the 1648 treaty and continued to fight until the Treaty of the Pyrenees in 1659.

[1] *Pannons*—Latin, *Pannonia* = now Hungary.
[2] *hare*—Misprint for *bare* = pillars of Hercules, or Gibraltar.

Saturne & Mars en Leo Espagne captifve,	Saturn and Mars in Leo, Spain is captive, taken in battle by a
Par chef Libyque au conflict attrapé,	Libyan leader. Near when Malta and (the knights of)
Proche de Malthe, Heredde prins vive,	Rhodes are captured alive, and the Roman power smitten by
Et Romain sceptre sera par coq frappé.	the cock.

NAPOLEON'S CAMPAIGNS, 1797–1807/8

The only time that Spain can be considered as captive is during the Peninsular War of 1807/8, when Napoleon's troops occupied both Spain and Portugal. The resistance of Spanish patriots led the British to send in an army under General Sir Arthur Wellesley, who succeeded in driving out the French after five years of fighting. The rest of the quatrain refers to events ten years earlier. In 1797 the first action of Napoleon's Egyptian campaign was the capture of Malta held by the Knights of Rhodes, Heredde being an anagram. Finally at the Treaty of Tolentino the Pope ceded part of the Vatican and Church states to the cock, the symbol of France.

15

En navigant captif prins grand pontife,	While sailing, the great Pope will be captured; great pre-
Grans aprets faillir les clercz tumultuez:	parations by the troubled clerics fail. The second elected absent,
Second esleu absent son bien debise,	his power declines, his favourite
Son favori bastard à mort tué.	bastard, put to death.

PIUS VII AND NAPOLEON, 1808

Pius VII was taken prisoner by the French in 1808 having travelled to crown Napoleon in Paris in 1804. He is the second Pope to be materially hurt by Napoleon, the first was Pius VI who died in exile at Valence. The trouble among the clergy describes the great religious discontent in France after the abolition of the established Church. The bastard of the final line is usually interpreted as Napoleon inheriting a crown that was not rightfully his, who having received the favours of the Pope, sacks Rome in 1808 and imprisons the Pope, although he doesn't kill him.

A son hault pris plus la lerme sabee,	The Sabine tears will no longer be of value, human flesh
D'humaine chair par mort en cendres mettre,	through death is burnt to ashes; the island of Pharos disturbed
A l'isle Pharos par croisars per-turbee,	by (man of) the cross, when at Rhodes a dreadful sight is seen.
Alors qu'à Rodes paroistra dur espectre.	

SECOND WORLD WAR. AFRICA AND GREECE

This quatrain seems to implicate Italy with the appalling deaths of Jews and others in the German concentration camps. It is important to remember that cremation was anathema to a 16th-Century man such as Nostradamus, and condemned not only by the Church but also socially. Pharos is an island opposite Alexandria and is probably used by Nostradamus to indicate Tobruk which is not far from there. It was disturbed several times by the men of the cross, the Nazis, as the battles in the African desert between the Allies and Rommel waged back and forth. The dreadful sight at Rhodes would be the invasion of Greece by Mussolini in 1940, followed by the Germans in 1941. Despite British evacuations, the Germans claimed 270,000 prisoners. In fact about 70,000 people were believed to have died.

17

De nuict passant le roi pres d'une Andronne,	The king, passing at night through a narrow lane, the man
Celui de Cypres & principal guette:	from Cyprus is the main guard;
Le roi failli la main fuict long du Rosne,	the king dies, the hand flees the length of the Rhône: the con-
Les conjurés l'iront à mort mettre.	spirators will put him to death.

Cyprus belonged to Venice until 1571, but the place of this conspiracy is obscure.

18

De deuil mourra l'infelix profligé,	The wretched man, destroyed, will die of grief. His victorious
Celebrera son vitrix l'hecatombe:	consort will celebrate the cere-
Pristine loi franc edict redigé,	monies. Former laws, free edicts
Le mur & Prince au septiesme jour tombe.	drawn up, both the Prince and the wall fall on the seventh day.

This quatrain implies that a man is destroyed by his actions, whereas his wife celebrates his death and brings an end to an oppressive régime. The wall may refer to the legal repressions, or may be understood literally. There is a hint that the wife may have helped towards his death. The seventh day means either a Sunday or, more literally, that the Prince took seven days to die.

19

Le grand Royal d'or, d'aerain augmenté,	The great golden Royal, augmented by brass breaks the covenant; war is started by a young man. The people are afflicted by a lamented leader, the land will be covered with barbarian blood.
Rompu la pache,[1] par jeune ouverte guerre:	
Peuple affligé par un chef lamenté	
De sang barbare sera converre terre.	

20

Dela les Alpes grand armée passera,	A great Army will cross over the Alps. A short while before a wretched monster will be born. In a strange way, suddenly, the great Tuscan will return to his native land.
Un peu devant naistre monstre vapin:	
Prodigieux & subit tournera,	
Le grand Tosquan à son lieu plus propin.	

NAPOLEON III, 1859

Napoleon III crossed the Alps against Austria in 1859. The evil monster is the Italian Revolution; it is interesting to note that one of the first results of the 1859 campaign was to drive the Grand Duke of Tuscany, Leopold II, from Florence. He was a Habsburg and retired to Austria to escape the Italians, thus fulfilling line 4 in retiring to his native land. The wretched monster is understood to refer to Garibaldi.

21

Par le trespas du monarque latin,	By the death of a Latin king. Those people whom he will have assisted during his reign; the fire glows, the booty is shared out; public death for the bold incursors.
Ceux qu'il aura par regne secouruz:	
Le feu luira, divisé le butin,	
La mort publique aux hardis incoruz.	

The Latin monarch is difficult to interpret. If it stands for the ruler of Latium it means the Pope. It could possibly refer to Mussolini and the Fascists.

[1] *pacha*—Provençal = treaty, covenant.

Avant qu'à Rome grand aie rendu l'ame,	Before the great man gives up his soul at Rome, there is much
Effrayeur grande à larmée estrangere:	fear among the foreign army. The ambush by the squadrons
Par Esquadrons, l'embusche pres de Parme,	takes place near Parma, then the two red ones will feast to-
Puis les deux rouges ensemble feront chere.	gether.

While a Pope lies dying some trouble occurs in Parma, in Northern Italy. At the same time two revolutionary leaders will be meeting each other in a festive way. It may continue in the next quatrain.

Les deux contens seront unis ensemble,	The two contented men are united together when most
Quand la pluspart à Mars seront conjoinct.	(planets) are conjunct with Mars. The African leader
Le grand d'Affrique en effrayeur & tremble:	trembles in terror. The twin alliance scattered by the fleet.
DUUMVIRAT par la classe desjoinct.	

TWO ALLIES

If the two mentioned here are a continuation of the two revolutionaries of V. 22, they are very soon involved in war with most other nations. Africa is troubled by the alliance which is finally broken through naval strength.

Le regne & lois souz Venus eslevé,	The kingdom and law raised under Venus, Saturn will domi-
Saturne aura sus Jupiter empire:	nate Jupiter. Law and empire
La loi & regne par le Soleil levé,	raised by the Sun, will endure
Par Saturnins endurera le pire.	the worst through those of Saturn.

This verse is similar to V. 11, but the meanings of Saturn and Venus are unclear. Nostradamus is probably using a configuration for dating purposes. The Sun could also stand for Charles V, or the Catholic Church. It is a very difficult quatrain to decipher.

Le prince Arabe Mars, Sol, Venus, *Lyon,* *Regne d'Eglise par mer succombera:* *Devers la Perse bien pres d'un million,* *Bisance, Egypte, ver. serp.[1] in-* *vadera.*	The Arab Prince, Mars, the Sun, Venus and Leo, the rule of the Church will succumb to the sea. Towards Persia very nearly a million men will invade Egypt and Byzantium, the true serpent.

1987?

When Mars, the Sun and Venus are in conjunction with Leo, the following predictions are forecast about a new Arabian Empire. It will attack Persia, Egypt, Constantinople (Byzantium) and the navies of Christendom. According to the commentator Lee McCann (1942) this conjunction will take place on 21st August 1987. This must therefore in some way link up with the quatrains about the uprising in Asia.

26

La gent esclave par un heur martial, *Viendra en haut degré tant esleuee:* *Changeront prince, naistre un pro-* *vincial,* *Passer la mer copie aux monts levee.*	The Slav people, through fortune in war, will become elevated to a high degree. They will change their Prince, one born a provincial; an army raised in the mountains to cross over the sea.

KING CONSTANTINE OF GREECE, 1917–20

The word *esclave* may mean either slave of Slav. The Russians were not regarded as Slavs in Nostradamus' day, this word was used to describe the Balkan peoples. The Greeks, partially Slav, rose against the Turks and landed troops at Smyrna in 1919 and stayed there until 1922. They also changed their king at this time as Nostradamus predicted. King Constantine, who was exiled in 1917, was recalled in 1920 but exiled again in 1922. Although of German origins Constantine was born in Athens. His rival was Premier Venizelos from Crete.

[1] *ver. serp.*—Suggested interpretation, *vera serpens* = true serpent.

Par feu & armes non loing de la marnegro,	With fire and weapons, not far from the Black Sea, he will
Viendra de Perse occuper Trebisonde:	come from Persia to occupy Trebizond. Pharos and Mytil-
Trembler Phatos Methelin, Sol alegro,	ene tremble, the Sun is bright, the Adriatic sea covered with
De sang Arabe d'Adrie couvert onde:	Arab blood.

Does this quatrain link up with V. 25? It is not clear whether the conquerors are the Arabs or Persians. Pharos is an island off Alexandria and Mytilene is the Greek island of Lesbos. Perhaps *Sol alegro* has a connection with a victorious crusade, which afterwards degenerates into a fight among the victors.

28

Le bras pendu & la jambe liée,	His arm hung and his leg
Visage pasle au seing poignard caché:	bound, with pale face and a dagger hidden in his breast:
Trois qui seront jurez de la meslee,	Three who will be sworn in the
Au grand de Gennes sera le fer lasché.	scuffle, against the great one of Genoa will the blade be drawn.

ASSASSINATION OF KING UMBERTO
OF ITALY, 1900

King Umberto was assassinated on 29th July 1900 by an unemployed smith called Acciarito. Genoa belonged to Savoy after 1815. Nostradamus seems to imply that the assassin had an arm in a sling, which was not the case in this instance. It is therefore possible that another assassination is referred to here.

29

La liberté ne sera recouvree,	Liberty will not be regained; it
L'occupera noir fier vilain inique:	will be occupied by a black, proud, villainous and unjust
Quand la matiere du pont sera ouvree,	man. When the matter of the Pope is opened by Hitler, the
D'Hister, Venise faschée la republique.	republic of Venice will be vexed.

HITLER, MUSSOLINI AND THE PAPACY

This quatrain describes Mussolini's intrigues to secure an alliance with Hitler between the years 1934–8. Hitler and Mussolini met at Venice—by this time a republic with Mussolini as its dictator. Note how accurate Nostradamus' details are. The adjective black probably refers to the Fascisti—the blackshirts. The matter of the Pope (Pontifex) refers to the Concordat drawn up between Mussolini and the Pope in 1928, which line 4 infers will bring trouble or war to Italy, as indeed it did.

30

Tout à l'entour de la grand Cité,
Seront soldats logez par champs &
villes:
Donner assaut Paris, Rome incité,
Sur le pont lors sera faicte grande
pille.

All around the great city soldiers will be billeted in fields and towns. Paris will make the assault, Rome incited: there will be great pillage made against the Pont(iff).

SACK OF ROME, 1797/1808

This verse describes Rome being sacked by the French which occured twice, in 1797 and 1808. The great pillage refers to the fact that the Pope was made to cede part of the Papal States in 1797, and in 1809 they were incorporated into the republic of France.

31

Par terre Attique chef de la sapience,
Qui de present est la rose du monde :
Pont ruiné & sa grand pre-
eminence,
Sera subdite & naufrage des undes.

From the land of Attica, source of all wisdom which at the present is the rose of the world: the Pont(iff) ruined, its great pre-eminence will be subjected and wrecked beneath the waves.

Apart from commentating that this is the third successive verse with the word Pont possibly implying the Papacy, I cannot decipher this verse. Attica if taken literally means South-eastern Greece, north of the Peloponnesus. It is not clear what ruins the Papacy.

Où tout bon est tout bien Soleil & Lune,	Where all is good, all well abundant, in Sun and Moon its
Est abondant sa ruine s'approche:	ruin approaches. It comes from
Du ciel s'advance vaner ta fortune,	heaven as you boast of your
En mesme estat que la septiesme roche.	fortune, in the same state as the seventh rock.

FRANCO-PRUSSIAN WAR, 1870–1

James Laver suggests that this refers to the Franco-Prussian war. The use of *ta fortune*, the second person singular is applied only to France by Nostradamus. When Paris is at the height of her fortune, the Exposition Universelle of 1867, etc; then the Prussians will declare war, as they did on 19th July 1870. The seventh rock is understood as a reference to the desolation of the seventh rock in the Apocalypse.

Des principaux de cité rebellee	Some of the principal citizens
Qui tiendront fort pour liberté ravoir:	of the rebellious city who will try hard to regain their liberty;
Detrencher masles, infelice meslee,	the men are cut up, unhappy
Cris hurlemens à Nantes piteux voir.	confusion; Cries, groans at Nantes pitiful to see.

ATROCITIES AT NANTES, 1793

During the excesses of the Revolution, Nantes suffered a series of appalling atrocities known as the Noyades. In 1793 its principal citizens had allied themselves with neighbouring districts and declared a Central Assembly of Resistance to Oppression. The National Convention quickly broke this counter-Revolution. Over 1,000 citizens were guillotined (cut up); others were tied, two together, face to face, naked, and placed in boats which were rowed to the middle of the river Loire and scuttled. The wretched victims were watched by their executioners as they drowned in a threshing mob of bodies.

Du plus profond de l'occident Anglois.	From the deepest part of the English West where is the
Où est le chef de l'isle Britannique:	leader of the British Isles; a
Entrera classe dans Gironde par Blois,	fleet will enter Gironde through Blois, through wine and salt,
Par vin & sel, feux cachez aux barriques.	fires hidden in casks.

It is unlikely that this quatrain refers to the West of England although these are the traditional lands of the heir to the English throne, c.f. Prince of Wales and the Duchy of Cornwall. Some interpret it as suggesting the Anglicization of North America, or even the Hundred Years War when the English held the West Coast of France for some decades. The wine and salt are suggested as metaphors for taxation, like the gabelle or salt tax. The fires in casks may be weapons. This quatrain is possibly still to be fulfilled.

35

Par cité franche de la grand mer Seline,
Qui porte encores à l'estomac la pierre:
Angloise classe viendra soubs la bruine
Un rameau prendre, du grand ouverte guerre.

For the free city of the great crescent sea, which still carries the stone in its stomach, an English fleet will come in under the mist to seize a branch, war opened by the great one.

This quatrain may connect with the preceding one and refer to a series of protracted encounters with English invaders. The crescent sea may have the usual meaning of Genoa, but is a rare theatre of operations for a British fleet.

36

De soeur le frere par simulte faintise,
Viendra mesler rosee en mineral:
Sur la placente[1] donne à vielle tardifve,
Meurt, le goustant sera simple & rural.

The sisters' brother through feigned deceit will come to mix dew into the mineral. On the cake given to the slow old woman who dies tasting it, she will be simple and rustic.

The only information I can offer here is that the *rosee*, dew, in the second line may stand for a Latin poison, *rosarius*, which was extracted from the laurel rose.

[1] *placente*—Latin, *placenta* = a cake.

Trois cents feront d'un vouloir &
accord,
Que pour venir au bout de leur
attaincte:
Vingt mois apres tous & records,
Leur Roi trahi simulant haine
saincte.

Three hundred will be of one agreement and accord to come to the execution of their end; twenty months later, after all remembrance, their king is betrayed pretending a feigned hatred.

Ce grand monarque qu'au mort
succedera,
Donnera vie illicite & lubrique,
Par nonchalance à tous concedera,
Qu'à la parfin faudra la loi
Salique.

He who succeeds upon the death of a great king will lead an illicit and debauched life. Through carelessness he will give way to all so that in the end Salic law will fail.

LOUIS XV

Louis XV succeeded to his great grandfather Louis XIV (great in both senses) and led a life of great debauchery and irresponsibility. An example of this was his famous *seraglio* at the Parc des Cerfs, and, of course, the influence of Madame de Pompadour. The *Encyclopaedia Britannica* says that it is difficult to find a European king whose life shows such a record of vulgar vice. His carelessness in state affairs was partially responsible for the troubles which were to come to a head under the Revolution. Salic law forbade the accession of women to the throne. Louis was succeeded by his son. Could the line possibly mean that France was effectively ruled by the mistresses and wives of both these men—Mme de Pompadour, Mme du Barry and finally (Louis XVI) by Marie Antoinette? Some historians would accept this view.

Du vrai rameau de fleur de lys issue
Mis & logé heretier de Hetrurie:
Son sang antique de long main tissu
Fera Florence florir en l'armoirie.

Issued from the true branch of the fleur de liys, placed and lodged as heir to Etruria, his ancient family line woven by many hands, will make the armorial bearings of Florence flower.

COUNT DE CHAMBORD

The Count of Chambord was the heir to Charles X and his legitimacy was questioned by the Duke of Orléans at his birth (see IV.

93). His mother the Duchess of Berry took her son into exile with her to Venice, Etruria standing for Italy. Here in 1846 he married the daughter of Duke Francis IV of Florence. The fleur de lis is part of the coat of arms of the house of Florence as well as the French royal line, and their marriage caused their united family lines to flower.

40

Le sang royal sera si tresmeslé,
Contrainct seront Gaulois de l'Hes-
perie:
On attendra que terme soit coulé,
Et que memoire de la voix soit
perie.

The Royal blood will be very mixed, the French will be restrained by the West. They will wait until his term of office has ended, and the memory of his voice has perished.

AMERICA, FRANCE AND THE COMMON MARKET

The first line probably indicates that the Royal blood in France is no longer truly royal, i.e. is not a ruling power, which brings the quatrain into the 20th Century. The restraint put on France by America (*Hesperie*) may well refer to the pressures to allow England to join the Common Market. Once de Gaulle's term of office has ended through his death, his policy, the famous '*Non*' is soon forgotten.

41

Nay souz les umbres & journée
nocturne
Sera en regne & bonté souveraine:
Fera renaistre son sang de l'antique
urne,
Renouvellant siecle d'or pour
l'aerain.

Born beneath the shadows on a dark day, he will be sovereign in ruling and in goodness. He will cause his blood to revive the ancient urn, renewing the century of gold for one of brass.

42

Mars esleue en son plus haut befroi,[1]
Fera retraire les Allobrox[2] *de*
France:
La gent Lombarde fera si grand
effroi,
A ceux de l'aigle comprins souz la
Balance.

A warlike man raised to the heights will bring about the return of Savoy to France. The people from Lombardy will cause such great fear to those of the Eagle included under the Balance.

[1] *befroi*—Literally a belfry.
[2] *Allobrox*—The Allobroges were a tribe that occupied what is present day Savoy.

Napoleon III and Cavour of Italy agreed between them that in return for French assistance for driving the Austrians (the Eagle) out of Italy (Libra), Savoy should be returned to France, which occurred on 22nd March 1860.

43

La grande ruine des sacrez ne s'esloigne,
Provence, Naples, Sicille, Seez & Ponce:
En Germanie, au Rhin & la Cologne,
Vexez à mort par ceux de Magonce.[1]

The great ruin of the clergy is not far off, Provence, Naples, Sicily, Sees and Pons. In Germany at the Rhine and Cologne, vexed to death by those of Maine.

In this far-reaching quatrain Nostradamus is probably inferring that Mainz and the other places would turn Protestant, possibly because Mainz was the centre of Gutenberg's city and the original centre of printing with all its inherent dangers. If so, a totally unsuccessful quatrain.

44

Par mer le rouge sera prins de pirates,
La paix sera par son moyen troublee:
L'ire & l'avare commettra par fainct acte
Au grand Pontife sera l'armee doublee.

On the sea the red one will be taken by pirates and because of him peace will be troubled. He will reveal anger and greed through a false act; the army of the great Pontiff will be doubled.

This prophecy was probably a contemporary one because it implies that a Cardinal (*le rouge*) will be captured by pirates— probably the corsairs of the Mediterranean. During the 16th Century Popes still had real armies. There is no record of its being fulfilled.

45

Le grand Empire sera tost desolé
Et translaté pres d'arduenne silve:
Les deux bastardz par l'aisné decollé,
Et regnera Aenodarb, nez de milve.

The great Empire will soon be desolated and changed near the forest of Ardennes. The two bastards will be beheaded by the oldest, Aenodarb, will rule, the hawk-nosed one.

---

[1] *Magonce*—Maguntiacum = Mainz or Mayenze.

The whole of the French empire was lost to the Germans in 1940 and there were great battles around the Ardennes forests, both then and in 1944/5. The two bastards may be the two 'unworthy' French generals who let the German advance through after the Battle of Sedan, André Georges Corap of the French 9th Army and the second-in-command, Henri Giraud, who was taken prisoner. The commander-in-chief, Maxime Weygand (*l'aisné*) then took over, but the battle was already lost for the Allies. The hawk-nosed man may refer to General de Gaulle. He was the only French general who, with the 4th Armoured Division, put up any real opposition to the Germans at Montcornet May 17th–19th. Dunkirk followed upon this crushing defeat.

46

Par chapeaux rouges querelles & *mouveaux scismes*	Quarrels and new schisms by the red hats when the Sabins
Quand on aura esleu le Sabinois:	will have been elected. They
On produira contre lui grans sophismes,	will produce great sophisms against him and Rome will be
Et sera Rome lesse par Albanois.	injured by those of Albania.

THE PAPACY

The red hats are the Cardinals who become divided among themselves when they elect a Pope from the land of the Sabines, north-east of Rome. The Albanians are a problem. Perhaps they cannot connect with this verse in that they are a people with strong links with Communist China which disturbs the Vatican?

47

Le grand Arabe marahera bien avant,	The great Arab will march well to the fore, he will be betrayed
Trahi sera par les Bisantinois:	by the Byzantians: ancient
L'Antique Rodes lui viendra au devant,	Rhodes will come forward to meet him and greater harm
Et plus grand mal par autre Pannonois.	through the other Hungarians.

The Byzantines are the Turks, since their capital was originally Byzantium. Nostradamus seems to imply that Rhodes in Greece will be the base for an operation against the Arabs. The Turkish conquest of Hungary is referred to in the final line. Probably a retroactive prophecy.

Apres la grand affliction du sceptre,
Deux ennemis par eux seront de-
faictz:
Classe d'Afrique aux Pannons
viendra naistre,
Par mer & terre seront horribles
faictz.

After the great affliction of the sceptre two enemies will be defeated by them. A fleet from Africa will come forth to the Hungarians; dreadful deeds will occur on land and sea.

This is almost certainly a continuation from the last quatrain. The fleet may be going to Fiume, now *Rijeka*, which used to belong to the Holy Roman Empire.

Nul de l'Espaigne mais de l'antique
France
Ne sera esleu pour le tremblant
nacelle,
A l'ennemi sera faicte fiance,[1]
Qui dans son regne sera peste
cruelle.

Not from Spain but from ancient France will he be elected for the trembling ship. He will make a promise to the enemy who will cause great plague during his reign.

FUTURE POPE

Since Nostradamus' day there have only been Italian Popes so this prediction may lie in the future. It indicates that there will be two main candidates for the Papacy, one Spanish and one French, when the Church is doing badly, 'trembling ship'. The French candidate will be elected and will try to compromise with his enemy, presumably Communism, with remarkably little success. See V. 46.

L'an que deux freres du lys seront en
aage,
L'un d'eux tiendra la grand
Romanie:
Trembler les monts, ouvert Latin
passage
Pache macher, contre fort d'Armenie.

The year that the brothers of the lily come of age one of them will hold great Romania. The mountains tremble, a Latin passage is opened; a treaty to march against the fort of Armenia.

The brothers of the lily are presumably sons of the French royal house. Romania is probably the Holy Roman Empire, and the

[1] *fiance*—O.F. = assurance, promise.

mountains, the Alps crossing to Rome. Armenia is difficult to interpret. In V. 94 it connects with Hitler and the Second World War.

51

La gent de Dace,[1] *d'Angleterre &*	The people of Dacia, England
Polonne	and Poland and Czechoslovakia
Et de Boesme[2] *feront nouvelle ligue:*	will form a new alliance. In
Pour passer outre d'Hercules la	order to pass beyond the
colonne	straights of Gibraltar the
Barcins,[3] *Tyrrens*[4] *dresser cruelle*	Spanish and the Italians will
brique.	hatch a cruel plot.

ALLIED ALLIANCE. SECOND WORLD WAR, 1939
One of Nostradamus' more interesting predictions. In March 1939 Britain allied with the Balkan countries. Her support of Poland started the war in September 1939. It was essential to keep the Mediterranean open for shipping for allied troops and supplies. The Italians were allied to Germany and the Spanish were technically neutral, their plot presumably the aid given to Hitlerian Germany.

52

Un Roi sera qui donra l'opposite,	There will be a king who will
Les exilez esleuez sur le regne:	give opposition, the exiles elec-
De sang nager la gent caste[5] *hyp-*	ted over the kingdom. The
polite,[6]	chaste, poor ones swim in blood
Et florira long temps soubs telle	and he will flourish for a long
enseigne.	time under this standard.

Line 3 probably refers to an order of mendicant Friars; otherwise this quatrain is unclear.

[1] *Dacia*—Now part of modern Rumania.
[2] *Boesme*—Modern Czechoslovakia.
[3] *Barcins*—Latin, *Barcino* = Barcelona; therefore Spanish.
[4] *Tyrrens*—Latin, *Tyrrheni* = the ancestors of the Tuscans and therefore Italians.
[5] *castus*—Latin = chaste, pure.
[6] *hyppolite*—Greek, *hypolitos* = poor, mean, little.

La loi du Sol, & Venus contendens,
Appropiant l'esprit de prophetie:
Ne l'un ne l'autre ne seront entendus,
Par Sol tiendra la loy du grand
   Messie.

The law of the Sun contending
with Venus, appropriating the
spirit of prophecy. Neither the
one nor the other will be understood; the law of the great
Messiah retained through the
Sun.

The Sun may stand here for Christianity and Venus for Islam.
This is a repetition of Nostradmus' belief that eventually Christianity would rule the world: unfortunately this is another of those
prophecies which now seem unlikely to reach fulfilment.

Du pont Euxine, & la grand
   Tartarie,
Un roi sera qui viendra voir la
   Gaule
Transpercera Alane & l'Armenie,
Et dans Bisance lairra sanglante
   Gaule.

From beyond the Black Sea and
great Tartary, there will be a
king who will come to see
France. He will pass through
Alania and Armenia and leave
his bloody rod in Byzantium.

THE MAN FROM THE EAST

Nostradamus says elsewhere that the Third Anti-Christ of this
century will come from Asia, and this quatrain seems to confirm this
view, as he will come from beyond Tartary, that is from China. His
route to France lies through Alania, Southern Russia, and Armenia
round the Balkan peninsula to Constantinople. The mention of a
bloody rod occurs also in connection with a man from the East and
France in II. 29. It may be intended as a weapon of some sort.

De la felice Arabie contrade,[1]
Naistra puissant de loi Mahome-
   tique:
Vexer l'Espaigne conquester la
   Grenade,
Et plus par mer à la gent Ligus-
   tique.[2]

In the fortunate country of
Arabia will be born one power-
ful in the laws of Mahomet. He
will trouble Spain and conquer
Grenada and most of the
Ligurian nation from the sea.

[1] contrade—Provençal, contrada = country.
[2] Ligustique—The Ligurians come from around Genoa.

Nostradamus seems to envisage a reconquest of Spain and Grenada by the Arabs who will extend their rule into Italy. Grenada was lost to the Moors in 1492.

56

Par le trespas du tres vieillart pontif, *Sera esleu Romain de bon aage:* *Qu'il sera dict que le siege debisse,* *Et long tiendra & de picquant ouvrage.*	Through the death of the very old Pope will be elected a Roman of good age. It will be said of him that he weakens the (Holy) Seat, but he will hold it long and with stinging effort.

NEW POPE

Instead of the usual aged Pope, one will be elected who is comparatively young and who, despite his detractors, reigns very effectively for a long time.

57

Istra du Mont Gaulfier & Aventin, *Qui par trou avertira l'armée:* *Entre deux rocs sera prins le butin,* *De SEXT. mansol faillir le renommee.*	There will go forth from Montgaulfier and the Aventine one, who through a hole will warn the army. The booty will be taken between two rocks. The renown of Sextus the celibate will fail.

MONTGOLFIER BALLOON AND THE BATTLE OF FLEURUS, 1794

The hot air balloon was invented by the Montgolfier brothers in 1783 and was used on a scouting party at the Battle of Fleurus 1794. The French victory at Fleurus was the turning point in the first coalition phase of the Revolutionary Wars paving the way for the sack of Rome and the Aventine. The word *mansol* is derived from *manens solus*—he who remains alone. Elsewhere Nostradamus calls monks and priests *les seuls*. *Sext.* is short for Sextus, and Pius VI who was captured by Napoleon, is the only Pope since Nostradamus' day, apart from the present one, Paul VI, to have this number. By the Treaty of Tolentino 1797, the Pope was deprived of much of his lands, the rocks on which his power was based.

De l'acqueduct d'Uticense,[1] Gardoing, Par la forest & mont inaccessible, En mi du pont sera tasché au poing, Le chef nemans & qui tant sera terrible.	By the aqueduct of Uzès by Gard, through the forest and inaccessible mountain; in the middle of the bridge he will be cut in the hand, the chief of Nîmes who will be very terrible.

1627

There is a famous Roman aqueduct in France which extended from Uzès to Nîmes. In 1627 the Duke de Rohan tried to support his fellow Calvinists who were besieged at Nîmes. He moved his artillery in by means of the aqueduct. Line 3 is interpreted as some of his soldiers cutting some of the supports of the bridge at Gard to widen the path for the cannons to be brought up. When Rohan arrived at Nîmes he was put in command. An impressive quatrain.

Au chef Anglois à Nimes trop sejour, Devers l'Espaigne au secours Aenobarbe: Plusieurs mourrant par Mars ouvert ce jour, Quand an Artois faillir estoille en barbe.[3]	The English chief stays too long at Nîmes, towards Spain Aenobarbe to the rescue. Many will die through war started on that day, when a bearded star falls in Artois.

Par teste rase viendra bien mal eslire, Plus que sa charge ne porte passera: Si grand fureur & raige fera dire, Qu'à feu & sang tout sexe trenchera.	Through the shaven heads he will be seen to have been wrongly elected. Burdened with a load he cannot carry. He will be made to proclaim with such great fury and rage that all one sex will be cut to pieces by fire and blood.

CROMWELL

Although many commentators interpret this verse as applying either to Napoleon or to the Popes, whose heads were shaven as

[1] *Uticense*—Castrum Uceciense, Uzès.
[2] *nemans*—Nemansus = Nîmes.
[3] *estoille en barbe* = comet or meteorite.

monks, I think it is more appropriately applied to Cromwell. Nostradamus says that Cromwell is elected to power, he did not rule by divine right. The fury and rage that cover Britain refers to the Civil War between Cavaliers and Roundheads (*testes rases*) which was a war both of politics and religion. A great number of men (*tant un sexe*) lost their lives during this time. There were comparatively few atrocities committed on women and children.

61

L'enfant du grand n'estant à sa naissance,	The child of the great man, not through his birth, will sub-
Subjugera les hauts monts Apennis:	jugate the high Apennine
Fera trembler tous ceux de la balance,	mountains. He will make all those under the Balance trem-
Et de monts feux jusques à mont Senis.	ble, fire from the mountains as far as Mount Cenis.

EUGÈNE DE BEAUHARNAIS

The nearest person to fulfil this quatrain to date is Eugène de Beauharnais, the son of Josephine. It states that the adopted son of a French ruler will vex the Habsburgs (Libra) in Spain and Italy and conquer Italy. Unfortunately it was Napoleon who conquered. Eugène only acted as ruler.

62

Sur les rochers sang on les verra plouvoir,	Blood will be seen to rain on the rocks, Sun in the East, Saturn
Sol Orient, Saturne Occidental:	in the West. War near Orgon,
Pres d'Orgon guerre, à Rome grand mal voir,	a great evil seen near Rome, ships sunken and the trident
Nefs parfondrees & prins le Tri-dental.[1]	taken.

One of Nostradamus' detailed but unintelligible quatrains. The Sun is probably Christianity and Saturn the Antichrist. Tridental refers to general sea power.

[1] *Tridental* = One who holds the trident: i.e. power of the seas.

*De vaine emprise l'honneur indue
  plaincte,
Galiotz errans par Latins froit,
  faim, vagues
Non loing du Timbre de sang la
  terre taincte.
Et sur humains seront diverses
  plagues.*

From the useless enterprise honour and undue complaint, boats wandering among the Latins, cold, hunger, waves; Not far from the Tiber the land stained with blood and there will be several plagues upon mankind.

*Les assemblés par repos du grand
  nombre,
Par terre & mer conseil contre-
  mandé:
Pres de l'Autonne Gennes, Nice de
  l'ombre
Par champs & villes le chef contre-
  bandé.*

Those assembled through the calm of the great number, countermanded by land and sea; near Autonne, Genoa, the shadow of Nice, revolution against the leader through fields and towns.

Autonne is one of Nostradamus' unsolved anagrams, written Antonne in some editions. The nearest equivalents phonetically are Nentone or Antibes (Antipolis) but do not clarify the meaning.

*Subit venu l'effrayeur sera grande,
Des principaux de l'affaire cachés:
Et dame en braise plus ne sera en
  veue
Ce peu à peu seront les grans fachés.*

Suddenly appeared, the terror will be great, hidden by the ringleaders of the affair. The women on the charcoal will no longer be seen; thus, little by little, the great ones will be angered.

*Soubs les antiques edifices vestaulx,
Non esloignez d aqueduct ruine:
De Sol & Lune sont les luisans
  metaulx,
Ardante lampe Traian d'or burine.*

Under the ancient buildings of the vestals not far from the ruin of the aquaduct. There will be the glittering metals of Sun and Moon, the golden lamp of Trojan burning, pillaged.

It has been suggested by Jaubert that the convent of St.-Sauveur-de-la-Fontaine at Nîmes was built on the site of a temple of Diana and that a lamp of gold and silver will eventually be dug up.

Quand chef Perouse n'osera sa tunique	When the great head of Perugia dare not risk his tunic, without
Sens au couvert tout nud s'expolier:	any cover and strip himself
Seront prins sept faict Aristocratique,	quite naked. The seven aristocrats will be taken, father and
Le pere & fils mors par poincte au colier.	son dead through a wound in the throat.

VATICAN AND FRANCE, 1585–9

The head of Perugia was the Pope, in this case Sixtus V who, in 1585, had excommunicated Henri de Navarre and was therefore reluctant to do the same to Henri III and risk losing France (stripping himself naked). When he was eventually forced to do so in 1589, he did not release his Catholic subjects from their oath of allegiance, because the Papacy had already lost the revenues of England and Northern Europe. The seven are again the children of Catherine de' Medici. Their father was already dead from a wound in the throat and his last ruling son, Henri III was to die from stab wounds, not in the throat but in the stomach in 1589. Possibly Henri's assassin Jacques Clément meant to get the king in the throat but missed.

68

Dans le Danube & du Rhin viendra boire,	The great Camel will come to drink of the Danube and the
Le grand Chameau ne s'en repentira:	Rhine, and will not repent of it. Those of the Rhône tremble
Trembler du Rosne & plus fort ceux de Loire,	and even more so those of the Loire; near the Alps the cock
Et pres des Alpes coq le ruinera.	will ruin him.

The great Camel also appears in IV. 85 and VI. 55. Nostradamus probably means an Arabian leader, or less possibly, a hunchback. Although this person sweeps aside German opposition, he will get his comeuppance in France.

69

Plus ne sera le grand en faux sommeil,	The great one will no longer be in a false sleep; unease will take
L'inquietude viendra prendre repoz:	the place of repose. The
Dresser phalange d'or, azur, & vermeil,	phalanx of gold, blue and vermillion to subdue Africa and
Subjuger Affrique la ronger jusques oz.	gnaw it down to the very bone.

Louis Philippe usurped his nephew's French crown in 1830, having waited for an opportune moment, line 2. He was the first legitimate Bourbon to accept the tricolour of red, white and blue. The French conquest of Algeria took place in the same year that he snatched the throne. Nostradamus says the flag is gold, red and blue. James Laver makes a charming comment, 'the old eyes of the prophet may be pardoned for being slightly colour blind'.

70

Des regions subjectes à la Balance,	Some of the regions subject to
Feront troubler les monts par grand guerre.	the Balance will trouble the mountains with a great war.
Captifz tout sexe deu & tout Bisance,	The entire sex will be captured, enthralled, and all Byzantium,
Qu'on criera à l'aube terre à terre.	so that at dawn they will call from land to land.

The Balance, Libra, as always is astrologically either Austria and Savoy, and sometimes England by Nostradamus' own reckoning. It appears that this country will overthrow the Ottoman empire. Possibly Austria's troubles in the Balkans in the early 1900s are hinted at in this verse?

71

Par la fureur d'un qui attendra l'eau,	By the fury of one who will wait for the water, by the great rage
Par la grand raige tout l'exercite esmeu:	that moves all the army; seventeen boats loaded with nobles,
Chargé des nobles à dix sept bateaulx,	the messenger comes too late along the Rhône.
Au long du Rosne, tard messagier venu.	

This quatrain has been tentatively applied to every would-be invader of Britain. Napoleon, Hitler etc.

72

Pour le plaisir d'edict voluptueux,	For the pleasure of an edict of
On meslera la poison dans l'aloy:	vice, poison will be mixed with
Venus sera en cours si vertueux,	the law. At Court, Venus will
Qu'obfusquera du soleil tout à loi.	be so virtuous, that all the glory of the sun will be obscured.

235

Nostradamus considered that the edict of Poitiers encouraged vice because it allowed the clergy to marry and legalized Calvinism. Henri III's court was very depraved; his openly flaunted homosexuality offended the country and his mignons were notorious for the fantastic wealth they acquired. The King was reputed to be a sorcerer with a familiar named Tarragon. Is the reference to the sun an oblique reference to the Roi Soleil, Louis XIV of the next century?

73

Persecutee sera de Dieu l'eglise,	The Church of God will be
Et les sainctz temples seront expoliez:	persecuted, and the holy temples will be pillaged; the mother
L'enfant la mere mettra nud en chemise,	will put out the child, naked in a shift. The Arabs will ally with
Seront Arabes aux Polons raliez.	the Poles.

74

De sang Troyen[1] naistra coeur Germanique	Of Trojan blood he will be born with a German heart and will
Qu'il deviendra en si haute puissance:	rise to very great power. He will drive out the foreign, Arabic
Hors chassera gent estrange Arabique	nation and return the Church to her early glory.
Tournant l'Eglise en pristine preeminence.	

75

Montera haut sur le bien plus à dextre,	He will rise high over his wealth, more to the right, he
Demourra assis sur la pierre quarree:	will remain seated on the square stone; towards the south placed
Vers le midi posé à la fenestre,	at the window, a crooked staff
Baston tortu en main, bouche serree.	in his hand, his mouth sealed.

A typically convoluted Nostradamus quatrain. A crooked staff normally refers to a bishop's crook.

[1] sang Troyen—Refers to the myth by which the French royal line were descended from Francus, son of Priam of Troy.

En lieu libere tendra son pavillon,	In a free place he will pitch his
Et ne voudra en citez prendre place:	tent, he will not want to stay in
Aix, Carpens l'isle volce, mont	the cities. Aix, Carpentras,
Cavaillon,	L'Ile Vaucluse, Montfavet,
Par tous ses lieux abolira sa trasse.	Cavaillon, in all these places he
	will abolish his trace.

All these places are quite close to Salon in Provence.

Tous les degrez d'honneur Eccle-	All degrees of ecclesiastical
siastique	honour will be changed to
Seront changez en dial¹ quirinal.²	Jupiter and Quirinus. A priest
En Martial quirinal flaminique,	of Quirinus in martial guise
Puis un Roi de France le rendre	then a king of France will make
vulcanal.	him a man of Vulcan.

Les deux unis ne tiendront longue-	The two will not remain allied
ment,	for long; within the thirteen
Et dans treize ans au Barbare	years they give in to barbarian
Satrappe:	power. There will be such a loss
Au deux costez seront tel perdement,	on both sides, that one will
Qu'un benira le Barque & sa	bless the bark (of Peter) and its
cappe.	leader.

ALLIANCE BETWEEN U.S.A. AND U.S.S.R.?

The alliance between the USSR and the USA, see II. 9, created because of Eastern developments will not last for more than thirteen years, maybe less. Then the barbarian hordes will cause them to fight. The scale of modern warfare makes Nostradamus' comment quite mundane, but it is interesting to see that he expects a Pope to play a singular and important part towards world peace. The prophecies of Malachy give four more Popes until the end of the world, and the name for the third is Gloria Olivae—the olive branch, which is traditionally a sign of peace. Most Popes are old men when elected. If we allow each an average of ten years this would bring us to the 1990s. The alliance should therefore occur in the late 1970s.

¹ *dial*—Latin, *Dialis* = of Jupiter.
² *Quirinus*—Sabine = Mars, identified with Romulus.

La sacree pompe viendra baisser les aisles,	The sacred pomp will come to lower its wings at the coming of
Par la venue du grand legislateur:	the great law giver. He will
Humble haulsera vexera les rebelles,	raise the humble and trouble
Naistra sur terre aucun aemulateur.	the rebellious; his like will not again appear on earth.

NAPOLEON

This is a general quatrain but the generalities do apply particularly well to Napoleon. He treated the Church and the Popes with arbitrary power. He originated the Code Napoléon, France's legal system. He made aristocrats from the lowly, and stamped out rebellion brutally. Line 4 may be an exaggeration, but he was a great man.

80

Logmion[1] grande Bisance approchera,	Ogmios will approach great Byzantium, the barbarian
Chasse sera la barbarique ligne:	league will be driven out. Of
Des deux loix l'une l'estinique[2] lachera,	the two laws the pagan one will fail, barbarian and freeman in
Barbare & franche en perpetuelle brigue.	perpetual struggle.

81

L'oiseau royal sur la cité solaire,	The royal bird over the city of
Sept mois devant fera nocturne augure:	the sun will give a nightly warning for seven months; the wall
Mur d'Orient cherra tonnerre esclaire,	in the East will fall, thunder and lightning, in seven days the
Sept jours aux portes les ennemis à l'heure.	enemies directly to the gates.

FRANCE. BERLIN WALL?

The royal bird is probably an eagle which flying over Paris or Rome will warn of a disaster to come. The wall in the East has been identified with the fall of France, the Maginot line and the Blitzkrieg, the seven days being 5th–11th June 1940. However, it may refer to the Berlin wall, and indicate that it will come down eventually, although other disasters will follow in its wake.

[1] *L'Omigon* was the Celtic Hercules.
[2] *l'estinique*—Latin, *ethnicus* = pagan.

*Au conclud pache hors de la for-
   teresse,*
Ne sortira celui en desespoir mis:
*Quand ceux d'Arbois, de Langres,
   contre Bresse,*
*Auront monts Dolle, bouscade[1]
   d'ennemis.*
	At the conclusion of the treaty outside the fortress he will not go who is overcome with despair. When the people of Arbois, Langres, against Bresse, will have an enemy ambush at the mountains of Dôle.

*Ceux qui auront entreprins sub-
   ventir,*
*Nompareil regne puissant & in-
   vincible:*
*Feront par fraude, nuictz trois
   advertir,*
*Quant le plus grand à table lira
   Bible.*
	Those who will have an undertaking to subvert an unparalleled kingdom, powerful and invincible. They will deceive, warn for three nights, when the greatest one is reading his Bible at the table.

The propaganda mentioned here could have many applications in this century.

*Naistra du gouphre & cité im-
   mesuree,*
*Nay de parents obscure & tene-
   breux:*
*Qui la puissance du grand roi
   reveree,*
*Voudra destruire par Rouen &
   Evereux.*
	Born of the gulf and the immeasurable city, born of parents both obscure and dark. He who will wish to destroy the power of the great, revered king through Rouen and Evereux.

Rouen and Evereux are linked also in **IV.** 100 as loyal to Napoleon III and the monarchy.

*Par les Sueves[2] & lieux circon-
   voisins,*
*Seront en guerre pour cause des
   nuees:*
Gamp marins locustes & cousins,
*Du Leman fautes seront bien
   desnuees.*
	Through the Swiss and surrounding areas they will war because of the clouds. A swarm of marine locusts and gnats, the faults of Geneva will be laid quite bare.

[1] *bouscade*—embuscade = ambush.
[2] *Sueves*—Latin, Suevi = ancestors of German Swiss.

LEAGUE OF NATIONS AND THE
SECOND WORLD WAR

This quatrain describes very accurately the failure of the League of Nations and the commencement of the Second World War. See also I. 47.

86

Par les deux testes, & trois bras separés,
La cité grande par eaux sera vexee:
Des grands d'entre eux par exile esgarés,
Par teste perse Bisance fort pressee.

Divided by the two heads and three arms, the great city will be troubled by water. Some of the great men among them, wandering in exile; Byzantium is hard pressed by the leader of Persia.

PARIS, PERSIA AND TURKEY
17th AND 18th CENTURIES

This probably describes Paris flooded by the Seine, which occurred reasonably frequently during the early 17th Century when the Turks (Byzantium) were hard pressed by Persia. There was further fighting in the East during the first half of the 18th Century.

87

L'an que Saturne hors de servage,
Au franc[1] terroir sera d'eau inundé:
De sang Troyen[2] sera son mariage,
Et sera ceur d'Espaignols circundé.

In the year that Saturn is freed from servitude the Frankish territory will be inundated by water. His marriage will be of Trojan blood and he will be closely encircled by the Spaniards.

The only clear factor here is that a French prince (or princess) will marry a Spaniard at the time of a great flood.

88

Sur le sablon par un hideux deluge,
Des autres mers trouvé monstre marin:
Proche du lieu sera faict un refuge,
Tenant Savone esclave de Turin.

Through a dreadful flood on the sand a marine monster will be found from other seas. A refuge will be made near the place, holding Savona the slave to Turin.

[1] *franc*—Either Frank, probably *Franche Comté*, or free.
[2] *sang Troyen*—Again the reference to the French royal line and its mythical descent from Francus, son of Priam.

In 1815 Savona, which was part of the State of Genoa, was given to the House of Savoy to whom Turin also belonged. The sea monster was not recorded.

89

Dedans Hongrie par Boheme, Navarre,	Into Hungary through Bohemia, Navarre and by the
Et par banniere fainctes seditions:	banner feigned sedition. The
Par fleurs de lys pays portant la barre,	country of the fleur de lis carrying the bar; they will
Contre Orleans sera emotions.	cause disturbances against Orléans.

The fleur de lis with a diagonal bar to each corner was the arms of the Bourbon family. The junior branches such as the Vendômes, who got the throne, and the Condés, just had a diagonal bar in the centre. It appears that Nostradamus is describing an expedition into Bohemia and Hungary led by one of the French royal line, possibly a Bourbon Vendôme of Navarre? It is all very obscure, and appears to be unfulfilled.

90

Dans les cyclades, en perinthe & larisse,	In the Cyclades, in Perinthus and Larissa, in Sparta and all
Dedans Sparte tout le Pelloponnesse:	of the Peloponnesus; a very great famine, plague through
Si grand famine, peste par faux connisse,[1]	false dust: it will last nine months throughout the whole
Neuf mois tiendra & tout le chevronesse.	peninsula.

CHEMICAL WARFARE IN GREECE AND THE BALKANS?

It is possible that by the words 'false dust' Nostradamus is trying to imply that the plague and famine described here are artificially induced? It appears to be a widespread disaster throughout the whole of Greece and the southern Balkans. This quatrain may tie in with the ones that predict trouble in the Middle East.

[1] *connisse*—Difficult, possibly Greek, *Konis* = dust, or Latin, *connissus* = exerted.

Au grand marché qu'on dict des
mensongiers,
Du tout Torrent[1] & champ
Athenien:
Seront surprins par les chevaux
legiers,
Par Albanois Mars, Leo, Sat. un
versien.[2]

At the great market, called that of the liars, of all Torrent and the field of Athens: they will be surprised by the light armed horses, by the Albanians, when Mars is in Leo, and Saturn in Aquarius.

Again a reference to an attack from the Albanians.

Apres le siege tenu dix sept ans,
Cinq changeront en tel revolu terme:
Puis sera l'un esleu de mesme temps,
Qui des Romains ne sera trop con-
forme.

After the See has been held seventeen years, five will change within the same period of time. Then one will be elected at the same time who will not be too agreeable to the Romans.

THE VATICAN AND ITS FUTURE

Nostradamus says that after a Pope rules for seventeen years there will be five Popes within the next seventeen years. If he is slightly out in his calculations this could apply to Pius XII who reigned for nineteen years. It is interesting to note that the Irish prophet, Malachy, with whom Nostradamus seems to agree to a remarkable degree, gives only another five Popes before the Final Coming. John XXIII ruled for five years, the present Paul VI has been in the Vatican since 1963 and is 75 years old. This allows a very short life span for the next three Popes but since most are elected as old men it may just be possible.

Soubs le terroir du rond globe
lunairs,
Lors que sera dominateur Mercure:
L'isle d'Escosse fera un luminaire,
Qui les Anglois mettra à decon-
fiture.

Under the land of the round moonlike globe, when Mercury is at the height of his powers. The island of Scotland will produce a leader, who will put the English into confusion.

[1] Torrent—It is unclear whether this is a proper name or not.
[2] versien—Verseau = Aquarius.

Most commentators apply this to Charles I, because he was born in Scotland in 1600 before the Stuarts came to the throne. But it seems more applicable to Bonnie Prince Charlie who did put the English into confusion for a while when he marched as far south as Derby.

94

Translatera en la grand Germanie, *Brabant & Flandres, Gand,* *Bruges & Bolongne,* *La traifue fainte, le grand duc* *d'Armenie,* *Assaillira Vienne & la Coloigne.*	He will change into the Greater Germany, Brabant and Flanders, Ghent, Bruges and Boulogne. The truce feigned, the great Duke of Armenia will assault Vienna and Cologne.

HITLER AND RUSSIA, 1939/40

The Greater Germany is, of course, the Third Reich. Hitler assimilated all the places mentioned in the quatrain during his march across Europe. The feigned truce probably describes the invasion of Poland under the guise of help, which Nostradamus elsewhere calls '*similé secours*'. The Duke of Armenia stands for Russia, who moved troops southwards into Germany.

95

Nautique rame invitera les umbres *Du grand Empire lors viendra con-* *citer* *La mer Aegee des lignes les en-* *combres,* *Empeschant l'onde Tirreme defflo-* *tez.*	The nautical oar will invite the shadows and then come to provoke the great Empire. In the Aegean sea the remains of (bits of) wood, obstruct the Tyrrhenian sea and impede it.

This seems to describe a few ships 'nautical oars', which grow in power into a mighty fleet and trouble the Empire, whether French or Roman is not clear. The end result is a devastating sea battle and great destruction in Italy.

96

Sur le milieu du grand monde la *rose,* *Pour nouveaux faicts sang public* *espandu:* *A dire vrai on aura bouche close,* *Lors au besoing viendra tard* *l'attendu.*	The rose upon the middle of the world, because of new deeds, public blood is shed; to speak the truth they will have closed mouths, then, at time of need the awaited one will come late.

Le nay defforme par horreur suf-foqué, *Dans la cité du grand Roi habi-table:* *L'edict severe des captifs revoqué,* *Gresle & tonnere, condon inestim-*	One born deformed, suffocated through horror in the city inhabited by the great king. The severe edict of the captives is revoked, hail and thunder, Condom too great.

THE MAN IN THE IRON MASK
It has been suggested that the first two lines refer to the man in the Iron Mask, reputed son of the Queen and Cardinal Mazarin. Line 3 is taken as a reference to the Edict of Nantes, 1685.

A quarante huict degré climaterique, *A fin de Cancer si grande seicheresse:* *Poisson en mer, fleuve, lac cuit hectique,* *Bearn, Bigorre par feu ciel en destresse.*	At the forty-eighth degree of the climacteric, the end of Cancer there is a very great drought. Fish in the sea, river and the lake boiled hectic, Bearn and Bigorre in distress from fire in the sky.

The 48° of the climacteric may mean 48° latitude, which runs through France near Rennes, Orléans and Langres. The drought is predicted as occurring after 22nd July when the sun leaves the sign of Cancer; there is another reference to fish cooking in the heat in II. 3. Fire in the sky is probably some form of freak electrical storm or an attack by bombs or rockets.

Milan, Ferrare, Turin & Aquil-laye, *Capne Brundis vexés par gent Celtique:* *Par le Lion & phalange aquilee* *Quant Rome aura le chef vieux Britannique.*	Milan, Ferrare, Turin & Aquileia, Capua and Brindisi vexed by the Celtic nation: by the lion and his eagle-like phalanx, when Rome will have the old British chief.

NAPOLEON AND THE LAST OF THE STUARTS, 1807
The cities mentioned cover all regions of Italy showing how complete was Napoleon's conquest. It is specifically dated to the time of Napoleon because it was in 1807 that Cardinal York, the last of the Stuarts, died in Rome.

Le boutefeu par son feu attrapé,
De feu du ciel à Carcas & Co-
  minge:
Foix, Aux, Mazere, haut veillart
  eschappé,
Par ceux de Hasse, des Saxons &
  Turinge.

The incendiary trapped in his own fire; fire from the sky at Carcassonne and Comminges: Foix Auch & Mazeres, the important old man escaped, through those of Hesse and Thuringia and some Saxons.

Yet another reference to fire in the sky, perhaps a battle, this time in South-western France. Not many Germans got as far South as this even during the Second World War, so this verse may still be unfulfilled.

CENTURY VI

1
2   1580 and 1703
3
4   Changes of French Border
5*F? A Manned Space Station. Fallout or Bacterial warfare
6*   Pope Leo XIII
7   Hitler and Mussolini
8
9
10
11* France, 1575–88
12   Europe?
13
14* King Sebastian of Portugal, 1578
15
16
17
18
19
20
21*F? Alliance between U.S.A. and U.S.S.R.
22
23   French Revolution
24F? 21st June 2002
25* Victor Emmanuel and Italian Revolution
26* Pope John XXIII
27
28* Pius VII
29* Catherine de' Medici and her children
30
31* Mussolini
32
33*F? Name of Third Antichrist?

34*   Bombing or rockets
35
36
37
38
39
40*   Holy Roman Empire, 1806
41
42
43
44*?   20th Century.
45
46
47
48
49*?   The swastika
50
51*?   Hitler
52*   Louis XVII?
53
54*?   1607
55
56*   Siege of Perpignan, 1597
57
58*   Philip II and Henri II
59
60
61
62   An erroneous quatrain
63*   Catherine de' Medici
64
65
66
67
68*   Duke of Alba
69*   Disbanding of Clergy after 1792
70
71
72*   Czarina Alexandra and Rasputin
73
74*   Elizabeth I
75*   Gaspard de Coligny
76

77

78   Retroactive prophecy?

79*   Battle of Lodi, 1796

80**F? War in Middle East. The Third Antichrist

81

82

83   Philip of Spain with France and Netherlands

84

85

86

87*   Emperor Ferdinand, 1558–62

88

89

90

91

92**   Death of Louis XVI

93

94

95

96

97*F? Bombing of New York?

98

99

100*   Incantation against stupid critics

KEY: * Of interest. F? Possibly referring to the future.

I

| Autour des monts Pyrenees grans amas, | Around the Pyrenean moun- |

Autour des monts Pyrenees grans
amas,
De gent estrange secourir roi nou-
veau:
Pres de Garonne du grant temple du.
Mas,
Un Romain chef le craindra dedans
l'eau.

Around the Pyrenean moun-
tains a great throng of foreign
people will help the new king.
Near the great temple of Mas
by the Garonne, a Roman
leader will fear him on the
water.

Le Mas d'Agenais has many famous Roman antiquities which
Nostradamus would have seen when he lived at Agen. The Roman
chief is unclear.

2

En l'an cinq cens octante plus &
moins,
On attendra le siecle bien estrange:
En l'an sept cens, & trois cieux en
tesmoings.
Que plusieurs regnes un à cinq
feront change.

In the year five hundred and
eighty more or less one will
await a very strange century.
In the year seven hundred and
three, the skies as witness that
several kingdoms, one to five,
will make a change.

1580 AND 1703

A daring quatrain with two dates, both of which seem accurate.
In 1580, Nostradamus nearly always leaves out the thousand for
reasons of scansion, France was torn by the Civil War called the
Seventh War and had little to look forward to. But by 1703
Louis XIV was defying Europe and fighting the war of the
Spanish Succession. The five kingdoms were probably the Two
Sicilies, Milan, the Netherlands, the Americas and Spain which
were inherited by the French grandson of Louis XIV, Philip V.

3

Fleuve qu'esprouve le nouveau nay
Celtique,
Sera en grande de l'empire discord:
Le jeune prince par gent ecclesias-
tique,
Ostera le sceptre coronel de concorde.

The river that the newborn
French heir attempts; there
will be great discord among the
empire. The young prince, because of the ecclesiastics will
remove peace from crown and
sceptre.

There is a legend that in former times new-born heirs to the French throne were put on a target and made to swim up the Rhine to see if they were lawfully begotten or not. (*Garancières*).

4

Le Celtiq fleuve changera de rivaige,
Plus ne tiendra la cité d'Agripine:[1]
Tout transmue ormis le vieil langaige,
Saturne, Leo, Mars, Cancer en rapine.

The French river will change course and no longer surround the city of Agrippina; all changed except the old language, Saturn in Leo, Mars plundering in Cancer.

CHANGES OF FRENCH BORDER

After the Franco-Prussian war and the surrender of Alsace and Lorraine to the Germans the Rhine—the French river—was no longer the border between France and Germany. The old language that remained was German; everything else will be changed by war.

5

Si grand Famine par unde pestifere.
Par pluie longue le long du pole arctique,
Samarobrin cent lieux de l'hemisphere,
Vivront sans loi exempt de pollitique.

A very great famine (caused) by a pestilent wave will extend its long rain the length of the Arctic pole. Samarobrin one hundred leagues from the hemisphere; they will live without law, exempt from politics.

MANNED SPACE STATION? FALLOUT OR BACTERIAL WARFARE

This quatrain has caused more comment than most in the Prophecies. It seems to indicate that a great pestilence, caused perhaps by fallout or bacterial warfare, will cover the Northern pole of the earth, and that it appears to come from the unidentified Samarobrin which is circling above at a height of approximately two hundred and seventy miles. Could Nostradamus possibly have foreseen a manned space station? The word Samarobrin may be the nearest he can get to its name. This quatrain may well fit the decade of the 1970s. Already there have been space stations manned for long periods sent up by both Russia and the U.S.A.

[1] *Agripine*—Colonia Agrippina = Cologne.

Apparoistra vers la Septentrion,	He will appear towards the
Non loin de Cancer l'estoille	North, not far from the bearded
chevelue:	star in Cancer; Susa, Siena,
Suze, Sienne, Boece, Eretrion,	Boetia, Eretria, the great man
Mourra de Rome grand, la nuict	of Rome will die, the night
disparue.	dispersed.

POPE LEO XIII

The great man of Rome was Pius IX who died in February 1878. He was succeeded by Pope Leo XIII whose family arms have a comet, a bearded star, and who is also called Lumen in Caelo, light in the sky, by the prophet Malachy.

Norneigre & Dace, & l'isle	Norway and Dacia and the
Britannique,	British Isles, will be troubled
Par les unis freres serong vexeés:	by the united brothers. The
Le chef Romain issue de sang	Roman leader, came from
Gallique,	French blood; the forces thrust
Et les copies au forestz repoulsées.	back into the forests.

HITLER AND MUSSOLINI

This quatrain is similar to V. 51. Hitler and Mussolini are the united brothers or allies who trouble Norway, Dacia (Rumania) and Great Britain during the Second World War. The forces in the forests are the famous Resistance Movements, which so troubled the Nazis.

8

Ceux qui estoient en regne pour	Those who were in the kingdom
scavoir,	for knowledge will become
Au Royal change deviendront apouv-	impoverished by a royal
ris:	change. Some exiled without
Uns exilez sans appui, or, n'avoir,	support, having no gold,
Lettrez & lettres ne seront à grand	neither learning nor the learned
pris.	will be held of much value.

A general comment on Nostradamus' belief that learning would decline during a period after his death.

Au sacrez temples seront faicts escandales,
Comptez seront par honneurs & louanges.
D'un que on grave d'argent, d'or les medalles,
La fin sera en torments bien estranges.

In the sacred temples scandals will be committed, they will be thought of as honours and praiseworthy. By one whom they engrave on silver, gold and medals; the end will be in very strange torments.

Un peu de temps les temples de couleurs
De blanc & noir des deux entre-meslee:
Rouges & jaunes leur embleront les leurs
Sang, terre, peste, faim, feu, d'eau affollee.

In a short time the colours of temples; with black and white, the two will be intermingled. The red and yellow ones will carry off their (possessions), blood, earth, plague, hunger, fire, maddened by thirst.

Des sept rameaux à trois seront reduicts,
Les plus aisnez seront surprins par mort,
Fraticider les deux seront seduicts,
Les conjurez en dormans seront morts.

The seven branches will be reduced to three, the elder ones will be surprised by death. Two will be attracted towards fratricidal (strife): the conspirators will die while asleep.

FRANCE 1575–88

A good quatrain. When Catherine de' Medici's seven children have been reduced to three, which occurred in 1575 when only Henri III, François d'Alençon and Marguerite of Navarre were alive, then Henri and his brother were involved in a series of complicated plots. François allied himself with the Leaguers, led by the Duc de Guise, and hoped to succeed to the throne. Both the de Guise brothers were murdered at Blois in the early morning on Henri's orders. See II. 18, III. 51 etc.

Dresser copies pour monter à l'Empire,	To raise forces to ascend to Empire from the Vatican the
Du Vatican le sang Royal tiendra:	Royal blood will hold fast.
Flamans, Anglois, Espaigne avec Aspire,[1]	Flemish, English, Spain with Aspire: he will fight against
Contre l'Italie & France contendra.	France and Italy,

EUROPE?

This is interesting because Europe is visualized in modern, not medieval, terms. Italy did not exist as such until 1870, and the Flemings were a Habsburg dependency until modern Belgium was created. The prophecy states three main points. The first will be an attempt to gain the Imperial throne. The second, a French Pope (possibly of Royal Blood). The third, the Habsburgs and English will ally against France and Italy, which occurred during the Napoleonic wars, as did the first point. We have not yet had a French Pope who occurs also in V. 49.

Un dubieux ne viendra loing du regne,	A doubtful one will not come far from the kingdom the
La plus grand part le voudra soustenir:	greater part will wish to support him. A Capitol will not
Un Capitole[2] *ne voudra point qu'il regne,*	want him to reign: he will not be able to bear his great
Sa grande charge ne pourra maintenir.	burden.

This has been generally applied to the fall of the House of Savoy, the rulers of Italy.

Loing de sa terre Roy perdra la bataille,	Far from his country, a king will lose the battle; quickly
Prompt eschappé poursuivi suivant prins,	escaped, he is followed and taken. The ignorant one taken
Ignare prins soubs la doree maille.	under the golden chain-mail
Soubs fainct habit & l'ennemy surprins.	under a false garment, and the enemy surprised.

[1] *Aspire*—Uncertain, possibly Speyer or Spires?
[2] *Capitole*—Probably the Pope, as the Capitol was the Roman citadel.

Here is another quatrain to support a romantic theory, such as V. 1. King Sebastian of Portugal decided to raise a Crusade despite the objections of the Pope and the Spanish king. He crossed to Morocco in 1578 and attacked the Army of the King of Fez and was obliterated at the Battle of Kasr Al-Kabir. He was reported killed but there were persistent rumours that he had escaped. Nostradamus seems to believe that he did so by changing armour with one of his followers. Although the Moors discovered this they did not reveal the news for political reasons. Nostradamus gives us a new slant on history!

15

Dessoubs la tombe sera trouvé le Prince, *Qu'aura le pris par dessus Nuremberg:* *L'Espaignol Roi en Capricorne mince,* *Fainct & trahi par le grand Uvitemberg.*	Under the tomb will be found a Prince, who will have taken him above Nuremberg. The Spanish king, Capricorn thin, deceived and betrayed by the great Wittemberg.

16

Ce qui ravi sera du jeune Milve, *Par les Normans de France & Picardie:* *Les noirs du temple du lieu de Negrisilve* *Feront aulberge & feu de Lombardie.*	That which the young hawk will carry off, by the Normans of France and Picardy. The black ones of the temple at the Black wood will make an inn and fire at Lombardy.

The black ones are almost certainly the Benedictines, sometimes known as the Black monks, who had a monastery at Harrenalb in the Black Forest. The rest is obscure.

17

Apres les limes[1] brusler les asiniers,[2] *Contraints seront changer habits divers:* *Les Saturnins bruslez par les meusniers,* *Hors la plupart qui ne sera convers.*	After the penances are burned the ass drivers will be forced to change into different clothing. Those of Saturn burnt by the millers, except the greater part which will not be covered.

[1] *limes*—O.F. = penance.
[2] *asniers*—Some texts have rasniers but both readings are doubtful.

Par les phisiques le grand Roy delaissé, *Par sort non art de l'Ebrieu est en vie,* *Lui & son genre au regne hault poussé.* *Grace donnee à gent qui Christ envie.*	The great king deserted by the physicians lives through chance not the skill of the Jew. He and his people placed high in the realm, pardon given to the race which denies Christ.

An interesting quatrain which unfortunately does not seem to have occurred. But it is worth remembering Nostradamus' Jewish background and beliefs. It does not sound as though he had relinquished them in this verse.

La vraie flamme engloutira l a dame, *Que voudra mettre les Innocens à feu:* *Pres de l'assaut l'excercite s'en-flamme,* *Quant dans Seville monstre en boeuf sera veu.*	The true flame will swallow up the woman who will want to put the Innocents to the fire. Near the assault, the army is inflamed, when in Seville a monstrous ox will be seen.

The ox and Seville are probably a reference to bull fighting, although the fanatic queen's identity is not clear.

L'union faincte sera peu de durée, *Des uns changés reformés la plus-part:* *Dans les vaissaux sera gent endurée,* *Lors aura Rome un nouveau liepart.*	The feigned union will last a short time, some changed, the greater part reformed. People will be suffering in the vessels, then when Rome has a new Leopard.

In heraldry a Leopard is a lion walking to the left with its head turned left to face the spectator. So possibly when a Pope has a Leopard in his coat of arms there will be great changes. It could equally refer to the English heraldic lion.

Quant ceux du polle artiq unis ensemble,	When those of the Northern pole are united together in the
En Orient grand effrayeur & crainte:	East will be great fear and dread. A new man elected,
Esleu nouveau, soustenu le grand tremble,	supported by the great one who trembles, both Rhodes and
Rhodes, Bisance de sang Barbare taincte.	Byzantium will be stained with Barbarian blood.

ALLIANCE OF U.S.A. AND U.S.S.R.

This quatrain must be linked with VI. 5 which describes the people of the northern pole as devastated by a possibly man-induced plague. Nostradamus does seem to indicate that the U.S.A. and U.S.S.R. will finally unite to form a new geopolitical group and that this will cause the East, China, to worry at the shift in the balance of power. This is followed by war, particularly in the Middle East. See V. 78, VI. 80.

Dedans la terre du grand temple celique,	In the land of the great heavenly temple, a nephew at
Nepveu à Londres par paix faincte meutri:	London is murdered through a false peace. The ship will then
La barque alors deviendra scismatique,	be schismatic, false liberty will be shouted abroad.
Liberte faincte sera au corn & cri.	

The above quatrain appears to describe England as the land of the great heavenly temple. The nephew of a ruler is asked to come to London on a peace treaty, and then murdered, so this rules out the two Pretenders. At the same time there will be trouble and schism in the Vatican. Some commentators have seen the death of Darnley, Mary Queen of Scots' second husband, in this verse. It is one of the most frustrating in all the Prophecies.

D'esprit de regne munismes des-criées,	Defences undermined by the spirit of the kingdom people
Et seront peuples esmuez contre leur Roi:	will be stirred up against their king. A new peace is made, holy
Paix, faict nouveau, sainctes loix empirées,	laws become worse, never was Paris in such great trouble.
Rapis onc fut en si tres dur arroi.	

FRENCH REVOLUTION

Rapis is Nostradamus' standard anagram for Paris. This verse is full of generalities which best apply to the French Revolution, new peace and new laws, with religious observations being controlled by the state, and Paris in a state of anarchy.

24

Mars & le sceptre se trouvera conjoinct,	Mars and the sceptre will be in conjunction, a calamitous war under Cancer. A short time afterwards a new king will be anointed who will bring peace to the earth for a long time.
Dessoubz Cancer calamiteuse guerre:	
Un peu apres sera nouveau Roi oingt,	
Qui par long temps pacifiera la terre.	

21st JUNE 2002

The sceptre here stands for Jupiter and, according to Wölner, the only time the conjunction will occur is on 21st June 2002. There will be a terrible war; this may be the war Nostradamus has already predicted for the end of this century, followed by a long era of peace.

25

Par Mars contraire sera la monar-chie,	With Mars adverse the monarchy of the great fisher-man will be in ruinous trouble. The young red king will take over the government. The traitors will act on a misty day.
Du grand pecheur en trouble ruineux:	
Jeune noir[1] rouge prendra la hierarchie,	
Les prodigeurs iront jour bruineux.	

VICTOR EMMANUEL AND ITALIAN REVOLUTION

The Vatican will be in trouble when its troops are defeated. This happened in 1796–1815 against Napoleon and again in 1860–70. The young king with politically socialist leanings probably stands for Victor Emmanuel and the Italian Revolution.

[1] Anagram for king as elsewhere.

Quatre ans le siege quelque bien peu tiendra,	For four years the seat will be held for some little good, one

Quatre ans le siege quelque bien peu tiendra,
Un surviendra libidineux de vie:
Ravenne & Pise, Veronne soustiendront,
Pour eslever la croix de Pape envie.

For four years the seat will be held for some little good, one will acceed to it who is libidinous in life: Ravenna and Pisa, Verona will support him, desirous of elevating the Papal Cross.

JOHN XXIII

A good Pope will die after four years to be succeeded by a worldly one. This might possibly refer to John XXIII who was Pope for just under four and a half years. He was probably a more popular Pope than any for several centuries. The present Paul VI appears more sophisticated and withdrawn.

27

Dedans les isles de cinq fleuves à un,
Par le croissant du grand Chyren Selin:
Par les bruines de l'aer fureur de l'un,
Six eschapés, cachés fardeaux de lin.

Within the islands of five rivers to one, by the crescent of the great Chyren Selin. Through the mists in the air the fury of one; six escaped, hidden in bundles of flax.

Although connected with the other Chyren Selin quatrains this remains undeciphered.

28

Le grand Celtique entrera dedans Rome,
Menant amas d'exilés & bannis:
Le grand pasteur mettra à mort tout homme,
Qui pour le coq estoient aux Alpes unis.

The great Celt will enter Rome, leading a crowd of exiled and banished. The great Pastor will put to death every man who was united over the Alps for the Cock.

PIUS VII

The Great Celt may refer to Napoleon's conquering of Rome and the subsequent return of the Pope Pius VII with his clergy who had been imprisoned in France. But the third line is totally incorrect as Pius VII was extraordinarily kind to his ex-captors and their adherents until his death in 1823.

La veuve saincte estendant les nouvelles,	The holy widow hearing the news of her offspring in trouble
De ses rameaux mis en perplex & trouble:	and distress: He who will be led to calm the quarrels by his
Qui sera duict appaiser les querelles,	pursuit will make the shaven
Par son pourchas des razes fera comble.	heads pile up.

CATHERINE DE' MEDICI AND HER SONS

Catherine de' Medici will learn of the problems and troubles of her children, in particular the massacre of St. Bartholomew and the murder of the Duke de Guise and of his brother by her son, Henri III. These actions all increased civil unrest and led to the eventual civil war between the Leaguers and the Huguenots.

Par l'apparence de faincte saincteté,	By the appearance of fake holiness, the seat will be betrayed
Sera trahi aux ennemis le siege:	to the enemies, in the night
Nuict qu'on cuidoit dormit en seureté,	when they thought to sleep safely; the people of Liège will
Pres de Braban marcheront ceux du Liege.	march near Brabant.

Liège was a province east of Brabant in the Netherlands. Normally the word seat in Nostradamus indicates the Vatican but here it is difficult to be sure.

Roi trouvera ce qu'il desiroit tant,	The King will find that which
Quand le Prelat sera reprins à tort.	he desires so greatly; when the
Responce au duc le rendra mal content,	Prelate will be wrongfully taken. The reply to the Duce
Qui dans Milan mettra plusieurs a mort.	will make him angry; in Milan he will put several to death.

MUSSOLINI

The king of Italy, gets what he desires when he angers the Duce, Mussolini. The executions at Milan probably refer to the deaths of Ciano and others. The Pope being wrongfully taken is understood as the Vatican, a neutral city, being completely surrounded by a hostile Fascist Italy.

32

Par trahison de verges à mort battu,	Beaten to death by rods for treason; captured he will be overcome because of his disorder. Frivolous advice is handed to the great captive, when Berich comes to bite his nose in a rage.
Prins surmonté sera par son desordre:	
Conseil frivole au grand captif sentu,	
Nez par fureur quant Berich viendra mordre.	

The name of Berich, possibly an anagram, remains unsolved to this day.

33

Sa main derniere par Alus sanguinaire
Ne se pourra par la mer guarantir:
Entre deux fleuves craindre main militaire,
Le noir[1] l'ireux le fera repentir.

His hand finally through the bloody Alus, he will be unable to protect himself by sea. Between two rivers he will fear the military hand, the black and angry one will make him repent of it.

NAME OF THIRD ANTICHRIST?

Alus is another unsolved mystery. I wonder whether it connects with the fearsome Mabus of II. 62? There is the repetition of the word main in connection with both. It may be an approximation of name of the third Antichrist tying up with the cryptic quatrain (II. 28) where Nostradamus seems to be trying to spell the letters of his name. See I. 50, II. 89, VIII. 77, X. 72.

34

Du feu volant la machination,
Viendra troubler au grand chef assiegez:
Dedans sera telle sedition,
Qu'en desespoir seront les profligez.

The machine of flying fire will come to trouble the great, besieged chief. Within there will be such sedition that those abandoned will be in despair.

BOMBING OR ROCKETS

A general quatrain describing the situation of any place besieged by modern weapons. However, the first line is very striking.

[1] noir—Possible anagram for king—roi.

35

Pres de Rion[1] & proche à la blanche laine,
Aries, Taurus, Cancer, Leo, la Vierge,
Mars, Jupiter, le sol ardra grand plaine,
Bois & citez, lettres cachez au cierge.

Near the Bear and close to the white wool, Aries, Taurus, Cancer, Leo, Virgo, Mars, Jupiter the Sun will burn the great plain, woods and cities; letters hidden in the candle.

The white wool is probably the Milky Way, but Nostradamus has produced too many constellations for one to be sure what he intended apart from a drought on a great plain.

36

Ne bien ne mal par bataille terrestre,
Ne parviendra aux confins de Perousse:
Rebeller Pise, Florence voir mal estre,
Roi nuict blessé sur mulet à noire house.

Neither good nor evil from the earthly battle will come to the borders of Perugia. Pisa to rebel, Florence seen to be in bad(times): a king on a mule, wounded by night, to the black covering.

37

L'oeuvre ancienne se parachevera,
Du toict cherra sur le grand mal ruine:
Innocent faict mort on accusera:
Nocent caiché taillis à la bruine.

The ancient work will be accomplished and from the roof evil ruin will fall on to the great man. Being dead, they will accuse an innocent of the deed, the guilty one hidden in the misty woods.

Although this is a detailed prophecy and seems likely to have occurred, I do not know of its ever having been fulfilled.

[1] *Rion*—Misprint for *Trion*, from Latin, Triones = the Bear Constellation.

Au profligez de paix les ennemis,
Apres avoir l'Italie superee:
Noir[1] sanguinaire, rouge sera com-
mis,
Feu, sang verser, eaue de sang
couloree.

The enemies of peace, the dis-
solute ones, having overcome
Italy the bloody black one, red
will be seen, fire, bloodshed,
water coloured with blood.

The exposure of the colour red presumably means revolution
although the colour did not contain this sense until the late 18th
Century. Before that it referred to the Spanish or to Cardinals of
the Church. Some of Nostradamus' concepts are surprisingly
modern.

39

L'enfant du regne par paternelle
prinse,
Expolié sera pour delivrer:
Apres du lac Trasimen l'azur
prinse,
La troupe hostaige pour trop fort
s'enivrer.

The child of the kingdom,
through his father's capture.
will be deprived to deliver him;
near Lake Trasimene the azure
captive, in order that the
hostage troop may become very
drunk.

40

Grand du Magonce[2] pour grand
soif estaindre,
Sera privé de sa grand dignité:
Ceux de Cologne si fort le viendront
plaindre,
Que le grand groppe[3] au Rin sera
getté.

To quench the great thirst the
great one of Mainz will be
deprived of his great dignity.
Those from Cologne will come
to complain so strongly that
the great rump will be thrown
into the Rhine.

HOLY ROMAN EMPIRE, 1806

The Archbishop of Mainz was one of the Electors of the Empire.
Mainz was captured by the French during the Revolution and
ceded by the Treaty of Campoformio to the French. However, the
Elector held his title until the formal end of the Holy Roman
Empire in 1806. The Archbishop of Cologne was also an elector,
whose office was abolished three years early in 1803, so he had the
right to complain.

[1] *Noir*—either black or king, the usual anagram.
[2] *Magonce*—Latin, *Maguntiacum* = Mainz or Mayence.
[3] *groppe*—Low Latin, *groppa* = haunches, rump.

Le second chef de regne d'Anne-marc,	The second leader of the king-dom of Annemarc, through
Par Ceux de Frise & l'isle Britannique,	those of Frisia and the British Isles, will spend more than one
Fera despendre plus de cent mille marc,	hundred thousand marks, attempting in vain a voyage to
Vain exploicter voyage en Italique.	Italy.

A difficult quatrain made interesting by the fact that when Nostradamus wrote, England and Frisia had the same ruler, Philip of Spain, husband to Mary of England and ruler of all the Netherlands. In IV. 89. Nostradamus foresees William of Orange, a Frisian, attaining to the English throne. A problem remains in the uninterpreted Annemarc, also in IV. 27.

A lomygon¹ sera laissé le regne,	To Ogmios the kingdom of the
Du grand Selin qui plus fera de faict:	great Selin will be left, who will do even more. He will extend
Par les Italies estendra son enseigne,	his banner throughout Italy
Regi sera par prudent contrefaict.	and it will be ruled by careful forgery.

Ogmios also appears in V. 80, VIII. 44, IX. 89, but his identity is not certain.

Long temps sera sans estre habitée,	For a long time it will remain
Ou Signe & Marne autour vient arrouser:	uninhabited around where the Seine and Marne come to
De la Tamise & martiaux tentée,	gush forth. Tried by Tamise and
Decevez les gardes en cuidant repouser.	soldiers, the guards deceived in believing it rebuffed.

Paris is the city between the Seine and Marne which Nostradamus seems to envisage here as uninhabited. The Tamise can mean the river Thames in London, or a town of that name near Antwerp.

¹ *lomygon*—Misprint for Ogmios, the Celtic Hercules.

De nuict par Nantes L'Iris appa- roistra, Des artz marins susciteront la pluie: Arabique goulfre grand classe par- foudra, Un monstre en Saxe naistra d'ours & truie.	By night the rainbow will appear near Nantes, the marine arts will raise up rain. In the Arabian Gulf a great fleet will flounder: in Saxony a monster will be born of a bear and a sow.

20th CENTURY?

This quatrain may apply to the 20th Century. In 1947 the scientists discovered how to produce artificial rain (line 2). At a time when a rainbow appears at Nantes a fleet will meet disaster either in the Red Sea, since there is no actual Gulf of Arabia, or in the Arabian sea, which lies to the south, or the Persian Gulf to the east.

Le gouverneur du regne bien scavant, Ne consentir voulant au faict Royal: Mellile classe par le contraire vent, Le remettra à son plus desloyal.	The very learned governor of the kingdom does not wish to consent to the Royal deed. The fleet at Melilla, by a contrary wind, will deliver him back to his most disloyal one.

Melilla is in Spanish Morocco; from this some commentators apply the quatrain to the Spanish Civil War.

Un juste sera en exile renvoyé, Par pestilence aux confins de Nonseggle, Response au rouge le fera desvoyé, Roi retirant à la Rane & à l'aigle.	A just one will be sent back into exile through pestilence to the confines of Nonseggle. His reply to the red one will mislead him, the king withdrawing to the Frog and the Eagle.

Nonseggle remains an unsolved proper name or anagram. The frog reappears here as in quatrains V. 3, and V. 95. The first line may refer to Louis XVIII during the Hundred Days but the rest is completely obscure.

Entre deux monts les deux grans assemblés *Delaisseront leur simulté*[1] *secrette:* *Brucelle & Dolle par Langres acablés,* *Pour à Malignes executer leur peste.*	The two great ones, assembled between two mountains will give up their secret quarrel. Brussels and Dôle overcome by Langres in order to execute their pestilence at Malines.

Brussels and Dôle and Malines were all in the Spanish Netherlands. This quatrain may therefore predict their being conquered by France, Langres.

La saincteté trop faincte & seductive, *Accompaigné d'une langue diserte* *La cité vieille & Parme trop hastive,* *Florence & Sienne rendront plus desertes.*	The holiness, too false and too attractive accompanied by an eloquent tongue: The old city, Parma too hasty, they will make Florence and Siena even more deserted.

De la partie de Mammer[2] *grand Pontife,* *Subjugera les confins du Danube:* *Chasser les croix par fer raffe ne riffe,* *Captifz, or, bagues plus de cent mille rubes.*	The great Pontiff by the warlike party who will subjugate the borders of the Danube. The cross pursued by hook or by crook; captives, gold, jewels, more than one hundred thousand rubies.

THE SWASTIKA?

The cross is described as *ne raffe ne riffe*, an expression which can mean by hook or by crook, but also, by extension, crooked. The crooked cross can only be the swastika. Hitler's party originated in Austria, the Danube. The last line is horribly reminiscent of the millions of pounds of personal jewellery, gold and possessions the Nazis stole from their victims, most of whom ended up in the concentration camps. The position of the Pope in the verse is not clear but Pius XII was criticized for not taking a stronger line

---

[1] *simulté*—O.F. = quarrel.

[2] *Mammer* = (*a*) Mamers, Sabine name for Mars. (*b*) Mamertini. People of Messina, Sicily.

against the Nazis and for allowing them refuge in the Vatican city after the war.

50

Dedans le puys seront trouvés les oz.	The bones will be found inside
Sera l'incest conmis par la maratre:[1]	the wells; it will be incest committed by the stepmother.
L'estat changé on querra bruict & loz,	The state changed he will seek renown and praise and will
Et aura Mars attendant pour son astre.	have Mars attendant as his star.

51

Peuple assemblé, voir nouveau expectacle,	The people gathered to see a new sight; Princes and Kings
Princes & Rois par plusieurs assistans:	among many onlookers. The pillars, walls, fall, but as if by a
Pilliers faillir, murs, mais comme miracle	miracle the King and thirty of those present are saved.
Le Roi sauvé & trente des instants.	

HITLER?

It would be curious to speculate whether this was the verse that caused Ernst Krafft, who worked on Nostradamus for Goebbels' Propaganda Ministry, to warn Hitler against an assassination attempt that was made upon him in November 1939. The bomb was hidden in a pillar behind the rostrum and it was by sheer chance that Hitler and some of his Party members left for Berlin unexpectedly early. The notoriety gained by Krafft after this was to eventually cost him his life.

52

En lieu du grand qui sera condemné,	In the place of the great one who will be condemned he is
De prison hors son ami en sa place:	outside prison, his friend in his place. The Trojan hope for
L'espoir Troien en six mois joinct, mortnay,	six months joined, the born, dead; the Sun in Aquarius,
Le Sol à l'urne seront prins fleuves en glace.	the rivers will be frozen.

[1] *maratre*—more likely stepmother than mother-in-law because of the incest theme.

Another tantalizing quatrain in which Nostradamus contradicts the little that is known of an historical mystery, the fate of Louis XVII, see V. I. Here he implies that another child dies in prison in 1795 in his place, the Trojan blood always referring to French royal blood because of the legend of Francus, son of Priam of Troy. Line 3 is difficult to interpret. Does it refer to the death of the fake king after six months, or to the death of the real king six months after his escape? The Sun in Aquarius applies from mid-February to mid-March. The Dauphin was reported dead on 8th June 1795, but this prophecy must refer to the earlier months.

53

Le grand Prelat Celtique à Roi suspect,	The great French Prelate suspected by the king by night
De nuict par cours sortira hors du regne:	will flee from his realm;
Par duc fertile à son grand Roi, Bretaigne,	through a Duke fertile to his great King, Britain, Byzantium
Bisance à Cipres & Tunes insuspect.	to Cyprus and Tunis undiscovered.

This quatrain appears to indicate that a French Cardinal or Bishop will flee to England and from there to Tunis via Constantinople and Cyprus. Very confused.

54

Au poinct du jour au second chant du coq,	At daybreak at second cockcrow, those of Tunis, Fez and
Ceulx de Tunes, de Fez, & de Bugie,	of Bougie; the Arabs captured
Par les Arabes captif le Roi Maroq,	by the king of Morocco in the year sixteen hundred and seven
L'an mil six cens & sept, de Liturgie.	by the Liturgy.

1607?

This quatrain seems to be one of Nostradamus' total failures. He appears to see the fall of the Ottoman Empire through a new European king, and also in Asia through new Persian and Arab Empires in the year 1607. The only point in Nostradamus' favour is that no commentator can agree about what is meant by 'the Liturgy'. This may alter the date as it now appears, but how is not clear. It could simply be an equivalent of Anno Domini, but Nostradamus was usually more convoluted than that.

55

Au chalme Duc, en arrachant l'esponce,	The calmed duke drawing up the contract, the Arabian sail is seen, a sudden discovery. Tripolis, Chios and those of Trabzon; the Duke captured, the Black Sea and the city deserted.
Voile Arabesque voir, subit descouverte:	
Tripolis Chio, & ceux de Trapesonce,	
Duc prins, Marnegro & la cité deserte.	

All one can say with certainty about this verse is that the action takes place in Asia Minor, the Black Sea and the Aegean (Chios).

56

La crainte armee de l'ennemi Narbon,	The dreaded army of the Narbonne enemy will greatly terrify the Hesperians. Perignan empty, through the blind one of Arbon, then Barcelona by sea will take up her weapons.
Effrayera si fort les Hesperiques;[1]	
Parpignan vuide par l'aveugle darbon,[2]	
Lors Barcelon par mer donra les piques.	

SIEGE OF PERPIGNAN, 1597

In this quatrain it appears that the Spaniards are being terrified by the French from Narbonne. Narbonne was only forty miles north of Perpignan, while Barcelona, sending supplies and relief, lies about one hundred miles to the south. Perpignan was besieged for a short while by the French in 1597.

57

Celui qu'estoit bien avant dans le regne,	He who was well to the front in the kingdom, having a red chief close to the seat of power. Harsh and cruel he will make himself most greatly feared; he will succeed to the sacred monarchy.
Ayant chef rouge proche à la hierarchie:	
Aspre & cruel, & se fera tant craindre,	
Succedera à sacré monarchie.	

[1] Hesperiques—(a) Spanish or Western. (b) American.
[2] Arbon (?) may be geographical. If so either in France or Switzerland.

A cruel cardinal will succeed to the Papacy. It is difficult to know if Nostradamus had any particular one in mind. The quatrain is very general.

58

Entre les deux monarques esloin-guez, *Lors que Sol par Selin clair perdue:* *Simulté grande entre deux indignez,* *Qu'aux Isles & Sienne la liberté rendue.*	Between the two distant monarchs when the clear Sun is lost by Selin; great enmity between two indignant ones, so that liberty is restored to the Islands and to Siena.

PHILIP II AND HENRI II

This was a quatrain contemporary with Nostradamus' lifetime. The sun and the chariot of Apollo were the devices of Philip II of Spain. The moon was that of Henri II of France, partly to honour his mistress, Diana of Poitiers, *Selin* meaning the Moon, line 2. Nostradamus seems to think France will conquer the Habsburgs. Siena was held by the French at this time and they were also trying to conquer Corsica. Does the restoration of Liberty mean the coming or the withdrawal of the French? Nostradamus is usually more patriotic than this.

59

Dame en fureur par rage d'adultere, *Viendra à son Prince conjurer non de dire:* *Mais bref cogneu sera le vitupere,* *Que seront mis dix sept à martyre.*	The lady, furious, in an adulterous rage, will come to conspire not to speak to her Prince. But the culprit will soon be known so that seventeen will be martyred.

60

Le Prince hors de son terroir Celtique *Sera trahi, deceu par l'interprete:* *Rouan, Rochelle par ceux de l'Armorique* *Au port de Blaue deceus par moine & prebstre.*	The Prince, outside his French territory will be betrayed, deceived by the interpreter. Rouen, La Rochelle, by those of Brittany at the port of Blaye deceived by monk and priest.

Le grand tappis plié ne monstrera,	Folded, the great carpet will
Fois qu'à demi la pluspart de l'histoire:	not show except by halves, the greater part of its history.
Chassé du regne loing aspre apparoistra	Driven far out of the kingdom he will appear harsh, so that
Qu'au faict bellique chascun le viendra croire.	each one will believe in his warlike act.

Trop tard tous deux les fleurs seront perdues,	Too late both of the flowers will be lost, the snake will not want
Contre la loi serpent ne voudra faire:	to act against the law; the forces of the leaguers con-
Des ligueurs forces par gallots¹ confondues,	founded by the French, Savona, Albenga through Monaco great
Savone, Albinque par monech grand martyre.	martyrdom.

AN ERRONEOUS QUATRAIN

Nostradamus seems to intend a league against the French in this verse in which the French triumph. But Monaco was bound to the Spanish by treaty and Savona and Albenga belonged to Genoa. Nostradamus probably had one of the 16th-Century Italian leagues in mind, but in this case, wrongly.

La dame seule au regne demuree,	The lady left alone in the
L'unic estaint premier au lict d'honneur:	kingdom, her only (spouse) first dead on the bed of honour.
Sept ans sera de douleur exploree,	For seven years she will be weeping with grief, then a long
Puis longue vie au regne par grand heur.	life for the good fortune of the kingdom.

CATHERINE DE' MEDICI

Nostradamus may have been prejudiced in this quatrain when he describes Catherine de' Medici as living for the good of her kingdom. Equally, knowing the prophet's writings she may have gone out of her way to fulfil the prediction. Catherine left off mourning for her husband on 1st August 1566, seven years after his death. She lived on until 1589 as Regent under Francis II and Charles IX, but lost most of her power under Henri III.

¹ gallots—O.F., gallot = Gallic or French.

On ne tiendra pache aucune arresté,
Tous recevans iront par tromperie:
De paix & trefve, terre & mer
* protesté'.*
Par Barcelone classe prins d'indus-
* trie.*

They will not keep any peace
agreed upon, all the receivers
will go through deceit. In peace
and truce land and sea having
protested, the fleet is seized
with skill by Barcelona.

Gris & bureau[1] demie ouverte
* guerre,*
De nuict seront assaillis & pillez:
Le bureau prins passera par la
* serre[2]*
Son temple ouvert, deux au plastre
* grillez.*

Grey and brown in half
declared war, at night they will
be besieged and pillaged. The
captured brown one will pass
through the prison, his temple
opened, two slipped in the
plaster.

It is likely that Nostradamus was describing a feud between two
monastic orders. The Franciscans wore grey habits, although
some were brown in subsidiary orders.

Au fondement de la nouvelle
* secte,*
Seront les os du grand Romain
* trouvés,*
Sepulchre en marbre apparoistra
* couverte,*
Terre trembler en Avril, mal
* enfouetz.*

At the founding of a new sect
the bones of the great Roman
will be found. A sepulchre
covered in marble will appear:
the earth will quake in April,
badly buried.

It appears that an April earth tremor may reveal the sepulchre
of an important Roman, probably a Pope. This is also mentioned
in III. 65. The sect is presumably Protestant.

[1] *bureau*—variant of *burel*. O.F. = brown.
[2] *serre*—Literally lock, or saw.

Au grand Empire parviendra tout un aultre	Quite a different man will attain to the great Empire,
Bonté distant plus de felicité:	distant from kindness, more so
Regi par un issue non loing du peaultre,	from happiness. Ruled by one not long come from his bed, the
Corruer regnes grande infelicité.	kingdom rushes to great misfortune.

There are two interpretations of the third line, either that the new Emperor is but a child having left the bed where he was born, or, that he leads a debauched life because *peaultre* can also mean a brothel. Possibly the Emperor Napoleon ruled by Josephine.

Lors que soldatz fureur seditieuse,	When the soldiers in a treacherous fury at night rise up and
Contre leur chef feront de niuct fer luire:	fight against their leader. The
Ennemi d'Albe soit par main furieuse,	enemy of Alba with furious hand then troubles Rome and
Lors vexer Rome & principaux seduire.	wins over the principals.

THE DUKE OF ALVA

This prediction was probably meant for the near future, i.e. 16th Century and the Duke of Alva (Alba). Nostradamus foresees him trying to suppress a revolt in the Spanish army, which he had to do soon afterwards in the Netherlands.

La pitié grande sera sans loing tarder,	The great pity will arrive before very long: those who gave will
Ceux qui donoient seront contrains de prendre.	be forced to take. Naked, starving with cold and thirst, they
Nudz affamez de froit, soif, soi bander,	band together to cross the
Les monts passer commettant grand esclandre.	mountains causing a great scandal.

DISBANDING OF THE CLERGY, *c.* 1792

Once France had declared the disestablishment of the Clergy in 1792 many priests found themselves in wretched circumstances. Instead of keeping themselves through their duties to their parishes they were constrained to beg to stay alive. Many did band together to cross the Alps and take refuge in the Vatican. Their plight naturally caused a scandal.

70

Au chef du monde le grand Chyren sera,
Plus oultre[1] apres aimé, craint, redoubté:
Son bruit & loz les cieux surpassera,
Et du seul titre victeur fort contenté.

The great Chyren will be chief of the world, after 'Plus oultre' loved, feared and dreaded. His fame and praise go beyond the heavens and he will be greatly satisfied with the sole title of victor.

The implication of line 2 is that the new hero Chyren will be greater in every way than the Emperor Charles V. It is tempting to equate Chyren with Henri IV of Navarre, the word being the obvious anagram from the old spelling of Henri, HENRYC. But the other Chyren quatrains will not bear this interpretation. Perhaps Nostradamus foresaw several great men named Henri?

71

Quand on viendra le grand roi parenter
Avant qu'il ait du tout l'ame rendue,
Celui qui moins le viendra lamenter,
Par Lions, d'aigles, croix, couronne vendue.

When they will come to give the last rites to the great king, before he has quite given up his soul, he who will come to lament him the last, through lions the cross and crown of the eagles sold.

This general description could apply to the deaths of many kings. Presumably the last line indicates the armorial bearings of those involved.

72

Par fureur faincte d'esmotion divine,
Sera la femme du grand fort violee:
Juges voulans damner telle doctrine,
Victime au peuple ignorant imolee.

Through feigned fury of a divine emotion the wife of the great one will be badly violated. The judges wishing to condemn such a doctrine, the victim is sacrificed to the ignorant people.

[1] 'Plus oultre Carol Quint' was the device of Charles V. It is in capitals in the 1605 edition which clarifies the reading.

Many modern commentators see in this verse a reference to the manner in which Rasputin dominated the wife of the Czar. The word violated should be taken metaphorically although rumours certainly went around the Russian Court that the Priest was the Czarina's lover. The whole family became victims of their ignorant people, when they refused to understand the doctrines of the times, which led eventually to their deaths.

73

En cité grande un moine & artisan, *Pres de la porte logés & aux* *murailles:* *Contre Modene secret, cave disant,* *Trahis pour faire souz couleur* *d'espousailles.*	In a great city a monk and an artisan are lodged near the gate and the walls; speaking vainly and secretly against Modena, betrayed for acting under the guise of a marriage.

74

La deschassee au regne tournera, *Ses ennemis trouvés des conjurés:* *Plus que jamais son temps tri-* *omphera,* *Trois & septante à mort trop* *asseures.*	She who was cast out will return to reign, her enemies found among conspirators. More than ever will her time be triumphant, at three and seventy to death very sure.

ELIZABETH I

Elizabeth was certainly rejected during her childhood and was the victim of conspiracies during her sister's reign. England rose to new heights during her reign. She died in her seventieth year in 1603. Most commentators want to insert a comma between *trois et septante*, indicating the first number as the year she died, 1603, and the second as her age. I leave it to the reader to decide.

75

Le grand pilot par Roi sera mandé, *Laisser la classe pour plus haut* *lieu attaindre:* *Sept and apres sera contrebandé,* *Barbare armée viendra Venise* *craindre.*	The great pilot will be commissioned by the King to leave the fleet to attain to higher rank. Seven years later he will be in rebellion, Venice will come to fear the barbarian army.

De Coligny was made Henry II's Admiral of the fleet (grand pilot) in 1552 and resigned the post seven years later, 1559, after the King's death to join up with the Calvinist party. He was one of the principal instigators of the Huguenot/Catholic wars in France. These events occurred at the same time that Venice was suffering the attacks of the Sultan Selim II, who took Cyprus from them in 1570.

76

La cité antique d'antenoree¹ forge.	The ancient city created by
Plus ne pouvant le tyran supporter:	Antenor is no longer able to
Le manchet² fainct au temple	support the tyrant; a false one-
couper gorge,	armed man in the temple will
Les siens le peuple à mort viendra	cut the throat, the people will
boucher.	come to put his followers to
	death.

Padua belonged to Venice which, as I have mentioned earlier, was governed by an hereditary office of podestas. But there does not seem to be any record of a murder in a church followed by the further killings of followers.

77

Par la victoire du deceu fraudulente,	Through the fraudulent victory
Deux classes une, la revolte Ger-	of the deceived, two fleets in
maine:	one, the German revolt. The
Le chef meurtri & son filz dans la	chief murdered with his son in
tente	the tent. Florence and Imola
Florence, Imole pourchassés dans	pursued into Romania.
Romaine.³	

During the 16th and 17th Centuries there were many revolts against the authority of the Emperor. *Romaine* is most likely to be Romagna because Imola is located there.

¹ *antenoree*—Anteor was the legendary founder of Padua.
² *manchet*—O.F. = one armed.
³ *Romania* = (*a*) Romagna, (*b*) The Holy Roman Empire, or (*c*) The Papal States.

Crier victoire du grand Selin croissant,[1]	To shout aloud the victory of the great crescent moon the
Par les Romains sera l'Aigle clamé,	Eagle will be proclaimed by the Romans. Pavia, Milan and
Ticcin, Milan, & Gennes n'y consent,	Genoa will not agree to it: then the great Lord is claimed by
Puis par eux mesmes Basil[2] *grand reclame.*	themselves.

RETROACTIVE PROPHECY?

This quatrain obviously refers to the Ottoman and Holy Roman Empires whose particular emblems were the crescent moon and the Eagle. The Sultan was known in Europe as the Grand Seignior, but not one has been captured by the Roman Empire since Nostradamus' day. The last was the Sultan Jem in the 15th Century, so this is possibly a retroactive prophecy.

Pres du Tesin les habitans du Loire,	Near the Ticino the inhabitants of the Loire, Garonne and
Garonne & Saonne, Seine, Tain, & Gironde:	Saône, the Seine, Tain and Gironde: Beyond the moun-
Outre les monts dresseront promontoire,	tains they will build a promontory; conflict engaged, Pau
Conflict donné Pau granci,[3] *submergé onde.*	seized, submerged by the wave.

BATTLE OF LODI, 10th MAY 1796

Many interpreters accept the word *Pau* in the last line as a shortened form of Napoleon, see VIII. 1. If so, this is a very precise description of an accident which befell Napoleon at the Battle of Lodi. While the bridge over the Adda was being stormed, Napoleon fell into the water (submerged by the wave) but was pulled out before he could drown.

[1] *croissant* = (*a*) Growing. (*b*) Crescent moon.

[2] *Basil*—Greed, *Basilous* = Lord, king, captain.

[3] *granci*—Either *grancito*, Tuscan for snatched, seized; or erratum for *grandi.*

De Fez le regne parviendra à ceux d'Europe,	From Fez the kingdom will stretch out to those of Europe.
Feu leur cité, & lame trenchera:	The city blazes, the sword will
Le grand d'Asie terre & mer à grand troupe,	slash; the great man of Asia with a great troop by land and
Que bleux, pers,[1] croix, à mort dechassera.	sea so that blues, perse, he will drive out the cross to death.

WAR IN MIDDLE EAST. THE THIRD ANTICHRIST
Nostradamus stated in VI. 54 that the King of Fez might be
captured by the Arabs, but I think this quatrain fits into a more
modern context. There is constant repetition of the theme of War
in the Middle East, connected with the man from Asia, who is
tentatively identified with Nostradamus' Third Antichrist.

Pleurs, cris & plaincts, hurlement effrayeur,	Tears, cries and wailing, howls and terror, an inhuman cruel
Cœur inhumain, cruel, noir & transi:	heart, black and cold. Lake Geneva, the Islands, the main
Leman, les isles de Gennes les majeurs,	people of Genoa; blood pours, hunger for wheat, mercy to
Sang epancher, frofaim[2] à nul merci.	none.

This may continue the horrors of the last quatrain, with the war
spreading to Switzerland, Italy and the Mediterranean islands.

Par les desers de lieu, libre & farouche,	Through the deserts of the free, wild place, the nephew of the
Viendra errer nepveu du grand Pontife:	Great Pontiff will wander. Killed by seven with a heavy
Assommé à sept avecques lourde souche,	club, by those who will afterwards occupy the chalice.
Par ceux, qu'apres occuperont le cyphe.	

[1] *perse*—A colour, either blue or blue green.
[2] *frofaim*—A Nostradamus word possibly from *froment-faim* meaning
hunger for wheat?

Celui qu'aura tant d'honneur & *caresses*	He who will have so much honour and affection at his
A son entree de la Gaule Belgique:	entry into Belgian Gaul; a
Un temps apres fera tant de *rudesses,*	while after he will act as crudely and will be very bellicose to-
Et sera contre à la fleur tant *bellique.*	wards the flower.

PHILIP OF SPAIN, FRANCE AND THE NETHERLANDS
When Charles V abdicated, Philip of Spain was well received in the Netherlands until his bigotry alienated the people to such a degree that they revolted in 1558. Then Francis Duke of Alençon was invited by the Netherlands to be their Protector in 1580 but stupidly he attempted to regain control of Antwerp and lost the loyalty of his subjects. The flower in the last line is presumably the fleur de lis of France, against which Philip went to war during 1589–98, against Henri of Navarre.

Celui qu'en Sparte Claude[1] ne peut *regner,*	The lame man who could not rule in Sparta, he will do much
Il fera tant par voie seductive:	seductive ways. That by the
Que du court, long, le fera araigner,	long and the short of it he will
Que contre Roi sera sa perspective.	be accused of aiming his objectives against the king.

The first line merely refers to the fact that the Spartans killed any children who were born imperfect. Then one must look for famous lame men in history; perhaps Talleyrand if one may read Emperor for king, or Lord Byron working with the Greek Freedom fighters?

La grand cité de Tharse par *Gaulois*	The great city of Tarsus by the Gauls will be destroyed, all
Sera destruite, captifs tous à *Turban:*	captured at Turban. Help from the sea from the great Portu-
Secours par mer du grand Portu- *galois,*	guese; the first day of summer, Urban's consecration.
Premier d'esté le jour du sacre *Urban.*	

[1] *Claude*—Latin, *claudus* = lame.

Nostradamus seems to envisage a French army capturing Tarsus in Asia Minor and continuing on into Asia. Portugal was one of the greatest sea powers in Nostradamus' day, and he envisages them as allies of the French. The dating of the last line is obscure. There are two main saints called Urban, one is celebrated on 25th May, the other on 23rd January: there are twelve other minor saints with this name but the first is most likely as summer begins on 21st June.

86

Le grand Prelat un jour apres son songe,
Interpreté au rebours de son sens:
De la Gascogne lui surviendra un monge,
Qui fera eslire le grand Prelat de sens.

One day the great Prelate, after his dream interpreted the opposite to its meaning; from Gascony a monk will come to him who will cause the great Prelate of Sens to be elected.

87

L'election faite dans Frankfort,
N'aura nul lieu Milan s'opposera:
Le sien plus proche semblera si grand fort
Que outre le Rhin és mareschz chassera.

The election made in Frankfurt will not be valid, Milan will oppose it. The closest follower will seem so very strong that he will drive him out beyond the Rhine into the marshes.

EMPEROR FERDINAND, 1558–62

The election at Frankfurt probably refers to the coronation of Ferdinand as Holy Roman Emperor which took place there in 1558. Philip, who was Ferdinand's rival had been given Milan by his Uncle Charles V before his death in 1542. Philip tries to drive Ferdinand out of Germany, line 4, and into the Netherlands. In fact he was not at all successful in this, but he did continue to intrigue against Ferdinand for the succession until 1562.

88

Un regne grand demourra desolé,
Aupres del Hebro se feront assem-
blees:
Monts Pyrenees le rendront consolé,
Lors que dans Mai seront terres tremblees.

A great kingdom will remain desolate, near the Ebro they will be gathered in assemblies. The Pyrenean mountains will console him when in May there will be earth tremors.

Entre deux cymbes[1] piedz & mains estachés,
De miel face oingt & de laict substanté:
Guespes & mouches, fitine[2] amour fachés,
Poccilateur[3] faucer, Cyphe[4] tempté.

Feet and hands bound between two boats, the face anointed with honey and touched with milk. Wasps and flies, fatherly love angered, the cupbearer lies, the goblet tried.

The fact that the face is anointed with milk and honey indicates that the victim was a crowned king for these are part of the Coronation service. The wasps may be an indirect reference to Napoleon's emblem of bees.

L'honnissement puant abhominable
Apres le faict sera felicité,
Grand excusé, pour n'estre favour-
able,
Qu'à paix Neptune ne sera incité.

The stinking and abominable shame, after the deed he will be congratulated. The great one excused for not being favour-able, that Neptune cannot be tempted towards peace.

Someone gets away with a deed of such skullduggery that it is almost incredible; and yet he is unsuspected and congratulated despite the fact that he cannot arrange for a naval peace. Presumably he was in communication with the enemy?

Du conducteur de la guerre navale,
Rouge effrené, severe horrible grippe,
Captif eschappé de l'aisné dans la
baste:
Quant il naistra du grand un filz
Agrippe.

Of the leader of the naval war, the red one unbridled, severe, horrible quarrel; captive escaped from the older one in the saddle, when the great Agrippa bears a son.

The Naval commanders in Nostradamus' time were the Baron de la Garde, and M. de la Mole, but the rest of the quatrain is obscure.

[1] *cymbe*—O.F. = boat.
[2] *fitine*—Gk., *phitus* = father.
[3] *Poccilateur*—Latin, *poccilator* = cup-bearer.
[4] *Cyphe*—Latin, *scyphus* = cup, goblet.

Prince de beauté tant venuste,	The Prince of such handsome
Au chef menee, le second faict trahi:	beauty, intrigues against his person, betrayed to the second
La cité au glaive de poudre face aduste,	rank. The city put to the sword, consumed with a powder that
Par le trop grand meutre le chef du Roi hai.	burns. By this, so great a murder, the head of the king is hated.

LOUIS XVI's DEATH

Louis XVI was considered to be very handsome as a youth. He finds intrigues (*menees*) directed against him and will be deposed to the second rank of a constitutional king. Then he is betrayed. The line *'poudre face aduste'* has been most interestingly interpreted by James Laver from the Latin, *fax*, a torch, and *adustus*, burned, as consumed by a powder that burns. It was into quicklime that the hated head of the King was thrown from the wicker basket after his execution on the guillotine. The third line *'cité au glaive'*, is an excellent description of revolutionary Paris.

Prelat avare d'ambition trompé.	The greedy prelate deceived by
Rien ne sera que trop viendra cuider:	ambition, he will think that nothing is too great (for him).
Ses messagiers, & lui bien attrapé,	He and his messengers, completely trapped, the man who
Tout au rebours voir, qui le bois fendroit.	cuts the woods sees all in reverse.

Un Roi iré sera aux sedifragues,[1]	A king will be angry with the
Quant interdicts seront harnois de guerre:	sedifragues[1] when warlike arms are prohibited; the poison
La poison taincte au succre par les fragues[2]	tainted with sugar in the strawberries, murdered by waters,
Par eaux meutris, mors, disant serre serre.	death, saying, close, close.

[1] *sedifragus*—A Nostradamus word; possible compounded from *sedem frangere*—which literally means to break a seat.

[2] *fragues*—Latin, *fraga* = strawberries.

The see breakers, if one has understood Nostradamus correctly, probably refer to the Protestants who broke up the unity of the See of Rome.

95

Par detracteur calumnie à puis nay.
Quant istront faicts enormes &
    martiaux:
La moindre part dubieuse à l'aisney
Et tost au regne seront faicts
    partiaux.

Calumny against the younger born by the detractor, when enormous, martial deeds will occur. The least part doubtful for the elder one, and soon in the kingdom there will be partisan actions.

96

Grande cité à soldatz abandonné,
Onques n'y eut mortel tumulte si
    proche,
O quel hideuse calamité s'approche,
Fors une offense n'y sera pardonnée.

A great city abondoned to the soldiers, there was never a mortal tumult so close; Oh what a dreadful calamity approaches; except for one offence it will not be forgiven.

This quatrain is so general that it could be applied to the sack of any city. Commentators are particularly fond of applying it to the sack of St. Quentin (1557) or Paris during the Revolution.

97

Cinq & quarante degrés ciel
    bruslera,
Feu approcher de la grand cité
    neufve,
Instant grand flamme esparse
    sautera,
Quand on voudra des Normans faire
    preuve.

The sky will burn at forty-five degrees, fire approaches the great New City. Immediately a huge, scattered flame leaps up when they want to have proof of the Normans.

BOMBING OF NEW YORK?

New York county lies between 40° and 45° parallel in the U.S.A. There are other references to it as the cité neufve. It appears that the attack is very widespread (scattered flame). The position of France when this occurs is unclear, but France is also involved in a similar quatrain, see X. 49 in particular and I. 91, IX. 92.

Ruine aux Volsques¹ de peur si fort terribles,	Ruin for the Volcae, so very terrible with fear, their great
Leur grand cité taincte, faict pestilent:	city stained by a pestilential deed. To plunder the Sun and
Piller Sol, Lune & violer leurs temples:	Moon and violate their temples and to redden the two rivers
Et les deux fleuves rougir de sang coulant.	running with blood.

The sun and moon plundered are gold and silver. The capital city of Languedoc would probably be Toulouse.

L'ennemi docte se tournera confus,	The learned enemy will turn
Grand camp malade, & de faict par embusches,	around confused, the great camp sick and defeated by
Monts Pyrenees & Poenus² lui seront faicts refus	ambushes. The Pyrenean Mountains and the Pennines
Proche du fleuve decouvrant antiques cruches.	will be refused to him, near the river discovering ancient urns.

LEGIS CANTIO CONTRA INEPTOS CRITICOS	INCANTATION OF THE LAW AGAINST INEPT CRITICS.
Quos legent hosce versus maturè censunto,	May those who read this verse think upon it deeply, let the
Profanum vulgus & inscium ne attrectato:	profane and ignorant herd keep away. Let all astrologers, idiots
Omnesq; Astrologi Blenni,³ Barbari procul sunto,	and barbarians stay far off, he who does otherwise, let him
Qui alter facit, is ritè, sacer esto.	be priest to the rite.

This verse is odd. Line 4 sounds vaguely like a threat or curse. If the verses were originally written in Latin, as I believe they were, this gives the reader a good idea of the type of construction and vocabulary used by Nostradamus. Why does Nostradamus include Astrologers among the people he damns? Is this yet another example of his trying to bluff the authorities?

¹ *Volsques*—People of Languedoc. Southern France.
² *Poenus*—Latin, *Alpes Poeninae* = the Pennine Alps.
³ *Blenni*—Greek, *Blennos* = simpleton, idiot.

CENTURY VII

1	
2	
3	
4*	Duke de Guise
5	
6	
7	
8	
9*	Duke de Guise and Diane de Poitiers
10*	Duke d'Aumale, 1573
11	
12	
13**	Napoleon
14*	National Assembly, 1789
15	
16*	Mary Tudor and the capture of Calais
17	
18	
19	
20*	Cavour in Paris, 1856
21	
22*	Pius VI, 1799
23	
24	
25	
26*	November 1555
27	
28	
29	
30	
31	
32*	de' Medici family
33*	France, 1940

34*	France, 1940 *continued*
35*	Henri III
36	
37	
38*	Death of Prince Ferdinand
39	
40	
41?	A haunted house?
42	

An incomplete Century.

KEY: * Of interest. F? Possibly referring to the future.

I

L'arc du thresor par Achilles deceu,
Aux procrées¹ sceu la quadrangu-
  laire:
Au faict Royal le comment sera sceu,
Cors veu pendu au veu du populaire.

The arc of the treasure deceived
by Achilles, the quadrangule
known to the procreators. The
invention will be known by the
Royal deed; a corpse seen hanging in the sight of the populace.

There are only two well-known Achilles in French history. The
first was Achille de Harlay, President of the Parlement de Paris
who contributed to the downfall of the Queen Regent's favourite,
Concini, who was assassinated in 1517. The other was Achille
Bazaine, a Marshal of France whose incapacity and defeatism
led to the fall of France in 1870.

2

Par Mars ouvert Arles ne donra
  guerre.
De nuict seront les soldartz
  estonnés:
Noir, blanc à l'inde dissimulés en
  terre,
Sous la faincte umbre traistres
  verez & sonnés.

Arles opened up by war will
not offer resistance, the soldiers
will be astonished by night.
Black and white concealing
indigo on land under the false
shadow you will see traitors
sounded.

3

Apres de France la victoire navale,
Les Barchinons, Saillinons,² les
  Phocens,
Lierre d'or, l'enclume serré dedans
  la basle,
Ceux de Ptolon³ au fraud seront
  consens.

After the naval victory of
France, the people of Barcelona
the Saillinons and those of
Marseilles; the robber of gold,
the anvil enclosed in the ball,
the people of Ptolon will be
party to the fraud.

Even the proper names are obscure in this quatrain. France is
clear and the Phocens who were from Marseilles. The Barchinons
may be from Barcelona. The Saillinons and Ptolons are unclear.
Garencières suggests that Ptolons should be from Toulon. It is

¹ *procrées*—There is a variant *procès* which would give a better reading
of 'in the documents'.
² *Saillinons*—Not identified.
³ *Ptolon* = Either the land of Ptolomy, Egypt, or Acre, earlier called
Ptolemais.

possible that the name could be contorted like this by Nostradamus.

4

Le duc de Langres assiegé dedans Dolle,
Accompaigné d'Ostun & Lyonnais:
Geneve, Auspour, joinct ceux de Mirandole,
Passer les monts contre les Anconnois.

The Duke of Langres besieged at Dôle accompanied by people from Autun and Lyons. Geneva, Augsburg allied to those of Mirandola, to cross the mountains against the people of Ancona.

THE DUKE DE GUISE

This complicated verse describes the Duke de Guise (*Langres*) with soldiers from Autun and Lyons being besieged in Dôle during an attack on the Spanish. At the same time armies of the Empires from Geneva, Augsburg and Northern Italy will invade the Papal States (Ancona belonged to the Pope).

5

Vin sur la table en sera respandu
Le tiers n'aura celle qu'il pretendoit:
Deux fois du noir[1] de Parme descendu,
Perouse à Pize fera ce qu'il cuidoit.

Some of the wine on the table will be spilt, the third will not have that which he claimed. Twice descended from the black one of Parma, Perouse will do to Pisa that which he believed.

Pisa belonged to Tuscany, Perugia and Parma to the Vatican, the latter being given to his bastard son Pierluigi Farnese by Pope Paul III in 1545. When the Farnese family died out Parma passed to the Bourbons. I cannot decipher this verse further.

6

Naples, Palerme, & toute la Secille,
Par main barbare sera inhabitee,
Corsicque, Salerne & de Sardeigne l'isle,
Faim, peste, guerre fin de maux intemptee.[2]

Naples, Palerma and all of Sicily will be uninhabited through Barbarian hands. Corsica, Salerno and the island of Sardinia, hunger, plague, war the end of extended evils.

[1] noir—The usual second meaning of *roi*, king, is possible here.
[2] intemptee—Latin, *intentatus* = extended, stretched.

This general verse predicts that Sicily and Southern Italy as well as Corsica and Sardinia will be ravaged by invasions of the Barbary pirates. There were many raids in the 16th Century both before and after Nostradamus wrote the Prophecies, so this may be a retroactive verse.

7

Sur le combat des grans cheveux, legiers,	Upon the struggle of the great, light horses, it will be claimed
On criera le grand croissant confond.	that the great crescent is destroyed. To kill by night, in the
De nuict tuer monts, habits de bergiers,	mountains, dressed in shepherds' clothing, red gulfs in the
Abismes rouges dans le fossé profond.	deep ditch.

The crescent moon was the emblem of the Turks and apparently Nostradamus sees them as suffering a great defeat. The third line suggests that some soldiers dress up as shepherds when attacking. The red gulfs almost certainly stand for rivers of blood.

8

Flora fuis, fuis le plus proche Romain,	Florence, flee, flee the nearest Roman, at Fiesole will be
Au Fesulan¹ sera conflict donné:	conflict given: blood shed, the
Sang espandu les plus grands prins à main,	greatest ones taken by the hand, neither temple nor sex will be
Temple ne sexe ne sera pardonné.	pardoned.

The quatrain seems to predict that Florence will suffer a severe attack by Vatican troops. Fiesole is only a few miles away and would naturally suffer the same fate.

9

Dame à l'absence de son grand capitaine,	The lady in the absence of her great master will be begged for
Sera priee d'amours du Viceroi,	love by the Viceroy. Feigned
Faincte promesse & malheureuse estraine,²	promise and misfortune in love, in the hands of the great Prince
Entre les mains du grand Prince Barrois.	of Bar.

¹ *Fesulan*—Latin, *Faesulae* = Fiesole.
² *estrenne*—O.F. = success in love, luck.

France has never had a Viceroy, the only comparable offices are those of the Constable, or the Lieutenant-General, which de Guise held when Nostradamus wrote. The title Duke de Bar was that given to the eldest son of the Duke de Lorraine. As the Duke was a child there was no holder at that period. It is unlikely that Dame refers to the Queen, Catherine de' Medici, but it may well describe Henri II's influential mistress, Diane de Poitiers, who would be in her late fifties.

10

Par le grand Prince limitrophe du Mans	By the great Prince bordering le Mans, brave and valliant
Preux & vaillant chef de grand excercite:	leader of the great army; by land and sea with Bretons and
Par mer & terre de Gallotz & Normans,	Normans, to pass Gibraltar and Barcelona to pillage the island.
Caspre passer Barcelone pillé isle.	

DUKE D'AUMALE, 1526–1573

Le Mans used to be the main city of Maine in North Western France, whereas Mayenne the next most important city, belonged to de Guise. In Nostradamus' lifetime it was held by de Guise's brother Claude, whose titles were Marquess of Mayenne and Duke d'Aumale. The latter did fight at Metz in 1552 and later at Calais, St. Denis, Dreux and Montcontour, but he never invaded Spain or North Africa. Nostradamus seems to have foreseen a much greater future for him that that which actually happened.

11

L'enfant Royal contemnera la mere,	The royal child will scorn his
Oeil, piedz blessés, rude, inobeis-sant,	mother, eye, feet wounded rude disobedient; strange and very
Nouvelle à dame estrange & bien amere,	bitter news to the lady; more than five hundred of her people
Seront tués des siens plus de cinq cens.	will be killed.

This quatrain seems to refer to the quarrels of a Queen Regent with her son. Since Nostradamus' lifetime there has been one notable example between Louis XIII and his mother Marie de' Medici. In the ensuing battle Garencières states that more than five hundred of the Queen's supporters were killed.

Le grand puisné fera fin de la guerre,	The great younger son will make an end of the war, he
Aux dieux assemble les excusés:	assembles the pardoned before the gods; Ahors and Moissac
Cahors, Moissac iront long de la serre,	will go far from the prison, a
Reffus Lestore, les Agenois razés.	refusal at Lectoure, the people of Agen shaved.

A cadet or younger son was usually used to refer to the younger brother, or descendent of a younger brother of a king or ruler. This may refer to a son of the Guise family which were cadets of the Dukedom of Lorraine, all the towns being quite close together in Gienne, South-western France.

13

De la cité marine & tributaire,	From the marine tributary city,
La teste raze prendra la satrapie:	the shaven head will take up
Chasser sordide qui puis sera contraire	the satrapy; to chase the sordid man who will then be against
Par quatorze ans tiendra la tyrannie.	him. For fourteen years he will hold the tyranny.

NAPOLEON, 1793
Bonaparte (the shaven head) will retake Toulon the marine city in 1793 from the English, led by Sir Arthur Wellesley, who have made it a tributary. He will then overthrow the Directory (the sordid one) and put an end to the Republic. He will enjoy absolute power for fourteen years (9th November 1799–13th April 1814). This interpretation was made by le Pelletier who adds that 'the sordid one' may well mean the English!

14

Faux esposer viendra topographie,	He will come to expose the false
Seront les cruches des monuments ouvertes:	topography, the urns of the tombs will be opened. Sect and
Pulluler secte saincte philosophie,	holy philosophy to thrive, black
Pour blanches, noirs, & pour antiques verts.	for white and the new for the old.

NATIONAL ASSEMBLY, 22nd DECEMBER 1789
On 22nd December 1789, the National Assembly changed the ancient regional districts of France into Departments. At St. Denis the tombs of the French kings will be violated and their ashes

scattered. Anti-christian sects flourish and take the place of religion. People will accept that black is white and will accept new ideas for the old traditions.

15

Devant cité de l'Insubre¹ contree,
Sept and sera le siege devant mis:
Le tres grand Roi y fera son entree,
Cité puis libre hors de ses ennemis.

Before the city of the Insubrian lands, for seven years the siege will be laid; a very great king enters it, the city is then free, away from its enemies.

Nostradamus here predicts a very long drawn out siege of Milan lasting seven years. The liberating king is probably a French one freeing Milan from its Spanish masters.

16

Entrée profonde par la grand Roine faicte
Rendra le lieu puissant inaccessible:
L'armee des trois lions sera deffaite,
Faisant dedans cas hideux &
terrible.

The deep entry made by the great Queen will make the place powerful and inaccessible; the army of the three lions will be defeated causing within a thing hideous and terrible.

QUEEN MARY AND THE CAPTURE OF CALAIS, 1558
The great Queen, Mary Tudor, held Calais 'engraved upon her heart' until it was recaptured by the Duc de Guise in 1558. England was at that time an ally of Spain through Mary's marriage and the three lions form part of the English Standard. This is a comparatively successful quatrain.

17

Le prince rare de pitié & clemence,
Viendra changer par mort grand cognoissance:
Par grand repos le regne travaillé,
Lors que le grand tost sera estrillé.

The prince who has little pity or mercy will come through death to change (and become) very knowledgeable. The kingdom will be attended with great tranquillity, when the great one will soon be fleeced.

¹ Insubre—Latin, Insubria = the area around Milan.

Les assiegés coulouleront leur paches,	The besieged will colour their
Sept jours apres feront cruelle issue	pacts, but seven days later they
Dans repoulsés feu, sang. Sept mis	will make a cruel exit: thrown
à l'hache	back inside, fire and blood,
Dame captive qu'avoit la paix	seven put to the axe the lady
tissue.	who had woven the peace is a
	captive.

An obscure quatrain which apparently describes a treacherous enemy who, while being besieged, pretends to sue for peace, but seven days later makes a disastrous attack. Line 4 is quite possible for that period. The peace of Cambrai, in 1529, was known as the Ladies' Charter because it was negotiated by the mother of Francis I and the aunt of Charles V.

Le fort Nicene ne sera combatu,	The fort at Nice will not engage
Vaincu sera par rutilant metal	in combat, it will be overcome
Son faict sera un long temps debatu,	by shining metal. This deed will
Aux citadins estrange espouvantal.	be debated for a long time,
	strange and fearful for the
	citizens.

Nice has been captured twice since Nostradamus wrote the Prophecies, in 1891 and 1705, both times by the French.

Ambassadeurs de la Toscane langue,	Ambassadors of the Tuscan
Avril & Mai Alpes & mer passer:	language will cross the Alps
Celui de veau[1] exposera l'harangue,	and the sea in April and May.
Vie Gauloise ne venant effacer.	The man of the calf will deliver
	an oration, not coming to wipe
	out the French way of life.

CAVOUR IN PARIS, 1856

The good relations which existed between Napoleon III and the Pope were spoiled when Cavour arrived in Paris in 1856 to plead the cause of Italian unity. The Congress at Paris took place in the months Nostradamus mentions, April and May. The reason for calling him man of the calf is obscure but fascinating, a typical

[1] *de veau*—Some commentators think this should be *de Vaud*, a Swiss Canton.

Nostradamus contortion of facts. Cavour was the envoy of Turin, and Torino means the city of the bull, it was called Augusta Taurinorum by the Romans, and Cavour is thus the offspring of the calf.

21

Par pestilente inimitié Volsicque,
Dissimulee chassera le tyran:
Au pont de Sorgues se fera la
traffique,
De mettre à mort lui & son adherent.

By the pestilential enmity of Languedoc, the tyrant dissimulated will be driven out. The bargain will be made on the bridge at Sorgues to put to to death both him and his follower.

Probably a bridge at Sorgues, the main town on the river of the same name. It belonged to the Vatican States until 1791. Languedoc was a large province to the west of the Rhône.

22

Les citoyens de Mesopotamie,[1]
Yrés encontre amis de Tarraconne,[2]
Jeux, ritz, banquetz, toute gent
endormie
Vicaire au Rosne, prins cité, ceux
d'Ausone.[3]

The citizens of Mesopotamia angry with their friends from Tarraconne; games, rites, banquests, every person asleep, the vicar at Rhône, the city taken and those of Ausonia.

POPE PIUS VI, 1799

Mesopotamia is used several times by Nostradamus but it is not wholly clear which town he meant. He does not seem to refer to modern Iraq, and therefore it probably describes a European town. The Venaissin between the Rhône and the Durance and Avignon in particular seem to fit the prediction very well. The vicar in line 4 was the Pope Pius VI whom Nostradamus had captured and imprisoned at Valence in 1799. The second part of line 4 describes how a French army led by General Chaupionnet recaptured Rome and then went on to Naples in 1799.

[1] *Mesopotamie*—Nostradamus means by this 'land between two rivers'. It could be modern Iraq or in France, Avignon, between the Rhône and the Durance, or Paris between the Seine and Marne.
[2] *Tarraconne*—Either from Latin, *Tarroca*, Tarragona in Catalonia, or from Tarraconensis, the north-eastern part of Roman Iberia.
[3] *Ausone*—Southern Italy, most probably Naples.

Le Royal sceptre sera contrainct de prendre, *Ce que ses predecesseurs avoient engaigé:* *Puis que l'aneau on fera mal entendre,* *Lors qu'on viendra le palais saccager.*	The Royal sceptre will be forced to take that which his predecessors had pledged. Because they do not understand about the ring when they come to sack the palace.

Hugh Allen, an unreliable commentator on Nostradamus, wrote in 1943 that the scene of this pawnbroking of Royal Jewels would take place in Buckingham Palace! This is a very obscure quatrain.

L'enseveli sortira du tombeau, *Fera de chaines lier le fort du pont:* *Empoisonné avec oeufz de Barbeau,* *Grand de Lorraine par le Marquis du Pont.*[1]	He who was buried will come out of the tomb, he will make the strong one out of the bridge to be bound with chains. Poisoned with the roe of a barbel, the great one from Lorraine by the Marquis du Pont.

The barbel is a freshwater fish found throughout most of Europe. The Grand one of Lorraine is probably the Duke of that name, Charles III, who was taken to be reared in the French Court. The Marquis du Pont-à-Mousson was held by the heir to the Duchy of Bar. After Bar passed to the house of Lorraine the title was given to the younger sons of the Duke of Lorraine. The quatrain predicts that among these families the Duke is to be poisoned by the Marquis, that is, by one of the younger sons.

Par guerre longue tout l'exercite expuiser, *Que pour souldartz ne trouveront pecune:* *Lieu d'or d'argent, cuir on viendra cuser,*[2] *Gualois aerain, signe croissant de Lune.*	Through long war all the army exhausted, so that they do not find money for the soldiers; instead of gold or silver, they will come to coin leather, Gallic brass, and the crescent sign of the Moon.

[1] *Marquis du Pont*—The younger son of the house of Lorraine had the title of Marquis de Pont-à-Mousson.
[2] *cuser*—Latin, *cusare*. O.F. cudere = to coin money.

It is suggested that this quatrain refers to soldiers being paid with money made from leather after a severe war. Line 4 is very obscure.

26

Fustes & galees autour de sept navires,	Foists and galleys around seven ships, a mortal war will be let
Sera livree une mortelle guerre:	loose. The leader from Madrid
Chef de Madric recevra coup de vivres,[1]	will receive a wound from arrows, two escaped and five
Deux eschapees & cinq menees à terre.	brought to land.

NOVEMBER 1555

In November 1555 some privateers from Dieppe attacked a Spanish fleet in the Channel. *Vivres* is then translated as *virer*, a nautical verb to attack. Apparently the privateers concentrated upon the Admiral's flagship and they succeeded in capturing it and four other ships who came to its aid and towed them to Dieppe.

27

Au cainct[2] *de Vast*[3] *la grand cavalerie,*	At the wall of Vasto the great cavalry are impeded by the
Proche à Ferrage empeschee au bagaige:	baggage near Ferrara. At Turin they will speedily commit such
Pompt à Turin feront tel volerie,	robbery that in the fort they
Que dans le fort raviront leur hostaige.	will ravish their hostage.

There are nine villages in France with the name of Vast plus a monastery near Arras and a harbour near Cherbourg. The reference may equally apply to Alphonso II, Marquis de Vasto (1502–44) who from 1537 onwards was Governor of Milan. He retired to Asti in 1554 and this may be what is meant by Ferrara, as it was a duchy of the house of Este—and was seized by the Papal States in 1597.

[1] *Vivres*—Alternative *vires* = arrows, seems better in context, or *virer* = to attack.

[2] *caint*—O.F., belt or waist. Possibly used here for encircling wall?

[3] *Vast*—Uncertain.

Le capitaine conduira grande proie,	The captain will lead a great
Sur la montaigne des ennemis plus	herd on the mountain closest
proche,	to the enemy. Surrounded by
Environné, par feu fera tel voie,	fire he makes such a way, all
Tous eschappez or[1] trente mis en	escape except for thirty put on
broche.	the spit.

Most commentators understand 'put on a spit' as meaning to be run through. I think it is Nostradamus' way of describing them being burnt alive.

Le grand Duc d'Albe se viendra	The great one of Alba will come
rebeller	to rebel, he will betray his great
A ses grans peres fera le tradiment :	forebears. The great man of
Le grand de Guise le viendra	Guise will come to vanquish
debeller,	him, led captive with a monu-
Captif mené & dressé monument.	ment erected.

This is at first sight a very clear quatrain, but it is not very accurate. The Duke of Alba was the main Spanish general, and the Duke de Guise the main French one. Unfortunately de Guise never triumphed over Alba, yet alone take him captive. It is doubtful whether Nostradamus saw Alba crossing over to the French side, but he did fight with the French from 1555–7 against the Vatican states.

Le sac s'approche, feu, grand sang	The sack approaches, fire and
espandu	great bloodshed. Po the great
Po, grand fleuves, aux bouviers[2]	rivers, the enterprise for the
l'entreprinse,	clowns; after a long wait from
De Gennes, Nice, apres long	Genoa and Nice, Fossano,
attendu,	Turin the capture at Savigli-
Foussan, Turin, à Savillon la	ano.
prinse.	

Nice, Fossano, Turin and Savigliano were all in Piedmont but all except Nice had been lost to the House of Savoy. Genoa was an independent state under Habsburg domination.

---

[1] *or*—Misprint, in all editions for *hors* = without, except for.
[2] *bouviers*—O.F. = either clowns or cowherdsmen.

De Languedoc, & Guienne plus de dix,	From Languedoc and Guienne more than ten thousand will
Mille voudront les Alpes repasser:	want to cross the Alps again.
Grans Allobroges[1] marcher contre Brundis	The great Savoyards march against Brindisi, Aquino and
Aquin & Bresse les viendront recasser.	Bresse will come to drive them back.

These place names are obscure because they are all so separate; Languedoc and Guienne were in South-western France. Bresse belonged to Savoy until 1601. Brindisi is in South Italy and together with Aquino, belonged to the kingdom of the Two Sicilies. The action is totally unclear.

Du mont Royal naistra d'une casane,[2]	From the bank of Montereale will be born one who bores and
Qui cave, & compte viendra tyranniser	calculates becoming a tyrant. To raise a force in the marches
Dresser copie de la marche Millane,	of Milan, to drain Faenza and
Favene, Florence d'or & gens espuiser.	Florence of gold and men.

DE' MEDICI FAMILY

This may have been directed at one of the de' Medicis who came from an area of Florence called Montereale. Milan belonged to the Habsburgs, Faenza was part of the Papal states and Florence, as above, belonged to the de' Medicis, but the action is again obscure.

Par fraude regne, forces expolier,[3]	The kingdom stripped of its forces by fraud, the fleet
La classe obsesse, passages à l'espie:	blockaded, passages for the spy; two false friends will come
Deux fainctz amis se viendront rallier,	to rally to awaken hatred for a
Esveiller haine de long temps assoupie.	long time dormant.

[1] *Allobroges* = inhabitants of Savoy.
[2] *casan*—low Latin, *casana* = bank.
[3] *expolier*—O.F. = plunder, strip, despoil.

This is one of Nostradamus' general prophecies which may have been fulfilled several times since it was written; mainly it is interpreted as the Fall of France in 1940, line 3 describing the Germans and the Russians, and the last line Anglo-French connections.

34

En grand regret sera la gent Gauloise	The French nation will be in great grief, vain and light-
Coeur vain, legier croirera temerité:	hearted, they will believe rash
Pain, sel, ne vin, eaue: venin ne cervoise	things. No bread, salt, wine nor water, venom nor ale, the
Plus grand captif, faim, froit, necessité.	greater one captured, hunger, cold and want.

FRANCE, 1940 *continued*

It is usually accepted that his quatrain carries on from the last, No. 33, and Nostradamus slipped up forgetting to change them about to muddle the reader as to their chronology. This is another general description of the Fall of France and its occupation under the Germans, which lasted until 1944.

35

La grand pesche viendra plaindre, plorer	The great fish will come to complain and weep for having
D'avoir esleu, trompés seront en l'aage:	chosen, deceived concerning his age: he will hardly want to
Guiere avec eux ne voudra demourer,	remain with them, he will be
Deçeu sera par ceux de son langaige.	deceived by those (speaking) his own tongue.

HENRI III

Henri III, the third son of Catherine de' Medici was elected King of Poland on the interpretation that Poland chose its kings in an unrestrained manner '*pesche*'. On the premature death of his brother Charles IX, he had to escape from Poland and resume his claim to the French throne. This upset the arrangements made by Poland and France to found dynasties. He was deceived (and also assassinated) by a fellow Frenchman, Jacques Clément.

36

Dieu, le ciel tout le divin verbe à l'unde,	God, the heavens, all the divine words in the waves, carried by seven red-shaven heads to Byzantium: against the anointed three hundred from Trebizond, will make two laws, first horror then trust.
Porté par rouges sept razes à Bisance:	
Contre les oingz trois cens de Trebisconde,	
Deux loix mettront, & l'horreur, puis credence.	

The seven red heads are almost certainly Cardinals, but what were they doing on their way to Constantinople? Perhaps they were trying to convert the Sultan? It seems very unlikely and there is no recorded incident that I can find to substantiate this.

37

Dix envoyés, chef de nef mettre à mort,	Ten sent to put the captain of the ship to death, are altered by one that there is open revolt in the fleet. Confusion, the leader and another stab and bite each other at Lerins and the Hyères, ships, prow into the darkness.
D'un adverti, en classe guerre ouverte:	
Confusion chef, l'un se picque & mord,	
Lerin, stecades[1] nefz cap dedans la nerte.[2]	

This dramatic quatrain heralds the attempted assassination of a naval commander. The Lerin Islands are off Cannes and the Hyères off Toulon.

38

L'aisné Royal sur coursier voltigeant,	The elder royal one on a frisky horse will spur so fiercely that it will bolt. Mouth, mouthfull, foot complaining in the embrace; dragged, pulled, to die horribly.
Picquer viendra si rudement courir:	
Gueulle, lipee, pied dans l'estrein pleignant	
Trainé, tiré, horriblement mourir.	

DEATH OF CROWN PRINCE FERDINAND, 1842
The heir of Louis Philippe was thrown and dragged by a frisky horse, and died on 13th July 1842.

[1] *stecades*—Latin, *Stoechades* = the Islands of Hyères.
[2] *nerte*—O.F. = Black, or Greek, *nerthe* = underneath.

Le conducteur de l'armeé Françoise,
Cuidant perdre le principal
   phalange:
Par sus pave de l'avaigne &
   d'ardoise,
Soi parfondra par Gennes gent
   estrange.

The leader of the French army
will expect to lose the main
phalanx. Upon the pavement of
oats and slate the foreign
nation will be undermined
through Genoa.

Dedans tonneaux hors oingz d'huile
   & gresse,
Seront vingt un devant le port
   fermés,
Au second guet par mont feront
   prouesse:
Gaigner les portes & du guet
   assommés.

Within casks anointed outside
with oil and grease twenty-one
will be shut before the harbour,
at the second watch; through
death they will do great deeds;
to win the gates and be killed
by the watch.

It seems as though Nostradamus is describing a second Trojan
horse which is trying to capture a seaport. They succeed in
entering the town but are killed by the guards.

Les oz des piedz & des main
   enserrés,
Par bruit maison long temps
   inhabitee:
Seront par songes concavent deterrés,
Maison salubre & sans bruit
   habitee.

The bones of the feet and the
hands locked up, because of
the noise the house is uninhabited for a long time. Digging
in dreams they will be un-
earthed, the house healthy and
inhabited without noise.

Nostradamus seems to have believed in ghosts, because this is a
description of a haunted house which is exorcized when the bones
of the victim are removed. Perhaps an occupant of the house
dreamt of the grave which led to the discovery of the skeleton?

Deux de poison saisiz nouveau venuz,	Two newly arrived have seized the poison, to pour it in the
Dans la cuisine du grand Prince verser:	kitchen of the great Prince. By the scullion both are caught in
Par le souillard tous deux au faicts congneuz	the act, taken he who thought to trouble the elder with death.
Prins que cuidoit de mort l'aisné vexer.	

This is a detailed, specific quatrain in which two conspirators on a Prince's kitchen staff try to poison him. They are caught red-handed by the kitchen boy but it appears that only one is captured so possibly his accomplice got away.

CENTURY VIII

1** Napoleon I
2
3 Duke de Mercoeur
4 Unsuccessful prediction
5
6* France, Switzerland, Savoy and England, c. 1560
7
8
9
10* Marxists or Calvinists
11*
12
13
14* Spanish riches in 16th Century
15** Germany and the Nazis
16
17*F? The Kennedy brothers
18
19* French Revolutionary Extremists
20
21? 20th Century?
22*? Communism in France
23** The Casket letters
24
25
26
27
28* Inflation and paper money
29
30*F Undiscovered treasure in Toulouse
31** Mussolini and Victor Emmanuel III
32
33** Mussolini

34
35
36
37** Charles I of England
38
39
40
41* Napoleon III
42* Louis Philippe d'Orléans
43* Defeat of Louis Napoleon, 1870
44
45
46**F? War linked with Paul VI and Kennedy Brothers
47
48? 1st February 2769?
49? 6th February 1971
50* Capture of Tunis, 1573
51
52
53* Napaoleon's failure to invade England
54
55
56* Scotland and Charles II
57* Napoleon I
58 James II and William of Orange, 1588
59*F? East and West in 20th Century?
60*? Napoleon II?
61?
62
63
64*? Nazis and Britain
65* Marshal Pétain, 1940-2
66
67
68* Death of Cardinal Richelieu and Louis XIII, 1642-3
69
70
71** 1607
72* Ravenna, 1512
73
74*F? The U.S.A.
75* Portuguese king and son assassinated, 1908
76* Cromwell

77**F? Antichrist, the Three Brothers and War
78
79
80* Russian Revolution
81* ?
82
83* The Fourth Crusade, 1202. Retroactive prophecy
84
85 Napoleon III's death
86 Navarre
87* Louis XVI
88* King of Sardinia, 1798–1802
89
90
91
92
93? 1590?
94* Bay of Cadiz, 1596
95
96* Flight of Jews, *c.* 1550
97? Kennedys?
98 Persecution of Clergy, 1792
99
100

KEY: * Of interest. F? Possibly referring to the future.

PAU, NAY, LORON plus feu	Pau, Nay, Loron will be more
qu'à sang sera.	of fire than blood, to swim in
Laude nager, fuir grand au surrez.	praise, the great one to flee to
Les agassas[1] entree refusera.	the confluence (of rivers). He
Pampon,[2] Durance les tiendra	will refuse entry to the magpies
enferrez.	Pampon and the Durance will
	keep them confined.

NAPOLEON I

Although the names in the first line are all small towns in Western France, Nostradamus does appear to be talking about a man rather than places. The capital letters also indicate a more fanciful reading by anagram, PAU, NAY, LORON becomes NAPAUL-ON ROY—Napoleon the King. The spelling of Napoleon's name with an 'au' instead of an 'o' was commonplace, and Nostradamus' orthography is not at all reliable. The connection of the *agassas* or Pius would refer to Pius VI and VII who were both imprisoned by Napoleon. The confluence of rivers refers to Valence where the Rhône and Isère meet and where Pius VI was taken to die in 1798–9. Pius VII was taken to Savona and then on to Fontainebleau in 1872, therefore neither was imprisoned near the Durance of line 4. But Durance did lie near Avignon which belonged to the Papacy until 1791, where the Rhône and the Durance meet.

2

Condon & Aux & autour de	Condom and Auch and around
Mirande	Mirande, I see fire from the sky
Je voi du ciel feu qui les environne.	which encompasses them. Sun
Sol Mars conjoint au Lion puis	and Mars conjoined in Leo,
marmande	then at Marmande, lightning,
Fouldre, grand gresle, mur tombe	great hail, a wall falls into the
dans Garonne.	Garonne.

All the towns mentioned are in the Departement of Gers in the south-west, except for Marmande which is about 50 miles north. The wall may be falling here or in some other Garonne town such as Bordeaux, Agen or Toulouse?

[1] *agassas*—Provençal, *agassa* = a magpie, known in French as pie, which is also the French spelling of Pius. A typical Nostradamus convolution.

[2] *Pampon*—Doubtful, possibly Gk., *Pamponeros* = all depraved?

Au fort chasteau de Viglanne[1] &
*   Resviers*
Sera serré le puisnay de Nancy:
Dedans Turin seront ards[2] les
*   premiers,*
Lors que de dueil Lyon sera transi.

Within the strong castle of Vigilance and Resviers the younger born of Nancy will be shut up. In Turin the first ones will be burned, when Lyons will be transported with grief.

THE DUKE DE MERCOEUR

The names in the first line of this quatrain are difficult to decipher, the best combinations are in Italy. There is a castle built by the Scaligers of Verona on the promontory at the south of Lake Garda. Another stands at Malescino. Also on the lake between San Vigilio and the Riviera is the monastery founded by St. Francis. Thus we have three possible sites on the Garda. Nancy is the capital of Lorraine, and the cadet a younger brother or branch of the family. It is most likely to refer to Nicholas, Duke of Mercoeur, the father-in-law of Henri III, who did not die until 1577. So what Nostradamus is trying to say can be summarized thus. The Duke of Mercoeur will be confined in a castle on Lake Garda. Turin, in line 3, belonged to the French when Nostradamus wrote. 'Ards' is a difficult word for which to find a definite meaning.

Dedans Monech[3] le coq sera receu,
Le Cardinal de France apparoistra
Par Logarion[4] Romain sera deceu
Foiblesse à l'aigle, & force au coq
*   naistra.*

The cock will be received into Monaco, the Cardinal of France will appear; He will be deceived by the Roman legation; weakness to the eagle, strength will be born to the cock.

This prediction did not come true, in fact just the opposite if one accepts that Logarion is a misreading for legation. It is concerned with the struggle for power in the Mediterranean between the French and Spanish. Monaco had nominal independence under the Grimaldis but was bound by Treaty to help Spain. Nostra-

[1] *Viglanne*—Most likely San Vigilio and the Riviera, but could be Rubbiera and Vignola.

[2] *ards*—Possibly from *ardere* = to burn, but uncertain.

[3] *Monech*—Monaceis = Monaco.

[4] *Logarion*—Other texts have legation, which reads much better in the context.

damus predicts that this protection will move to Franco, which occurred in 1614. The French Cardinal who intrigued so much during Nostradamus' time is probably a reference to Charles, second Cardinal of Lorraine (1524–74). Reading Logarion as legate, there were two in France, the viceregal legate at Avignon and another as Papal Ambassador. Nostradamus describes a legate deceiving the French, but in spite of this he foresees the Habsburg power declining and that of France growing. In fact the exact opposite occurred. Monaco became a closer ally to the Spanish when a garrison took over from 1605–41, and the French were driven out of Italy in 1559.

5

Apparoistra temple luisant orné,	There will appear a shining
La lampe & cierge à Borne &	ornate temple, the lamp and
Bretueil.	candle at Borne and Breteuil.
Pour la lucerne le canton destorné,	For the canton of Lucerne
Quand on verra le grand coq au	turned aside, when one will see
cercueil.	the great cock in his shroud.

This seems to predict that the Canton of Lucerne will be overcome, and that at the same period a great French king would die. This has not occurred.

6

Charte fulgure à Lyon apparente	Lightning and brightness are
Luisant, print Malte subit sera	seen at Lyons shining, Malta
estainte,	is taken, suddenly it will be
Sardon,¹ Mauris² traitera decep-	extinguished. Sardon, Maurice
vante,	will act deceitfully, Geneva to
Geneve à Londes à coq trahison	London, feigning treason to-
fainte.	wards the cock.

FRANCE, SWITZERLAND, SAVOY AND ENGLAND
c. 1560

Malta was an independent state until the Revolution. The Turks attacked it in 1565. Maurice, according to legend, was a saint, a leader of a Theban legion who were annihilated because they refused to murder Christians. His cult is strong in Switzerland and Savoy. Sardon may stand for Sardinia which belonged to the House of Savoy after 1720. Nostradamus thus indicates that the

¹ *Sardon*—Sardinia is the most likely interpretation for this word.
² *Mauris*—Probably St. Maurice, patron Saint of much of French Alps and of Savoy.

Savoy held both regions. The connection between Geneva and London probably describes Elizabeth I's involvement with Calvin in the Conspiracy of Amboise (1566).

7

Verceil, Milan donra intelligence,	Vercelli, Milan will give the
Dedans Tycin[1] sera faite la paye.[2]	news, the wound will be given
Courir par Siene eau, sang, feu par	at Pavia. To run in the Seine,
Florence.	water, blood and fire through
Unique choir d'hault en bas	Florence, the unique one falling
faisant maie.[3]	from high to low calling for
	help.

Very obscure except for the fact that Vercelli and Pavia belonged to the Duchy of Milan and was finally taken over by the Habsburgs until the 19th Century.

8

Pres de Linterne[4] dans de tonnes	Near Focia enclosed in some
fermez,	tuns Chivasso will plot for the
Chivaz[5] fera pour l'aigle la menee,	eagle. The elected one driven
L'esleu cassé lui ses gens enfermez,	out, he and his people shut up,
Dedans Turin rapt espouse em-	rape with Turin, the bride led
menee.	away.

The village of Focia which occupies the old site of Linternum is unlikely to be the subject of this. Chivasso, a few miles north-east of Turin, was occupied by the French, and Nostradamus sees it plotting on behalf of the Emperor. Is the leader of the Chivasso plot exiled or sent to another town?

[1] *Ticin*—Latin, *Ticinum* = Pavia.
[2] *la paye*—Possible alternative is the plague.
[3] *maie* = (*a*) Kneading-trough. (*b*) *Ma aie*, help me!
[4] *Linterne*—Now Focia near Naples.
[5] *Chivaz* = Chivasso.

Pendant que l'aigle & le coq à Savone	While the eagle is united with the cock at Savona, the Eastern
Seront unis Mer Levant & Ongrie,	Sea and Hungary. The army at
L'armee à Naples, Palerne, Marque d'Ancone	Naples, Palermo, the marches of Ancona, Rome and Venice
Rome, Venise par Barb'[1] horrible crie.	a great outcry by the Barbarian.

At Savona Nostradamus foresees an alliance between the Emperor and the French. Both the Levant and Hungary belonged to the Turks except for the small area the Habsburgs retained and paid for. Naples and Palermo were in the Habsburg kingdom of the Two Sicilies, and Ancona belonged to the Papal States. Does Nostradamus envisage a Moslem invasion of Italy which will suddenly unify the Christian faces?

Puanteur grande sortira de Lausanne,	A great stench will come from Lausanne, but they will not
Qu'on ne seura l'origine du fait,	know its origin, they will put
Lon mettra hors toute le gente loingtaine	out all the people from distant places, fire seen in the sky, a
Feu veu au ciel, peuple estranger deffait.	foreign nation defeated.

MARXISTS OR CALVINISTS

The stench from Lausanne probably refers to the Calvinist centre that it became in the 16th Century, and in particular while Calvin's second-in-command, de Bèze, was teaching there. A more modern meaning applies it to the very frequent meetings of early Marxists there.

Peuple infini paroistra à Vicence	A multitude of people will
Sans force feu brusler la Basilique	appear at Vicenza without
Pres de Lunage deffait grand de Valence,	force, fire to burn the Basilica. Near Lunage the great one of Valenza defeated: at a time
Lors que Venise par more prendra pique.	when Venice takes up the quarrel through custom.

[1] *Barb'*—short for either barbarian, or the enigmatic Aenobarb = the red bearded one. See I. 74, II. 49, V. 45 etc.

Vincenza was in the Republic of Venice, Valenza in Habsburg Milan and Valence the town where the Rhône and Isère join. During the lifetime of Nostradamus the title of Valentinois belonged to Diane de Poitiers, Henri II's erstwhile mistress. It passed to the Grimaldis of Monaco and at the moment is held by the son of Grace Kelly and her husband.

12

Apparoistra aupres de Buffaloree	He will appear near to
L'hault & procere entré dedans	Buffalora the highly born and
Milan	tall one entered into Millan.
L'abbé de Foix avec ceux de saint	The Abbe of Foix with those of
Morre	Saint-Meur will cause damage
Feront la forbe abillez en vilan.	dressed up as serfs.

Buffalora is a tiny village west of Milan, so small that it is unlikely that Nostradamus would know about it, unless he passed through it on his Italian wanderings. Those of St. Mark mean the Benedictines, because St. Maurus founded the order in France, while the Abbey at Foix belonged to the Augustinians. Quite what they hope to accomplish in line 4 is difficult to imagine.

13

Le croisé frere par amour effrenee	The crusader brother through
Fera par Praytus Bellesophon	impassioned love will cause
mourir,	Bellerophon to die through
Classe à mil ans la femme	Proetus; the fleet for a thousand
forcenee,	years, the maddened woman,
Beu le breuvage, tous deux apres	the potion drunk, both of them
perir.	then die.

A story of poisoning based on the myth of Bellerophon and Proetus, king of Argos whose wife was furious when her advances to Bellerophon were refused. The Queen Anteia persuaded Proetus to send Bellerophon on a mortal mission in a sealed message to Lobates, king of Lycia. Lobates sent Bellerophon to kill the monster Chimaera, and he succeeded with the help of his flying horse, Pegasus. In Nostradamus' situation the cuckold husband is poisoned as well as the wife.

Le grand credit d'or, d'argent l'abondance	The great credit of gold and abundance of silver will cause
Fera aveugler par libide honneur	honour to be blinded by lust;
Sera cogneu d'adultere l'offense,	the offence of the adulterer will
Qui parviendra à son grand deshonneur.	become known, which will occur to his great dishonour.

SPANISH MONEY IN 16th CENTURY

The first two lines appear to be a general condemnation of the great riches flowing from the Spanish-American mines into Europe, which caused great inflation throughout the 16th Century. Nostradamus apparently connects monetary lust very closely to sexual lust.

Vers Aquilon grans efforts par hommasse	Great exertions towards the North by a man-woman to vex
Presque l'Europe & l'univers vexer,	Europe and almost all the
Les deux eclipse mettra en tel chasse,	Universe. The two eclipses will be put into such a rout that
Et aux Pannons vie & mort renforcer.	they will reinforce life or death for the Hungarians.

GERMANY AND THE NAZIS

This quatrain almost certainly ties up with a prediction Nostradamus made in the preface as to the great German expansion. The mannish-woman may be understood as Germania. Many commentators apply this to the Nazi empire.

Au lieu que HIERON feit sa nef fabriquer,	At the place where HIERON has his ship built, there will be
Si grand deluge sera & si subite,	such a great sudden flood, that
Qu'on n'aura lieu ne terres s'atacquer	one will not have a place nor land to fall upon, the waters
L'onde monter Fesulan Olympique.	mount to the Olympic Fesulan.

I cannot decipher *HIERON* although some commentators change it to *JASON* to fit the Greek atmosphere of the quatrain. It is hard to find any connection between that and *Fesulan* (Fiesole) in central Italy. As for the flooding Fiesole is 970 feet above sea level, whereas Mount Ołympia is 9,570 feet above it.

Les bien aisez subit seront desmis
Par les trois freres le monde mis en
   trouble,
Cité marine saisiront ennemis,
Faim, feu, sang, peste & de tous
   maux le double.

Those at ease will suddenly be cast down, the world put into trouble by three brothers; their enemies will seize the marine city, hunger, fire, blood, plague, all evils doubled.

THE KENNEDY BROTHERS?

It appears that when three brothers appear in positions of power during a century, those at ease, i.e. America will suddenly suffer trouble. The marine city seized by their enemies, whom I doubtfully connect with the Asian Antichrist, could be Formosa or even Singapore or Hong Kong. It will be fascinating to see what the youngest Kennedy brother will do during the next few years. Nostradamus also mentions the three brothers in his Epistle which will appear in full in the following book.

De Flora issue de sa mort sera
   cause,
Un temps devant par jeune & vieille
   bueira,
Par les trois lys lui feront telle
   pause,
Par son fruit sauve comme chair
   crue mueire.

The cause of her death will be issued from Florence, one time before drunk by young and old; by the three lilies they will give her a great pause. Save through her offspring as raw meat is dampened.

Florence belonged to the de' Medicis and several daughters of that name, Catherine and Marie in particular, married into the Royal Family of France, as denoted by the fleur de lis. The last line probably means that poison was put into the meat—after all the Medicis were renowned for their mastery of poison.

A soubstenir la grand cappe[1] *troublee,*	To support the great troubled Cappe; the reds will march in
Pour l'esclaircir les rouges mar-cheront,	order to clarify it; a family will be almost overcome by death,
De mort famille sera presque accablee.	the red, red ones will knock down the red one.
Les rouges rouges le rouge assome-ront.	

EXTREMISM IN THE FRENCH REVOLUTION

Cappe here probably is the shortened form of Capulet, the name of the French Royal family line. The French are described as not supporting the great Caputian family troubled by the Revolution. Republicans will march against them so that the family has to take enforced refuge in the Temple. The Royal Family will be almost completely destroyed except for the King's sister, Elizabeth, and possibly the eldest son, Louis XVII (see V. 1). Then the extremists, the red, red ones will guillotine the more moderate revolutionaries, the Girondins. Possibly the name of Robespierre (the red stone) is hinted at in the last line?

Le faux messaige par election fainte	The false message about the rigged election to run through
Courir par urban rompu pache arreste,	the city stopping the broken pact; voices bought, chapel
Voix acheptees, de sang chappelle tainte,	stained with blood, the empire contracted to another one.
Et à un autre l'empire contraicte.	

This apparently describes the election of a Holy Roman Emperor who uses bribery 'voices bought' to attain his ends. The false election will be followed by a short war, which ends when the Pretender is murdered.

Au port d'Agde trois fustes entreront	Three foists will enter the port of Agde carrying the infection
Portant d'infect non foi & pesti-lence	and pestilence, not the faith. Passing the bridge they will
Passant le pont mil milles embleront,	carry off a million, the bridge is broken by the resistance of a
Et le pont rompre à tierce resistance.	third.

[1] *cappe*—Here stands for Capulet instead of the more usual meaning of Pope.

The enormity of the figure of these victims of the plague make the quatrain somewhat suspect. The figures are more suitable for the 20th Century, as for instance Biafra and Pakistan. Agde is a sea-port in the south-west of France, between Narbonne and Marseilles. Could it possibly be an indirect reference to the Second World War?

22

Gorsan, Narbonne, par le sel advertir	Coursan, Narbonne through the salt to warn Tuchan, the grace of Perpignan betrayed; the red town will not wish to consent to it, in a high flight, a copy flag and a life ended.
Tucham, la grace Parpignam trahie,	
La ville rouge n'y vouldra consentir.	
Par haulte vol drap gris vie faillie.	

COMMUNISM IN FRANCE?

A difficult quatrain. There are many Communist strongholds in present-day France around Perpignan, the red town. The rest is obscure.

23

Lettres trouvees de la roine les coffres,	Letters are found in the queen's chests, no signature and no name of the author. The ruse will conceal the offers; so that they do not know who the lover is.
Point de subscrit sans aucun nom d'hauteur	
Par la police[1] seront caché les offres.	
Qu'on ne scaura qui sera l'amateur.	

THE CASKET LETTERS

Unfortunately there is no proper noun to finally determine this quatrain but in that Nostradamus knew of Mary Queen of Scots and probably met her, while summoned to the Court in 1556, it may apply. The Casket Letters were documents relating to the murder of Darnley and events of 1567. The Earl of Morton pro-duced them before commissions in London and York. The originals disappeared after 1584 and their authenticity has always been held in doubt.

[1] *police*—O.F. = (*a*) Ruse. (*b*) Government.

Le lieutenant à l'entree de l'huis,	The lieutenant at the door of
Assommera la grand de Perpignan,	the house, will knock down the
En se cuidant saulver à Monpertuis.	great man of Perpignan. Think-
Sera deceu bastard de Luisgnan.	ing to save himself at Mont-
	pertuis, the bastard of Lusignan
	will be deceived.

The family of Lusignan died out before Nostradamus' time but ruled Jerusalem and Cyprus until 1489, its titles passing to the house of Savoy. Nostradamus' patron, the Count de Tende, Governor of Provence, was the son of the Grand Bastard of Savoy, as he was known. If this is so then Montpertuis is almost certainly the Perthus Pass in the Pyrenees, and Nostradamus must have envisaged Tende defeating the Spanish around Rousillan (Perpignan) and then finding himself trapped in the Pyrenees with the Spanish blocking his return route to France.

Coeur de l'amant ouvert d'amour fertive	The heart of the lover, awakened by furtive love will
Dans le ruisseau fera ravir la Dame,	ravish the lady in the stream. She will pretend bashfully to
Le demi mal contrefera lassive,	be half injured, the father of
Le pere à deux privera corps de l'ame.	each will deprive the body of its soul.

A possible history of incest and rape among Royalty? The plot is clear but the references too general to be of any use.

De Caton es[1] trouves en Barcellonne,	The bones of Cato found in
Mis descouvers lieu retrouvers & ruine,	Barcelona, placed, discovered, the site found again and ruined.
Le grand qui tient ne tient vouldra Pamplonne.	The great one who holds, but does not hold, wants Pamplona,
Par l'abbaye de Montferrat bruine.	drizzle at the abbey of Mont- serrat.

None of Cato's famous family died at Barcelona, and only C. Pacius Cato died in Spain, at Tarragona.

[1] *es*—Alternative reading, *os* = Bones. O.F., *ez* means planks or boards.

La voye auxelle l'une sur l'autre
    forniz[1]
Du muy desert hor mis brave &
    genest
L'escript d'empereur le fenix[2]
Veu en celui ce qu'à nul autre n'est.

The auxiliary way, one arch upon the other, Le Muy deserted except for the brave one and his genet. The writing of the Phoenix Emperor, seen by him which is (shown) to no other.

This is set in Provence and the aqueduct is probably the one which ran from the River Saigne to Fréjus. A jennet is a small black horse. The commander with the Phoenix-like qualities is more of a problem.

Les simulacres d'or & argent enflez,
Qu'apres le rapt au lac furent gettez
Au desouvert estaincts tous &
    troublez.
Au marbre script prescript inter-
    getez.

The copies of gold and silver inflated, which after the theft were thrown into the lake, at the discovery that all is exhausted and dissipated by the debt. All scrips and bonds will be wiped out.

INFLATION AND PAPER MONEY

This quatrain may well be describing the monetary inflation which hit Europe during the nineteen twenties and again in the sixties and seventies. It is one of the few quatrains I have not translated literally, as it is too complex, and have used that of Dr. Fontbrune (1939). It is an interesting idea for a man who lived long before paper money (the copies of gold and silver) were ever used.

Au quart pillier l'on sacre[3] à
    Saturne.
Par tremblant terre & deluge fendu
Soubz l'edifice Saturnin trouvee
    urne,
D'or Capion ravi & puis rendu.

At the fourth pillar which they dedicate to Saturn split by earthquake and by flood; under Saturn's building an urn is found gold carried off by Caepio and then restored.

[1] forniz = (a) Arch. (b) Brothel. In this case Nostradamus is describing an aqueduct.
[2] fenix = (a) The Phoenix. (b) The Phoenician.
[3] sacrere—O.F. = to dedicate.

Saturn's building presumably means a temple dedicated to him, or the Church of Saint Saturnin (Sernin) in Toulouse. Under the fourth pillar an urn of gold will be found, stolen by Caepio who was a Roman consul who plundered Toulouse (106 BC). The treasure never reached Rome, for which Caepio was impeached and expelled from the Senate.

30

Dedans Tholoze non loing de Beluzer[1]	In Toulouse, not far from Beluzer making a deep pit a palace of spectacle, the treasure found will come to vex everyone in two places and near the Basacle.
Faisant un puis long, palais d'espectacle,[2]	
Tresor trouvé un chacun ira vexer,	
Et en deux locz & pres del vasacle.[3]	

UNDISCOVERED TREASURE IN TOULOUSE

Beluzer is as yet unidentified by all Nostradamus' commentators. Quatrain 29 indicated that gold would be found when a pillar was struck by lightning, but here it seems more likely to be the result of men digging or a chance find, perhaps the two places referring to two different discoveries. This may be a quatrain yet to be fulfilled.

31

Premier grand fruit le prince de Perquiere	The first great fruit of the prince of Perchiera, then will come a cruel and wicked man. In Venice he will lose his proud glory, and is led into evil by the younger Selin.
Mais puis viendra bien & cruel malin,	
Dedans Venise perdra sa gloire fiere	
Et mis à mal par plus joune Celin.	

MUSSOLINI AND VICTOR EMMANUEL III

When Mussolini led the Fascists in revolt the first prize that fell to him was the Prince of Pescheria, i.e. Victor Emmanuel himself, who, at Pescheria did one of the noblest acts of his reign. He had gone to the front after Caporetto, and took command in person rejecting all proposals of surrender and determined to fight it out.

[1] Beluzer—Unidentified name, or anagram?
[2] Nostradamus presumably means a theatre.
[3] vasacle = The mill section of Toulouse, also of the castle protecting the main bridge and gate to the city.

The Council of War was also held at Pescheria. The cruel one is Mussolini, who will lose his glory in Venice and be delivered to the hands of the younger Selin. Since Selin means crescent or moon, Nostradamus foresaw some connection with Islam, which did not occur.

32

Garde toi roi Gaulois de ton nepveu
Qui fera tant que ton unique fils
Sera meutri à Venus faisant voeu,
Accompaigné de nuit que trois & six.

French king, beware of your nephew who will do so much that your only son will be murdered while making his vows to Venus; accompanied at night by three and six.

A clear prophecy which does not seem to have taken place.

33

Le grand naistra de Veronne &
  Vincence,
Qui portera un surnon bien indigne.
Qui à Venise vouldra faire
  vengeance.
Lui mesme prins homme du guet &
  signe.

The great one who will be born of Verona and Vincenza who carries a very unworthy surname; he who at Venice will wish to take vengeance, himself taken by a man of the watch and sign.

MUSSOLINI

The great one born in the North of Italy, where both towns mentioned are situated, bearing an unworthy name, is Mussolini which literally means muslin maker. The vengeance he desires was against those powers who frustrated his dream of Mare Nostrum. The last line, more difficult, implies that he is taken in a snare by a man who watches and ambushes—presumably Hitler, who became Mussolini's inspiration.

Apres victoire du Lyon au Lyon	After the victory of the Lion
Sur la montaigne de JURA	over the Lion, there will be
Secatombe[1]	great slaughter on the mountain
Delues[2] *& brodes*[3] *septieme million*	of Jura; floods and dark-
Lyon, Ulme à Mausol mort &	coloured people the seventh (of
tombe.	a million), Lyons, Ulm at the
	mausoleum death and the
	tomb.

The Jura mountains run through Franche-Comté which belonged to the Habsburgs until 1674. If *brodes* can be understood as dark-haired people, rather than dark skinned, this may refer to the Spanish. However this is another quatrain where the vast amount of the figure suggests the present century.

Dedans l'entree de Garonne &	At the entrance to Garonne
Baise	and Baise and the forest not
Et la forest non loing de Damazan	far from Damazan, discoveries
Du marsaves[4] *gelees, puis gresle &*	of the frozen sea, then hail and
bize	north winds. Frost in the
Dordonnois gelle[5] *par erreur de*	Dardonnais through the mis-
mezan.[6]	take of the month.

This seems to be a general summary of unseasonable weather which will occur in all the above mentioned places.

[1] *Secatombe*—An obvious misprint for hecatombe.
[2] *Delues*—Uncertain, possibly from Latin, *diluvies* = flood/destruction
[3] *brodes*—Yet again these strange people derived from the O.F., *brode* = black, brown and decadent.
[4] *marsaves*—Compound word made up from O.F., *mar* = sea and O.F., *save* = discovery.
[5] *gelle*—O.F., without extra syllable for scansion = frost.
[6] *mesan*—From Latin, *mensa* = a month by metathesis.

Sera commis conte oingdre aduché[1]	It will be committed against
De Saulne & sainct Aulbin &	the anointed brought from
Bell'oeuvre[2]	Lons le Saulnier, Saint Aubin
Paver de marbre de tours loing	and Bell'oeuvre. To pave with
espluché	marble taken from distant
Non Bleteram resister & chef	towers, not to resist Bletteram
d'oeuvre.	and his masterpiece.

A difficult quatrain with an enigma, see footnote. Bletterans is in Franche Comté which used to belong to the Habsburgs until 1647.

La forteresse aupres de la Tamise	The fortress near the Thames
Cherra par lors le Roi dedans serré,	will fall when the king is locked
Aupres du pont sera veu en chemise	up inside. He will be seen in his
Un devant mort, puis dans le fort	shirt near the bridge, one facing
barré.	death then barred inside the
	fortress.

CHARLES I

One of Nostradamus' more exciting quatrains, and reasonably exact too. After his defeat and captivity Charles I was taken to Windsor Castle overlooking the Thames, in December 1648. He remained there until 9th January 1649. In a sense the castle did fall because it was in the hands of the Parliamentarians. On 30th January after a trial, Charles was beheaded dressed in a white shirt. The nearest bridge would be London Bridge, for Westminster Bridge was not built at this time. This quatrain is definitely connected with IX. 49.

[1] *aduché*—Provençal, *aducha* = brought.
[2] *Bell'oeuvre*—Most probably an enigmatic place-name or it may translate literally 'beautiful work'.

Le Roi de Blois dans Avignon regner	The King of Blois will reign in
Un autre fois le peuple emonopole[1]	Avignon, once again the people
Dedans le Rhosne par murs fera	covered in blood. In the Rhône
baigner	he will make swim near the
Jusques à cinq le dernier pres de	walls up to five, the last one
Nolle.[2]	near Nolle.

Qu'aura esté par prince Bizantin,	He who will have been for the
Sera tollu par prince de Tholoze.	Byzantine prince will be taken
La foi de Foix par le chef Tholentin,	away by the prince of Toulouse.
Lui faillira ne refusant l'espouse.	The faith of Foix through the
	leader of Tolentino will fail
	him, not refusing the bride.

The identity of the characters here is completely unclear. A Byzantine prince is either a Sultan or a Moslem leader; the prince of Toulouse may be its Archbishop or any one of the hereditary Montmorency family. Tolentino is part of the Papal States so presumably its leader is the Pope. Foix belonged to the House of Navarre.

Le sang du Juste par Taurer la	The blood of the Just for Taur
daurade,[3]	and La Duarade in order to
Pour se venger contre les Saturnins[4]	avenge itself against the Satur-
Au nouveau lac plongeront la	nines. They will immerse the
marinade.[5]	band in the new lake, then they
Puis marcher contre les Albanins.[6]	will march against Alba.

If one accepts that the two churches stand for Toulouse, the quatrain seems to imply that the inhabitants are fighting both Calvin-

[1] *emonopole*—A difficult compound Nostradamus word. Probably the nearest is the Greek, *aimapnoos* meaning bloodthirsty, or *aimatopotes*, blood drinker.

[2] *Nolle*—Probably an enigmatic proper name; possible Nola in Italy, but it does not fit the context.

[3] *Taurer la daurade* = Two Churches in Toulouse. (*a*) St. Saturnin du Taur. (*b*) Sainte Marie de la Daurade.

[4] *Saturnins*—Either those of Saturn or of St. Saturnin.

[5] *marinade*—Provençal, *marinada* = (*a*) Band. (*b*) Servants, household.

[6] *Albanins*—Probably the troops of the Duke of Alba, the Habsburg general for Emperors Charles V and Philip II. Just possibly Albanian mercenaries.

ism, or the Huguenots, as well as a Spanish attack led by the Duke of Alba.

41

Esleu sera Renad ne sonnant mot,	A fox will be elected without
Faisant le faint public vivant pain d'orge,[1]	speaking one word, appearing saintly in public living on
Tyranniser apres tant à un cop,[2]	barley bread, afterwards he will suddenly become a tyrant
Mettant à pied des plus grans sus la gorge.	putting his foot on the throats of the greatest men.

NAPOLEON III

Napoleon III was indeed as cunning as a fox and when elected President was known as *'le Taciturne'*. The prediction of line 3 was fulfilled by the *coup d'état* he exerted to make way for the Second Empire, 2nd December 1851. He certainly used his newly acquired power to fulfil line 4.

42

Par avarice, par force & violence	Through avarice, through force
Viendra vexer les siens chiefz d'Orléans,	and violence the chief of Orléans will come to vex his
Pres saint Memire[3] *assault & resistance.*	supporters. Near St. Memire, assault and resistance. Dead in
Mort dans sa tante diront qu'il dort leans.	his tent they will say he is asleep inside.

LOUIS PHILIPPE D'ORLÉANS

Louis Philippe will upset his supporters and will engage in combat around St. Merri (not *Memire*). That Nostradamus got the title of Orléans is astonishing because the founder of the House was the brother of Louis XIII, born long after Nostradamus' death. After his victory Orléans is unable to cope and sleeps like a dead man within his tent.

[1] *vivant pain d'orgue*—Has a secondary meaning—to feather one's nest, which is singularly appropriate.

[2] *cop*—Alternative spelling of coup, for the rhyme.

[3] *St. Memire*—An unidentified place name.

Par le decide[1] de deux choses bastars
Nepveu du sang occupera le regne
Dedans lectoyre seront les coups de dars
Nepveu par peur plaire l'enseigne.

Through the fall of two bastard creatures the nephew of the blood will occupy the throne. Within Lectoure there will be blows of lances, the nephew through fear will fold up his standard.

THE DEFEAT OF LOUIS NAPOLEON, 1870

The only important nephew in French history occurred over 300 years after Nostradamus' death; Louis Napoleon, son of King Louis, of Holland who was the brother of Napoleon I. The two bastards that fall are presumably the government of Louis Philippe, for whom Nostradamus has little liking, and that of the Second Republic. Lectoyre is an anagram of Le Torcey, a suburb of Sedan, the scene of Louis Napoleon's defeat by the Germans and Prussians. He ordered a flag of surrender to be hung on Sedan's church and then on its citadel, after which the Emperor formally surrendered to the Germans at Douchery two miles away from Le Torcey, in 1870.

44

Le procreé naturel dogmion,[2]
De sept à neuf du Chemin destorner
A roi de longue & ami au mi-hom,
Doit à Navarre fort de PAU prosterner.

The natural offspring of Ogmios will turn off the road from seven to nine. To the king long friend of the half man, Navarre must destroy the fort at Pau.

Ogmios turns up in several quatrains; he was the Celtic equivalent of Hercules or Mercury. Apart from this, the only clear fact seems to be the destruction of the fortress at Pau when Henri IV of Navarre was born.

[1] *decide*—From Latin, *decidere* = to fall.
[2] *Ogmion* = the Celtic Hercules.

La main escharpe & la jambe bandes,	With his hand in a sling and his leg bandaged, the younger
Longs puis nay de Calais portera.	brother of Calais will reach far.
Au mot du guet la mort sera tardee	At the word of the watch, the
Puis dans le temple à Pasques saignera.	death will be delayed, then he will bleed at Easter in the Temple.

Pol mensolee mourra trois lieus du Rosne[1]	Paul the celibate will die three leagues from Rome, the two
Fuis les deux prochains tarasc destrois:	nearest flee the oppressed monster. When Mars will take
Car Mars fera le plus horrible trosne,	up his horrible throne, the Cock and the Eagle, France
De coq & d'aigle de France, freres trois.	and the three brothers.

WAR LINKED WITH PAUL VI AND KENNEDY BROTHERS

The last Pope Paul before the present Paul VI died in 1621. The linking of the present Pope with the three Kennedy brothers helps us to date the quatrain in the near future. The present Pope will die either just outside Rome, or in France if the Rhône is intended. At this point the two allies (cf. V. 78 and VI. 50) are troubled, threatened by a great war. The Cock stands for France who appears to have an important role to play, and the Eagle stands for U.S.A. the home of the Kennedy brothers.

Lac Trasmenien portera tesmoignage,	Lake Trasimene will bear witness of the conspirators locked
Des conjurez serez dedans Perouse,	up inside Perugia. A fool will
Un despolle contrefera le sage,	imitate the wise one, killing the
Truant Tedesque de sterne & minuse.	Teutons, destroying and cutting to pieces.

[1] possible misspelling for Rome or Rhône.

Saturne en Cancer, Jupiter avec Mars,
Dedans Feurier Chaldondon¹ salva-terre.
Sault Castalon² affailli de trois pars,
Pres de Verbiesque³ conflit mortelle guerre.

Saturn in Cancer, Jupiter with Mars in February 'Chaldondon' salva tierra. Sierra Morena besieged on three sides near Verbiesque, war and mortal conflict.

According to Wöllner the astrologer, the closest we will come to this conjunction is 1st February 2769. I cannot offer a further opinion on this very difficult verse.

Saturn: au beuf joue en l'eau, Mars en fleiche,
Six de Fevrier mortalité donra,
Ceux de Tardaigne⁴ à Briges si grand breche,
Qu'à Ponteroso⁵ chef Barbarin mourra,

Saturn in Taurus, Jupiter in Aquarius. Mars in Sagittarius, the sixth of February brings death. Those of Tardaigne so great a breach at Bruges, that the barbarian chief will die at Ponteroso.

According to Wöllner again, this conjunction occurred in 1736 and not again in the foreseeable future. However McCann (1942) says that it occurred on 6th February 1971 so Nostradamus seems to have been wrong on both counts, unless it refers to those Mafia chiefs who were put on an island off Sardinia in enforced exile in 1971?

La pestilence l'entour de Capadille,
Un autre faim pres de Sagont s'appreste:
Le chevalier bastard de bon senille,
Au grand de Thunes fera trancher la teste.

The plague around Capellades, another famine is near to Sagunto; the knightly bastard of the good old man will cause the great one of Tunis to lose his head.

¹ *Chaldondon*—Possibly from Latin, *Chaldens* = a soothsayer, otherwise incomprehensible.
² *Sault Castalon*—Probably Latin, *Saltus Castulonensis* = Sierra Morena.
³ *Verbiesque*—An unsolved place name, probably near to Sierra Morena.
⁴ *Tardaigne*—Almost definitely misreading for Sardaigne = Sardinia.
⁵ *Ponteroso*—Unidentified, may mean the red bridge.

This quatrain is a very successful hit for Nostradamus. In 1573 (after Nostradamus' death in 1566), Don John of Austria, the bastard son of Charles V the old man, recaptured Tunis for his half-brother, Philip of Spain. Although there is no record of a famine, Spain was suffering from sporadic outbursts of plague between 1570–4.

51

Le Bizantin faisant oblation,	The Byzantine makes an obla-
Apres avoir Cordube à soi reprinse:	tion after having taken back
Son chemin long repos pamplation,[1]	Cordoba. A long rest on his
Mer passant proi par la Colongna[2]	road, the vines cut down, at
prinse.	sea the passing prey captured
	by the Pillar.

In this, Nostradamus seems to predict that the leader of Constantinople, whatever nation it might be, will invade Spain near Cordoba, having first made an offering to the Gods. Cordoba had belonged to the Arabs until 1031, and then to the Moslems until 1236. Line 4 may suggest that this Turkish leader, or whatever, is likely to be caught when returning through the Pillars of Hercules, i.e. Gibraltar.

52

Le roi de Blois dans Avignon regner,	The king of Blois to reign in Avignon, from Amboise and
D'amboise & seme[3] *viendra le long de Lyndre*	'Seme' the length of the Indre: claws at Poitiers holy wings
Ongle à Poitiers sainctes aesles ruiner	ruined before Boni. . . .
Devant Boni.[4]	

Line 1 is identical to the first line of VIII. 38. The various rivers are in France. Either the final line was not completed or was cut by the Catholic censor because it was dangerous or heretical. It is a pity because, with it, one might have gleaned some meaning from this quatrain.

---

[1] *pamplation*—Dubious, probably from Latin, *pampinatio* = to cut vines.

[2] *Colongna*—From *Collonnes d'Hercule* = Gibraltar.

[3] *seme*—Possibly the Seine, otherwise not identified.

[4] *Boni*—Incomplete line.

Dedans Bolongne vouldra laver ses fautes, *Il ne pourra au temple du soleil,* *Il volera faisant choses si haultes* *En hierarchie n'en fut oncq un pareil.*	Within Boulogne he will want to wash away his misdeeds, he cannot at the temple of the Sun. He will fly away, doing very great things: In the hierarchy he had never an equal.

NAPOLEON'S FAILURE TO INVADE ENGLAND

Many commentators apply this to Napoleon by reading Bolongne as Boulogne, but there is just a possibility that it may mean Bologna in the Papal States. Westminster Abbey, which Napoleon could not enter by conquest, was traditionally built on the Temple of Apollo, which was destroyed by an earthquake in AD 154. Napoleon flew so high as to think of taking Russia as well as England. Certainly he had no equal during his lifetime.

Soubz la colleur du traicte mariage, *Fait magnamine par grand Chyren selin,* *Quintin, Arras recouvrez au voyage* *D'espaignolz fait second banc macelin.*	Under the colour of the marriage treaty, a magnanimous act by the 'Chyren selin': St. Quintin and Arras recovered on the journey; By the Spanish a second butcher's bench is made.

Entre deux fleuves se verra enserré, *Tonneaux & caques unis à passer outre,* *Huict poutz rompus chef à tant enferré,* *Enfans parfaictz sont jugetez en coultre.*[1]	He will find himself shut in between two rivers, casks and barrels joined to cross beyond: eight bridges broken, their chief run through so many times, perfect children's throats slit by the knife.

Specific details of an unknown battle.

[1] *coultre*—O.F. = knife.

La bande foible le terre occupera	The weak band will occupy the
Ceux de hault lieux feront horribles	land, those of high places will
cris,	make dreadful cries. The large
Le gros troppeau d'estre coin	herd of the outer corner
troublera	troubled, near Edinburgh it
Toute pres D. nebro descouvers les	falls discovered by the writings.
escris.	

SCOTLAND AND CHARLES II

Dinebero is taken as meaning Edinburgh, through a phonetic pun, 'Edinbro''. This quatrain then describes very clearly the battle of Dunbar which took place 25 miles east of the city. Charles II landed in Scotland in 1650. The highlanders (line 1) were more numerous than the Cromwellians but their position was weak. (The phrase *estre en coin* is interesting because before the battle the Scots boasted they had Cromwell cornered 'in a pound'.) Therefore the weaker band, the Cromwellians, routed the Scots on 3rd September. Perhaps line 4 can be explained by the fact that Cromwell took possession of all the papers in the Scottish War Office?

De soldat simple parviendra en	From simple soldier he will
empire,	attain to Empire, from the short
De robe courte parviendra à la	robe he will grow into the long.
longue	Brave in arms, much worse
Vaillant aux armes en eglise on plus	towards the Church, he vexes
pire	the priests as water fills a
Vexer les prestres comme l'eau fait	sponge.
l'esponge.	

NAPOLEON I

From a simple lieutenant Napoleon attained to the government of the French Empire. He exchanged his short consular robe for the long robe of Imperial Majesty. Although brave in battle he mishandles the Clergy, and troubles the priests by the abolition of the Clergy just as much as water fills a sponge. An explicit quatrain to describe Napoleon's progress.

Regne en querelle aux freres divisé,	A kingdom divided by two
Prendre les armes & le nom	quarrelling brothers to take the
Britannique	arms and the name of Britain.
Tiltre Anglican sera guard advisé,	The Anglican title will be
Surprins de nuict mener à l'air	advised to watch out, surprised
Gallique.	by night (the other is), led to
	the French air.

JAMES II AND WILLIAM OF ORANGE, 1688

Since Nostradamus' death there have been no brothers fighting for the English throne, the loser fleeing to France. The nearest this came to fulfilment was when James II and his son-in-law, the Anglican William of Orange, came to open disagreement in 1688. The Anglican Church may well have exerted influence on the Catholic James II, but nevertheless he fled to France 'to take the Gallic air'.

Par deux fois hault, par deux fois	Twice put up and twice cast
mis à bas	down, the East will also weaken
L'orient aussi l'occident faiblira	the West. Its adversary after
Son adversaire apres plusieurs	several battles chased by sea
combats,	will fail at time of need.
Par mer chassé au besoin faillira.	

EAST AND WEST, 20th CENTURY

This seems again to describe the geopolitical state of the 20th Century better than any other. From this quatrain it appears that Asia will make two violent attacks upon the Western Powers which will affect them somewhat. But finally the East will lose at sea.

Premier en Gaule, premier en	First in Gaul, first in Roumania,
Romanie	over land and sea against the
Par mer & terre aux Anglois &	English and Paris. Marvellous
Paris	deeds by that great troop,
Merveilleux faitz par celle grand	violent, the wild beast will lose
mesnie	Lorraine.
Violent terax perdra le NOR-	
LARIS.	

Napoleon II is the only French leader to lose the Lorraine, but the rest of the quatrain does not fit him well. James Laver applies it to Napoleon I, saying he can be described as first in France and in Rome. This may be a split quatrain describing father and son, or maybe Nostradamus was confused, and saw the two men as one.

61

Jamais par le descouvrement[1] du jour
Ne parviendra au signe sceptrifere[2]
Que tous ses sieges ne soient en sejour,
Portant du coq don du TAG[3] amifere.

Never by the revelation of daylight will he attain the mark of the sceptre bearer. Until all his sieges are at rest, bringing to the Cock the gift of the armed legion.

The Cock bearing the gift of arms is the Cock symbolizing France, which was an obscure symbol until the Revolutionaries adopted it. The rest most commentators apply to Napoleon III; although I am not happy with this interpretation I cannot find a better.

62

Lors qu'on verra expiler[4] le saint temple,
Plus grand du rosne leurs sacrez profaner:
Par eux naistra pestilence si ample.
Roi fuit injuste ne fera condamner.

When one sees the holy temple plundered, the greatest of the Rhône profaning their sacred things; because of them a very great pestilence will appear, the king, unjust, will not condemn them.

A very general quatrain in which an unjust king commits sacrilege which results in a plague.

63

Quand l'adultere blessé sans coup aura
Merdri la femme & le filz par despit,
Ferme assoumee l'enfant estranglera:
Huit captifz prins, s'estouffer sans respit.

When the adulterer wounded without a blow will have murdered his wife and son out of spite; his wife knocked down, he will strangle the child; eight captives taken, choked beyond help.

[1] *descouvrement*—O.F. = discovery.
[2] *sceptrifere*—Latin = sceptre bearing, i.e. royal.
[3] *TAG*—Variant in editions, *tagma* = body of soldiers or legion.
[4] *expiler*—Latin, *expilare* = to rob, plunder.

Too general to identify.

64

Dedans les isles les enfans transportez, *Les deux de sept seront en desespoir,* *Ceux terrouer[1] en seront supportez,* *Nom pelle[2] prins des ligues fui l'espoir.*	The infants transported into the islands, two out of seven will be in despair. Those of the soil will be supported by it, the name 'shovel' taken, the hope of the leagues fails.

NAZIS AND BRITAIN

This quatrain is applied by most modern commentators to Britain, besieged by the Nazis in the Second World War. But even with this, *pelle* is not satisfactorily deciphered.

65

Le vieux frustré du principal espoir, *Il parviendra au chef de son empire:* *Vingt mois tiendra le regne à grand pouvoir,* *Tiran, cruel en delaissant un pire.*	The old man disappointed in his main hope, will attain to the leadership of his Empire. Twenty months he will hold rule with great force, a tyrant, cruel, giving way to one worse.

MARSHAL PÉTAIN, 1940–2

If one accepts that most general quatrains are assumed to occur in France, as I do, this may well refer to that country in 1940. In that year on 10th July, a rump session of the French Assembly invested Pétain with plenary powers until a new constitution could be formed. After increasing pressure from the Germans to collaborate he handed most of his powers over to Laval on April 1942.

[1] *terrouer*—O.F. = soil, land, ground.
[2] *pelle*—This has never been deciphered. Garencières got nearest with his suggestion of Montpellier.

Quand l'escriture D.M.[1] trouvee,	When the inscription D.M. is
En cave antique à lampe descouverte,	found in the ancient cave,
Loi, Roi, & Prince Ulpian[2]	revealed by a lamp. Law, the
esprouvee	King and Prince Ulpian tried,
Pavillon rogne & Duc sous la	the Queen and Duke in the
couvert.	pavilion under the cover.

Many commentators have suggested very ingenious solutions for
D.M., but as I say in the footnote, it is just the equivalent of There
Lies . . . in English. James Laver takes it to mean *du manuscrit,*
of the manuscript. It probably ties in with the puzzling quatrain
of IX. 84.

PAR. CAR. NERSAF, à ruine	Paris, Carcassone, France to
grand discord,	ruin in great disharmony,
Ne l'un ne l'autre aura election,	neither one nor the other will
Nersaf du peuple aura amour &	be elected. France will have
concorde.	the love and good will of the
Ferrare, Callonne grande protection.	people, Ferara, Colonna great
	protection.

Par. and *Car.* probably stand for Paris and Carcassonne, but
NERSAF is not a very good anagram for France, although by the
rules one is allowed to change one letter. Although Ferara was
joined with the Franco-Papal troops fighting Spain in 1557,
Colonna was always firmly pro-Spanish. The key to this quatrain
lies in the word *Nersaf.*

Vieux Cardinal par le jeune deceu,	The old Cardinal is deceived by
Hors de sa change se verra desarmé,	the young one, he will find him-
Arles ne monstres double soit	self disarmed, out of his
aperceu,	position: Do not show, Arles,
Et Liqueduct & le Prince em-	that the double is perceived,
bausmé.	both Liqueduct and the Prince
	embalmed.

[1] *D.M.*—Probably stands for Latin inscription, *Diis Manibus* which
was put on many Roman tombstones.

[2] *Ulpian*—Ulpius a Roman name, e.g. Trojan's was Marcus Ulpius
Trojanus.

Cardinal Richelieu is supplanted by the younger Cinq Mars and loses the favours of Louis XIII and has to resign. But at Arles he will receive a copy of a treaty with Spain, signed by Cinq Mars and the king's brother, in 1642. He tells the king of this treachery, and although very ill, travels to Paris on a barge. *Liqueduct* means literally 'led by the water', an excellent description of the Cardinal's voyage. But the Cardinal died at the end of 1642 and the king five months later, and as Nostradamus says, both bodies were embalmed.

69

Aupres du jeune le vieux ange baisser	Beside the young one the old
Et le viendra surmonter à la fin:	angel falls, and will come to rise
Dix ans esgaux au plus vieux rabaisser,	above him at the end; ten years equal to most the old one falls
De trois deux l'un huitiesme seraphin.	again, of three two and one, the eighth seraphin.

This quatrain seems to describe the rivalry of favourites; apart from this it is very obscure.

70

Il entrera vilain, mechant, infame	He will enter, wicked, un-
Tyrannisant la Mesopotamie,	pleasant, infamous, tyrannizing
Tous amis fait d'adulterine d'ame,	over Mesopotamia. All friends
Terre horrible, noir de phisonomie.	made by the adulterous lady, the land dreadful and black of aspect.

Usually Mesopotamia has described Avignon, at the joining of the Rhône and the Durance. If this is so, the villain is the Cardinal Legate governing it in place of the Pope.

71

Croistra le nombre si grand des astronomes	The number of astrologers will grow so great, that they will be
Chassez, bannis & livres consurez,	driven out, banned, and their
L'an mil six cents sept par sacre glomes	books censored. In the year 1607 by sacred assemblies so
Que nul aux sacres ne seront asseurez.	that none will be safe from the holy ones.

This dating appears successful when reading other commentators who all apply it to the Council of Malines of 1607 which banished astrology. But I can find no record of this Council existing at all. It was probably invented by a prejudiced commentator of Nostradamus! Therefore this quatrain must be counted as a definite failure, despite the dating.

72

Champ Perusin d'enorme deffaite
Et le conflit tout au pres de Ravenne,
Passage sacre lors qu'on fera la feste,
Vainqueur vaincu cheval manger la venne.

Oh what a huge defeat on the Perugian battlefield and the conflict very close to Ravenna. A holy passage when they will celebrate the feast, the conquerer banished to eat horse meat.

RAVENNA, 1512

This is probably a retrospective quatrain which had already occurred when Nostradamus wrote the Prophecies. Both Perugia and Ravenna were Papal States and this quatrain describes accurately enough the victory of Gaston de Foix at Ravenna in 1512.

73

Soldat barbare le grand Roi frappera,
Injustement non esloigné de mort,
L'avare mere du fait cause fera
Conjurateur & regne en grand remort.

The king is struck by a barbarian soldier, unjustly, not far from death. The greedy will be the cause of the deed, conspirator and realm in great remorse.

If used correctly the word '*barbare*' refers to the pirates from Barbary (Algeria), but it is used widely for Moslems and others not of the Christian faith.

74

En terre neufue bien avant Roi entré
Pendant subges lui viendront faire acueil,
Sa perfidie aura tel recontré
Qu'aux citadins lieu de feste & receuil.

A king entered very far into the new land while the subjects will come to bid him welcome; his treachery will have such a result that to the citizens it is a reception instead of a festival.

The new land is an interesting phrase because it was one of the names for America in Nostradamus' day. If the U.S.A. is meant, the verse implies that a world leader comes to that country and is given an excellent welcome whereas the whole time the guest is planning treachery. I wonder if the Chinese will visit the U.S.A. in the near future?

75

Le pere & fils seront meurdris ensemble	The father and son will be murdered together, the leader within his pavilion. The mother at Tours will have her belly swollen with a son, a verdure chest with little pieces of paper.
Le prefecteur dedans son pavillon	
La mere à Tours du filz ventre aura enfle	
Criche verdure de failles papillon.	

ASSASSINATION IN PORTUGAL, 1908?

The first line of this quatrain is very clear, the murder of a father and son. It cannot apply to France as no French kings and Dauphins were assassinated together. In the case of Louis XVI and his son there was over two years between the king's and his son's presumed death. There was no pregnant widow at Tours involved with the family. The most important father and son assassination outside France was in 1908, when Carlos I and Louis Philippe of Portugal were murdered at Lisbon. But still no explanation of the widow at Tours or the puzzling last line.

76

Plus Macelin[1] que roi en Angleterre	More of a butcher than a king in England, born of obscure rank will gain empire through force. Coward without faith, without law he will bleed the land; His time approaches so close that I sigh.
Lieu obscure nay par force aura l'empire:	
Lasche sans foi, sans loi saignera terre,	
Son temps approche si presque je soupire.	

OLIVER CROMWELL

Apparently Nostradamus had little sense of time because Oliver Cromwell did not appear until over 30 years after his death (1599–1658). He is described as more of a butcher than a king

[1] *Macelin*—Latin, *macellum* = a meat basket. Used elsewhere with the above meaning by Nostradamus.

because of the bloodshed of the Civil War. He was of the Protestant faith and Nostradamus regards him as a heretic. He was of comparatively humble origins and attained his position through military force. The reference to his being a coward is interesting as Cromwell was supposed to wear a corselet of some kind, because he was afraid of assassination.

77

L'antechrist trois bien tost an-niehilez,	The antichrist very soon an-nihilates the three, twenty-seven years his war will last. The unbelievers are dead, captive, exiled; with blood, human bodies, water and red hail covering the earth.
Vingt & sept ans sang durera sa guerre.	
Les heretiques mortz, captifs, exilez.	
Sang corps humain eau rougi gresler terre.	

ANTICHRIST AND THREE BROTHERS. LENGTH OF THE WAR

Three separate Antichrists appear in Nostradamus' Epistle. It is usually accepted that Napoleon was the first and Hitler the Second, so the Third is still to come. Line 1 can be read either as 'the third Antichrist will soon be annihilated' or 'the Antichrist will soon annihilate the three', implying by this the three Kennedy brothers, two of whom are already dead. It makes more sense in this context to assume that the Antichrist is a way of life, i.e. Russian Communism or Chinese Communism, since obviously one man did not kill both brothers. It seems as though Edward Kennedy must be a psychological assassinee since even Nostradamus foresaw his death four hundred years ago! The war is a long one of attrition; it may refer to the length of time needed before the cities would be safe from harmful radioactive fallout. After the atomic bombing of Nagasaki and Hiroshima large black raindrops fell, full of dust. This was recorded by survivors so perhaps Nostradamus is not so far out when he speaks of red rain.

78

Un Bragamus[1] avec la langue torte	A soldier of fortune with twisted tongue will come to the sanctuary of the gods. He will open the door to heretics and raise up the Church militant.
Viendra des dieux le sanctuaire,	
Aux heretiques il ouvrira la porte	
En suscitant l'eglise militaire.	

[1] *Bragamus*—O.F. = broadsword, or Provençal, *Briamanso* = a soldier of fortune.

This is a general quatrain that can be applied either to France during the Wars of Religion (1562–98) or to Germany during the Thirty Years War (1618–48).

79

Qui par fer pere perdra nay de Nonnaire,[1]	He who loses his father by the sword, born in a Nunnery,
De Gorgon sur la sera sang perfetant[2]	upon this Gorgon's blood will conceive anew; in a strange
En terre estrange fera si tant de taire,	land he will do everything to be silent, he who will burn
Qui bruslera lui mesme & son enfant.	both himself and his child.

The legendary Gorgon was a hateful monster, who turned everyone who looked at her into stone. Nostradamus is therefore describing an appalling woman who causes a man to kill himself and the child he has had by her. An interesting footnote is that Hugh Allen in his book on Nostradamus 1943, applies this quatrain to himself, on page xii!

80

Des innocens le sang de vefue & vierge.	The blood of innocents, widow and virgin, so many evils com-
Tant de maulx faitz par moyen se grand Roge	mitted by means of the Great Red One, holy images placed
Saintz simulacres tremper en ardent cierge	over burning candles, terrified by fear, none will be seen to
De frayeur crainte ne verra nul que boge.	move.

THE RUSSIAN REVOLUTION

The great Red One of line 2 is a revolution, but it is difficult to decide if the French or Russian Revolution is meant. I am inclined to accept the latter as the Communist Party is described as Red, and Nostradamus describes the French Revolutionary tricolour elsewhere. The first line would then refer to the deaths of the Czar and Czarina and their 'virgin' children. Line 3 smacks faintly of the influence of the Church through the priest Rasputin. The last line would then imply that Anastasia did not escape assassination, and that those who claim to be her are pretenders.

[1] *Nonnaire*—Low Latin, *nonneria* = nunnery.
[2] *perfetant*—Latin, *superfetens* = to conceive while pregnant.

Le neuf empire en desolation	The new empire in desolation
Sera changé du pole aquilonaire.	will be changed from the
De la Sicile viendra l'esmotion	Northern Pole. From Sicily will
Troubler l'emprise à Philip tribu-	come such trouble that it will
taire.	bother the enterprise tributary
	to Philip.

The first two lines make this quatrain sound very modern by the sheer scope of their concept. A ravaged empire moves itself and its civilization southwards, this might well occur after an atomic war. But the last two lines bring us back to 16th-Century Europe where Nostradamus seems to see a Habsburg civil war between Philip and Ferdinand over the division of Charles V's empire. The uprising against Philip is predicted as starting in Sicily.

Ronge long, sec faisant du bon valet,	Thin tall and dry, playing the
A la parfin n'aura que son congie[1]	good valet in the end will have
Poignant poison & lettres au collet	nothing but his dismissal; sharp
Sera saisi eschappé en dangie.[1]	poison and letters in his collar,
	he will be seized escaping into
	danger.

A valet who tries to poison his master is caught and dismissed.

Le plus grand voile hors de port de	The largest sail set out of the
Zara,	port of Zara, near Byzantium
Pres de Bisance fera son entreprinse,	will carry out its enterprise.
D'ennemi parte & l'ami ne sera,	Loss of enemy and friend will
Le Tiers à deux fera grand pille &	not be, a third will turn on both
prinse.	with great pillage and capture.

FOURTH CRUSADE, 1202
Another retroactive prophecy describing the atrocities of the Fourth Crusade, 1202. Venice agreed to cross to Egypt with the Crusaders for a large sum of money and half the plunder. The Crusaders could not raise the money and so they captured Zara (then Hungarian, now in Yugoslavia). The Pope excommunicated the whole Crusade, whereupon they sacked Constantinople (Byzantium) and set up Romania, the Roman Empire of the East.

[1] *congie* and *dangie*—The latter word shortened to keep the rhyme.

Paterne orra de la Sicile crie,
Tous les aprests du Goulphre de
  Trieste,
Qui s'entendra jusque à la Trina-
  crie[1]
Tant de voiles, fui, fuiz, l'horrible
  peste.

Paterno will hear the cry from
Sicily, all the preparations in
the Gulf of Trieste; it will be
heard as far as Sicily flee oh
flee, so many sails, the dreaded
pestilence!

The Spanish empire of the two Sicilies owned Catonia and Paternum, whereas Trieste belonged to Venice of the Habsburg branch.
So this is probably a continuation of VIII. 81.

Entre Bayonne & à Saint Jean de
  Lux
Sera posé de Mars la promottoire[2]
Aux Hanix[3] d'Aquilon Nanar[4]
  hostera lux,[5]
Puis suffocqué au lict sans ad-
  jutoire.[6]

Between Bayonne and St. Jean
de Luz will be placed the
promontory of Mars. To the
Hanix of the North, Nanar will
remove the light, then suffocate
in bed without assistance.

NAPOLEON III'S DEATH?

Nostradamus foresees a war zone (Mars) between Bayonne and
St. Jean de Luz in South-west France. The difficulty of interpretation lies in Hanix and Nanar, see below. Another suggestion is that
the promontory is Biarritz, where Napoleon III, like Mars the God
of War, retired into the arms of loving women when the North
wind ceases to blow. *Hanix* would then come from the Greek,
ansiscus, without force. Napoleon died from an operation for the
stone, but his weak physical condition, because of his debauchery,
may have made him much weaker.

[1] *Trinacrie* = Trinicia, poetic name for Italy.
[2] *promottoire*—Variant spelling of *promontoire*.
[3] *Hanix*—Possibly from Gk., *anikatos* = unconquerable, or Latin,
Hamaxaeci = the nomads of Northern Europe.
[4] *Nanar*—Possibly Latin, *nonaria* = prostitute?
[5] *lux*—Latin = light.
[6] *adjutoire*—O.F. = assistance, aid.

Par Arani Tholoser ville franque,	Through Emani, Tolosa and
Bande infini par le mont Adrian,	Villefranche, an infinite band
Passe riviere, Hutin¹ par pont la	through the mountains of
planque	Adrian. Passes the river, Cam-
Bayonne entrera tous Bihoro² criant.	bat over the plank for a bridge,
	Bayonne will be entered all
	crying Bigoree.

NAVARRE

The three towns of line 1 and the mountain of Adrian in line 2 are all close together on the south-western tip of the Spanish Pyrenees. The only river to the north between them and Bayonne is the Bidassoa. As I have said before, Bigorre was the battle cry of the Huguenots of Navarre, and the original Navarre covered the area south of the Pyrenees and north into France. It became a separate state in 1515 until it was reunified with France by the accession of Henri IV of Navarre to the French throne after Nostradamus' death.

Mort conspiree viendra en plein	A death conspired will come to
effect,	its full effect, the charge given
Charge donnee & voiage de mort,	and the voyage of death.
Esleu, crée, receu par siens deffait.	Elected, created, received
Sang d'innocence devant foi par	(then) defeated by his followers,
remort.	in remorse the blood of in-
	nocence in front of him.

LOUIS XVI

The conspiracy to rob Louis XVI of both his crown and life is successfully carried off. The change to the position of constitutional king and his flight to Varennes (voyage of death) will be the final cause of his death. He will be defeated by his own nation who earlier elected him. His innocent blood will be a source of remorse to the French.

¹ *Hutin*—O.F. = dispute, combat, hostility.
² *Bihoro*—Bigorre was the battle cry of the Huguenots of Navarre.

Dans la Sardaigne un noble Roi viendra	A noble king will come to Sardinia, who will only rule for three years in the kingdom. He will join with himself several colours; he himself, after taunts, care spoils slumber.
Que ne tiendra que trois ans le royaume,	
Plusieurs couleurs avec soi conjoindra,	
Lui mesmes apres soin someil marrit[1] scome.[2]	

KING OF SARDINIA, 1798–1802

King Charles Emmanuel IV, when the French Republic took most of his lands retired to Sardinia where he reigned for three years (1798–1802). He then abdicated in favour of his brother, Victor Emmanuel I. He then went to Rome humiliated and unhappy and joined the Jesuit Order with whom he stayed until his death in 1819. This is one of the few times in modern history that Sardinia had its own king and not a titular one.

Pour ne tumber entre mains de son oncle,	In order not to fall into the hands of his uncle who slaughtered his children in order to reign. Pleasing with the people, putting his foot on 'Peloncle', dead and dragged between armoured horses.
Qui ses enfans par regner trucidez.[3]	
Orant[4] au peuple mettant pied sur Peloncle[5]	
Mort & traisné entre chevaulx bardez.	

I have not been able to decipher *Peloncle* and therefore the quatrain remains unbroken.

[1] *marrit*—O.F. = to afflict, spoil.

[2] *scome*—Latin, *scomma* = scoff, taunt, jeer.

[3] *trucidez*—Latin, *trucidare* = to slaughter, massacre.

[4] *Orant*—Latin, *orans* = pleading, arguing.

[5] *Peloncle*—Doubtful, possibly Pellonia, the goddess who put enemies to flight?

Quand des croisez un trouvé de sens trouble	When those of the cross are found their senses troubled,
En lieu du sacre verra un boeuf cornu	in place of sacred things he will see a horned bull, through the
Par vierge porc son lieu lors sera comble	virgin the pig's place will then be filled, order will no longer
Par roi plus ordre ne sera soustenu.	be maintained by the king.

The men of the cross are either Crusaders, or Nazis. The bull may mean in Taurus, and the Virgin, Virgo, but it doesn't get us much further.

Frymy[1] les champs des Rodans[2] entrees	Entered among the fields of the Rhône (dwellers) where those
Ou les croisez seront presque unis,	of the cross are almost united,
Les deux brassieres[3] en Pisces rencontrees	the two lands meeting in Pisces and a great number
Et un grand nombre par deluge punis.	punished by the flood.

The conjunction of Pisces with Venus is the time clue for this quatrain, linked with flooding above the Rhône.

Loin hors du regne mis en hazard voyage	Far distant from his kingdom, sent on a dangerous journey,
Grand host[4] duira[5] pour soi l'occupera,	he will lead a great army and keep it for himself. The king
Le roi tiendra les siens captif ostrage	will hold his people captive and hostage, he will plunder the
A son retour tout pays pillera.	whole country on his return.

A very clear and dramatic quatrain which does not seem to have been fulfilled.

[1] *Frymi*—Misprint in some editions for *Parmi* = among.
[2] *Rodans*—Latin, *Rhodanus* = the Rhône, or possibly its people.
[3] *brassieres*—lead strings, probably standing for Venus who was bound to Mars by an unbreakable thread forged by Vulcan.
[4] *host*—O.F., *ost* = army.
[5] *duira*—O.F., *duire* = to lead.

Sept mois sans plus obtiendra prelature	For seven months, no longer, will he hold the office of prelate,
Par son deces grand scisme fera naistre:	through his death a great schism will arise; for seven months
Sept mois tiendra un autre la preture	another acts as prelate near Venice, peace and union are
Pres de Venise paix union renaistre.	reborn.

1590?

The only popes to live for less than seven months after election were Sixtus V, Urban VII, who died after two weeks, followed by Gregory XIV, who died after ten months, all in 1590. But unfortunately there is no record of a schism.

Devant le lac ou plus cher fut getté	In front of the lake where the
De sept mois, & son host desconfit	dearest one was destroyed for
Seront Hispans par Albanois gastez	seven months and his army
Par delai perte en donnant le conflict.	routed; Spaniards will be devastating by means of Alba, through delay in giving battle, loss.

BAY OF CADIZ, 1596

Ward applies this quatrain to the English attack on Cadiz by Essex, Howard and Raleigh in June 1596. In line 1 the word *cher* becomes treasure or valuables, because the ships were heavy with booty having come in from a seven months' voyage. Cadiz bay is called a lake because the word Gaddir, from which Cadiz comes, means 'an enclosed space'. Forty galleons and thirteen warships were destroyed. What makes this quatrain so interesting is that Nostradamus must have foreseen the war between Spain and England, whereas when he wrote England's queen was the wife of Spain's king (Mary Tudor).

Le seducteur sera mis en la fosse	The seducer will be placed in a
Et estaché jusques à quelque temps,	ditch and will be tied up for
Le clerc uni le chef avec sa crosse[1]	some time. The scholar joins
Picante droite attraira[2] les contens.	the chief with his cross. The sharp right will draw the contented ones.

[1] *crosse*—O.F. = possibly abbey; or cross.
[2] *attraire*—O.F. = to draw, attract.

La synagogue sterile sans nul fruit	The sterile synagogue without
Sera receu entre les infideles	any fruit, will be received by
De Babylon la fille du porsuit	the infidels, the daughter of the
Misere & triste lui trenchera les	persecuted (man) of Babylon,
aisles.	miserable and sad, they will
	clip her wings.

FLIGHT OF JEWS TO MOSLEMS, *c.* 1550–1566

This prophecy was already partly fulfilled in Nostradamus' lifetime. After the wave of persecution that they were suffering in Christian countries, the Sultan of Turkey, Suleiman the Magnificent, offered hospitality to Jews who came and settled in Constantinople, and Salonika in particular. One of them became very powerful and in 1566, the year of Nostradamus' death, Don Joseph Nassi was created Duke of Naxos and became the principal adviser to Selim II.

A fin du VAR changer le pompotans,	At the end of the Var the great
Pres du rivage les trois beaux enfants	powers change; near the bank
naistre.	three beautiful children are
Ruine ay peuple par aage competans.	born. Ruin to the people when
Regne ay pays changer plus voir	they are of age; in the country
croistre.	the kingdom is seen to grow
	and change more.

KENNEDYS?

In X. 100 '*pempotan*' stands for England. The problem is to decide whether it does so in this case, probably not. The river Var flows into the Mediterranean between Cannes and Nice and it was the approximate border of Savoy in Nostradamus' time. The three beautiful brothers who bring trouble to the nation may link up with the Kennedy theme. Certainly the U.S.A. was changing during their lifetimes and presumably was growing in influence to become a world power.

Des gens d'eglise sang fera espandu,	Of the church men the blood
Comme de l'eau eu si grand	will be poured forth as abun-
abondance;	dant as water in (amount); for
Et d'un long temps ne sera restranche	a long time it will not be res-
Ve, ve[1] au clerc ruine & doleance.	trained, woe, woe, for the clergy
	ruin and grief.

[1] *Ve, ve*—Latin, *vae* = alas, woe.

Another quatrain about the Persecution of the Clergy *c.* 1792 in France.

99

Par la puissance des trois rois tempoulz,
En autre lieu sera mis le saint siege:
Où la substance & de l'esprit corporel,
Sera remis & receu pour vrai siege.

Through the powers of three temporal kings, the sacred seat will be put in another place, where the substance of the body and the spirit will be restored and received as the true seat.

The only time that the Pope's seat has been moved from the Vatican to date is when Pope Pius VI was moved to Valence and died there. Pius VII managed to return to Rome. Maybe one of the future Popes will move out of the Vatican. Lines 3 and 4 imply a revival of religious fervour.

100

Pour l'abondance de larme respandue
Du hault en bas par le bas au plus hault.
Trop grande foir par jeu vie perdue
De soif mourir par habondant deffault.[1]

By the great number of tears shed, from top to bottom and from the bottom to the very top, a life is lost through a game with too much faith, to die of thirst through a great deficiency.

A nonsensical quatrain to present-day readers.

[1] The whole of this line is difficult. It probably means drowned, or even to drink oneself to death.

CENTURY IX

1
2
3
4
5*   National Assembly, 1848
6
7
8
9   Nîmes, 1557
10
11*   England, 1649–56
12
13
14
15
16***   General Franco and de Rivera
17*   French Revolution
18**   Louis XIII
19
20***   Louis XVI flight to Varennes
21
22
23*   Louis XVI and his son
24
25
26
27*   Louis XVII?
28
29*   Capture of Calais, 1558
30
31?
32
33

34*** Louis XVI and Saulce
35*   Ferdinand of Bulgaria, 20th Century
36*F? Kennedy brothers
37
38
39
40*   Battle of St. Quentin, 1557
41
42*** Battle of Lepanto, 1571
43
44
45
46
47?   Francis II, 1559–60?
48*?
49**   Execution of Charles I, 1649
50*   Henri IV
51**   20th Century?
52*   Peace of Cateau Chambresis, 1559
53
54
55**   Influenza epidemic, 1918
56
57
58
59
60
61
62   Magic practices?
63
64
65***F? The Space Race
66
67
68*   The sack of Lyons, 1793
69
70
71
72
73*?   18th February 1981
74
75
76

77***   Fates of Marie Antoinette and Mme. du Barry
78
79
80
81
82
83*F?   An earthquake on 10th April?
84**   Tomb of St. Peter?
85
86*   3rd July 1851
87
88*   1557. Calais
89*   Louis Philippe, 1830–48
90**   Hitler
91
92**F?   New York?
93**   Louis XIV
94
95
96
97
98
99*   Napoleon's retreat from Moscow
100**?   Pearl Harbour, 1941

KEY: * Of interest. F? Possibly referring to the future.

Dans la maison du traducteur de Bourc[1]	In the house of the translator from Bourg letters will be found on the table. One-eyed, red- and white-haired will hold the course, which will change for the new constable.
Seront les lettres trouvees dur la table	
Bourgne, roux, blanc chanu tiendra de cours,	
Qui changera au nouveau connestable.	

This is a fascinating quatrain. One of the best known 16th-Century French scholars was a man called Etienne de la Boétie. If '*Bourc*' stands for Boétie then the prophecy makes some sort of sense, in that the latter had a famous quarrel with the then Constable of France, Anne de Montmorency over the publication of a book, 'La Servitude Voluntaire'. Nostradamus seems to predict that Boétie would have even more trouble with the Constable's successor, Henri de Montmorency. This did not occur as Boétie died four years before Anne de Montmorency, in 1563. See also IX. 81.

Du hault du mont Aventin voix ouie,	A voice is heard from the top of Aventine Hill. Go, go, all on both sides! The anger will be appeased by the blood of the red ones. From Rimini and Prato, Colonna expelled.
Vuidez, vuidez de tous les deux costez,	
Du sang des rouges sera l'ire assomie,[2]	
D'Arimin Prate, Columna[3] *debotez.*[4]	

Another quatrain centred around the feuds of the Vatican states with the great Italian families, the Colonnas and the Orsinis etc. In Nostradamus' time they were allied to the Spanish and thus got deeply involved with the Vatican's anti-Spanish policies of Pope Paul IV.

[1] *Bourc* = Bourg, north of Bordeaux; the inhabitants were called Bourcais.

[2] *assomie*—O.F. = to appease.

[3] *Columna*—Original spelling of the Colonnas of Rome.

[4] *desbotez*—O.F., *debouter* = expell, drive out.

La magna vaqua[1] à Ravenne grand trouble,
Conduictz par quinze enserrez à Fornase
A Rome naistre deux monstres à teste double
Sang, feu, deluges, les plus grands à l'espase.

The Magnavacca near Ravenna in great trouble, led by fifteen shut up at Fornese; at Rome two monsters with double heads are born, blood, fire, floods, the greatest in the air.[2]

This is similar to the last quatrain with the added enigma of *magna vaqua*, literally 'the great cow'. It seems to be involved with the Papal states and the Vatican, together with hanging and two-headed monsters, two of which were shown to Nostradamus in his capacity of prophet in the early 1560s near Salon, when he declared them to predict a disunited France to come.

L'an ensuivant descouvertz par deluge,
Deux chefs esluez le premier ne tiendra
De fuir ombre à l'un d'eux le refuge,
Saccager case[3] qui premier maintiendra.

The following year revealed by a flood, two leaders elected, the first will not hold on; for one of them refuge in fleeing shadows, the victim plundered who maintained the first.

Another quatrain describing a discovery, or treasure, combined with vague threats.

Tiers doit du pied au premier semblera.
A un nouveau monarque de bas hault
Qui Pise & Lucques Tyran occupera
Du precedant corriger le deffaut.

The third toe will look like the first one of a new king, of low height, he who will occupy as a tyrant Pisa and Lucca, to correct the fault of his predecessor.

[1] *magna vacca*—Either the valley and port named Magnavalca between Ravenna and Ferrara, or an unsolved name?
[2] i.e., hanged.
[3] *case*—Provençal *casa* = victim of hunt or the hunt.

The third estate, established for a second time in 1848, will seem no more than a toe of the first, i.e. very insignificant. Louis-Napoleon found it easier to deal with than did Napoleon I. In 1831 Louis Napoleon was involved with Italian revolutionaries and helped to try to seize Civila Castellana which is in Tuscany as are Pisa and Lucca. The fault of Napoleon's predecessor was Napoleon II's failure to obtain real power.

6

Par la Guienne infinité d'Anglais.
Occuperont par nom d'Anglaquitaine
Du Languedoc Ispalme[1] Bourdelois.
Qu'ils nommeront apres Barboxitaine.[2]

A great number of English in Guienne will occupy it, calling it Anglaquitain. In Languedoc, Ispalme, Bordelais which they will name after Barboxitaine.

The English occupied Guienne, the Languedoc and Bordelais steadily between the 12th and 15th Centuries, but not since Nostradamus' lifetime. Bordelais was one of the centres of English dominance in southern France. Perhaps Ispalme is a misprint for Lapalme near Narbonne? Barboxitaine seems to mean 'the Beard's' south-western France, the Beard being the man variously referred to as Bronze Beard or Aenobarbe (see V. 59). Not a successful quatrain on the whole.

7

Qui ouvrira le monument trouvé
Et ne viendra le serrer promptement.
Mal lui viendra & ne pourra prouvé,
Si mieux doit estre roi Breton ou Normand.

The man who opens the tomb when it is found, and who does not come and shut it immediately; evil will come to him, no one will be able to prove it. It might have been better were he a Breton or a Norman King.

Another quatrain about the discovery of a tomb, and it may be linked with I. 27. The last line is suitably enigmatic: I. 27 is regarded by some as being a threat against the opening of Nostradamus' tomb which happened all the same in 1813.

[1] *Ispalme*—Unidentified place name.
[2] *Barboxitaine*—Probably derived from Barbe-Occitanie, Barbe referring to the enigmatic Bronzebeard and Occitanie, the medieval name for the Mediterranean coast.

Puisnay Roi fait son pere mettre à mort, *Apres conflit de mort tres inhoneste:* *Escrit trouvé soubson donra remort,* *Quand loup chassé pose sus la conchette.*	The younger son will put his father, the king to death, after the quarrel, to a death very dishonest. Writings found, suspicion will bring remorse, when the chased wolf lies on the bedcover.

Although the statement of a younger son taking over his father's throne, in a way that involves murder, sounds quite reasonable, it is hard to find any possible fulfilment since Nostradamus' lifetime, and also of the strange details of the last two lines.

9

Quand lampe ardente de feu inextinguible, *Sera trouvé au temple des Vestales,* *Enfant trouvé feu, eau passant par trible:*[1] *Perir eau Nimes, Tholose cheoir les halles.*	When the lamp burning with eternal fire, will be found in the temple of the Vestals. A child found (in the) fire water passing through the sieve, Nîmes to perish in water, the markets will fall in Toulouse.

1557

Nostradamus may have cheated on this verse because in 1557 the most enormous cloudburst occurred over Nîmes (popularly held to be the site of a Temple of Diana, tended by the Vestal Virgins). The water was over six feet deep in some places and many of the beautiful monuments were uncovered. But nothing remarkable occurred in Toulouse around that time.

10

Moine moinesse d'enfant mort exposé, *Mourrir par ourse & ravi par verrier.*[2] *Par Foix & Pamyes le camp sera posé.* *Contre Tholose Carcas, dresser forrier.*	The child of a monk and a nun will be exposed to die, to die by a she bear, and carried off by a boar; the army will be camped near Foix and Parmiers, Carcassonne will raise the pillage against Toulouse.

[1] *trible*—Mod. French, *crible* = a sieve.
[2] *verrier*—Probably made up by Nostradamus from Latin, *verez* = a boar.

A quatrain set in South-west France, the first part describing the tragic circumstances and death of a baby, the second part great military events.

11

Le juste à tort à mort l'on viendra mettre	They will come to put the just man wrongfully to death, pub-
Publiquement & du millieu estaint:	licly in the midst he is ex-
Si grande peste en ce lieu viendra naistre,	tinguished. So great a plague will be born in this place that
Que les jugeans[1] fouir seront constraint.	the judges will be forced to flee.

ENGLAND, 1649–56

This quatrain is usually applied to England. It states that after someone is unjustly executed, a great plague occurs in that place causing the people who caused the death to flee. It is understood to describe Charles I who was beheaded in 1649, his death to be followed by the great plague of London 1655–6.

12

Le tant d'argent de Diane & Mercure	The great amount of silver of Diana & Mercury, the images
Les simulacres au lac seront trouvez,	will be found in the lake. The sculptor looking for new clay,
Le figulier cherchant argille neufve	both he and his followers will
Lui & les siens d'or seront abbrevez.	be soaked in gold.

Another treasure quatrain relating in particular to that in Toulouse of VIII. 28–30.

13

Les exilez autour de la Soulonge	The exiles around Sologne, led
Condus de nuit pour marcher à Leuxois,	by night to march into Auxas, two from Moderna for the
Deux de Modene truculent[2] de Boulogne,	cruel one of Bolognia; put, discovered, by the fire of the
Mis descouvers par feu de Burancois.	Buzançais.

[1] *jugeans* = judges, again invented by Nostradamus.
[2] *truculent*—From Latin, *truculentus* = ferocious, hard, cruel.

Mis en planure chaulderone d'in- fecteurs,[1]	The dyers' cauldrons put in a flat place, wine, honey and oil
Vin, miel & l'huile, & bastis sur forneaulx	and built over furnaces. They will be drowned, without saying
Seront plongez sans mal dit mal facteurs	or doing an evil thing, seven of Borneaux, the snake extin-
Sept. sum extaint au canon des borneaux.	guished from the cannon.

A typical, unintelligible Nostradamus quatrain at its worst.

Pres de Parpan les rouges detenus	The red ones detained near
Ceux du milieu parpondrez menez loing:	Perpignan, those in the middle, ruined, led far away. Three cut
Trois mis en pieces, & cinq mal soustenus,	into pieces and five badly supported for the Lord and
Pour le Seigneur & Prelat de Bourgoing.	Prelate of Burgundy.

Perpignan belonged to Spain until 1659, and red was the colour
of the Spanish. Nostradamus seems to foresee a Franco-Spanish
struggle around the Pyrenees. The Governor of Burgundy, in
Nostradamus' time the Duke of Aumale died in 1573, the country
had four (not five) bishops under him.

De castel[2] *Franco sortira l'assem- blee*	From Castille Franco will bring out the assembly, the ambassa-
L'ambassadeur non plaisant fera scisme:	dors will not agree and cause a schism. The people of Riviera
Ceux de Ribiere seront en la meslee	will be in the crowd, and the
Et au grand goulphre desnier ont l'entree.	great man will be denied entry to the Gulf.

FRANCO AND DE RIVERA

This is an extraordinary verse with the names of two personages in
it. The Dictator Primo de Rivera and also Francisco Franco, who
helped depose him, and was exiled to Morocco, returning trium-
phantly when his party came to power. The last line is held to
describe Franco's exile when he was not allowed to cross the Medi-

[1] *infector*—Latin, dyer.
[2] *castel* = Castille.

terranean (*goulphre*) to his native Spain. Castel should be read a Castille. See III. 8.

17

Le tiers premier pis que ne fait Neron,	The third one firstly does worse than Nero, go, flow, brave
Vuidez vaillant que sang humain respandre:	human blood. The furnace will be rebuilt, a golden century;
R'edifier sera le forneron,	(then) death, a new king and
Siecle d'or, mort, nouveau roi grand esclandre.	great scandal.

THE FRENCH REVOLUTION

The third first is the National Convention of the Tiers État in Revolutionary France. Nostradamus describes it as being far crueller than Nero's reign with blood flowing freely from the guillotines. The machine will be put at the Place de la Révolution opposite the Tuileries, where formerly tile kilns were built. The golden century of the Kings Louis XIV–XVI is over! The great scandal is possibly a reference to the killing of the Royal Family. See also III. 59.

18

Le lis Dauffois portera dans Nancy	The lily of the Dauphin will be
Jusques en Flandres electeur de l'empire,	taken as far as Nancy, the elector of the empire as far as
Neufve obturee au grand Montmorency,	Flanders. A new prison for the great Montmorency, to the
Hors lieux provez delivre à clere peyne.	usual place delivered up to Clerepeyne.

LOUIS XIII

Louis XIII was the first bearer of the lilies of France and the title of Dauphin since Nostradamus' death. He entered Nancy in September 1633. The city of Treves had been recovered the year before by the Maréchal d'Estrées who re-established the authority of the Elector. However in 1633 the Elector was carried off by the Spanish and taken as a prisoner to Brussels (*Flandres*). At the same time 1632, a revolt was led in southern France by the great Montmorency. His family pleaded for his release in vain, but did obtain the doubtful privilege of execution by a private, rather than public, executioner. He was beheaded in the court of the prison Hôtel de Ville, quite recently built, i.e. 'not in the usual place'. '*Delivre à clere peyne*' has two meanings. It means delivered to clear

356

punishment, but also *clere peyne* is declared by some commentators to be the name of the executioner. A typical Nostradamus pun. I have not been able to verify the name. It first appears in a commentary by Jaubert, 1656.

19

Dans le millieu de la forest Meyenne,	In the middle of the Mayenne forest, the Sun in Leo, the
Sol au lyon la fouldre tombera.	lightning will fall. The great
Le grand bastard issu du Grand du Maine,	bastard born of the great man of Maine, on that day a point
Ce jour fougeres pointe en sang entrera.	will enter the blood of Fougères.

Mayenne in North-western France has a large forest west of the city. Fougères is about twenty miles further west, the seat of a great family bearing the name which died out in the 13th Century. It was used in the 15th Century by Diane de Poitiers, Henri II's mistress, and also by Henri III when he was still Duke of Anjou. No other great families are connected with the house, and the Fougères line was long dead, unfortunately for Nostradamus.

20

De nuict viendra par la forest de Reines,	By night will come through the forest of Reins two partners, by
Deux pars vaultort Herne[1] la pierre blanche,	a roundabout way, the Queen, the white stone. The monk-
Le maine noir[2] en gris dedans Varennes	King dressed in grey at Varennes the Elected Capet causes
Esleu cap. cause tempeste feu sang tranche.	tempest, fire and bloody slicing.

LOUIS XVI's FLIGHT TO VARENNES, 1791

The royal couple, Louis XVI and his wife, Marie Antoinette, will go by night through the forest of Reins, having fled from the Tuileries through a secret door in the Queen's apartment. They lost their way and chose an extremely bad route (*vaultort*), The *pierre blanche* probably refers to the affair of the diamond necklace which demolished Marie Antoinette's fragile popularity with the French people. It may also refer to the fact that her lady in waiting said that the Queen's hair turned white overnight, and that she normally wore white dresses. The King was wearing a

[1] *Herne*—Anagram for *Reine*.
[2] *noir*—Usual anagram for king.

simple grey suit (perhaps the word monk refers to his earlier impotence), when they entered Varennes. He was a Capet, an elected king, the first France had ever had, and as Nostradamus declares, was the cause of a revolution and the shedding of blood. *Tranche* is the verb meaning to slice, and the sound is particularly apposite in this context of the guillotine.

21

Au temple hault de Blois sacre Solonne,	At night, the high temple of Blois at Sacré Solonne a priest
Nuict pont de Loire, prelat, roi pernicant[1]	on the Loire bridge, a king dying; a messenger, victory for
Curseur[2] *victoire aux marestz de la lone*[3]	the marshes on the water. Destruction for a priestly gift
Don prelature de blancs à borméant.[4]	from the whites.

Sacré Solonne is the church of Saint Solenne, the Cathedral at Blois. Nostradamus repeats in several quatrains his conviction that France would gain a king from Blois.

22

Roi & sa court au lieu de langue halbe,[5]	The king and his court in the place of the clever tongue, in
Dedans temple vis à vis du palais.	the temple, facing the palace.
Dans le jardin Duc de Mantor & d'Albe.	In the garden the Duke of Mantua and Alba, Alba and
Albe & Mantor poignard langue & palais.	Mantua dagger, tongue and the palace.

The key to this quatrain lies in the identities of Mantor and Alba. In 1536 the places of Alba and Mantua had been joined together by Charles V. The ruler from 1550–87 was Gonzaga who did suffer an assassination attempt at Casale, but not at Blois. Also the famous Château de Blois does not face the Cathedral.

[1] *pernicant*—From either Latin, *pernecare* = to kill, or *pernix* = swift.
[2] *curseur*—O.F. = runner, messenger.
[3] *lone*—Provençal, *lona* = a pool, still water.
[4] *abormeant*—Latin, *aboriri* = to miscarry. Provençal, *abouriment* = destruction.
[5] *halbe*—O.F., *habler* = to talk a lot.

Puisnay jouant au fresch dessouz la tonne,	The younger son playing out-doors under the arbour, the
Le hault du toict du milieu sur sa teste,	top of the roof on the middle of his head. The father king in the
Le pere roi au temple fait Solonne,	Temple is solemn, sacrificing,
Sacrifiant sacrera fum de feste.	he will consecrate the smoke of the feast.

LOUIS XVI AND HIS SON

The younger child is the second son of Louis XVI and his wife who was allowed out to play in the Temple gardens while Louis was imprisoned in a tower away from the rest of his family. Line 3 actually repeats this fact, and we continue on to the King's gloomy future when he will be sacrificed to the Festival of Revolution.

Sur le palais au rochier[1] des fenestres	At the palace from the balcony of the windows, the two little
Seront ravis les deux petits royaux,	royal ones will be carried off.
Passer aurelle[2] Luthece[3] Denis cloistres	To pass Orléans, Paris and the cloisters of Saint Denis, a nun,
Nonain, mallods[4] avaller verts noiaulx.	the flies devouring the green pits.

St. Denis was about ten miles from Paris in Nostradamus' age. All that is clear in this verse is the fact that two young royal children are kidnapped.

[1] *rochier*—Derived from roche, and in the context of windows probably means a balcony.
[2] *aurelle*—Latin Aurelianum, Orléans.
[3] *Luthece*—Latin, Lutetia, Paris.
[4] *mallods?*—O.F., *malots* = flies? *malois* = wicked? or Latin, *malum* = an apple?

Passant les ponts venir pres des rosiers,[1]	Crossing the bridges to come near the Roisiers, sooner than
Tard arrivé plustot qu'il cuidera,[2]	he thought, he arrived late.
Viendront les noves[3] *espaingnolz à Beziers,*	The new Spaniards will come to Béziers, so that this chase
Qui icelle chasse emprinse[4] *cassera.*	will break the enterprise.

Nostradamus' new Spaniards are the interesting point in this quatrain. Béziers was on the Spanish invasion route about fifty miles north-east of the pre-1659 border. The river is probably the one which became the Canal du Midi.

Nice sortie sur nom[5] *des letres aspres,*	Departed by the bitter letters the surname of Nice, the great
La grande cappe[6] *sera present son sien,*	Cappe will present something, not his own; Near Voltai at the
Proche de Vultry aux murs de vertes capres	wall of the green columns, after Piombino the wind in good
Apres plombin[7] *le vent à bon essien.*	earnest.

De bois la garde vent chez rond pont sera,	The forester, the wind will be close around the bridge, re-
Hault le receu frappera le Daulphin,	ceived highly, he will strike the Dauphin. The old craftsman
Le vieux teccon[8] *bois unis passera,*	will pass through the woods in a company, going far beyond the
Passent plus oultre du duc le droit confin.	right borders of the Duke.

LOUIS XVII

This quatrain may be another confirming the escape of the Dauphin who was reported dead in June 1795. It implies that he is taken out of France, but the method is very obscure. The possible

[1] *rosiers*—Either the place or rosebushes.
[2] *cuiderer*—O.F. = to think.
[3] *noves*—O.F. = new.
[4] *emprinse*—O.F. = enterprise.
[5] *sur nom*—Either surname or 'under the name of'.
[6] *cappe*—Referring to Pope as a Cope, modern French, Cape.
[7] *plombin*—Either of Piombino, or leaden, from lead.
[8] *teccon*—O.F. = a game played with a ball. Possibly from Gk., *tekton*, a craftsman?

reference to a ball game would be in context with amusing a ten-year-old child. See V. 1.

28

Voille Simacle[1] *port Massiliolique,*[2]	The Allied fleet from the port of
Dans Venice port marcher aux Panons:	Marseilles, in Venice harbour to march against Hungary. To
Partir du goulfre & Sinus[3] *Illirique,*	leave from the gulf and the bay of Illyria, devastation in Sicily,
Vast[4] *à Socile, Ligures coups de canons.*	for the Ligurians, cannon shot.

This quatrain covers a lot of ground, geographically. We have Panonia, Hungary, Marseilles, and the gulf of Illyria which is the Adriatic sea, but despite so many place names I cannot decipher it.

29

Lors que celui qu'à nul ne donne lieu,	When the man will give way to none, will wish to abandon a
Abandonner vouldra lieu prins non prins:	place taken, yet not taken; Ship afire through the swamps,
Feu nef par saignes, butiment[5] *à Charlieu,*	bitumen at Charlieu, St. Quintin and Calais will be recap-
Seront Quintin Balez[6] *reprins.*	tured.

CAPTURE OF CALAIS, 1558

The last line of this quatrain is interesting. The fall of Calais to the French was unexpected when the Duke de Guise recaptured it on 6th January 1558. St. Quentin was given back to the French in the general settlement of 1559.

[1] *Simacle*—Gk., *symmachos* = allied with, auxiliary.
[2] *Massiliolique*—Latin, *Masilioticus* = of Marseilles.
[3] *Sinus*—Latin = a bay.
[4] *Vast*—Latin, *vastum* = destruction, devastation.
[5] *butiment*—O.F. = bitumen—a mineral pitch, asphalt.
[6] *Balez*—Probably anagram for Calais.

Au port de P.U.O.L.A. & de saint Nicolas,	At the port of Pola and Saint Nicolo, a Normand will punish
Perir Normande au goulfre phanatique,[1]	in the Gulf of Quarnero: Capet to cry alas in the streets of
Cap.[2] *de Bizance raues crier helas,*	Byzantium, help from Cadiz
Secours de Gaddez[3] *& du grand Philipique.*	and the great Philip.

All the places mentioned, except Cadiz, are in Yugoslavia. If Philip is intended to be Philip II, Nostradamus was predicting a Franco-Turkish attack on the Habsburgs in the south, with the Spaniards helping against the French.

31

Le tremblement de terre à Montara,	The trembling of the earth at Mortara the tin island of St.
Cassich[4] *saint George*[5] *à demi perfondrez,*	George half sunk; drowsy with peace, war will arise, at Easter
Paix assoupie, la guerre esveillera,	in the temple abysses opened.
Dans temple à Pasques abismes enfondrez.	

The St. George islands here seem unlikely to be Great Britain because it is unusual to suffer earthquakes so far outside the earthquake zone, and secondly an earthquake in Mortara would incur a disturbance of over 1,000 miles from Britain. This one is left for the reader.

[1] *phanatique?*—Latin, *Sinus Flanaticus* = the Gulf of Quaerno?

[2] *Cap*—Probably apocope of Capet, the French Royal line.

[3] *Gaddez*—Latin, *Gades* = Cadiz.

[4] *Cassich*—probably from Greek Cassiterides, the tin islands, a name given to Cornwall and the Scilly Isles.

[5] *saint George*—Probably England, as he was adopted as patron saint in the 14th Century.

De fin porphire profond collon trouvee	A deep column of fine porphyry is found, inscriptions of the
Dessoubz la laze[1] escriptz capi- tolin:[2]	Capitol under the base; bones, twisted hair, the Roman
Os poil retors Romain force prouvee,	strength tried, the fleet is stirred at the harbour of
Classe[3] agiter ay port de Methelin.	Mitylene.

Hercules Roi de Romme & d'Annemarc[4]	Hercules, king of Rome and of 'Annemarc' three times the
De Gaule trois Guion[5] surnommé	leader of France to be surnamed
Trembler l'Italie & l'unde de sainct Marc[6]	(de Gaule). Italy will tremble and the waters round St. Mark,
Premier sur tous monarque renommé.	the first to be renowned over all (the) kings.

Perhaps a reference to General de Gaulle? For Annemarc see also IV. 27.

Le part solus mari sera mitré,	The partner, solitary but married, will be mitred, the
Retour conflict passera sur le thuille:	return, fighting will cross over the Tuileries. By five hundred
Par cinq cens un trahir sera tiltré,	one traitor will be ennobled,
Narbon & Saulce par conteuax avons d'huile.	Narbonne & Saulce, we will have oil for knives.

LOUIS XVI AND SAULCE

This is one of the most extraordinary of the quatrains. When Louis XVI and Marie Antoinette were stopped at Varennes (IX. 20) they passed the night at the house of a man named Saulce (line 4). The Sauces (modern spelling) have been chandlers and *marchands-épiciers* there since the 16th Century. The fact that the king alone is mitred refers to Louis' return to the Tuileries on 20th June 1792 when the mob invaded the palace, and the king

[1] *laz*—Greek = foot or base.
[2] *capitolin*—Belonging to the Capital of Rome—i.e. latin.
[3] *Classe*—Latin, *classis* = fleet.
[4] *Annemark?* Hungary and Bohemia, Moravia.
[5] *Guion.* O.F. guide, chief, leader.
[6] *Saint Marc.* Venice, of whom he is the patron.

was forced to wear the revolutionary cap of liberty, which looks very like a mitre. It is thought that *couteaux* in line 4 should be read as *quartants*, which means oil sold in retail, which was exactly what Saulce did. In Thiers' History of France, he states that the mob when they returned (*retour*) to the Tuileries (*thuile*), for a second time, numbered exactly five hundred. A very convincing quatrain.

35

Et Ferdinand blonde sera descorte,[1]
Quitter la fleur suivre le Macedon.[2]
Au grand besoin faillira sa routte,
Et marchera contre le Myrmidon.[3]

And the fair-haired Ferdinand will be detached to abandon the flower and to follow the Macedonian. In great need his course will fail him and he will march against the Myrmidons.

FERDINAND OF BULGARIA, 20th CENTURY
This may well describe King Ferdinand of Bulgaria with the Macedonians, Germans and Greeks during the Second World War.

36

Un grand Roi prins entre les mains
d'un Joine,
Non loing de Pasque confusion coup
coultre:[4]
Perpet.[5] *captifs temps que fouldre*
en la husne,
Lorsque trois freres se blesseront &
meutre.

A great king captured by the hands of a young man, not far from Easter, confusion, a state of the knife. Everlasting captives, times when the lightning is on the top, when three brothers will be wounded and murdered.

KENNEDYS?
If this refers to the Kennedys, the theme of three bothers from America, which runs through the Prophecies, this verse indicates that the brothers are murdered and that this may happen around Easter. Since J. F. Kennedy died on 22nd November 1963 and Robert Kennedy on 6th June 1968, perhaps another assassination

[1] *descorte*—O.F. = detached, in disagreement.
[2] *Macedon*—Nostradamus probably means the Spanish.
[3] *Myrmidons*—Achilles' tribe, renowned for their obedience to all commands.
[4] *coultre*—Latin, *culter* = a knife.
[5] *Perpet*—Probably apopope of Latin, *Perpetualis* = everlasting.

may occur around April, with perhaps a storm thrown in, 'the lightning on the top'. Equally the lightning may refer to a gun on the top of a tall building, as happened at Dallas in 1963.

37

Pont & malins en Decembre versez,	Bridges and milk overturned in
En si haut lieu montera la Garonne:	December, the Garonne will
Murs, edifices, Tholose renversez,	rise to a very high place. Walls,
Qu'on ne scaura son lieu avant	buildings, Toulouse over-
matronne.[1]	thrown, so that none will know
	his place before Matronne.

38

L'entree de Blaye par Rochelle &	The entry at Blaye for la
l'Anglois,	Rochelle and the English, the
Passeraontre le grand Aemathein[2]	great Macedonia will pass
Non loing d'Agen attendr le	beyond; not far from Agen the
Gaulois,	Gaul will wait,[3] help from
Secours Narbonne deceu par entre-	Narbonne misled by a con-
tien.	versation.

39

En Arbissel à Veront[4] *& Carcari,*	In Albisobla to Veront &
De nuict conduitz pour Savonne	Carcara, led by night to seize
attrapper,	Savona, the swift Gascon, La
Le vifz Gascon Turbi, & la	Turbie and l'Escarene, to seize
Scerry	the old and new palace behind
Derrier mur vieux & neuf palais	the wall.
gripper.	

[1] *matronne*—May well be disguised place name.

[2] *Aemathein*—Latin, *Emathia* = poetic name for Macedonia and Thessaly.

[3] will wait—Alternatively, he will wait for the Frenchman . . .

[4] *Veront*—Not Verona as other places close to Albisola; unsolved place name?

Pres de Quintin dans la forest bourlis¹	Near St. Quentin, deceived in the forest, in the Abbey the
Dans l'abbaye seront Flamens ranches,²	Flemish will be cut up. The two youngest half-stunned by blows,
Les deux puisnays de coups mi estourdis	their followers crushed, and the guard all cut to pieces.
Suitte oppressee & garde tous aches.	

BATTLE OF ST. QUENTIN, 1557

Before the battle of St. Quentin in 1557 the Spaniards seized the Abbey of Vermandois: this was followed by the battle on 10th August 1557.

Le grand Chyren³ soi saisir Avignon,	The great 'Chyren' will seize Avignon, from Rome will come
De Romme letres en miel plein d'amertume.	honeyed letters full of bitterness. The letter and embassy to
Letre ambassade partir de Chanignon,⁴	leave from Chanignon, Carpentras taken by the Black
Carpentras pris par duc noir rouge plume.	Duke with the red feather.

Henri II is here seen to capture Avignon, which belonged to the Papacy, but unfortunately it did not come into French hands until 1791, although it was twice occupied in 1663–4 and 1768–74. The letters are doubtless from an irate Vatican. Chanignon is still undeciphered. Carpentras is near Avignon and was part of the Pope's lands.

¹ bourlis?—Possibly a proper name or derivative of boucle = deceived?
² ranches—Error for tranches in all editions.
³ Chyren—Anagram for Henryc?
⁴ Chanignon—Unsolved place or proper name.

De Barcellonne, de Gennes & *Venise,*	From Barcelona, from Genoa and Venice, from Sicily a
De la Secille peste Monet[1] unis	pestilence allied with Monaco;
Contre Barbare classe[2] prendront la *vise*	they will take aim against the barbarian fleet, the barbarian
Barbare, pulse bien loing jusqu'à *Thunis.*	driven as far back as Tunis.

BATTLE OF LEPANTO, 7th OCTOBER 1571

This prophecy was well fulfilled in 1571 when the allied fleets of the Papacy, Venice and Spain crushed the Turks at Lepanto. By 1573 Don John of Austria the leader of the expedition went on to recapture Tunis. Much of the Turkish fleet was composed of ships from their ally the Algerian Barbari, or pirates.

Proche à descendre l'armee Cruci- *gere[3]*	Ready to land, the army of the Cross will be watched for by the
Sera guettez par les Ismaëlites[4]	Ismaelites; struck from all sides
De tous cottez batus par nef *Raviere[5]*	by the ship Raviere, quickly attacked by ten chosen galleys.
Prompt assaillis de dix galeres *eslites.*	

This is probably a continuation of the last quatrain.

Migres migre de Genesve trestous,	Leave, leave Geneva everyone,
Saturne d'or en fer se changers,	Saturn will change from gold
Le contre RAYPOZ[6] exterminera *tous,*	into iron. Those against RAY-POZ will all be exterminated.
Avant l'a ruent de ciel signes fera.	Before the rush the sky will show signs.

[1] *Monet*—Unusual spelling for Monech, Monaco from Latin, *Herculi Monoeciis.*

[2] *classe*—Latin = fleet.

[3] *Crucigere*—Bearing a cross, a Crusader.

[4] *Ismaëlites*—Biblical name for the Arabs.

[5] *Raviere*—O.F., *raviere* = impetuosity. Nostradamus must be hinting at an unsolved name here.

[6] *RAYPOZ*—An anagram, but not solved except for one suggestion. Zopyre who betrayed Babylon to Darius.

Geneva was famous in Nostradamus' time as being the Protestant equivalent of the Vatican because Calvin made it his centre. Nostradamus is either warning the victims of a Calvinist purge, or warning them that they will be attacked by Philip II. Raypoz is another unsolved personal name.

45

Ne sera soul jamais de demander,
Grand Mendosus[1] obtiendra son Empire
Loing de la cour fera contremander,
Pimond, Picard, Paris, Tyrron[2] le pire.

There will never be a single person to ask, great Mendosus will attain his Empire. Far from the court he will have countermanded Piedmont, Picardy, Paris, Tuscany the worst.

Mendosus is an anagram for the family of Vendôme, earlier spelt Vendosme, in which case the quatrain should describe either Henri IV, or his father Anthony de Navarre, Duke de Vendosme. Unfortunately despite this excellent lead the rest of the quatrain is very obscure. Piedmont was Italian and belonged to Savoy, Picardy is a Normandy province of France.

46

Vuidez, fuyez de Tholose les rouges
Du sacrifice faire expiation,
Le chef du mal dessouz l'ombre des courges
Mort estranger carne omination.[3]

Be gone, flee from Toulouse the red ones, make expiation for the sacrifice. The main cause of evil in the shadow of the gourds, dead, to strangle the prognostication of flesh.

47

Les soulz signez d'indigne delivrance,
Et de la multe auront contre advis,
Change monarque mis en perille pence,[4]
Serrez en caige se verront vis à vis.

The undersigned to an infamous delivery, and receiving contrary advice from the crowds; a monarch changes, thoughts are put in danger, shut in a cage they will see each other face to face.

[1] *Mendosus*—Erroneous, or an anagram for Vendosme, the Bourbon branch who won the French throne in 1594.

[2] *Tyrron*—Probably from Latin, *Tyrrheni* = the Etruscans.

[3] *carne ominatio*—Prognostic of flesh.

[4] *pence*—This may either be from *penser*, to think, or if Nostradamus knew some English, pence.

Possibly this quatrain can be applied to Francis II, 1559–60?

48

La grand cité d'occean maritime,	The great city of the maritime
Environnee de maretz en cristal:	ocean, surrounded by a swamp
Dans le solstice hyemal¹ & la	of crystal; in the winter solstice
prime²	and the spring will be tried by a
Sera tempté de vent espouvantal.	dreadful wind.

This is described by Allen (1943) as the destruction of Central Park, and by Boswell (1941) as the destruction of Tokyo, but by Russian chemical bombs. The latter was almost correct in his own prediction i.e. Nagasaki and Hiroshima 1945.

49

Gand & Bruceles marcheront contre	Ghent and Brussels march
Envers	against Antwerp; the Parlia-
Senat du Londres mettront à mort	ment of London will put their
leur Roi	king to death; the salt and wine
Le sel & vin lui seront à l'envers,	will oppose him; because of
Pour eux avoir le regne en dessarroi.	them he will have the kingdom
	in trouble.

EXECUTION OF CHARLES I, 1649

This quatrain implies that lines 1 and 2 are simultaneous. Charles I was executed in 1649 new style, or 1648, old style, when New Year's day was held on 25th March. Philip IV made great attempts to reconquer the Netherlands but by 1648 they were anxious to get the Dutch out of the war, and ceded to them several key towns. By doing this, they closed the Scheldt which ruined Antwerp. Note that the quatrain is also numbered 49, the date of King Charles' death, a very fortunate coincidence. See VIII. 37.

50

Mandosus tost viendra à son hault	Mendosus will soon come to
regne	his great reign putting behind
Mettant arriere un peu de Nolaris:	somewhat the Nolaris; the pale
Le rouge blaisme, le masle à	red one, the man in the in-
l'interregne	terregnum, the frightened
Le jeune crainte & frayeur Bar-	young man and the fear of the
baris.	Barbaric ones.

---

¹ *hymal*—Latin, *hiemalis* of winter.
² *prime*—O.F., springtime.

Mendosus as we saw in IX. 45 and X. 18, is an anagram of Vendosme, and Nolaris one of the Lorraine, the home of the Guise family. The quatrain says that Vendosme, Henri IV, will soon come to the throne and relegate the house of Guise to the wings. The *'rouge blesme'* is probably the old Cardinal of Bourbon, pallid from age and red in his Cardinal's robes. He was proclaimed King Charles X in 1589 but died the next year. The *'masle'* is the Duke de Mayenne who was Lieutenant-General during the interregnum. The young man is the Duke de Guise, and Barbaris is Philip II of Spain who claimed the throne of France through his daughter Isabella.

51

Contre les rouges sectes se banderont,	Against the red ones sects will
Feu, eau, fer, corde par paix se minera,[1]	unite, fire, water, iron, the rope will weaken through peace.
Au point mourir, ceux qui machineront,	Those who plot are at the point of dying except one who above
Fors un que monde surtout ruinera.	all will ruin the world.

20th CENTURY

This quatrain must have a 20th-Century interpretation. The Reds here fit in a modern politico-social setting better than anywhere else. The conditions described existed between the two World Wars. In line 1 are Fascism, Nazism, Communism etc., and in line 2 the rope obviously refers to the Corde Sanitaire. Line 3 describes the wretched western statesmen, most of whom were appeasers like Chamberlain and Pétain. The exception is Hitler in line 4 who certainly attempted to fulfil this prediction.

52

La paix s'approche d'un costé, & la guerre	Peace approaches from one side; and war never was the
Oncques ne feut la poursuitte si grande,	pursuit of it so great. Men and women moan, innocent blood
Plaindre homme, femme, sang innocent par terre	on the land, and this will be throughout the whole of
Et ce fera de France à toute bande.	France.

PEACE OF CATEAU CAMBRESIS, 1559

On 13th April 1559, the King of France declared that he would stop fighting the Spanish and turn his attention to liquidating the

---

[1] *se miner*—O.F. = to ruin, destroy, spoil.

heretics in France. The peace is between France and Spain, the war the civil war between Catholics and Huguenots, declaring a time of bloodshed for all of France.

53

Le Neron jeune dans les trois cheminées
Fera de paiges vifs pour ardoir[1] getter,[2]
Hereux qui loing sera de telz menees,
Trois de son sang le feront mort guetter.

In three chimneys the young Nero will make the living pages thrown out to burn. He is happy who will be far from such happenings; three of his family will ambush him to death.

There is one record of a young man being thrown into a fireplace by his prince in the historical novels of Rafael Sabatini; otherwise I can offer no clue.

54

Arrivera au port de Corsibonne,[3]
Pres de Ravenne qui pillera la dame,
En mer profonde legat de la Ullisbonne
Souz roc cachez raviront septante ames.

There will arrive at Porto Corsini, near Ravenna, one who will plunder the lady. The legate from Lisbon in the deep sea; hidden under a rock they will carry off seventy souls.

The Dame here may well be the Catholic Church that is plundered at Porto Corsini, eight miles north of Ravenna.

55

L'horrible guerre qu'en l'occident s'apreste
L'an ensuivant viendra la pestilence,
Si fort horribles que jeune, vieux, ne beste,
Sang, feu, Mercure, Mars, Jupiter en France.

The dreadful war which is prepared in the West, the following year the pestilence will come, so very horrible that young, nor old, nor animal (will survive) blood, fire, Mercury, Mars, Jupiter in France.

[1] ardoir—O.F. = to burn.
[2] getter—O.F. spelling of jeter = to throw.
[3] Corsibonne = Porto Corsino, the port of Ravenna.

This quatrain is usually applied to the First World War which was followed by the dreadful influenza epidemic of 1917–18, governed by the conjunction of Mercury, Mars and Jupiter.

56

Camp pres de Noudam passera Goussan ville, *Et à Maiotes¹ laissera son ensigne,* *Convertira en instant plus de mille,* *Cherchant les deux remettre en chaine & legne.²*	The army near Noudan will pass Goussainville, and will leave its mark at Maiotes; in an instant more than a thousand will be converted, looking for the two to put back chain and firewood(?).

Houdan and Goussainville are both to the west of Paris. But Maiotes is still unsolved and I cannot find a clear meaning for *legne.*

57

Au lieu de DRUX³ un Roi reposira, *Et cherchera loi changeant d'Ana-theme,* *Pendant le ciel si tres fort tonnera,* *Porter neufve Roi tuera soimesme.*	In the place of DRUX a king will rest, and will look for a law to change Anathema. While the sky thunders so loudly the king will kill himself at the new gate.

58

Au costé gauche à l'endroit de Vitry Seront guettez les trois rouges de France; *Tous assomez rouge, noir non murdri* *Par les Bretons remis en asseurence.*	To the left side of the place of Vitry the three red ones of France will be watched. All those killed red, the black not murdered, in safety reassured by the Bretons.

¹ *Maiotes*—Either a place name, Mantes? or from the Greek, *memaotes* = keen soldiers.

² *legne*—Possibly Provençal, *legna* = firewood, Loomis?

³ *DRUX*—Possibly anagram for Dreux?

A la Ferté prendra la Vidame	At the Ferté Vidame he will
Nicol tenu rouge qu'avoit produit la	take, Nicol the red who had
vie.	produced life; to the great
La grand Loisne naistra que fera	Louise who acts secretly one
clame.[1]	will be born, who gives Bur-
Donnant Bourgongne à Bretons par	gundy to the Bretons through
envie.	envy.

Conflict Barbar en la Cornere noire.	In a black head-dress the
Sang espandu trembler la d'Almatie,	Barbarian fights, blood shed,
Grand Ismaël[2] *mettra son pro-*	Dalmatia trembles. The great
montoire,	Ismaël will make his pro-
Ranes[3] *trembler secours Lusitanie.*	montory, Frogs tremble under
	aid from Portugal.

La pille faite à la coste marine,	The plunder taken on the sea
La cita nova & parents amenez	coast, in the new city and
Plusieurs de Malte par le fait de	relations brought forward;
Messine,	Several of Malta through the
Estroit serrez seront mal guardon-	deeds of Messina, will be closely
nez.	shut up, poorly rewarded.

Au grand de Cheramon agora	To the great one of Cheramon
Seront croisez par ranc tous	agora will all the crosses by
attachez,	rank be attached, the long
Le pertinax[4] *Oppie,*[5] *& Man-*	lasting Opium and Mandrake,
dragora,[6]	the Rougon will be released on
Rougon[7] *d'Octobre le tiers seront*	October the third.
laschez.	

MAGIC PRACTICES?

A very odd verse. Ceramon-agora was actually the name of a town in Asia Minor which is believed to be present-day Usak.

[1] *clame*—Latin, *clam* = secretly.
[2] *Ismaël* = An ancestor of the Arab nation, therefore Arabs.
[3] *ranes*—Latin, *rama* = a frog.
[4] *pertinax*—Latin = long lasting.
[5] *Oppie*—Greek = opium.
[6] *Mandragoras*—Gk. = mandrake.
[7] *Rougon*—Unsolved place name.

Both the herbs of opium and mandrake had mysterious virtues and were used in occult practices.

63

Plainctes & pleurs cris & grands urlemens	Complaints and tears, cries and great howls, near Narbonne and Bayonne and in Foix; oh what dreadful calamities and changes, before Mars has revolved a few times.
Pres de Narbon à Bayonne & en Foix	
O quel horrible calamitz changemens,	
Avant que Mars revolu quelques fois.	

Each revolution of Mars lasts 687 days, which may be relevant if the quatrain is to be taken literally. The rest is obscure.

64

L'Aemathion[1] passer montz Pyrenees,	The Aemathian will cross the Pyrenees in March, Narbonne will not make any resistance. He will carry on a very great intrigue by land and sea, Cap. having no land in which to stay safely.
En Mars Narbon ne fera resistance,	
Par mer & terre fera si grand menee	
Cap.[2] n'ayant terre seure pour demeurance.	

65

Dedans le coing de luna[3] viendra rendre,	He will come to take himself to the corner of Luna, where he will be taken and placed on foreign land. The unripe fruit will be the subject of great scandal, great blame, to the other great praise.
Ou sera prins & mis en terre estrange,	
Les fruitz immeurs seront à la grand esclandre	
Grand vitupere à l'un grande louange.	

SPACE RACE?

If Luna is to be taken literally as the moon, this quatrain makes surprising sense. The first two lines describe the astronaut deliberately going to the moon, 'taken' in his capsule and landing. The 'unripe fruit' may intend to imply that the rockets are not yet

[1] *Aemathian*—Either Macedonian or Thessaly as before IX. 38.
[2] *Cap.*—Nostradamus' usual shortening of the Capetian name of the French royal line.
[3] *luna*—Possibly Lunigiana, or even the Moon?

ready for such intensive flight. The scandals and blame are the deaths and dangers suffered by all astronauts whether American or Russian. Note that Nostradamus is aware that one country or side gets great praise and benefit from the space race, but that the other receives only blame from its citizens. The USA has halted its space programme while that of the USSR is continuing apace.

66

Paix, union sera & changement,	There will be peace, union and change, estates and offices (that were) low, (are) high, those high, very low. To prepare for a journey torments the first child; war to cease, legal processes, debates.
Estatz, offices bas hault, & hault bien bas.	
Dresser voyage le fruict premier torment,	
Guerre cesser, civil proces debatz.	

This could apply to any post-war period.

67

Du hault des montz à l'entour de Lizer	From the top of the mountains around Isère, a hundred assembled at the gate to the Valencian rock; from Château-neuf, Pierrelatte, in Douzère; against the Crest, Romans assembled in faith.
Port à la roche Valen cent assemblez	
De chasteau neuf pierre late en donzere	
Contre le crest Romans foi assemblez.	

Crest is probably a shortening of Chrestiens, Christians, which makes this obscure verse imply some sort of religious strife.

68

Du mont Aymar[1] sera noble obscurcie,	The noble of Mount Aymar will become obscure, the evil will come at the junction of the Saone and the Rhône, soldiers hidden in the woods on Lucy's day, there never was so horrible a throne.
Le mal viendra au joinct de sonne & rosne.[2]	
Dans bois caichez soldatz jour de Lucie,[3]	
Qui ne fut onc un si horrible throsne.	

[1] *Mont Aymar*—Possibly Montelimart? or by the mountain of slaughter.
[2] Junction of the rivers is at Lyons.
[3] *Lucie*—St. Lucy's day, 13th December.

Two facts are obvious in this quatrain, Lyons and December the 13th. This is probably describing the sack of Lyons in 1793 which was performed by the Revolutionary soldiers and was a great scandal at the time. Mount Aymar is still unclear.

69

Sur le mont de Bailly & la Bresle[1]	On the mountain of Sain Bel and l'Arbresle[1] will be hidden
Seront caichez de Grenoble les fiers,	the proud people of Grenoble.
Oultre Lyon, Vien. eulx si grande gresle,	Beyond Lyons, at Vienne there will be such great hail, locust
Langoult[2] en terre n'en restera un tiers.	on the land, not a third of it will remain.

70

Harnois trenchant dans les flambeaux cachez	Sharp armour hidden in the torches at Lyons, on the day
Dedans Lyon le jour du Sacremont,[3]	of the sacrament; all those of
Ceux de Vienne seront trestous hachez	Vienne will be cut to pieces by the Latin cantons, Mâcon
Par les cantons Latins[4] Mascon ne ment.	does not lie.

71

Au lieux sacrez animaux veu à trixe,[5]	Animals with hair seen at the holy places with one who does
Avec celui qui n'osera le jour:	not dare (to face) the day;
A Carcassonne pour disgrace propice,	Carcassonne is suitable for the disgrace, and will be left for a
Sera posé pour plus ample sejour.	longer stay.

[1] The most likely two combinations.

[2] langoult—O.F., langouste = a locust, not a lobster as in modern French.

[3] jour du Sacrament—Understood as Corpus Christi, the first Thursday after Trinity Sunday.

[4] Latins—Possibly the Grisoné where most of the Italian-speaking Swiss live.

[5] trixe—Greek, thrix = hair or wool, possibly sheep in this context?

Encor seront les saincts temples pollus,	Again the holy temples will be polluted and plundered by the
Et expillez par Senat Tholossain,	Senate of Toulouse; Saturn
Saturne deux trois cicles revollus,	having completed two or three
Dans Avril, Mai, gens de nouveau levain.[1]	cycles in April and May there will be people of a new leaven.

The cycle of Saturn is 29·5 years, so two or three cycles can be added presumably to the date of the sack of Toulouse. Nostradamus appears to think that the Calvinists will take over and despoil the churches. It is possible that line 3 means two × three cycles of Saturn, i.e. six, which would be 177 years, a figure Nostradamus mentions also in the Preface.

Dans Foix entrez Roi ceiulee[2] *Turbao,*	The king enters Foix wearing a blue turban, he will reign for
Et regnera moins revolu Saturne,	less than a revolution of Saturn;
Roi Turban blanc Bisance coeur ban,	the king with the white turban, his heart banished to Byzan-
Sol, Mars, Mercure pres de la hurne.[3]	tium, Sun, Mars and Mercury near Aquarius.

18th FEBRUARY 1981

This verse apparently describes a Moslem or Eastern invasion, because of the turbans. Foix is understood to belong to a blue-turbaned man, king for less than 29·5 years. Then the white figure appears, in some way connected with Constantinople (Byzantium). According to McCann (1942) this quatrain is dated by the planets as 18th February 1981.

[1] *levain*—i.e. Protestants disputing the Eucharist.
[2] *ceiulee*—Latin, *caeruleus* = blue.
[3] *hurne*—Variant spelling of *l'urne*, Aquarius.

Dans la cité de Fersod[1] *homicide,*	In the homicidal city of Fert-
Fait & fait multe beuf arant ne	sod, again and again many
macter,[2]	oxen plough, not sacrificed;
Retour encores aux honneurs d'Arte-	again a return to the honours of
mide,	Artemis, and to Vulcan the
Et à Vulcan corps morts sepultures.[3]	corpses of the dead to bury.

De l'Ambraxie & du pays de	From Arta & the country of
Thrace	Thrace, people ill by sea, help
Peuple par mer mal & secours	from the Gauls; in Provence
Gaulois,	their perpetual trace and rem-
Perpetuelle en Provence la trace,	nants of their customs and laws.
Avec vestiges de leur coustume &	
loix.	

This seems to describe the Greeks returning to ask aid from Southern France, and particularly Provence, of which their early colonial settlers were particularly fond.

Avec le noir[4] *Rapax & sanguin-*	With the rapacious and bloody
aire,	king, sprung from the pallet of
Issu du peaultre[5] *de l'inhumain*	inhuman Nero; between two
Neron	rivers, the military on the left
Emmi[6] *deux fleuves main gauche*	hand, he will be murdered by a
militaire,	bald young man.
Sera murtri par Joine cheulveron.[7]	

[1] *Fertsod?—La Ferté—*Sodom?
[2] *macter,* Latin, *mactare* = to slaughter.
[3] *sepultrer—*O.F. to bury.
[4] Anagram for *roi,* king, or the black one?
[5] *peaultre* = pallet, brothel, rudder, (Laver).
[6] *emmi—*O.F., = between.
[7] *chaulveron—*Diminutive of *chauve* = bald.

Le regne prins le Roi conujera,[1]	The kingdom taken, the King will plot, the lady taken to death by those sworn by lot; they will refuse life to the Queen's son, and the mistress suffers the same fate as the wife.
La dame prinse à mort jurez à sort,	
La vie à Roine fils on desniera,	
Et la pellix[2] *au sort de la consort.*	

FATE OF MARIE ANTOINETTE AND MME. DU BARRY

After the Royal Family's imprisonment, Louis XVI was executed in January 1793. He was condemned by the Convention who elected these powers to itself. However, the Queen, who was not executed until the following October, had a newly created revolutionary tribunal to judge her which was served by a jury selected by lot. This was an institution unknown to France in Nostradamus' day. The third line tells the fate of Louis XVII whether he died or lived abroad is irrelevant, his kingdom was denied to him. Finally the most interesting line of all. While the Queen was imprisoned in the Conciergerie, the old mistress of Louis XV, Mme. du Barry, was taken for a while to the prison of Sainte Pelagie. An impressive quatrain.

La dame Greque de beauté laydique,[3]	The Greek lady of the beauty of Lais is made happy by innumerable suitors; transferred out to the Spanish kingdom she is captive taken to die a wretched death.
Hereuse faicte de procs innumerable,	
Hors translater au regne Hispanique,	
Captive prinse mourir mort miserable.	

It has been suggested that the incomparable lady is in fact democracy, which was founded in Greece, and which starts to die out in Europe beginning with Spain in 1936.

[1] *conjuera*—Alternative, will make advances?

[2] *pellex*—Latin = mistress or concubine.

[3] *laydique*—Lais was the most beautiful woman in Corinth. Possibly means ugly from *laid*?

Le chef de la classe[1] par fraude
 stratageme,
Fera timides sortir de leurs galleres,
Sortis meutris chef renieur de
 cresme,
Puis par l'embusche lui rendront les
 saleres.

The leader of the fleet through deceitful trickery will make the scared ones come out of their galleys. Come out, murdered, the leader to renounce the holy oil. Then through an ambush they give him his deserts.

Le Duc voudra les siens exterminers
Envoyera les plus forts lieux
 estranges,
Par tyrannie Pize & Luc ruinera,
Puis les Barbares sans vin feront
 vendanges.

The Duke will wish to kill his followers, he will send the strongest to the strangest places; through tyranny he ruins both Pisa and Lucca, then the Barbarians will harvest grapes without wine.

Le Roi rusé entendra ses embusches
De trois quartiers ennemis affaillir,
Un nombre estranges larmes de
 coqueluches[2]
Viendra Lemprin[3] du traducteur
 faillir.

The crafty king will understand his ambushes, from three sides the enemies threaten; a large amount of strange tears from the hooded (ones), the splendour of the translator will fail.

Perhaps the translator in this quatrain is the same as in IX. 1, in trouble with the church and the state?

Par le deluge & pestilence forte
La cité grande de long temps
 assiegee,
La sentinelle & garde de main
 morte,
Subite prinse, mais de nul oultragee.

By the flood and the great plague the great city is assailled for a long time. The sentry and guard killed by hand, suddenly captured, but none wronged.

Another vague, general quatrain; a great city which is suffering from the plague and flooding, is seized by a surprise attack at night.

 [1] *classe*—Latin = fleet.
 [2] *coqueluches* = hooded men, i.e. monks.
 [3] *Lemprin?*—Greek, *lampros* = splendour.

Sol vingt de Taurus si fort terre trembler.	The sun in twenty degrees of Taurus, there will be a great
Le grand theatre rempli ruinera,	earthquake; the great theatre
L'air ciel & terre obscurcir & troubler	full up will be ruined. Darkness and trouble in the air, on sky and land, when the infidel calls
Lors l'infidelle Dieu & sainctz voguera.	upon God and the Saints.

AN EARTHQUAKE ON 10th APRIL

The day but not the year of this great earthquake is given; such an apocalyptic verse makes one think of the Los Angeles fault. '*Sol vingt de Taurus*' means twenty days after the sun moves into Taurus which is April 10th

84

Roi exposé parfaira l'hecatombe,	The king discovered will complete the slaughter once he has
Apres avoir trouvé son origine,	found his origin: a torrent to
Torrent ouvrir de marbre & plomb la tombe	open the tomb of marble and lead, of a great Roman with the
D'un grand Romain d'enseigne Medusine.[1]	Medusine device.

TOMB OF ST. PETER?

Yet another verse about the discovery of a tomb. The key lies in the word Medusine. If it is an anagram of Deus in me, this would mean it was the real tomb of St. Peter, as that was his emblem, and that the one which was declared to be found some years ago is of another early Pope.

85

Passer Guienne, Languedoc & le Rosne,	To pass Guienne, Languedoc and the Rhône from Agen,
D'Agen tenans de Marmande & la Roole,	holding Marmande and La Réole; to open the wall through
D'ouvrir par foi par roi[2] *Phocen*[3] *tiendra son trosne*	the king, Marseilles will hold its throne a battle near St.
Conflit aupres saint Pol de Mauseole.[4]	Paul-de-Mausole.

[1] *Medusine*—Device of Medusa? Device of Pegasus? Device of 'Deus in me'?

[2] *par roi*—Possibly *parroi* = wall?

[3] *Phocen* = Marseilles.

[4] *St. Paul de Mausole*—A convent, then an asylum (where Van Gogh stayed) just outside St. Rémy.

Du bourg Lareyne ne parviendront	From Bourge-la-Reine they will
droit à Chartres	not come straight to Chartres,
Et feront pres du pont Anthoni	they will pause near the Pont
panse,[1]	d'Anthony: seven as crafty as
Sept pour la paix cantelleux comme	martens for peace they will
martres.	enter with weapons into a
Feront entree d'armee à Paris	closed Paris.
clause.	

3rd JULY 1815

The seven allied nations who joined against Napoleon were Austria, England, Prussia, Portugal, Sweden, Spain and Russia, they entered Paris on 3rd July 1815. The city was stripped of its troops when the French army was evacuated to Chartres taking up positions on the way to the Loire, passing Bourge-la-Reine and the Pont d'Anthony under which it is reputed to have camped.

87

Par la forest du Touphon[2] *essartee,*	In the cleared forest of Tou-
Par hermitage sera posé le temple,	phon the temple will be placed
Le duc d'Estampes par sa ruse	near the hermitage. The Duke
inventee,	of Étampes through the ruse he
Du mont Lehori prelat donra	invented will give an example
exemple.	to the priest of Montlhery.

The clue to this verse probably lies in the title in line 3. Three of the kings of France's greatest mistresses held the title, first Anne de Pisseleu, then Diane de Poitiers, and later Henri IV's Gabrielle d'Estrées. I cannot get any further with this.

[1] panse. should be *pause* to rhyme with line 4.
[2] *Touphon*—Doubtful. There is a place called Forfou but it has no forest. Possibly from the Gk., *tophion* = a plaster quarry, or French, *touffe* = a clump.

Calais, Arras secours à Theroanne,	Calais & Arras help to Théro-
Paix & semblant simulera les- *coutte,*[1]	uanne, the spy will simulate peace and semblance; the
Soulde[2] *d'Alabrox*[3] *descendre par* *Roane*	soldiers of Savoy go down by Roanne; those people who
Destornay peuple qui deffera le *routte.*[4]	would stop the rout turned away.

1557

This quatrain must be dated 1557 since Calais fell to the French in 1558. Both Arras and Théronanne belonged to Spain. When Calais fell, Philip II, husband of the English Queen, lost all rights to Calais. On 5th February 1556 the Treaty of Vaucelles was declared between France and Spain. Therefore this quatrain was probably written between the Truce and the Spanish attack of 1557. Savoy (Allobrox) was almost completely French occupied at this period, so it is possible that a garrison of soldiers was sent up after St. Quentin. The borders of Savoy were only thirty-five miles from Rouanne.

89

Sept ans sera Philip fortune pro- *spere,*	Fortune will favour Philip for seven years, he will cut down
Rabaissera des Arabes l'effaict,	again the exertions of the
Puis son midi[5] *perplex rebours* *affaire*	Arabs. Then, in the middle a perplexing, contrary affair,
Jeune ognion[6] *abismera son fort.*	young Ogmios will destroy his stronghold.

LOUIS PHILIPPE, 1830–48

The first seven years of Louis Philip's reign, 1830–8 were extremely fortunate. He managed to subdue the Arabs and consolidate the French occupation of Algeria. In the middle of his reign, 1838–40, he will be troubled by the Eastern question and the result will be shameful for him. Finally the French proclaiming the new republic, 24th February 1848, will dethrone him and keep him under guard.

[1] *l'escoute*—O.F. = a spy.
[2] *soulde*—O.F. = pay or mercenaries.
[3] *Allobrox* = classical inhabitants of Savoy.
[4] *routte*—Either O.F., *route* = rout; or route—road?
[5] *son midi*—Either in middle age, or to the South?
[6] *ogmios*—The Celtic Hercules.

Un capitaine de la grand Germanie	A captain of the greater Germany will come to deliver false help; king of kings; to support Hungary; His war will cause a great shedding of blood.
Se viendra rendre par simulé secours	
Un roi des rois aide de Pannonie,[1]	
Que sa revolte fera de sang grand cours.	

HITLER

The Greater Germany sounds uncannily like the Grossendeutschland of Hitler's Third Reich. The second line is brilliant. Hitler invaded Poland under the pretence of giving help, as Nostradamus says elsewhere. Hitler for a time was a king of kings, lord of all he surveyed. He also captured Hungary and the war he started killed about 14 million people among the soldiers of both sides, and according to some estimates as many again among the civilian population, and quite probably more.

L'horrible peste Perynte[2] *& Nicopolle,*[3]	The dreadful plague at Perinthus and Nicopolis will take the Peninsula and Macedonia; it will lay waste Thessaly and Amphipolis, an unknown evil, and refused by Anthony.
Le Chersonnez[4] *tiendra & Marceloyne,*[5]	
La Thessalie vastera l'Amphipolle,[6]	
Mal incogneu & le refus d'Anthoine.	

The Anthony here may be Anthony of Navarre, father of Henri IV, but the setting of the quatrain in Greece makes this unlikely.

[1] *Panonia*—Classical Hungary.
[2] *Perinthus*—Modern Eski Eregli
[3] *Nicopolis*—Modern Preveza.
[4] *Chersonnez*—Either the Gallipoli peninsular (Chersonese) or the Poloponnesus.
[5] *Marceloyne*—Probably error for Macedoine.
[6] *Amphipolis*—Near modern Salonika.

Le roi vouldra dans cité neuf entrer	The king will want to enter the
Par ennemis expugner[1] lon viendra	new city, they come to subdue
Captif libere faulx dire & per-	it through its enemies; a captive
petrer	falsely freed to speak and act;
Roi dehors estre, loin d'ennemis	the king to be outside, he will
tiendra.	stay far from the enemy.

NEW YORK?

This may refer to New York, as in I. 87, VI. 97 and X. 89, and
continue the three quatrains describing the city being attacked
during the next war. This is a logical possibility which must be
futuristic as it has not occurred to date. The king far from the
enemy is probably the President in some secret underground
shelter from which he will continue to direct the war.

Les ennemis du fort bien eslongnez,	The enemies are very far from
Par chariots conduict le bastion,	the strong man, the bastion is
Par sur les murs de Bourges	brought by wagons. Above the
esgrongnez,	crumbled walls of Bourges
Quand Hercules battra l'Haema-	when Hercules strikes the
thion.[2]	Macedonian.

LOUIS XIV

This quatrain tells that when Aemathion, who can here stand for
Louis XIV, has pushed back his enemies and consequently en-
larged the borders of France, bastions of earth were constructed
in the fortification system of Vauban. At this time Bourges falls
into decay when its Grosse Tour (great tower) fell into ruin during
Louis' reign. The final line refers to a labour of Hercules, which
was in this case the lengthy Languedoc canal. Started in 1666
and finished in 1681 at a cost of 34,000,000 francs it was the wonder
of the times. It also freed the French from dependency on the
Western area of the Mediterranean and became their equivalent
of the Pillars of Hercules, i.e. Gibraltar.

[1] *expugnare*—Latin = to subdue, capture, storm, violate etc.
[2] *Haemathion*—As Aemathion, Macedonian or from Thessaly.

Foibles galleres seront unies
ensemble,
Ennemis faux le plus fort en
rampart:
Faible assaillies Vratislaue tremble,
Lubecq & Mysne tiendront barbare
part.

Weak galleys will be joined
together, the false enemy is
strongest on the ramparts.
Bratislava trembles, the weak
attacked, Lubeck & Meissen
will take the Barbarian's side.

95

Le nouveau faict[1] conduira l'exercite,[2]
Proche apamé[3] jusques au pres de
rivage,
Tendant secour de Milannoile[4]
eslite,
Duc yeux privé à Milan fer de cage.

The new fact will lead the
army, almost cut off as far as
to the river bank, holding for
help from the Milanese élite;
the Duke loses his eyes in an
iron cage in Milan.

Milan belonged to the Habsburgs until 1859. A lot of commentators equate the last line with Mussolini but the quatrain is
really too general.

96

Dans cité entrer excercit[5] desniee,
Duc entrera par persuasion,
Aux foibles portes clam[6] armee
amenee,
Mettront feu, mort de sang
effusion.

The army denied entry to the
city, the Duke will enter
through persuasion; secretly
the army led to the weak gates,
they put it to fire, death and
flowing of blood.

97

De mer copies[7] en trois parts
divisees,
A la seconde les vivres failliront,
Desesperez cherchant champs Heli-
sees,
Premier en breche entrez victoire
auront.

The forces at sea divided into
three parts, the second one
will run out of supplies; in
despair looking for the Elysian
Fields, the first entering the
breach will have victory.

[1] Or the newly made one?
[2] exercitus—Latin = army.
[3] apamé—Greek, apamao = to cut off.
[4] Almost certainly means Milanese.
[5] exercite—Latin, exercitus = army.
[6] clam—Latin = secretly.
[7] copies—Latin, copia = troops, army.

Here are two battles; we start with a naval one and end up on land. Apart from the fact that the Elysian Fields were the Greek heaven, I cannot decipher this muddled quatrain.

98

Les affligez par faute d'un seul taint,	Those afflicted through the fault of a single infected one,
Contremenant[1] à partie opposite,	the transgressor will be in the opposite party. He will send
Au Lygonnois mandera que contraint	to the Lyonnais and compel
Seront de rendre le grand chef de Molite.[2]	that they should be given up to the great leader of Molite.

99

Vent Aquilon fera partir le siege,	The north wind will cause the
Par murs gerer cendres, chauls, & pousiere,	seige to be raised, to throw over the walls cinders, lime and
Par pluie apres qui leur fera bien piege,[3]	dust; afterwards through rain which does them much harm,
Dernier secours encontre leur frontiere.	the last help is met at their frontier.

RETREAT FROM MOSCOW?

If Aquilon is a synonym for North, most commentators take this as describing Napoleon's retreat from Moscow. He finds help only at the frontiers of his empire having lost so many men on the expedition (the rain and snow which does them such harm).

100

Navalle pugne[4] nuit sera superee,[5]	A naval battle will be overcome at night. Fire in the
Le feu naves[6] à l'Occident ruine:	ruined ships of the West, a new
Rubriche neufue la grand nef coloree	coding the great ship coloured
Ire à vaincu, & victoire en bruine.	anger to the vanquished and victory in a mist.

[1] *Contremenant*—Error for *contrevenant*.
[2] *Molite?*—either from Melita, Malta, or Greek, *molos* = war?
[3] *piege*—Provençal, *piegi* = worse, harmful.
[4] *pugne*—Latin, *pugna* = battle.
[5] *superee*—Latin, *superatus* = overcome.
[6] *naves*—Latin = ships.

PEARL HARBOUR, 1941

Pearl Harbour was attacked in the very early morning by the Japanese planes. The great tankers were set alight to the ruin of America, the West. I think 'the new coding' of line 3 is the formula for this new type of attack which finally brings anger to a defeated Japan and hazy glimpses of victory to a stunned America. The 'colour' of the ship probably refers to camouflage.

CENTURY X

1	France. Vichy Régime
2	
3	
4*	Battle of Worcester, 1651
5	
6*	9th September 1557
7	
8*	15th June 1856
9	
10*	Napoleon
11	
12*	1591 ?
13	
14	
15	
16*	Louis XVIII
17*	Madame Royale, 1787–99
18*	Henri of Navarre
19*	Elizabeth of England ?
20	Post-Fascist Italy ?
21	
22**	Abdication of Edward VIII, 1936
23	Louis XVIII
24*	The Hundred Days, 1815
25	
26**	Death of Robert Kennedy. Britain and Common Market
27	
28	
29	
30	
31	
32	

33
34** Napoleon and the King of Naples
35
36 British Isles?
37
38** Henri of Navarre
39*** Mary Queen of Scots and Francis II
40** Abdication of Edward VIII, 1936
41
42* Pax Britannica
43* Louis XVI
44* Henri III
45* Henri of Navarre
46
47
48* Spanish Civil War followed by World War II
49***F? New York's water supply poisoned?
50
51* France and Germany, 1871
52
53
54
55** Francis II and Mary Queen of Scots
56
57
58* Louis XIV
59* 1560
60
61
62
63
64* Italy 19th Century
65
66** Polaris in Scotland from U.S.A.
67
68
69
70
71*? The U.S.A.?
72*F? The Third Antichrist and War
73
74** War in 20th Century, probably at end of 1970s
75** *continued*

76
77*   Italy and Russia, 1945
78
79
80
81 ?   Spanish wealth, or American Wealth?
82
83
84*   Elizabeth I
85*   France, 1940–3
86*   Allied Forces, 1815
87
88
89*   Louis XIV
90   Napoleon on St. Helena
91 ?
92
93   Pius VI, 1799
94
95*   Philip II of Spain
96 ?
97 ?
98*   French Third Republic
99
100**   Great Britain

KEY: * Of interest. F? Possibly referring to the future.

A l'ennemy l'ennemy foi promise *Ne se tiendre les captifs retenus:* *Prins preme[1] mort & le rest en chemise,* *Damné le reste pour estre soustenus.*	To the enemy, the enemy faith promised will not be kept, the captives retained; one is taken near to death and the rest in their shirts, the rest damned for being supporters.

FRANCE—VICHY RÉGIME

This is usually read as a general quatrain about the Vichy régime, when the Germans failed to make collaboration a two-way proposition to the French people.

2

Voille gallere voil de nef cachera, *La grande classe[2] viendra sortir la moindre.* *Dix naves[3] proches le tourneront poulser,* *Grande vaincue unis à foi joindre.*	The ships sail will hide the sailing galley, the great fleet will cause the lesser one to go out. Nearby ten ships will turn to drive it back, the great one conquered united to join in faith.

There seems possibly to be a connection between this quatrain and IX. 100. It describes a naval battle with ships either camouflaged or hidden by a smoke screen. The great one who is conquered may then refer to the U.S.A. who joins the Allies after Pearl Harbour. Alternatively it may apply to one of the many actions in the Mediterranean 1940–1943.

3

En apres cinq troupeau ne mettra hors un *Fuytif pour Penelon[4] l'aschera,* *Faulx murmurer secours venir par lors,* *Le chief le siege lois habandonnera.*	After the fifth will not put out a flock, a fugitive will be turned loose for Penelon. Falsely to murmur, then to come in aid, then the chief will abandon the siege.

The key word in this quatrain is Penelon which is not definitely deciphered, see below.

[1] *preme*—O.F. = next, close, near.
[2] *classe*—Latin, *classis* = fleet.
[3] *naves*—Latin, *navis* = ship.
[4] *Penelon?*—Possibly an anagram for Polone, Poland?

Sus la minuict conducteur de l'armee	At midnight the leader of the army will run away, suddenly
Se saulvera, subit evanoui,	disappeared. Seven years later,
Sept ans apres la fame non blasmee	his reputation unblemished, to
A son retour ne dira oncq oui.	his return 'yes' will not once be said (i.e. many times).

BATTLE OF WORCESTER, 1651

After his defeat at the Battle of Worcester, Charles II fled to France via Scotland, in disguise. His usurper Cromwell actually reigned for seven years, and Charles was restored in 1560. It is a general quatrain but can be applied to these events quite accurately.

Albi & Castres feront nouvelle lique,	Albi & Castres will make a new alliance, nine Arians Lisbon
Neuf Arriens[1] Lisbons & Portugues,	and the Portuguese; Carcassonne, Toulouse will join their
Carcas, Tholosse consumeront leur brigue	intrigue when a new chief is the monster from the Lauragues.
Quand chef neuf monstre de Lauragues.	

The new Arians are the interesting subject here. Unfortunately it is most likely that Nostradamus was reverting to the Crusade (1208–13) of the Albigensians.

Sardou[2] Nemans si hault desborderont,	The Gardon will flood Nîmes so high that they will think
Qu'on cuidera[3] Ducalion renaistre,	Ducalion has been reborn.
Dans le collosse la plus part fuiront,	In the colossus the greater part will flee, Vesta's fire appears
Vesta sepulchre feu estaint apparoistre.	extinguished in the tomb.

[1] *Arriens* = (a) The 13th Century heretics. (b) People now dwelling in Afghanistan.
[2] *Sardon*—Error for Gardon.
[3] *cuider*—O.F. = To think, believe.

According to Jaubert a storm broke out at Nîmes in 1557 which lasted from 5 a.m. to 9 p.m., and this combined with a flood from the Gardon. Apparently many antiquities were revealed when the flood waters withdrew. Menard's History of Lyons confirms the flood as 1 p.m. to 9 p.m. but does not mention the Gardon.

7

Le grand combat qu'on appreste à Nancy,	The great fight that they prepare at Nancy, Aemathien will
L'aemathieu dira tout je soubmetz,	say I subjugate all; the British
L'isle Britanne par vin, sel, en solci,	Isles through wine and salt are in trouble, Hem. mi Philip
Hem. mi deux Phi. long temps ne tiendra Metz.	two, Metz will not hold for long.

The reference to wine and salt connect this quatrain in some manner to England, see IX. 49. But I am not happy with any of the ingenious comments to date. It seems more probable that '*deux Phi.*' refers to Philip II attacking French-occupied Lorraine. Metz was finally ceded in 1648 but was in French control from 1552, in which case Nostradamus is only stating a known fact. Nancy was handed back to its Duke in 1661 having been occupied for twenty-seven years.

8

Index & poulse parfondra[1] le front	With index finger and thumb
De Senegalia le Conte à son filz propre	he will wet the forehead, the Count of Seneglia to his own
Les Myrnarmee[2] par plusieurs de prin front	son, through several, Venus in short order, three are wounded
Trois dans sept jours blesses mors.	to death in seven days.

15th JUNE 1856

On this date the Prince Imperial, son of Napoleon III, was baptized. His godfather was Pope Pius IX who was the son of Count Mastoi Ferretti of Senigallia. Venus is interpreted as the Empress Eugenie but line 4 is still unexplained.

[1] *perfundere*—Latin = to sprinkle, moisten.
[2] *Mimnermia*—A surname of Venus.

De Castillion figuires jour de brune,	In the Castle of Figueras on a
De fame infame naistra souverain prince.	misty day a sovereign prince will be born of an unworthy
Surnon de chausses perhume lui posthume,	woman. The surname of Chausses on the ground will
Onc Roi ne faut si pire en sa province.	make him posthumous, never was a king so bad in his province.

See X. 11 also for this verse. Loomis suggests this verse describes one of Nostradamus' Antichrists.

10

Tasche de murdre enormes adulteres,	Stained with murder and enormous adulteries, great enemy
Grand ennemi de tout le genre humain	of all mankind, he will be worse
Que sera pire qu'ayeulx, oncles ne peres	than his ancestors, uncles and fathers, in steel, fire and water,
En fer, feu, eau, sanguin & inhumain.	bloody and inhuman.

NAPOLEON

The epithet of line 2 was applied to Napoleon Bonaparte by the Venetian ambassador, Morenigo.

11

Debbouz louchere du dangereux passage	In the dangerous passage underneath Junquera, the post-
Fera passer le posthume sa bande,	humous one will cross his men.
Les monts Pyrens passer hors son bagaige	To cross the Pyrenean mountains without his baggage the
De Perpignam courira duc à tende.	duke will hasten to Perpignan from Tende.

This obscure verse seems to be related to X. 9, particularly the reference to the posthumous child.

Esleu en Pape, d'esleu sera mocqué,	Elected as Pope, he will be
Subit soudain esmeu prompt &	mocked when elected, suddenly
timide,	and unexpectedly moved,
Par trop bon doulz à mourir pro-	prompt and timid: Caused to
vocqué,	die through too much goodness
Crainte estainte la nuit de sa mort	and kindness he will fear for the
guide.	guide killed on the night of his
	death.

1591?

This is normally applied to the Cardinal Santa Severina who was elected Pope Gregory XIV, but died two months later in 1591, the election being declared illegal. However his successor Innocent IX also died in under two months.

13

Soulz la pasture d'animaux rumi-[1]	Beneath the food of ruminating
nant[1]	animals, led by them into the
Par eux conduicts au ventre herbi-	centre of the food place;
polique[2]	soldiers hidden, their weapons
Soldatz caichez les armes bruit	being noise, tried not far from
menant,	the city of Antibes.
Non loing temptez de cité Anti-	
polique.	

14

Urnel Vaucile[3] *sans conseil de soi*	'Urnel Vaucile' without a plan
mesmes.	of his own, bold, timid for fear
Hardit timide par crainte prins	of being taken and captured;
vaincu,	accompanied by several pale
Accompaigné de plusieurs putains	whores converted in the Car-
blesmes	thusian convent at Barcelona.
A Barcellonne aux chartreux con-	
vaincu.	

The interpretation here depends on the *Urnel Vaucile* line, which has no connections to date with the monastery at de Urgel, near Llanos to the town of the same name. The Carthusian monastery mentioned is that of Mont Allegro.

[1] i.e. under a load of hay.
[2] Into the market place?
[3] *Urnel Vaucile?*—Llanos de Urgel? Plain of Urgel?

Pere duc vieux d'ans & de soif chargé,	The father duke old in years and troubled with thirst, on
Au jour extreme filz desniant les guiere[1]	the last day his son denying him the jug: into the well
Dedans le puis vif mort viendra plongé,	plunged alive he will become dead: the Senate to the son a
Senat au fil[2] *la mort longue & legiere.*	death long and light.

A son is hanged for giving his thirsty father an excess of water, by putting him down the well! Impossible to place this quatrain.

Heureux au regne de France, heureux de vie	Happy in the kingdom of France, happy in life, ignorant
Ignorant sang mort fureur & rapine,	of blood, death, anger and rage. By a flattering name he will
Par nom flateurs seras mis en envie,	be envied, a king robbed, too
Roi desrobé trop de foi en cuisine.[3]	much faith in the kitchen.

LOUIS XVIII

When he is happily re-established on the French throne, Louis XVIII will not die a violent death but lives happily. He was given the name of Louis le Desiré (line 3). His guilt will lie in the fact that he does not sufficiently occupy himself with the public good, and that he is a renowned glutton.

La roine Ergaste[4] *voiant sa fille blesme,*	The barren queen, seeing her pale daughter because of un-
Par un regret dans l'estomac encloz,	happiness locked up in her stomach. Lamentable cries will
Cris lamentables seront lors d'Angoulesme,	then come from Angoulême and the marriage to the cousin
Et au gemain mariage fort clos.	greatly impeded.

MADAME ROYALE, 1787–99

The *Roine Ergaste* is a queen confined to the manual labour found in any penitentiary. When imprisoned in the Temple Marie

[1] *l'aiguiere*—Mod. French = jug.
[2] *fil*—Probably should read *filz* = son.
[3] i.e. in his servants.
[4] *Ergaste*—Ergastulus = penitentiary?

Antoinette was compelled to sew her own clothes. The adjective can also mean captive, which indeed the Queen was. She sees her daughter, Madame Royale, pale with the family misfortunes. Madame Royale was betrothed to the Duke of Angoulême in 1787, and married him in 1799. It is suggested that her childless marriage '*l'estomac enclos*' was due to her sufferings with her family in the Temple.

18

Le ranc Lorrain fera place à Vendosme,	The house of Lorraine will make way for Vendôme, the high put low and the low exalted. The son of Hamon will be elected in Rome, and the two great ones will be put at a loss.
Le hault mis bas & le bas mis en hault,	
Le filz d'Hamon[1] sera esleu dans Rome,	
Et les deux grands seront mis en deffault.	

HENRI DE NAVARRE

This is a very successful prophecy for Nostradamus. Henri IV, Duke of Vendôme will eclipse the house of Lorraine, and Henri IV, earlier known as '*le petit Béarnais*' will be elevated to the high rank of king of France. This son of Hamon, i.e. heretic, will be accepted as King in Rome. The two great ones who lose out on this are the two Pretenders, the Duke de Guise and the Duke de Mayenne.

19

Jour que sera par roine saluee Le jour apres le salut, la priere, Le compte fait raison & valbuee,[2] Par avant humbles oncques ne feut si fiere.	The day she will be saluted as queen, the prayer the day after the blessing. The account is right and valid, once humble, there was never a woman so proud.

Suggested as applying to Elizabeth I of England when she succeeded to her sister, the childless Mary Tudor.

[1] *Hamon*—Mamon in some editions.
[2] *valbuee*—Unsolved word. *Valable* is suggested as an alternative?

Tous les amis qu'auront tenu parti,	All of the friends who have belonged to the party, put to
Pour rude en lettres mis mort & saccagé,	death and looked for the uncouth letters. The public possessions, the great one anni-
Biens publiez pat sixe grand neanti,[1]	hilated by six, never were the
Onc Romain peuple ne feut tant outragé.	Roman people so wronged.

POST-FASCIST ITALY

This quatrain applies accurately to post-Fascist Italy, and in Nostradamus' day it made little sense. The drastic remedy makes it appear more modern.

21

Par le despit du Roi soustenant moindre,	Through the king's spite in supporting the lesser one, he
Sera meurdri lui presentant les bagues,	will be murdered presenting the jewels to him. The father
Le pere au filz voulant noblesse poindre	wishing to impress his son with nobility did what the Magi
Fait comme à Perse jadis feirent les Mague:	once used to do in Persia.

22

Pour ne vouloir consentir à divorce,	For not wanting to consent to
Qui puis apres sera cogneu indigne,	the divorce, which then afterwards will be recognized as
Le Roi des Isles sera chassé par force	unworthy, the King of the islands will be forced to flee,
Mis à son lieu que de roi n'aura signe.	and one put in his place who has no sign of kingship.

ABDICATION OF EDWARD VIII, 1936.
10th DECEMBER

Edward VIII's abdication was not popular among the British people, who had little love for Mrs. Simpson. Edward was therefore forced to leave Britain because of her social standing, '*cogneu indigne*'. Finally George VI, who was not in line for the kingship is forced to accede to the throne. See also X. 40.

---

[1] *neantir*—to annihilate.

Au peuple ingrat faictes les remon- strances, *Par lors l'armee se saisira d'Antibe,* *Dans l'arc Monech feront les* *doleances* *Et à Frejus l'un l'autre prendra* *ribe.*[1]	Remonstrances are made to the ungrateful people, then the army will seize Antibes. In the arch of Monaco the complaints will occur, and at Fréjus the shore will be taken by one from the other.

LOUIS XVIII

When Louis XVIII issued a proclamation urging fidelity to the
new régime the only place that remained loyal to Napoleon was
Antibes. Both Louis and Napoleon used Fréjus; the former to
embark for England, the latter when embarking for Elba.

Le captif prince aux Italles vaincu *Passera Gennes par mer jusqu'à* *Marseille,* *Par grand effort des forens[2] sur-* *vaincu* *Sauf coup de feu barril liqueur* *d'abeille.*	The captive prince conquered in Italy will cross from Genoa to Marseilles by sea; by a great effort the foreigners will be overcome except for a gun shot, a barrel of bees' honey.

THE HUNDRED DAYS, 1815

This quatrain must be linked with IV. 26 in which Napoleon's
emblem of bees also appears. Napoleon, a closely guarded prisoner
on Elba, escapes by sea in March and lands at Cannes, near
Marseilles. He is overcome again at Waterloo, where he seeks
death in vain, and the bees of his emblem spill all their sweetness.

Par Nebro ouvrir de Brisanne[3] *passage,* *Bien eslongez el tago fara muestra,* *Dans Pelligauxe[4] sera commis* *l'outrage* *De la grand dame assise sur* *l'orchestra.*	Through the Ebro will be opened a passage to Brissane far away the Tago will make a demonstration. The outrage will be committed in Pelligoux, of the great lady sitting in the orchestra.

[1] *ribe*—Provençal, *riba* = bank, shore.
[2] *forens*—O.F. = foreigner, stranger.
[3] *Brisanne*—Unsolved place name.
[4] *Pelligaux*—Unsolved place name.

Le successeur vengera son beau frere,	The successor will avenge his handsome brother and occupy
Occupera regne souz umbre de vengeance,	the realm under the shadow of vengeance, he, killed, the
Occis ostacle son sang mort vitupere,	obstacle of the blameworthy dead, his blood; for a long time
Long temps Bretaigne tiendra avec la France.	Britain will hold with France.

DEATH OF SECOND KENNEDY BROTHER.
BRITAIN AND COMMON MARKET

The quatrain seems to indicate that Robert Kennedy will die following the death of his handsome brother, J. F. Kennedy. It is interesting to note that Nostradamus foresees two brothers killed within a short period of time. Robert Kennedy's stand in the name of his dead brother does him no good. One wonders what it will bring to Edward Kennedy. The last line seems to imply that once de Gaulle is dead, Britain's relationship with the Common Market is a particularly successful one. See I 26, VIII. 46, 77.

Par le cinquieme & un grand Hercules	Through the fifth and a great Hercules they will come to
Viendront le temple ouvrir de main bellique,	open the temple with the hand of war; one Clement, Julius
Un Clement, Iule & Ascans recules,	and Ascans put back, the sword, the key, the eagle never
Lespe, clef, aigle n'eurent onc si grand picque.	once felt so great a dislike.

Second & tiers qui font prime musicque	Second and third make first class music they will be sub-
Sera par Roi en honneur sublimee,	limely honoured by the king:
Par grasse & maigre presque demi eticque	Through fat and thin, even half emaciated, to be made
Rapport de Venus faulx rendra deprimee.	debased by the false report of Venus.

De Pol MANSOL dans caverne caprine[1] *Caché & prins extrait hors par la barbe,* *Captif mené comme beste mastine* *Par Begourdans amenee pres de Tarbe.*	In the great cave of Saint Paul de Mausole, hidden and seized, pulled out by the beard, the captive led like a mastiff animal, by the people of Bigorre brought near to Tarbes.

St. Paul de Mausole is just outside Nostradamus' birthplace of St. Rémy. The quatrain seems to describe the capture of a goat, or goatboy, who is taken to Bigorre in Navarre.

30

Nepueu & sang du sainct nouveau venu, *Par le surnom soustient arcs & couvert* *Seront chassez mis à mort chassez nu,* *En rouge & noir convertiront leur vert.*	Nephew and of the blood of the newly created saint, through his surname he will sustain the arches and the roof. They will be driven out naked and chased to their deaths, their green will be converted to red and black.

31

Le saint Empire viendra en Germanie *Ismaelites*[2] *trouveront lieux ouverts.* *Anes vouldront aussi la Carmanie,*[3] *Les soustenens de terre tous converts.*	The Holy Empire will come to Germany, the Arabs will find open places; the asses will also want Carmania, the supporters completely covered with earth.

32

Le grand empire chacun an devoir estre *Un sur les autres le viendra obtenir,* *Mais peu de temps sera son regne & estre,* *Deux ans aux naves se pourra soustenir.*	The empire each year should become great. One will come to hold (power) over all the others. But his kingdom and life will last a short time. In two years he will be able to maintain himself in his ships.

[1] *caprinus*—Latin adjective = pertaining to goats.
[2] *Ismaelites*—Not Jews but Arabs, who claim descent from Ishmaël, son of Abraham.
[3] *Carmanie*—Either the Persian province at the entrance to the Persian Gulf, or an unsolved anagram.

La faction cruelle à robbe longue,	The cruel party with long robes
Viendra cacher souz les pointus poignars	will hide sharp daggers under- neath. The Duke to seize
Saisir Florence le duc & lieu diphlongue[1]	Florence and the place of two words. Its discovery through
Sa descouverte par immeurs & flaugnards.[2]	young ones and flatterers.

Gaulois qu'empire par guerre occu- pera	The Gaul who gains his empire through war will be betrayed
Par son beau frere mineur sera trahi,	by his younger brother-in-law. He will be dragged by an
Par cheval rude voltigiant trainera,	untrained nervous horse, for the act the brother will be
Du fait le frere long temps sera haï.	hated for a long time.

NAPOLEON AND THE KING OF NAPLES

The King of Naples, Joachim Murat, married Napoleon's younger sister Caroline. He first betrayed Napoleon in 1814, but sided with him in 1815. He was also a renowned cavalry leader. Apparently, according to Robb (1942) this quatrain converted the eminent Professor Jacques Barzun of Colombia University, and Professor Siceloff, who stated that the chances of this quatrain being fulfilled were 'about zero'.

Puisnay royal flagrand d'ardent libide,	The younger son of a king flagrant with burning lust to
Pour se jouir de cousine germaine,	enjoy his first cousin. Women's
Habit de femme au temple d'Arthemide:	attire in the temple of Diana going to be murdered by the
Allant murdri par incognu du Marne.	unknown man from Marne.

The last line suggests that a Duke of Mayenne or Maine will be involved in a royal scandal, but unfortunately though a probable situation, it does not seem to tie in with anything specific.

[1] *diphlongue*—Erratum for *diphtongue* = double word.
[2] *flaugnards*—Provençal = flatterer or wheedler.

Apres le Roi du saucq guerres parlant,	After the king (of the stump?) speaks of wars, the United
L'isle Harmotique[1] le tiendra à mespris,	Island will despise him. For several years the good one
Quelques ans bous rongeant un & pillant	gnaws and pillages, through tyranny on the island its values
Par tyrranie à l'isle changeant pris.[2]	change.

The United Islands may well be the British Isles, bringing the date to after 1603. Line 3 probably describes the privateers of the late 16th Century and early 17th Century, such as Drake, Hawkins and Raleigh. But it is difficult to interpret the adjective '*de soucq*' as applying to James I.

L'assemblee grande pres du lac de Borget,	The great crowd near to the lake of Le Bourget, they will
Se ralieront pres de Montmelian,	rally near to Montmelian,
Marchans plus oultre pensifz feront proget	going further ahead the thoughtful ones draw up a plan,
Chambry, Moraine combat sainct Julian.	Chambery, St. Julian de Maurienne, fight.

Amour alegre non loing pose le siege,	'Light of love' will not hold the
Au sainct barbar seront les garnisons,	siege for long, for the converted barbarian will be all the
Ursins[1] Hadrie pour Galois feront plaige,	garrisons; the Ursins and Adria give security for the French, for
Pour peur rendus de l'armee du Grisons.[3]	fear of the army being handed over to the Grisons.

HENRI OF NAVARRE

Henri's usual nickname among his contemporaries was 'Vert Galant', which is very close to Nostradamus' '*armour allegre*'. During the Siege of Paris, 1590, Henri could not hold the siege for longer than four complete months, because of the advance of the Duke of Parma from Flanders. Nostradamus describes the city garrison as devoted to things converted and barbarous, by

[1] *Harmotique*—Dubious probably from Greek, *armoskitos* = joined together, fitting together?

[2] *pris*—Mod. French, *prix*.

[3] *Grisons* = The people of South-east Switzerland.

which he means that they were the clerical revolutionaries. Henri also changed his religion to get the French throne. The last two lines are unclear.

39

Premier fils veufve malheureux marriage,	The first son, a widow, an unfortunate marriage without
Sans nuls enfans deux isles en discorde,	any children: two islands thrown into discord. Before
Avant dixhuict incompetant eage,	eighteen years of age, a minor:
De l'autre pres plus bas sera l'accord.	of the other even lower will be the betrothal.

MARY QUEEN OF SCOTS AND FRANCIS II

This is one of Nostradamus' notoriously successful quatrains, and appears to have been understood by the French Court of the time. Francis II, the eldest son of the widowed Catherine de' Medici, marries Mary Stuart, an unfortunate marriage which was childless. Because of Mary's return to Scotland she caused discord between England and her own country. Francis was still not quite eighteen years old when he died (seventeen years, ten months, fifteen days). His younger brother Charles IX was betrothed to Elizabeth of Austria when only eleven years old. This quatrain is quite astonishingly accurate.

40

Le jeune nay au regne Britannique,	The young born to the realm of Britain, which his dying father
Qu'aura le pere mourant recommandé,	had commended to him. Once
Icelui mort LONOLE[1] donra topique,	he is dead, London will dispute with him, and the kingdom
Et à son fils le regne demandé.	will be demanded back from the son.

ABDICATION OF EDWARD VIII, 1936

This refers back to X. 22. Edward VIII is the true heir to the British throne which was left to him by his dying father. But he will cause scandal (*topique*) in London by his behaviour with Mrs. Simpson, and public hostility towards her earlier divorce caused the King to abdicate, the kingdom taken back from him by the people and given to his brother.

[1] *Lonole*—Probably erratum for *Londres* = London.

En la frontiere de Caussade &
Charlus,
Non guieres loing du fonds de la
vallee,
De ville franche musicque à son de
luths,
Environnez combouls[1] & grand
mytee.[2]

On the boundary of Caussade
and Caylus, not very far from
the depths of the valley, music
from Villefranche to the sound
of lutes, surrounded by cymbals
and a great (deal) of stringed
(instruments).

All the places mentioned are small villages within fifty miles of
Agen where Nostradamus once lived. Perhaps here he is just
describing a festival he witnessed?

Le regne humain d'Anglique geni-
ture,
Fera son regne paix union tenir,
Captive guerre demi de sa closture,
Long temps la paix leur fera
maintenir.

The human reign of English
offspring will cause the kingdom to remain united in peace.
Half captured in his enclosure
in the war, for a long time peace
will be maintained by them.

PAX BRITANNICA

This is a general but very apt quatrain, which describes Britain
and the Pax Britannica of the 19th Century, or possibly the long
peace England enjoyed under Walpole and the early Georges.
The first is more acceptable because of England's vast influence in
the 19th Century.

Le trop bon temps trop de bonté
royalle:
Fais & deffois prompt subit
negligence,
Legier croira faux despouse loyalle,
Lui mis à mort par sa benevolence.

Too much of good times and
too much royal bounty, made
and quickly undone by sudden
negligence. He will lightly
believe false his loyal wife
whom in his benevolence he
puts to death.

LOUIS XVI

Louis XVI was put to death because he did not bother to apply
himself properly to affairs of state. The weakness and irresolution
of character that he displayed, and the great ease with which he

[1] *combouls*—Greek, *kumbalon* = cymbal.
[2] *mytee*—Dubious, possibly from *mitos* = a stringed instrument?

believed reports that his wife, Marie Antoinette was involved, other than as a dupe, in the affair of the Diamond Necklace; all these, plus his kindness, left him defenceless before the Revolutionaries.

44

Par lors qu'un Roi sera contre les siens,	Where a king is (chosen) against his people a native of
Natif de Blois subjugera Ligures.	Blois will subdue the League.
Mammel,[1] *Cordube & les Dalmatiens,*	Mammel, Cordoba and the Dalmatians; of the seven then
Des sept puis l'ombre à Roi estrennes[2] *& lemurs.*[3]	a shadow to the King, new money and dead ghosts.

HENRI III
See VIII. 38 and 52 which also discuss a king from Blois. It probably refers to Henri III of France who will subjugate the League (line 2). He was descended from the Court of Blois and Nostradamus elsewhere calls him *'le grand du Blois'*. The seven in the final line is yet another reference to the seven children of Catherine de' Medici.

45

L'ombre du Regne de Navarre non vrai,	The shadow of the kingdom of Navarre is not true, it will make
Fera la vie de fort illegitime:	the life of a strong man illegal.
La veu promis incertain de Cambrai	The uncertain vow promised at Cambrai,[4] the king at Orléans
Roi Orleans donra mur legitime.	will give a lawful boundary (wall).

HENRI IV OF NAVARRE
Henri of Navarre has still only a shadow of a kingdom since he has not yet gained true possession of France. He did lead an irregular life with many mistresses, including the wife of Balagny, the governor of Cambrai, to whom Henri gave in return the hereditary possession of the town (line 3). Orléans may represent here either the family or the town.

[1] *Mammel*—Unsolved place name; perhaps Mamel, in the Baltic?
[2] *estrennes* = Handsel, earnest money, or New Year money.
[3] *lemur*—Latin, *lemures* = spirits of the dead.
[4] Cambrai—A reference to the Peace of Cambrai 1529 when the French gave up their claims to Flanders.

Vie sort mort de L'OR vilaine indigne, *Sera de Saxe non nouveau electeur:* *De Brunsuic mandra d'amour signe,* *Faux le rendant aux peuple seducteur.*	Because of the gold, the life, fate and death of an unworthy, sordid man: he will not be the new Elector of Saxony. From Brunswick he will send for a sign of love, the false seducer giving it to the people.

This quatrain appears to be set in Germany, and to state that Saxony will not have a new Elector. Maurice did not enter the fight against Charles V until 1552 while the Duchy of Brunswick played no significant role in the 16th Century, so maybe this quatrain is reasonably accurate.

De Bourze ville à la dame Guirlande, *L'on mettra*[1] *sus par la trahison faicte,* *Le grand prelat de leon par Formande,*[2] *Faux pellerins & ravisseurs defaicte.*	In the town of Burgos, at the Garland lady they will give the verdict on the treason committed; the great prelate of Leon through Formande, undone by false pilgrims and thieves.

Du plus profond de l'Espaigne enseigne, *Sortant du bout & des fins de l'Europe,* *Troubles passant aupres du pont de Laigne,* *Sera deffaicte par bands sa grand troppe.*	Banners from the furthest corners of Spain, coming out from the ends and borders of Europe. Trouble passing near the bridge of Laigne, its great army will be routed by bands (of men).

SPANISH CIVIL WAR FOLLOWED BY WORLD WAR II

The first lines describe well enough the Spanish Civil War and the involvement of the Germans and Italians. Nostradamus sees this trouble growing, i.e. the Second World War, until it is stretched all over Europe. Laingnes a town forty odd miles north-west of Dijon was occupied by the Germans. It is interesting to note that

[1] *mettra*—Literally, impose a verdict.
[2] *Formand?*—Formentera, the Balearic island?

Nostradamus sees the occupying army as being routed by its enemies the Allied Forces, as it was in 1944 and 1945.

49

Jardin du monde au pres du cité neufve,	Garden of the world near the New City, in the road of the hollow mountains. It will be seized and plunged in the tank, forced to drink water poisoned with sulphur.
Dans le chemin des montaignes cavees,	
Sera saisi & plongé dans la Cuve,	
Beuvant par force eaux soulfre envenimees.	

NEW YORK POISONED THROUGH ITS WATER SUPPLY?

This is a fascinating quatrain with the idea of a water supply of a whole city being poisoned, more suited to James Bond than Nostradamus. The *cité neuf* is New York. The *jardin du Monde* is probably a way of describing it as a world centre. The next line is interesting. Could a road of hollow mountains be the nearest Nostradamus could get towards describing a skyscraper? I am not quite sure what the tank is, perhaps Nostradamus is trying to indicate the controls or reservoir of the water supply poisoned with sulphuric acid? See IV. 97, IX. 92.

50

La Meuse au jour terre de Luxembourg.	By day, the Meuse in the land of Luxembourg, will find Saturn and three in Aquarius; mountain and plain, town, city and borough; flood in Lorraine betrayed by the great urn.
Descouvrira Saturn & trois en lurne,	
Montaigne & plein, ville, cité & Bourg,	
Lorrain deluge trahison par grand hurne.	

51

Des lieux plus bas du pays de Lorraine,	Some of the lowest places in the county of Lorraine will be united with the lower Germanies. Through the people of the seats of Picardy, Normandy and Maine, they will be reunited to the cantons.
Seront des basses Allemaignes unis,	
Par ceux du siege Picards, Normans, du Maisne,	
Et aux cantons ce seront reunis.	

FRANCE AND GERMANY, 1871

Lorraine and the regions to the South (*plus bas*) such as Alsace, were united to Lower Germany with the consent of those defeated in the Siege of Paris in 1871, the people of France, Picards, Normans and from Maine. All those areas suffered German occupation. Lorraine did not return to France until 1919.

52

Au lieu[1] où LAYE & Scelde se marient,
Seront les nopces de longtemps maniees,
Au lieu d'Anvers où la crappe[2] charient[3]
Jeune vieillesse consorte intaminee.

At the place where the Laye and the Scheldt join the marriage will be arranged a long time ago. At the place in Antwerp where the chaff is carried a young undefiled wife, and old age.

An obscure marriage between a very young girl and an old suitor which takes place at Ghent.

53

Les trois pellices de loing s'entre-batron,
La plus grand moindre demeurera à l'escoute:
Le grand Selin n'en fera plus patron,
Le nommera feu pelte blanche routte.

Three prostitutes will quarrel for a long time; the greatest will remain to hear the least. The great Selin will no longer be her patron, she will call him fire, shield, a white rout.

If Selim does refer to Henri II here this would describe his many royal mistresses, presumably rivals to Diane de Poitiers, such as Gabrielle d'Estrées. I imagine 'white rout' is intended to mean a lily-livered coward!

54

Nee en ce monde par concubine fertive,
A deux hault mise par les tristes nouvelles,
Entre ennemis sera prinse captive,
Et amené à Malings & Bruxelles.

Born into this world of a furtive concubine, at two raised high by the bad news. She will be taken captive among enemies and brought to Malines and Brussels.

[1] *lieu*—Ghent.
[2] *crappe*—O.F. = chaff.
[3] *charier*—O.F. = to carry, to cast about.

Les malheureuses nopces celebreront,	The unfortunate marriage will
En grand joye mais la fin mal-	be celebrated with great joy,
heureuse:	but the end is unhappy. The
Mary & mere nore desdaigneront.	mother will despise the
Le Phybe mort & nore plus	daughter-in-law Mary, the
piteuse.	Apollo dead and the daughter-
	in-law more pitiful.

FRANCIS II AND MARY QUEEN OF SCOTS, 1558–60

The word Mary is spelt with a *y* in the original, and this makes it
quite likely to refer to Mary Queen of Scots and her unhappy
wedding, see X. 39. Catherine de' Medici disliked Mary intensely
and the latter called the Queen Mother 'a merchant's daughter'.
The strange word Phybe may well mean Francis II, Mary's
husband, if one takes the first syllable (*Phy*) (*phi*) for F. and the *be*
for beta, second letter of the alphabet, thus F II, Francis II. They
married in 1558 and Francis died in 1560.

Prelat royal son baissant trop tiré,	The royal priest bowing too
Grand fleux de sang sortira de sa	low, a great flow of blood will
bouche,	come out of his mouth. The
Le reign Anglique par regne	Anglican reign, a realm breath-
respiré,	ing, for a long time dead as a
Long temps mort vif en Tunis	stump, living in Tunis.
comme souche.	

Le soublevé ne cognoistra son	The uplifted one will not know
sceptre,	his sceptre, he will disgrace
Les enfants jeunes des plus grands	the young children of the
honnira:	greatest ones. There was never
Oncques ne fut un plus ord[1] cruel	so filthy and cruel a being, for
estre,	their wives, the king will banish
Pour leurs espouses à mort noir[2]	them to death.
bannira.	

[1] *ord*—O.F. = filth.
[2] *noir*—Usual Nostradamus anagram for king.

Au temps du dueil que le felin monarque,	At a time of mourning the feline monarch will make war
Guerroiera le jeune Aemathien:	with the young Aemathien.
Gaule bansler perecliter la barque[1]	France to shake, the bark will
Tenter Phossens[2] *au Ponant entretien.*	be in danger, Marseilles to be tried, a talk in the West.

LOUIS XIV

Aemathien, the child of the dawn, that is the sun, must refer here to Louis XIV who adopted the sun as his device and was also called the Sun King. When there is a time of mourning for Louis XIII, the wily monarch, Philip IV of Spain, will go to war against Aemathien. France is shaken by the civil war of the Fronde, and the bark of the Papacy is threatened by the development of Jansenism. Phossen is Marseilles, which Louis XIV entered by breaching the walls in 1660. A year earlier he went to the West of France (Ponant means Occident) and on the island of Bidussoa concluded the peace of the Pyrenees and his marriage with the Infanta Maria Theresa. The island is still called l'Isle de la Conférence.

Dedans Lyons vingt cinq d'une alaine,	In Lyons, twenty-five of the same breath, five citizens, Germans, Bressans, Latins, under a noble they will lead a long train and are discovered by the barking of the mastiffs.
Cinq citoyens Germains, Bressane, Latins,	
Par dessous noble conduiront longue traine,	
Et descouverts par abbois les matins.	

1560

In September 1560 five citizens from Lyons and twenty others, including some German Protestants, entered into a conspiracy to hand over the city to the Huguenots. It was suspected at the time that the main people behind the plot were the Prince de Condé and the Vidame de Chartres. It was discovered in time by the guards.

[1] *la barque* — the Papacy, bark of St. Peter.
[2] *Phossens* = Phoceans, founders of Marseilles.

Je pleure Nisse, Mannego, Pize,
Gennes,
Savone, Sienne, Capue, Modene,
Malte:
Le dessus sang & glaive par
estrennes,
Feu, tremblera terre, eau, mal-
heureuse nolte.[1]

I weep for Nice, Monaco, Pisa,
Genoa, Savona, Siena, Capua,
Modena and Malta. The blood
and sword above for a gift, fire,
the earth will tremble, water,
an unhappy reluctance.

Betta,[2] *Vienne, Emorre,*[3] *Sacar-*
bance,[4]
Voudront livrer au Barbares Pan-
none:
Par picque & feu, enorme violance,
Les conjurez descouvers par mat-
rone.

Betta, Vienna, Emort, Sopron,
they will want to deliver
Hungary to the Barbarians;
great violence through pike and
fire, the conspirators discovered
by a matron.

This quatrain appears to be linked with the following ones, X. 62
and 63, but they are all very obscure.

Pres de Sorbin pour affaillir
Ongrie,
L'herault de Bude les viendra
advertir:
Chef Bizantin, Sallon de Sclav-
onie,
A loi d'Arabes les viendra con-
vertir.

Near Sorbia in order to assail
Hungary, the herald of Brudes
will come to warn them. The
Byzantine chief, Salona of
Slavonia, he will come to
convert them to Arab law.

[1] *nolte*—Probably from Latin, *noluntas* = unwillingness.
[2] *Betta?*—Possibly Baetis, the Guadalquivir River?
[3] *Emmore*—Uncertain place name.
[4] *Sacarabance*—Latin, *Scarbantia* = modern Sapron.

Cydron,[1] *Raguse,*[2] *la cité au sainct Hieron.*[3]
Reverdira le médicant succours,
Mort fils de Roi par mort de deux heron,[4]
L'Arabe Ongrie feront un mesme cours.

Cydonia, Ragusa, the city holy to Hieron, the healing help will make it green again, the king's son dead because of the death of two heroes, Arabia and Hungary will take the same steps.

Pleure Milan, pleure Luques, Florance,
Que ton grand Duc sur le char montera,
Changer le siege pres de Venise s'advance,
Lors que Colomne[5] *à Rome chang-era:*

Weep Milan, weep Lucca and Florence, when your great Duke climbs into the chariot. To change the seat it advances close to Venice when at Rome the Colonnas will change.

ITALY 19th CENTURY

When the Grand Duke left Italy, Austria abandoned the province of Venetia to Napoleon III, who gave it in turn to Victor Emmanuel. Florence became the latter's new capital until the seat of all Italian government was moved to Rome, when the temporal powers of the Papacy declined.

O vaste Romone ta ruine s'approche,
Non de tes murs de ton sang & substance;
L'aspre par lettres fera si horrible coche,
Fer poinctu mis à tous jusques au manche.

O great Rome your ruin draws near, not of your walls but of your blood and substance; the harsh one in letters will make so horrid a notch, pointed steel wounding all up to the sleeve.

[1] *Cydonia*—Now modern Canea.
[2] *Ragusa*—Now Dubrovnik.
[3] *Hieron?*—Dubious personal name?
[4] *heron*—Mostly regarded as a false rhyme for heroes.
[5] *Colonne*—A great Roman family, the Colonnas.

Le chef de Londres par regne l'Americh,	The London premier through American power will burden
L'isle de l'Escosse tempiera par gellee:	the island of Scotland with a cold thing. Reb the King will
Roi Reb auront un si faux antechrist	have so dreadful an antichrist who will bring them all into
Que les mettra trestous dans la meslee.	the troubles.

POLARIS IN SCOTLAND AND U.S.A.

A most interesting quatrain. The Premier of London at the time specified was Harold Macmillan who had a good relationship with America. It was during his office that Scotland was burdened with the cold thing (the Polaris submarines). Roi Reb sounds strange but links this even firmly with another antichrist to come who will lead all of them, i.e. Britain and U.S.A. into trouble.

Le tremblement si fort au mois de Mai,	A very great trembling in the month of May, Saturn in
Saturne, Caper, Jupiter, Mercure au beuf:	Capricorn. Jupiter and Mercury in Taurus. Venus also in
Venus aussi Cancer, Mars en Nonnay,[1]	Cancer, Mars in Virgo, then hail will fall greater than an
Tombera gresse lors plus grosse qu'un euf.	egg.

The accumulation of planets in the zodiac here referred to is apparently very rare, but all it predicts here is an earthquake in May and a great fall of hail. The dates are April 1929 or May 3755.

[1] *Nonnay* = Virgo, as *nonnay* comes from *Nonne,* or *Nonnain* a nun, and virgin.

L'armee de mer devant la cité tiendra
Puis partir sans faire langue alee,
Citoyens grande proie en terre prendra,
Retourner classe,[1] *reprendre grand emblee.*[2]

The army of the sea will stand before the city then depart without making a long passage. A great prey of citizens will be taken on land, the fleet returns to seize (by) great robbery.

69

Le fait luisant de neuf vieux esleué
Seront si grand par midi aquilon,
De sa seur propre grande alles[3] *levé.*
Guyant meurdri au buisson d'ambellon.[4]

The shining deed of the new old one exalted, will be so great in the south and north. Raised by his own sister great crowds arise, fleeing is murdered in the bushes at Ambellon.

70

L'oeil par object ferra telle excroissance,
Tant & ardente que tumbera la neige,
Champ arrousé viendra en descroissance,
Que le primat succumbera à Rege.

Because of an object the eye will swell so much, burning so greatly that the snow will fall. The watered fields will start to shrink when the Primate dies at Reggio.

71

La terre & l'air gelleront si grand eau,
Lors qu'on viendra pour jeudi venerer,
Ce qui sera jamais ne feut si beau,
Des quatre pars le viendront honnorer.

The earth and air will freeze so much water when they come to venerate on Thursdays. He who will come will never be as fair as the few partners who come to honour him.

U.S.A.?

This is interesting in that the Christian Sabbath is Sunday, for Jews it is Saturday, and for Muslims, Friday. Could Thursday possibly refer to the United States unique tradition of Thanksgiving, which is held on a Thursday?

[1] *classe*—Latin, *classis* = a fleet.
[2] *emblee*—O.F. = robbery or thieving.
[3] *alles*—O.F. = trip, speed, crowd.
[4] *ambellon?*—Dubious, possibly village of Ambel?

L'an mil neuf cens nonante neuf sept mois,	In the year 1999, and seven months, from the sky will come the great King of Terror. He will bring back to life the great king of the Mongols. Before and after War reigns happily.
Du ciel viendra un grand Roi deffraieur.	
Resusciter le grand Roi d'Angolmois.[1]	
Avant que Mars regner par bonheur.	

3rd ANTICHRIST WAR

In this gloomy prediction Nostradamus seems to foresee the end of the world at the Millennium, the year 2000. He was greatly influenced in this by medieval thinking which held all millenniums in great dread. From the verse it appears that first we must suffer the Asian antichrist 'the King of Mongols' before the advent of this new and terrifying figure. Note that Nostradamus expects war both before and after his coming. See IV. 50, X. 74, 75.

Le temps present avecques le passé	The present time together with the past will be judged by the great man of Jupiter. Too late will the world be tired of him and disloyal through the oath-taking clergy.
Sera jugé par grand Jovialiste,	
Le monde tard lui sera lassé,	
Et desloyal par le clergé juriste.	

By *Jovialiste* Nostradamus means a follower of Jupiter, and, by extension, a pagan. The quatrain has been applied to both Rabelais and Voltaire, but was probably intended as a dig at Calvin, Nostradamus' arch enemy.

An revolu du grand nombre septiesme	The year of the great seventh number accomplished, it will appear at the time of the games of slaughter, not far from the age of the great millennium, when the dead will come out of their graves.
Apparoistra au temps Jeux d'Hecatombe,	
Non esloigné du grand eage milliesme	
Que les entres sortiront de leur tombe.	

[1] *Angolmois*—Not Angoumois in Western France but the anagram of the O.F., *Mongolois.*

WAR IN THIS CENTURY, 1979–80?

At the time of the seventh number (could this mean at the end of the 1970s?), war will break out again on an immense scale. The date will not be far from the millennium, which it isn't, see X. 72. The last line is purely horrific unless Nostradamus had some vision of the last judgment.

75

Tant attendu ne reviendra jamais	Long awaited he will never
Dedans l'Europe, en Asie appar-	return in Europe, he will
oistra	appear in Asia; One of the
Un de la ligue islu du grand	league issued from great
Hermes,	Hermes, he will grow above all
Et sur tous rois des orientz croistra.	other powers in the Orient.

WAR IN THIS CENTURY (*continued*)

This may refer to the last quatrain, The King of Horror will appear in Asia, not Europe and will wax powerful over the Eastern countries? See X. 72.

76

Le grand senat discernera la pompe	The great Senate will see the
A l'un qu'apres sera vaincu chassé,	parade for one who afterwards
Ses adherans seront à son de	will be driven out, vanquished.
trompe,	His adherents will be there at
Biens publiez ennemis deschassez.	the sound of a trumpet, their
	possessions for sale, the enemies
	driven out.

No setting is given to the reader for these general events.

77

Trente adherens de l'ordre des	Thirty members of the order of
quiretres[1]	Quirites, banished, their
Bannis leurs biens donnez ses	belongings given to their bold
adversaires,	adversaries. All their good
Tous leurs bienfais seront pour	actions will be taken as wrong,
desmerites	the fleet scattered, delivered up
Classe[2] *espargie*[3] *delivrez aux*	to the Corsairs.
consaires.	

[1] *quiretres* = (*a*) Roman citizens in their civil capacity. (*b*) Low Latin, renowned warriors.
[2] *classe*—Latin, *classis* = a fleet.
[3] *espargie*—O.F., *espargier* = tò sprinkle, dispense.

This is usually accepted as referring to post-Fascist Italy, and the corsairs are then understood to be the Russians, who received a large part of the Italian navy.

78

Subite joie en subite tristesse	Sudden joy into sudden sadness
Sera à Romme aux graces embras-	will beat Rome for the graces
sees.	embraced; Mourning, cries,
Deuil, cris, pleurs, larm. sang	tears, weeping, blood, excellent
excellent liesse	rejoicing, contrary bands sur-
Contraires bandes surprinses &	prised and trussed up.
troussees.	

79

Les vieux chemins seront tous	The old roads will all be
embelis,	improved, they will go to (a
L'on passera à Memphis somentrée,[1]	place) similar (to) Memphis.
Le grand Mercure d'Hercules fleur	The great Mercury of Hercules'
de lis	fleur de lis, will cause land, sea
Faisant trembler terre, mer &	and country to tremble.
contree.	

80

Au regne grand du grand regne	In the kingdom of the great one
regnant	reigning with a great rule by
Par force d'armes les grands portes	force of arms he will cause to
d'airain	be opened the great gates of
Fera ouvrir le roi & duc joignant,	brass; the king and duke allied
Port demoli nef à fons jour serain.	the port demolished, the ship
	(sunk) to the bottom and a
	serene day.

81

Mis tresor temple citadins Hesperi-	Treasure is placed in a temple
ques	by Western citizens withdrawn
Dans icelui retiré en secret lieu,	therein to a secret place, the
Le temple ouvrir les liens fameli-	temple to open by hungry
ques.	bonds, recaptured, ravished, a
Reprens ravis proie horrible au	terrible prey in the midst.
milieu.	

[1] *somentré*—From Greek, *symmetros* = like, resembling.

During the 16th Century gold poured into Spain from her possessions in the New World. Could Nostradamus be taken literally in this case, that a great amount of treasure is hidden in some Spanish Cathedral? However, problems arise with line 3. How can a bond be hungry? It has been suggested that this is an imaginative description of economic crisis in the United States (Hesperiques' other meaning) to be followed by a riot at Fort Knox, the greatest gold hoard in the world.

82

Cris, pleurs, larmes viendront avec coteaux
Semblant fouir donront dernier assault.
Lentour parques planter profons plateaux,
Vifs repoulsez & meurdris de prinsault.[1]

With the knives will come cries, tears and weeping, seeming to flee they will make a final assault around the parks they will set up high platforms, the living pushed back and murdered instantly.

83

De batailler ne sera donné signe,
Du parc seront contraint de sortir hors,
De Gand lentour sera cogneu l'ensigne,
Qui fera mettre de tous les siens à mors.

The signal will not be given to fight, they will be obliged to go out of the park; the banner around Ghent will be recognized, he who will put all his followers to death.

84

La naturelle à si hault hault non bas
Le tard retour fera marris contens,
Le Recloing[2] ne sera sans debatz
En empliant & pendant tous son temps.

The illegitimate girl so high, high not low, the late return will make the grieved ones contented. The Reconciled one will not be without disputes by employing and wasting all his time.

ELIZABETH I

Some people regard line 1 as describing Elizabeth Tudor whom Pope Paul IV declared to be a bastard through the illegality of her

[1] de prinsault—O.F. = firstly, at once, immediately, etc.
[2] Recloing—Dubious? Possibly derived from Latin, recolligo = to regain, be reconciled?

mother's marriage. She was considered to be one also by most English Catholics.

Le vieil tribung au point de la trehemide.	The old tribune on the point of trembling will be pressed not
Sera pressee captif ne deslivrer,	to give up the captive. The old,
Le veuil non veuil ne mal parlant timide	not old speaking timidly of the evil to free his friends in a law-
Par legitime à ses amis livrer.	ful manner.

FRANCE, 1940–3

This quatrain has been mentioned as a general description of France between 1940–3 when Marshal Pétain was negotiating with the Germans about prisoners of war who were being used as slave labour.

86

Comme un griphon viendra le roi d'Europe	The king of Europe will come like a griffon, accompanied by
Accompaigné de ceux d'Aquilon,	those of the North; he will lead
De rouges & blancz conduira grand trappe	a great troop of red and white, they will go against the king of
Et iront contre le roi de Babilon.[1]	Babylon.

ALLIED FORCES, 1815

The King of Europe was the Allied Forces which marched against Napoleon, the king of Egypt, before he was made first Consul. The great army of red and white uniforms are the tunics of the English and the Austrians. The English may well be described as from the North, as also Russia.

87

Grand roi viendra prendre port pres de Nisse	A great king will come to anchor near Nice, the death of
Le grand empire de la mort si enfera	the great empire is thus accom- plished. He will place his
Aux Antipolles posera son genisse,	heifer in Antibes, plunder at
Par mer la Pille tout esvanoira.	sea, all will vanish.

[1] *Babylon*—In medieval texts the King of Egypt is often called the King of Babylon.

Piedz & cheval à la seconde veille	Foot and horse at the second
Feront entree vastient tour par la mer,	watch, they will make an entry laying waste all at sea. He will
Dedans la poil[1] entrera de Marseille,	enter the port of Marseilles, tears, cries and blood, never a
Pleurs, cris, & sang onc nul temps si amer.	time so bitter.

De brique en marbre seront les murs reduits	The walls will change from brick to marble, seventy-five
Sept & cinquante annees pacifiques,	peaceful years. Joy to people,
Joie aux humains renoué Laqueduict,	the aqueduct reopened, health abundant fruit, joy and melli-
Santé, grandz fruict joye & temps melifique.[2]	fluous times.

LOUIS XIV

This general quatrain seems to describe the prosperity of France under her great King Louis XIV.

Cent fois mourra le tyran inhumain.	A hundred times the inhuman
Mis à son lieu scavant & debonnaire,	tyrant will die and a wise and carefree man put in his place.
Tout le senat sera dessoubz sa main,	He will have the whole senate
Faché sera par malin themeraire.	in his hands, he will be troubled by a wretched scoundrel.

NAPOLEON IN ST. HELENA

Napoleon is dying a hundred deaths through his enforced captivity; in his place is elected Louis XVIII, often called '*le debonnaire*'. Both houses of Parliament, the Senate, will profess devotion to their new king down to the last man. The trouble referred to in the final line was the assassination of the Duke de Berry in line for the throne through his father, Charles X.

[1] *poil*—Usually regarded as erratum for *port*.
[2] *melific*—From Latin, *mellificus* = honey making. Nostradamus probably meant to write *mellifluus*.

Clergé Romain l'an mil six cens &	In the year 1609, the Roman
neuf,	Clergy at the head of the year
Au chef de l'an feras election	will have an election; one of
D'un gris & noir de la Compagne	grey and black come forth from
issu,	Campania, never was there one
Qui onc ne feut si maling.	as wicked as he.

Pope Paul V reigned from 1605 to 1621 as Pope. But in the year 1609 he fell ill, and according to contemporary reports, there was a great deal of intriguing going on in the Courts of France and Rome should the Pope die an opportune death.

Devant le pere l'enfant sera tué:	In front of the father the child
Le pere apres entre cordes de jonc,	will be killed, the father after-
Genevois peuple sera esvertué	wards between ropes of rushes.
Gisant le chief au milieu comme un	The people of Geneva will be
tronc.	exerted, the chief lying in their
	midst like a trunk.

La barque neufve recevra les	The new Bark will go on
voyages,	voyages, there and nearer they
Là & aupres transferont l'empire,	will transfer the empire. Beau-
Beaucaire, Arles retiendront les	caire & Arles will retain the
hostages	hostages near where two
Pres deux colomnes trouvees de	columns of porphyry are found.
paphite.	

PIUS VI, 1799
This quatrain implies that the Papacy will be moved as in I. 32, and V. 45 etc. Both Beaucaire and Arles are near the Rhône river which borders Valence where Pope Pius VI died in captivity in 1799.

De Nismes, d'Arles, & Vienne contemner,
N'obei tant à l'edict Hespericque:[1]
Aux labouriez[2] *pour le grand condamner,*
Six eschappez en habit seraphicque.[3]

Scorn from Nîmes, Arles and Vienne, not to obey at all the Western edict; in order that the great may condemn the tormented, six escape in Franciscan garb.

Dans les Espaignes viendra Roi trespuissant,
Par Mer & terre subjugant or midi,
Ce mal fera rabaissant le croissant,
Baisser les aesles à ceux du vendredi.[4]

Into Spain will come a very powerful king, he will subjugate the south by land and sea. This evil will cause a lowering of the crescent again, a lowering of the wings of the people of Friday.

PHILIP II OF SPAIN

The nearest this appears to come to fulfilment is Philip II of Spain who persecuted the Moors, made several futile expeditions to North Africa and was involved in the Battle of Lepanto 1571.

Religion du nom des mers vaincra,
Contre le secte fils Adaluncatif,[5]
Secte obstinee deploree craindra,
Des deux blessez par Aleph & Aleph.

The religion called after the seas will overcome, against the sect of the son Adaluncatif; the stubborn lamentable sect will fear the two men wounded by A & A.[6]

This quatrain should be easy to solve but is not. The anagram for Adaluncatif is still unbroken. The A's in line 4 are not much help since a great number of Arab names begin with A.

[1] *Hesperique*—Western? American? Spanish?
[2] *labourier*—O.F. = to be tormented.
[3] *seraphique*—The true name of the Franciscan order is the Order of Seraphim.
[4] The Mahometans celebrate their Sabbath on a Friday.
[5] *Adaluncatif*—Unsolved name, possibly containing Calif among the anagram?
[6] A & A—Aleph, letter A in Hebrew. Alif in Arabic.

Triremes pleines tout aage captif,
Temps bon à mal, le doux pour
amertume;
Proie à Barbares trop tost seront
hastifs,
Cupid de veoir plaindre au vent la
plume.

Triremes full of captives of all
ages good times for bad, sweet
ones for the bitter; hasty they
will be too quickly prey for
the Barbarians anxious to see the
plume (of smoke) wail in the
wind.

La splendeur claire à pucelle
joyeuse,
Ne luira plus long temps sera sans
sel:
Avec marchans,[1] ruffiens loup
odieuse,
Tous pesle mesle monstre univer-
selle.

For the joyful maiden the
bright splendour will shine no
more, for a long time she will
lack salt. With merchants,
bullies, odious wolves all confusion the universal monster.

FRENCH THIRD REPUBLIC

The Third Republic in France was typified as Marianne, and so
might refer in a general way to France between 1940–4, lacking
wisdom 'salt' in her behaviour. The confusion and beasts refer to
the Nazi invasion.

La fin le loup, le lyon, beuf, &
l'asne,
Timide dama[2] seront avec mastins,
Plus ne cherra à eux la douce
manne,
Plus vigilance & custode aux
mastins.

The end of the wolf, the lion,
ox and the ass, the timid deer
will be with the mastiffs. No
longer will the sweet manna
fall upon them; more vigilance
and guarding for the mastiffs.

[1] *marchands*—May mean mercenaries here?
[2] *dama*—Latin = a deer.

Le grand empire sera par Angleterre,
Le pempotam[1] des ans plus de trois cens:
Grandes copies[2] passer par mer & terre,
Les Lusitains[3] n'en seront pas contens.

A great empire will be for England, the all powerful for more than 300 years. Great forces cross by land and sea. The Portuguese will not be content.

GREAT BRITAIN

In this interesting quatrain Nostradamus foresees a great future for Britain lasting for three hundred years. Most people take it from the reign of Elizabeth to that of Victoria, fifty years longer than prophesied. It is unclear what the Portuguese have to do with this, and line 3 is also tricky, does it refer to English forces, or to the forces that will end Britain's greatness? A good ambiguous twist with which to end in the typical Nostradamus tradition.

[1] *pempotam*—From the Greek, *pan* = all, and the Latin, *potens* = powerful.

[2] *copies*—Latin, *copia* = troops.

[3] *Lusitains*—Classical name for Portuguese.

INDEX

Abercromby, Sir Richard, 109
Acciarito, 219
Acre, 109
Aemathien, 412
Aenobarbe, 352
Aerial warfare, 183
Africa, 159, 160, 217
  and World War II, 215
Agde, 315
Agen, 194, 406
Air battles, in twentieth century, 53–54
Air travel, in twentieth century, 53
Alba (Alva), Duke of, 203, 273, 297, 323, 358
Albanians, 226, 242
Albenga, 271
Albigensians, Crusade of the, 393
Alchemy, 120
Alençon, Duc François d', 110, 162, 253, 279
Alexander I, of Russia, 104, 338
Alexandra, Czarina, 275, 338
Algeria, French conquest of, 235, 383
Ali Pasha, 66
Allen, Hugh, 295, 338, 369
Allied Forces (1815), 421
Alphonso II, 296
Alsace, 251
Alva, Duke of. See Alba, Duke of
Amboise, Conspiracy of, 26–27, 309
America, 111. See also United States

attack on, 112
future war in, 65
Anabaptists, 149, 153
Anastasia, Princess, 338
Ancona, 310
Anglican Church, 330
Angoulême, Duke of, 41, 50, 398
Anjou, Duke of, 357
Anne, Queen, 110
Annemarc, 363
Anthony de Navarre, 368
Antibes, 233, 400
Antichrist, 46, 111, 229, 261, 278, 337, 395, 415, 417
Antioch, 57
Antwerp, 172, 369
Aqualeia, 192
Aquino, 298
Arab empire, 268. See also United Arab Republic
Arabs, 226, 230, 278
Araxes, Battle of, 134
Arles, 423
Arras, 383
Artois, Count of, 61
Ashraf, Shah, 154
Asia, 186, 202
Atomic explosions, 72–73
Augsburg, Battle of, 213
August II, 46
Augustinians, 311
Aumale, Duke of, 41, 290, 355
Austria, 48–49, 90, 140, 216, 235, 382, 414, 421
  and World War I, 60–61
Avignon, 334

Bacterial warfare, 251

Balagny, 407
Balennes, 85
Balkans, 241
Bar, Duc de, 290
Barbarossa, 57, 105, 176
Barbary pirates, 105, 120, 132, 335, 367
Barchinons, 287
Barry, Madame du, 223, 224, 379
Barzun, Jacques, 403
Bastille, 210
Bazaine, Achille, 287
Beaucaire, 423
Beauharnais, Eugène de, 232
Beauregard, Marquis de, 108
Bellerophon, myth of, 311
Beluzer, 318
Benedictines, 255, 311
Berich, 261
Berlin, 183
Berlin Wall, 238
Bernhard, Duke of Saxe Weimar, 213
Berry, Duchess de, 68, 159, 201
Berry, Duke of, 50, 360, 422
  assassination of, 61, 193
Bèze, Théodore de, 310
Biafra, 315
  famine in, 55
Bigorre, 194
Bletterans, 321
Blitzkrieg, 238
Blois, 358
Blücher, Gebhard Lebericht von, 31
Boétie, Etienne de la, 350
Boleyn, Anne, 132
Bologna, 328
Bombings, 211, 261
Bonaparte, Caroline, 403
Bonaparte, Josephine, 13, 51, 90, 131, 189, 232, 273
Bonaparte, Louis, III, 52
Bonaparte, Napoleon. See Napoleon Bonaparte
Bordelais, 352
Bordeaux, 124

Bordeaux, Duke of, 41, 152, 159
Bothwell, James, 62
Bourbons, 241
Bourges, 385
Bourgogne, Duke of, 41
Boyne, Battle of the, 100, 101
Bresse, 298
  French occupation of, 23
Bretagne, Duke of, 127
Brindisi, 298
Brunswick, duchy of, 408
Burgundy, Duke of, 127
Buffalora, 311
Byron, Lord, 279

Cadiz, 362
Cadiz, Bay of, 344
Caepio, Quintus Servilius, 318
Calais, fall of, 292, 361, 382, 383
Calvin, John, 309, 368, 417
Calvinism, 44, 94, 99, 153, 171, 231, 236, 276, 310, 377
Cambrai, peace of, 293
Camisard rebels, 190
Campoformio, Treaty of, 263
Caputian family, 314
Carcassonne, 333
Carlos I, 336
Carpentras, 366
Casau, Charles de, 158
Casket Letters, 315
Castille, 356
Cateau Cambrésis, Peace of, 370–71
Catholic Church, 22, 27, 63, 75, 76, 77, 85, 94, 110, 153, 171, 194, 196, 217, 227, 234, 263, 276, 371. See also Clergy; Papacy; Papal States
Catholics. See Catholic Church
Cato, 316
Cato, C. Pacius, 316
Catonia, 340
Cavaliers, 232
Cavour, Count Camillo Benso di, 225, 293–94

Central Park, destruction of, 369
Centuries (Nostradamus), 10–11, 45
  history of, 12–15
Ceramon-agora, 373
Cevennes, 98
Châlon, 150
Chamberlain, Nevile, 370
Chambord, Comte de, 68, 201, 223–24
Chanignon, 366
Charles I, of England, 94, 155, 189, 243, 321
  execution of, 354, 369
  and Parliament, 63
Charles II, of England, 168, 393
  and Scotland, 329
Charles III, of France, 295
Charles V, Holy Roman Emperor, 36, 217, 274, 280, 293, 299, 327, 339, 358, 408
Charles IX, of France, 11, 138, 185, 271, 299, 405
Charles X, of France, 41, 50, 61, 106, 152, 159, 198, 201, 223, 370, 422
Charles XII, of Sweden, 46
Charles, second Cardinal of Lorraine, 308
Charles Emmanuel IV, 342
Charlie, Bonnie Prince, 243
Chartres, 189
Chartres, Vidame de, 412
Châteauneuf, 122
Chaupionnet, General, 294
Chavigny, Jean Aymes de, 9, 77
Chemical warfare in Europe, 153
China, 84, 146, 212, 226, 257
Chivasso, 309
Churchill, Winston, 72
Cimbrians, 123
Cing Mars, 335
Civila Castellona, 352
Clément, Jacques, 67, 110, 142, 234, 299
Clergy, abolition of, in France, 43, 48, 76, 77, 176–77, 273–74, 329, 346
Coligny, Gaspard de, 184, 276
Cologne, Archbishop of, 263
Colonna, 333
Colonna family, 350
Common Market, 57, 186, 401
Communism, 161, 180, 227, 315, 338, 370
Concentration camps, 151–52
Concini, Concino, 287
Condé, Louis Bourbon, death of, 41
Condé, Prince de, 412
Constantine, King, 158, 218
Constantinople, 339, 377
Corap, André Georges, 226
Corde Sanitaire, 370
Cordoba (Cordova), 327
Cordova, Gonsalvo Fernandez de, 129
Corsica, 181, 289
Cosimo, Duke, 169
Cremona, 32
Cromwell, Oliver, 155, 189, 231–32, 329, 336–37, 393
Crusade, Fourth, 339
Crusaders, 343
Cuban missile crisis, 172
Cult of Reason, 43, 48, 77
Cyprus, 15, 168, 215, 276

Dalmatia, 85, 108
Damiens, Robert François, 126
Danton, Gêorges Jacques, 21, 146
Dardanelles, 72
Darlan, Jean L. X. F., 163
Darnley, Lord, 315
  death of, 257
De Demonibus (Psellus), 42
De Gaulle, Charles, 57, 84, 163, 175, 224, 226, 363, 401
De Mysteriis Egyptorum (Iamblichus); 9, 20
De Urgel, 396
Dieppe, 296
Directoire, 146, 177–78

Divination, 20–21, 42–43
Dôle, 288
Doria, Charles, 158
Douro River, 147
Drake, Francis, 404
Dreyfus, Alfred, 23
Dreyfus case, 23
Dunkirk, 42, 226

Earthquake, 381, 415
Edward VIII, abdication of, 399,
    405
Egypt, 67–68, 109, 421
Eisenhower, Dwight D., 172
Elba, 400
Electricity, discovery of, 139
Elizabeth, Princess, of Spain, 314
Elizabeth I, of England, 132,
    275, 309, 420–21, 426
Elizabeth of Austria, 11, 405
Elizabeth of Valois, 131
Elyne, 79
Elysian Fields, 387
England, 63, 94, 121, 140, 151,
    155, 160, 182, 199, 202, 222,
    232, 235, 252, 254, 257, 264,
    275, 292, 308, 344, 345, 352,
    354, 362, 382, 394, 399, 404,
    406, 415, 421, 426
  and Civil War, 336–37
  and Common Market, 401
  German blockade of, 151
  history, 145
  and Napoleonic Wars, 291
  Napoleon's failure to invade,
    328
  and Nazis, 332
  and World War II, 173, 209
Enosis, 158
Entragues, Balzac d', 142
Epirus, 57
Essex, Earl of, 344
Estrées, Gabrielle d', 382, 410
Estrées, Maréchal d', 356
Europe, 254
  chemical warfare in, 153
Eugénie, Empress, 394

Evereux, 239
Exposition Universelle, 221

Faenza, 153, 298
Famagusta, 168
Famine, 55, 104
Farnese, Pierluigi, 288
Fascists, 216, 220, 318, 370
Ferdinand I, Holy Roman Em-
    peror, 280, 339
Ferdinand II, Holy Roman Em-
    peror, 213
Ferdinand V, of Castile, 129
Ferdinand, Archduke of Austria,
    assassination of, 49
Ferdinand of Bulgaria, 364
Ferdinand, Crown Prince of
    France, 300
Ferretti, Count Mastoi, 394
Ferrière, Chevalier de la, 157
Fiesole, 289
Flemings, 254
Fleurus, Battle of, 230
Fleury, 126
Floods
  and drought, 28
  general, 125
Florence, 153, 209, 289, 298, 414
Florinville, Seigneur de, 8
Focia, 309
Foix, 322, 377
Foix, Gaston de, 335
Fontbrune, Dr., 317
Fossano, 297
Fougères family, 357
France, 23, 56, 59, 84, 87, 90, 95,
    104, 106, 123, 126, 127, 130,
    131, 133, 134, 140, 141, 142,
    143, 155, 156, 160, 169, 172,
    181, 190, 192, 196, 198, 213,
    220, 221, 225, 230, 231, 234,
    235, 238, 251, 253, 254, 266,
    269, 270, 271, 276, 279, 280,
    283, 287, 209, 291–92, 296,
    297, 308, 310, 325, 327, 333,
    335, 336, 340, 341, 342, 352,

354, 355, 357, 358, 359, 361, 362, 363–64, 370–71, 378, 382, 383, 385, 397, 404–5, 407, 422. *See also* French Revolution; Napoleon Bonaparte
abolition of clergy in, 43, 48, 76, 77, 177, 273–74, 346
in Algeria, 160
archaeological treasures in, 55
capitulation of, 175, 189, 299, 332, 392, 421
and Common Market, 57, 224
Communism in, 315
famine in, 55
Fronde civil war, 412
and Germany, 147, 409–10
and Hitler, 37
invasion of Italy, 42, 47, 65
in North Africa, 29
and Pius VI, 40
Seventh War, 250
Third Republic, 425
and Vatican, 234
Wars of Religion, 338
and World War II, 56, 123, 226, 238, 245
Franche-Comté, 320, 321
Francis, Duke of Lorraine, 209
Francis I, of France, 293
Francis II, of France, 11, 27, 271, 405, 411
Francis IV, Duke of Florence, 224
Franciscans, 272
Franco, Francisco, 143, 355–56
Franco-Prussian war, 52, 65, 152, 190, 204, 221, 251
Francus, 29, 268
Franklin, Ben, 139
Frederika, Queen, 158
Fréjus, 400
French Revolution, 21, 27, 48, 76, 77, 146, 177, 198, 210, 221, 258, 314, 338, 356–57, 359, 363–64, 379
Frisia, 264

Garde, Baron de la, 281
Gardon river, 394
Garibaldi, Giuseppe, 216
Gauric, Luc, 38
Geiger counter, 182
Gemelle, Anne Ponsart, 9
Geneva, 368
Genoa, 182, 191, 219, 222, 241, 297
George I, of England, 109–10
George VI, of England, 399
Germany, 5, 14, 90, 145, 172, 174, 181, 183, 196, 226, 251, 299, 324, 408. *See also* Hitler, Adolf
blockade of Great Britain, 151–52
and Europe, 87
and France, occupation of, 123, 147, 332, 392, 409–10, 421
and Italy, 148
Third Reich, 384
Thirty Years War, 338
World War II, 134, 215, 364
Gers, Departement of, 44, 306
Gibraltar, 327, 385
Giraud, Henri, 226
Girondins, 5, 34
Glanum, 55
Goebbels, Joseph, 5, 267
Goebbels, Frau Dr., 5, 14
Gomez, 212
Gonzaga, Guglielmo, 358
Gorgon, 338
Goussainville, 372
Greece, 158, 218, 378, 379
chemical warfare in, 241
Italian occupation of, 61
and World War II, 215, 364
Greek fire, 176
Gregorian calendar, institution of, 42–43
Gregory XIV, Pope, 344, 396
Grenada, 129, 230
Greslot, Jerôme, 149
Grimaldi, House of, 124, 307, 311
Grouchy, Emmanuel de, 194

Guienne, 298, 352
Guise, Duc de, 26, 95, 137, 174,
    253, 260, 288, 290, 291, 292,
    297, 361, 370, 398. *See also*
    Guise brothers
Guise brothers, assassination of,
    39, 62, 79, 142, 144. *See also*
    Guise, Duc de

Habsburgs (Hapsburgs), 254, 270,
    309, 310, 320, 321, 339, 362,
    386
Harlay, Achille de, 287
Hawkins, John, 404
Henri II, of France, 10, 80, 131,
    133, 188, 195, 270, 276, 290,
    311, 357, 366, 410
    death of, 38, 144
Henri III, of France, 11, 62, 79,
    86, 106, 110, 141, 142, 144,
    162, 234, 236, 253, 260, 271,
    299, 307, 357, 407
    assassination of, 25, 39, 67
Henry IV, of Navarre, 12, 22, 95,
    98, 110, 131, 132, 174, 181,
    194, 196, 234, 274, 279, 324,
    341, 368, 370, 382, 398, 404-5,
    407
    assassination of, 125
    and Duke of Parma, 25
    and siege of Paris, 24, 25
Henrietta Maria, of France, 63
Hime, H., 176
Hiroshima, 74, 337, 369
History of France (Thiers), 364
History of Lyons (Menard), 394
Hitler, Adolf, 14, 53, 82, 87, 123,
    135, 143, 145-46, 148, 183,
    191, 196, 228, 235, 252, 266,
    267, 319, 337, 370, 384
    and France, 37
    and Mussolini, 220
    and Russia, 243
Holland, 121. *See also* Nether-
    lands
Holy League, 137, 151, 407. *See
    also* Catholicism

Holy Roman Empire, 37, 143,
    227, 263, 277
Houdan, 372
Howard, Charles, 344
Howe, Ellic, 82
Huguenots, 22, 29, 75, 121, 131,
    138, 185, 194, 196, 263, 276,
    323, 341, 371, 412
Hundred Years War, 222
Hungary, 146, 226, 310, 361
    1956 revolution, 111-12
Hyerès, 300

Iamblichus, 20
Idris, King, 57, 189
Ile du Diable, 74
Illyria, 361
Imola, 153
Imperial, Prince, 394
India, famine in, 55
Inflation, 317
Influenza epidemic, 372
Inge, Dr., 15
Innocent IX, Pope, 396
Inquisition, 174
Iran, 188
Ireland, famine in, 55
Isabella, 129, 370
Israel, creation of, 161-62
Istanbul, 92
Italian Revolution, 216, 258
Italy, 42, 87, 90, 103, 136, 137,
    139, 156, 157, 169, 174, 182,
    211, 219, 220, 225, 243, 244,
    254, 260, 288, 289, 308, 414
    and Germany, 148
    and Greece, occupation of, 61
    post-Fascist, 399, 419
    in twentieth century, 150
    and World War II, 78, 134,
    209, 212, 215, 228
Ivry, Battle of, 98, 110

James I, of England, 151, 404
James II, of England, 100-1,
    199-200, 330

James III, 202
Jansenism, 412
Japan
  and Pearl Harbor, 388
  and World War II, 212
Jarnac, Battle of, 138
Jem, Sultan, 277
Jews, 345
  in Spain, 129
John XXIII, Pope, 242, 259
John of Austria, Don, 106, 134, 327, 367
Journée des Barricades, 141–42

Kasr Al-Kabir, Battle of, 255
Kelly, Grace, 311
Kennedy, Edward, 325, 337, 345, 401
Kennedy, John F., assassination of, 33, 96, 114, 172, 325, 337, 345, 364–65, 401
Kennedy, Robert F., assassination of, 33, 114, 325, 337, 345, 364, 401
Khrushchev, Nikita, 96
Knights of Rhodes, 214
Krafft, Ernst, 267

Ladies' Charter, 293
Laingnes, 408
Languedoc, 294, 298, 352
Languedoc canal, 385
Lapalme, 352
La Rochelle, 124
Laval, Pierre, 332
La Vallette, 116
Laver, James, 64, 134, 196, 221, 235, 282, 331, 333
Law, John, 126
League of Nations, 45, 240
Le Mans, 290
Le Mas d'Agenais, 250
Leo XIII, Pope, 90, 252
Leoni, Edgar, 103, 130
Leopold II, Grand Duke of Tuscany, 216

Lepanto, Battle of, 66, 106, 120, 133–34, 367, 424
Lerin Islands, 300
Lesbos, 219
Le Torcey, 324
Levant, the, 310
Libertat, Pierre, 158
Liège, 260
Libyan Revolution, 57
Lodi, Battle of, 277
Loire towns, occupation of, 30
London
  Great Fire of, 93, 94
  Plague, 94, 354
Loomis, 395
Lorraine, 251, 291, 394, 410
Lorraine, Charles de, 142
Lorraine, Duke of, 209, 290
Los Angeles, 381
Loubet, Emile, 23
Louvel, 161
Louis XII, of France, 168
Louis XIII, of France, 125, 162, 290, 323, 334, 356, 412
Louis XIV, of France, 24, 47, 86, 98, 126, 127, 168, 169, 223, 236, 250, 356, 385, 412, 422
Louis XV, of France, 126, 127, 223, 379
Louis XVI, of France, 14, 15, 27, 39, 50, 61, 77, 198, 208, 210, 223, 282, 336, 341, 356, 357–58, 359, 363–64, 379, 406–7
Louis XVII, of France, 198, 208, 268, 314, 360, 379
Louis XVIII, of France, 39, 50, 65, 76, 90, 99, 156, 265, 397, 400, 422
Louis, King of Holland, 128, 324
Louis de Condé, death of, 138
Louis Napoleon, 76, 324, 352
Louis Philippe, 41, 190, 211, 235, 300, 323, 383
Louis Philippe of Portugal, 336
Lucca, 128, 129, 352
Lucerne, 308
Lusignan, 316

Lutherans, 153
Lyons, 108, 140, 412
  sack of, 376

Mabus, 98
Macedonia, and World War II,
  364
Mâcon, 150
Magic practices, 373–74
Maginot Line, 196, 238
Mahomet, 83
Mainz, 225
Mainz, Archbishop of, 263
Malachy, 237, 242
Malines, Council of, 335
Malta, 92, 116, 191, 214, 308
  siege of, 25
Mantua, 358
  siege of, 32
Marguerite of Navarre, 25, 38,
  110, 253
Maria Theresa, 412
Marie Antoinette, 39, 208, 210,
  223, 357, 359, 363, 379, 397–
  98, 407
Marie Louise of Austria, 90, 187
Marlborough, Duke of, 200
Marseilles, 158, 361
  downfall of, 154
Marxists, 310
Mary I, of England, 131, 264,
  292, 344
Mary II, of England, 202
Mary Queen of Scots, 11, 62,
  257, 315, 405, 411
Matignon, Marshal de, 133
Maurice of Nassau, 308, 408
Mayenne, 357
Mayenne, Duc de, 39, 62, 95, 370,
  398, 403
Mazarin, Jules, 13, 244
McCann, Lee, 218, 326, 377
Media, 148
Medici family, de', 298
Medici, Alessandro de', 209
Medici, Catherine de', 10–11–12,
  25, 29, 38, 78, 79, 110, 189,

234, 253, 260, 271, 290, 299,
  405, 407, 411
Medici, Marie de', 125, 290
Medicine, 30
Mediterranean, 392
Melilla, 200, 265
Mercoeur, Duke of, 307
Mercure Français, 125
Metz, 394
  capitulation of, 82–83
Middle East, wars in, 257, 278
Milan, 136, 150, 292, 298, 386
Milky Way, 262
Minorca, 105
Miollis, General, 22
Missiles, 204
Mole, M. de la, 281
Monaco, 124, 271, 307–8
Money, paper, 317
Mont Allegro, 396
Montesquiou, 138
Montgolfier balloon, 230
Montgomery, 144
Montgomery, Count of, 133
Montmorency family, 322, 356
Montmorency, Anne de, 133, 350
Montmorency, Henri de, 350
Montpertuis, 316
Moors, 230, 424
Morenigo, 395
Morton, Earl of, 315
Moscow, 90, 194, 197
  Napoleon's retreat from, 387
Moslems, 335, 345
Mount Aventine, 128
Mount Aymar, 376
Mussolini, Benito, 78, 148, 150,
  191, 215, 216, 252, 260, 318–
  19, 386
  and the Papacy, 220
Murat, Joachim, 21, 131, 403
Mytilene, 219

Napoleon Bonaparte, 47, 51, 58,
  65, 76, 90, 96, 101, 104, 106,
  128, 135, 142, 156, 159, 181,

187, 192, 211, 214, 230, 231, 235, 238, 244, 273, 281, 291, 306, 329, 331, 337, 352, 382, 395, 400, 403, 421
and Bourbons, 50
campaigns, 214
and church, 27
coup d'état, 177
death, 146
Egyptian campaign, 40, 42, 67–68, 107, 113, 214
on Elba, 36
England, failure to invade, 328
Italian compaign, 65, 113, 136, 142, 182, 258, 259
Italian Republic, president of, 47
Lodi, Battle of, 277
Peninsular campaign, 214
and Pius VII, 22, 214
Russian campaign, 115, 197, 387
on St. Helena, 36, 40, 422
at Villa Nova, 32
at Waterloo, 31, 40, 99, 102, 184, 194
Napoleon II, 331, 352
Napoleon III, 51, 112–13, 128, 190, 193, 204, 210, 216, 225, 239, 293, 323, 331, 394, 414
assassination attempt, 211–12
death, 340
at Sédan, 184
Nagasaki, 74, 337, 369
Nagy, Imre, 111
Nancy, 394
Nantes, 265
atrocities at, 221
Nantes, Edict of, 98, 169, 244
Naples, 153, 310
Narbonne, 269
Nassi, Don Joseph, 345
National Assembly of 1789, 291–92
National Assembly of 1848, 352
Navarre, 131, 341
Naxos, Duke of, 345

Nazis, 75, 151, 215, 266–67, 332, 343, 370, 425
Negrepont, 80
Nelson, Horatio, 59
Nentone, 233
Netherlands, 279. See also Holland
revolt in, 93
New York City, 283, 385, 409
attack on, 63
Ney, Michel, 109
Nice, 297
Nicholas, Duke de Mercoeur, 307
Nîmes, 231, 353, 394
Nola, 153
Nonseggle, 265
Normandy, Duke of, 50
North Africa, 132
and World War II, 29
North Atlantic Treaty Organization (NATO), 81
Norway, 252
Nostradamus
birth and life, 5–12
opening of tomb, 352
Nostradamus and the Nazis, (Howe), 82
Nostredame, César, 9
Nostredame, Jacques, 5
Nostredame, Jean, 5–6
Nostredame, Pierre de, 5
Noyades, 221
Nuremberg Trials, 87

Occult, 177, 178, 179, 180
Ogmios, 264, 324
Orléans, 189, 407
Orléans, Duke of, 39, 68, 126, 127, 162, 201, 223
Orsini family, 350
Orsini, Felice, 212
Orange, 173
Oswald, Lee Harvey, 33
Ottoman Empire, 277. See also Turks

Padua, 276
Pakistan, 315
Palermo, 310
Panonia, 361
Papacy, 169, 192, 226, 227, 230,
    412, 414
Papal States, 22, 23, 288, 296,
    310, 350, 351, 366
Paris, 162, 240, 258, 264, 282,
    283, 293, 333, 382
    siege of, 24, 25, 95, 404
Paris, Comte de, 68, 152
Paris peace talks, 84
Parma, 217, 288
Parma, Duke of (Duc de Parme),
    25, 98, 172, 174, 404
Parthis, 148
Pasteur, Louis, 32–33
Pasteur Institute, 32–33
Paternum, 340
Paul III, Pope, 288, 350, 420
Paul V, Pope, 423
Paul VI, Pope, 230, 242, 259, 325
Pavia, 309
    Battle of, 102–3, 136
Pearl Harbor, 34, 388, 392
Peninsular Wars, 64, 192, 214
Peretti, Felice, 8
Perigord, 194
Perpignan, 355
    siege of, 269
Persia, 114, 154, 240, 268
Perugia, 288, 335
Pétain, Henri, 59, 189, 332, 370,
    421
Peter the Great, 46
Pharos, 219
Philip II, of Spain, 38, 57, 129,
    131, 158, 203, 213, 264, 270,
    279, 280, 327, 339, 362, 368,
    370, 383, 394, 424
Philip III, of Spain, 203
Philip IV, of Spain, 369, 412
Philip V, of Spain, 168, 169, 250
Phocens, 287
Picardy, 368
    Spanish invasion of, 121

Piedmont, 368
Pieri, 212
Pisa, 288, 352
Pisseleu, Anne de, 382
Pius, VI, Pope, 88, 156, 214, 230,
    294, 306, 346, 423
    death of, 114
    and France, 40
Pius VII, Pope, 22, 47, 50, 88,
    214, 259, 306, 346
Pius IX, Pope, 252, 394
Pius XII, Pope, 242, 266
Plancus, Lucius Munatius, 140
Poitiers, Diane de, 188, 195, 270,
    290, 311, 357, 382, 410
Poitiers, Edict of, 236
Poland, 145, 146, 299
Polaris ballistic missiles, 35, 415
Pompadour, Madame de, 223
Pont-à-Mousson, Marquis du,
    295
Porto Corsini, 371
Portugal, 255, 280, 336, 382
Portuguese succession, 203
Prognostications (Nostradamus),
    9
Prophecies (Nostradamus), 9, 10,
    11, 13, 14, 15, 45, 188
Protestants, 94, 149, 153, 173,
    193, 194, 213, 225
Provence, 317
    Huguenot struggles in, 22
Prussia, 30, 140, 324, 382
Psellus, Michael, 42
Ptolons, 287
Pyrenees, Treaty of the, 213

Qaddafi, Muammai al-, 189

Rabelais, François, 417
Radar, 200–1
Radio, 200–1
Raleigh, Walter, 344, 404
Rasputin, Gregory, 275, 338
Ravaillac, François, 125
Ravenna, 85, 335
Raypoz, 368
Religion, 229

Religious beliefs, 77
Religious revival, 67, 75
Reynaud, Paul, 59
Rhodes, 92
Rhône, 343
Rian, Jean de, 157
Richelieu, Cardinal, death of, 334
Rivera, Primo, de, 355
Robespierre, Maximilien, 21, 146, 314
    death of, 89
Robine river, 156
Rockets, 204, 261
Rohan, Duke of, 231
Romania, 339
Rome, 113
    sack of, 156, 220
Rommel, Irwin, 34, 212, 215
Roosevelt, Franklin, 75
Rouen, 124, 174, 189, 239
Roundheads, 63, 191, 232
Rousseau, Waldeck, 23
Royale, Madame, 397–98
Rudio, 212
Rumania, 252
Russia, 30, 111–12, 140, 202, 275, 369, 382, 419. *See also* Union of Soviet Socialists Republic
    and Allies, 87
    and Hitler, 243
    and World War II, 209
Russian Revolution, 48, 338

Sabatini, Rafael, 371
Saillinons, 287
St. Bartholomew massacre, 185, 260
St. Bernard Pass, 182
St. Denis, 359
St. Francis, 307
St. George Islands, 362
St. Maurus, 311
St. Paul de Mausole, 402
St. Peter, tomb of, 148–49, 381
St. Quentin, 283, 361, 383
    battle of, 169, 170, 366

St. Rémy, 178, 402
St. Rémy, Reyniere de, 5
Saint Saturnin, Church of, 318
Saint Solenne Cathedral, 358
St. Theresa, 174
St. Urban, 280
Salon, 237
Sardinia, 289, 342
Saviglione, 297
Savona, 241, 271
Savoy, House of, 241, 254, 297
Savoy, 235, 308–9, 383
    return of, to France, 225
Savoy, Duke of, 38
Scaliger, Julius-César, 7
Scaligers, 307
Scholarship, 52, 252
Scotland, 329, 415
Sebastian I, of Portugal, 255
Second Empire, 323
Sedan, Battle of, 226
Selim II, 66, 134, 276, 345
Selim III, 47
Severina, Cardinal Santa, 396
Sextus V, Pope, 8
Sicily, 289, 310
Siena, 58
Simpson, Wallis, 399, 405
Sixtus V, Pope, 234, 344
Sorgues, 294
Space race, 374–75
Space stations, 251
Spain, 129, 131, 140, 168, 169, 213, 214, 230, 292, 333, 335, 340, 344, 350, 355, 356, 360, 362, 366, 367, 370–71, 379, 382, 383, 420
    and twentieth century, 150
    and World War II, 228
Spanish Civil War, 123, 143, 265, 408
Spanish monarchy, downfall of, 36

Third Republic, 42, 152
Third World leader, 98

Third World War, 73–74, 88–89, 91
Thirty Years War, 213, 338
Tobruk, 215
and World War II, 34–35
Tokyo, destruction of, 369
Tolentino, 322
Treaty of, 214, 230
Torné, Abbé, 13, 86, 196
Toulon, 96
Toulouse, 284, 318, 322, 353, 354
Battle of, 140
sack of, 377
Trafalgar, Battle of, 59
Traité des Fardmens (Nostradamus), 8
Trevor-Roper, Hugh, 146
Trieste, 340
Tripartite Pact, 191
Tunis, capture of, 327
Turin, 297
French occupation of, 23
Turkey, 96, 240
Turks, 105, 106, 108, 109, 114, 120, 132, 134, 139, 154, 168, 218, 226, 240, 289, 308, 310, 367
Tuscany, 181
Tuscany, Duke of, 68
Twentieth century, 265, 315, 330, 370

Umberto, King of Italy, assassination of, 219
Unigenitus, Papal Bull, 169
Union of Soviet Socialist Republics (USSR), 161, 180, 251, 299. See also Russia
and space race, 375
and United States, 237, 257
United Arab Republic, 161–62, 182
United Provinces, 94
United States, 30, 103, 173, 174, 224, 251, 325, 336, 345, 415, 416, 420
and Asia, 186

and Pearl Harbor, 392
and Russia, 237, 257
and space race, 375
and United Arab Republic, 182
and war, 202
Urban VII, Pope, 344
Usak, 373

Valence, 311
Valenza, 311
Valois children, 11, 25
Var river, 345
Vast, 296
Vatican, 113. See also Papacy; Papal States
and France, 234
and future, 242
States, 115
Vauban, Marquis de, 385
Vaucelles, Treaty of, 383
Venaissin, 294
Vendôme family, 368
Venice, 367
Venizelos, Eleutherios, 218
Vercelli, 309
French occupation of, 23
Vermandois, Abbey of, 366
Verona, 85–86
Versailles, Treaty of, 383
Vichy government, 37, 56, 87. See also France
Victor Emmanuel I, 258, 342, 414
Victor Emmanuel III, 318
Victoria, Queen, 426
Vidal, Frère, 77
Villar, Marshal, 190
Villeneuve, Pierre C.J.B.S. de, 59
Vincenza, 311
Voltaire, 417
Volturno river, 85

Walewska, Marie, 187
Walpole, Horace, 406
Wars, twentieth century, 28, 417, 418

Warsaw Pact, 111
Waterloo, Battle of, 31, 40, 99, 102, 184, 194, 400. *See also* Napoleon Bonaparte
Wellesley. *See* Wellington, Duke of
Wellington, Duke of, 31, 64, 140, 192, 194, 214, 291
Westphalia, Treaty of, 213
Weygand, Maxime, 226
Wilhelm II, Kaiser, 184
William III, of England (William of Orange), 94, 100, 101, 199–200, 202, 264, 330
William the Silent, 173
Windsor, Duchess of. *See* Simpson, Wallis

Wohl, Louis de, 14
Worcester, Battle of, 393
World War I, 49, 72, 90, 372
World War II, 29, 34, 36, 56, 78, 87, 88, 123, 134, 151, 160, 173, 191, 196, 209, 212, 215, 228, 240, 252, 315, 332, 364, 392, 408–9. *See also* Third World War

Yalta Conference, 87
York, Cardinal, 244
Yugoslavia, 362

Zara, 339